The NVA machine gunner opened fire. The first burst killed Allen and drove everyone ahead of me to the ground. I hit the ground slightly to the left with my feet still on the trail. Several AK-47s joined the enemy machine gun almost immediately. I raised my helmet-covered head in an attempt to pinpoint the source. In an instant, the NVA gunner answered my unasked question. A burst clipped off a bush near my neck a split second before the next burst filled my face with stinging gravel as the bullets ricocheted past.

A moment later Snyder came into view. He hurried forward in a crouch, keeping right of the trail for the little protection that a termite hill offered. Dropping to one knee as he drew even with me, Snyder looked directly into my eyes, a look that haunts me still. "Goodbye," his eyes seemed to say. He leaped forward and threw himself onto the path, and the machine gunner shifted his fire from me to Snyder.

Books published by The Ballantine Publishing Group are available at quantity discounts on bulk purchases for premium, educational, fund-raising, and special sales use. For details, please call 1-800-733-3000.

IT TOOK HEROES

A CAVALRY CHAPLAIN'S MEMOIR OF VIETNAM

CLAUDE D. NEWBY

BALLANTINE BOOKS • NEW YORK

Sale of this book without a front cover may be unauthorized. If this book is coverless, it may have been reported to the publisher as "unsold or destroyed" and neither the author nor the publisher may have received payment for it.

A Presidio Press Book
Published by The Ballantine Publishing Group
Copyright © 1998, 2000 by Claude D. Newby

All rights reserved under International and Pan-American Copyright Conventions. Published in the United States by The Ballantine Publishing Group, a division of Random House, Inc., New York, and simultaneously in Canada by Random House of Canada Limited, Toronto. This work was originally published as two separate volumes: *It Took Heroes* published by Bonneville Book in 1998 and *It Took Heroes Volume II* published by Tribute Enterprises in 2000.

Presidio Press and colophon are trademarks of Random House, Inc.

www.ballantinebooks.com

ISBN 0-345-45913-X

Manufactured in the United States of America

First Edition: March 2003

OPM 10 9 8 7 6 5 4 3 2 1

Contents

Preface

"It doesn't take a hero to order men into battle. It takes a hero to be one of those men who goes into battle," said General H. Norman Schwarzkopf. He knew firsthand of what he spoke, and this book is about those of whom he spoke, as I knew them.

My Vietnam memoirs began as part of my autobiography. Sometime before 1995, I listed several good reasons for writing my life story. These reasons included a desire to leave a chronicle of my life that my posterity may "know" me, gain some advantage from the lessons life taught me, and cherish their heritage. I also wanted to pay tribute to and give credit to key people for their influence in my life. Deeper inside me, though, something gnawed at me, some motivation these stated reasons failed to satisfy. Do I crave recognition? Yes, at some level of human weakness, but this answer doesn't assuage the gnawing.

In November 1972 a military man wrote me: "The Vietnam War is over, and it's time to forget it. Please quit telling war stories, and let's leave the war behind us." These well-intended words pained me deeply—the gnawing increased. *If even military people want to bury and forget the faithful sacrifices rendered in Vietnam, does anyone care? Can we forget the event and still remember those who served and sacrificed so much?*—There was a connection between Vietnam and the gnawing inside me, but I missed it.

In 1969 President Richard M. Nixon began pulling combat forces out of Vietnam. By 1973 the process was complete except for a few advisors, and "peace with honor" was declared. We Army Chaplains in Europe, where I then served, were ordered to celebrate the peace with special religious services. *"No!"* I declared. "Rather, I will conduct a final memorial service for the soldiers and civilians who died and will yet die—on both sides—in Vietnam, and for their grieving loved ones," I wrote.

So in memorial services and on countless other speaking engagements, I shared my memories of many of the heroes who went into battle in Vietnam. As I shared these memories, the gnawing inside me eased. Finally, in 1995, I recognized the connection.

My serendipitous awakening occurred the day I finished the first draft of the chronicle of my tours in Vietnam. Suddenly, a great weight lifted from me—a mental, emotional, spiritual burden of near tangible proportions. That's when I first realized the gnawing had been there all along because I needed to preserve "the rest of the story" in writing.

Thus, with my war memories on paper and in the computer—making up two-thirds of almost a thousand pages of double-spaced manuscript—the gnawing almost ceased for the first time in more than a quarter of a century, and I felt free of a vague melancholy. It was as if I'd been properly relieved from some lonely guard post, of some awesome burden, which burden I never fully appreciated until it lifted off of me. *I don't have to remember anymore. Now, whatever happens to me, the story is preserved, lest we forget.*

As for American involvement in the Vietnam War, my strong feelings are—should they show through—incidental. This is about heroes, about whole life spans compressed into months, days, hours. It is about grunts, a tribute to them and to those who supported them up close and personal. As a chaplain in Vietnam, I served no war, just or unjust. I served soldiers—heroes—faithful souls who stepped forward when called upon by their country, while others received accolades for refusing to serve. It took a special kind of hero to step forward in the decade of the sixties. And I owe those special heroes for much more than memories. I owe them my life, literally.

This book is not about tenets of religion or points of religious doctrine. However, considering its source, an Army chaplain (retired), it is occasionally necessary to refer to my own and other chaplains' and soldiers' faith and religious affiliation. To do otherwise and remain true to the facts and context of the events and people described is impossible. A "prime directive" of each of America's military chaplaincies is that the chaplain will not attempt to win soldiers from other religious denominations to his or her own. While retirement released me from this "rule of engagement," I adhere to it in the pages of this book because my purposes are quite non-denominational.

By the way, adherence by chaplains to the prime directive is not a sellout, because their commission is to provide or coordinate spiritual and religious support for soldiers and their families without regard to one's religious affiliation or lack thereof. In other words, the role of a military chaplain, in most respects, is an institutional one rather than an ecclesiastical one.

Of course, each chaplain must be endorsed to serve by a church or group of religious bodies, and he or she must be ordained in whatever way that church or body of churches describes. A chaplain is not required to violate the tenets of his religious vows or faith to support the soldier. However, he is expected to do all in his power to bring to bear those resources that are necessary to meet those spiritual needs of the soldier that he cannot personally provide. In this way, I was as responsible for the Baptist and athiest as I was for those of my own faith.

The chronology of this memoir rests firmly on my personal journal, which provides the framework and foundation for the memories. I augmented these by interviewing fellow soldiers, by personal and official journals, and by other sources. Not to brag, but my memory is verifiably exceptional, especially for directions, lay-of-the-land and chronology. This ability I've validated through research and revisits to places of long ago. Almost always, my recollections of sites and events are accurate as to geographic orientation. And usually sites and layouts are the way I remembered them— schools, houses, farms, streams, roads, and dates and sequences. This holds true back to when I was a toddler, before I knew of compass directions. Apparently, this talent is inborn in me, perhaps a psychological need to know where—and when—I am. Whatever its source, my gift served me well in combat and in writing this memoir.

In the preface to the first edition I wrote that "the hardest thing about writing this book has been stopping, because every action and story has as many facets and perspectives as there were individuals involved in it. I've discovered that every veteran I contact adds detail that helps clarify and clear up seeming inconsistencies, and deserves at least a chapter of his own. I hope I didn't stop writing too soon. I trust I'll be forgiven by my grunts, medics, LRRPs (rangers) and scouts, aviators and former leaders when my memories, notes and perspective differ from theirs, for I have been faithful to my memories and journal and strove to verify and validate every detail and name whenever I could."

As it turned out my grunts, medics, pilots and leaders were very kind to me and forgiving and helpful. Many of their valuable perspectives and suggestions are incorporated into this edition. A few non-veterans questioned the jargon-like style of the notes at the end of some of the chapters. None of these notes are critical to the text.

Rather, they are included for the benefit of soldiers and their families who might be benefitted in their dealing with the Veterans Administration and as they try to find each other and so forth. When compared to the text, the notes also provide a glimpse of how the official record compares to the actual action.

Republic of Vietnam

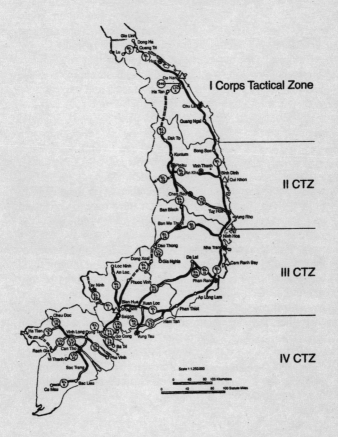

I Corps Tactical Zone

II CTZ

III CTZ

IV CTZ

Gio Linh
Dong Ha
Quang Tri
Ca Lu
Hue
Da Nang
Ha Tan
Chu Lai
Quang Ngai
Dak To
Kontum
Pleiku
An Khe
Vinh Thanh
Binh Dinh
Qui Nhon
Cheo Reo
Ban Blech
Tuy Hoa
Ban Me Thuot
Vung Rho
Ninh Hoa
Dao Thong
Nha Trang
Dong Xoai
Gia Nghia
Da Lat
Loc Ninh
An Loc
Cam Ranh Bay
Tay Ninh
Phuoc Vinh
Phan Rang
Bien Hua
Xuan Loc
Ap Long Lam
Cho Gao
Saigon
Phan Thiet
Chau Doc
Ham Tan
Ha Tien
Vinh Long
Dong
Vung Tau
Go Cong
Ba Tri
Rach Gia
Vi Thanh
Can Tho
Phu Vinh
Soc Trang
Ca Mau
Bac Lieu

Scale 1:1,250,000

0   40   80   100 Kilometers
0   40   80   100 Statute Miles

IT TOOK HEROES

Ambush! screamed my brain the instant geysers of dirt began sprouting up on the right shoulder of the road ahead of the jeep. A fraction of a second later, my ears confirmed what my eyes saw. An AK-47 on full automatic was kicking up those geysers. The enemy had hit us when we were about 200 feet from where the road curved left at the top of the hill.

One enemy gunner had opened up as we entered the kill zone, firing ahead of our jeep—leading us—and no doubt expecting us to try to speed away from the kill zone as quickly as possible. Had we sped up as expected, we would have driven straight into almost certain death. Martinez, however, reflexively slammed on the brakes and brought the chugging, laboring jeep to an instant halt, sparing our lives.

As Martinez hit the brakes, I leaped from the jeep and down a bank into the elephant grass. A fraction of a second later, Preacher landed almost on top of me. Almost simultaneously, Martinez threw himself down across the seat I'd just vacated, beating by a fraction of a second a burst of machine-gun fire from a second concealed position straight ahead, where the road curved to the left. Three bullets tore through the windshield and dash and passed on, missing Martinez. Other rounds punctured the radiator and a tire.

With the AK-47 and machine gun blazing away, Martinez slithered from the jeep and joined us in the grass. Hot lead cracked continually over our heads. My first thought was *the gunners will keep us pinned down while others sneak up and frag us. We've got to move away from the road!*

one

"Marching as to War"

(From the hymn "Onward Christian Soldiers")

Braniff Airline Charter Flight W243B departed Travis Air Force Base, California, at 2:38 p.m. September 14, destination South Vietnam with stops on the way in Alaska and Japan. As the airplane plunged forward toward whatever awaited, my pained thoughts hung tightly to the wife and five children I left behind. I could hardly believe I was here, an Army chaplain headed into war.

The final leg of this journey really began a year and a half earlier on a Sunday evening in February 1965. Helga was already in bed when I decided to visit Alan Smith, a fellow seminary teacher and neighbor. During the visit I informed Smith that I had tendered my resignation from my teaching position, effective at the end of the current school year.

"Why don't you return to the Army as a chaplain?" Smith asked.

"No thanks," I snapped, "I've had enough of the Army." Between 1952 and 1958 I had been an enlisted soldier and was currently a medic on a Special Forces A-team in the National Guard.

Not to be put off by my reflexive response, Smith referred me to an article in the latest edition of the *Deseret News*. The piece announced that for the first time since the Korean War, the military services were accepting chaplaincy applications from Latter-day Saints. By an agreement worked out between the military services and the LDS Church, acceptable applicants could enter the chaplaincy under an educational waiver of the requirement that all chaplains have 90 hours of graduate credit and a divinity-school degree. This requirement had been an almost impossible barrier for LDS candidates because their church had neither divinity schools nor professional clergy. For Mormons, a bachelor's degree would henceforth be sufficient. So read the announcement—I had one of those!

Though I'd reflexively rejected Alan's suggestion about the chaplaincy, I had second thoughts as I walked home from his house. For one thing, being in the National Guard, I knew American involvement was heating up in Vietnam, and experienced soldiers would soon be in demand. With my Army background, I reasoned, I'd have an edge in understanding soldiers' lives and challenges and in serving those of all faiths. And I'd earn at least $500 per month as a lieutenant, before taxes.

At home, my mind swirling, I crawled into bed next to Helga and nudged her until she acknowledged my intrusion into her dreams. "What is it?"

"How would you like to go back in the Army and earn five hundred dollars a month?" I asked.

In response, Helga mumbled something that I chose to interpret as agreement and fell back to sleep. She doesn't remember this conversation.

Moments later, in the living room, I penned a letter to apply to become a chaplain. The letter highlighted those aspects of my background that I believed would make my application stand out. I expressed preference for the Army and infantry and added that I had received the Good Conduct Medal as an enlisted man.

I seriously doubted I'd be accepted for the chaplaincy. After all, my seminary-teaching career was less than spectacular. An ecclesiastical leader, upon learning of my intentions, advised me to not get my hopes up because he had failed to be selected to be a chaplain, despite his having much better credentials than I had. But I tried and dared hope, with nothing to lose. Meanwhile, to be on the safe side, I continued to seek employment elsewhere for the coming summer and school year.

*   *   *

Excitement reigned in our home the day we were called to come for an interview at church headquarters in Salt Lake City. I was the first of a hundred applicants to be interviewed because we had planned to be in Tennessee come June, the scheduled time for the interviews.

Elder Boyd K. Packer, a general or church headquarters-level leader, interviewed me alone, and then Helga and me together. During the private interview, Elder Packer asked, in effect, "Have you ever done anything that would cause you to be unworthy to represent the church as a chaplain," a pause while my life flashed before my eyes, "since you joined the church?"

"No," I answered honestly.

We left Elder Packer's office quietly convinced we'd better keep looking elsewhere for employment, which conviction we shared with each other a few nights later during a drive-in movie date.

In May 1965, I accepted the junior position in a two-teacher school in Kiana, Alaska. Kiana is situated on the banks of the Kobuk River, 40 miles north of the Arctic Circle and 80 miles inland from the frigid Bering Sea. The boys and I looked eagerly toward Alaska. Helga and Jeannie looked forward with dread and trepidation. But wonderful companion that she was, is, Helga prepared resolutely for two years in the cold north wilderness. The reprieve, when it came, was very welcome.

Upon returning home from our June trip to Tennessee, we solidified plans for the move to Alaska and readied ourselves to receive the packers. That's when the telephone rang. We received the call on a wall telephone in our small kitchen. Helga came close when she heard me say, "Elder Packer." Standing face to face with her, I heard him say:

"I regret to inform you (pause for effect), you've been selected to be a chaplain in the Army. Do you accept?"

With barely controlled emotions and feigned dignity, I accepted. *The Army, my first choice!*

The main business attended to, Elder Packer instructed me to attend an orientation meeting at church headquarters where I would receive further instructions.

Helga's beautiful eyes sparkled with joy as she interpreted my side of the conversation. Cool dignity dissolved as I hung up the telephone; Helga did a little dance of glee as we melted joyfully into each other's embrace. We were in, we thought. Little did we suspect the obstacles between the telephone call and *being in*.

War clouds loomed heavy when, on July 25, 1965, we eleven endorsed candidates gathered at church headquarters. Infantry divisions were going to Vietnam, screamed the headlines that day—the next step in Secretary of Defense Robert McNamara's policy of limited war and gradual escalation, a policy obviously doomed in the opinion of many professional soldiers.

As part of a daylong orientation, Elder Packer said, looking straight at me, "You were not selected for the chaplaincy because you are necessarily the best qualified applicants. You were selected because you are who the Lord wants." These words would motivate me for more than a quarter of a century.

Upon completion of the orientation, H. Richard Thomas gave to each candidate a set of military application forms and a formal military letter. My letter, dated 29 July 1965, authorized me to obtain an Army physical examination at the nearest military induction center. I was further instructed to send my application and physical exam results to the Office of the Army Chief of Chaplains. Once I had active-duty orders in hand, I was to return to church headquarters and be set apart (an LDS ordinance similar to ordination in many churches). The process of "getting in" seemed simple enough.

I reported to Fort Douglas, Utah, for a physical examination on August 2, 1965, and flunked it because of high-frequency deafness in both ears. How could that be? I'd passed hearing tests to enter and exit the Army, to become a correctional officer at Alcatraz, to be a police officer, and within the past year to enlist in the National Guard. But the previous hearing tests each consisted of a doctor clicking coins together and asking me if I heard it, which I always had. This time, the Army had tested my hearing with me inside an electronic box and declared me unfit for military service.

Reluctantly, sorrowfully, I returned and shared the sad news with Helga. She was wonderful. First, she assured me the Lord was aware of us, that He was bound to bless us because we faithfully paid an honest tithe, and we tried to keep His commandments. "And," she reflected, "do you really have to have perfect ears to be a chaplain?" Perhaps not.

A letter dated 11 August 1965 informed me that my request for a waiver of my hearing disability had been forwarded to the Office of the Surgeon General of the Army with a recommendation that it be approved. The chaplain who signed the letter promised to cooperate with me in every possible way, and said, "I trust whatever the news may be, it will be God's will for you."

The waiver was approved in late August. "Commissioning and active duty awaits only completion of a security check on you. You should be on active duty by early September [1965]," read an official letter.

Meanwhile, times were getting very tight, financially. We'd canceled the move to Alaska, and almost three months had passed since our last paycheck. Even the monthly National Guard drill pay had ended in May due to my impending move to Alaska, and that, alas, just before I was to have attended paratrooper training at Fort Benning, Georgia. To make matters worse, I couldn't find decent employment without being dishonest. For example, Sears declined to hire me because I "might" enter the Army soon. Other potential employers turned me away because I was "overqualified."

September came and went without any further word from Washington. We were desperate. With little money for house payments, utilities, food, we were falling deeper and deeper in debt. Between June and October we racked up more than $3,000 in medical bills alone, a fortune even had paychecks been regular. Fortunately, with the new school year came the opportunity to earn a little—about $500 over four months—as a substitute teacher.

Our financial condition became so bad that by late fall I was forced to seek help from our bishop. He gave us food orders to be filled at the Bishop's Storehouse. Thus, I continued to feed my family, though the mortgage payments and other bills were very difficult to meet. In exchange for help from the church—between substitute teaching and job hunting—I helped out at a church welfare warehouse, cannery and dairy and delivered coal to churches. Doing her part and more, Helga did ironing and sewing jobs assigned to her by the bishop. Thus, we kept our dignity by earning the assistance we received.

About mid-October, having heard nothing from Washington, I called on H. Richard Thomas, the Servicemen Committee secretary at church headquarters. He greeted me with, "Hello, Brother Newby. I'm glad you are here, but I have bad news for you."

The chaplaincy had rejected my application, along with another one, Thomas said. I, like the other candidate, would not be allowed to enter the chaplaincy on an education waiver because I lacked a master's degree and hadn't completed a full-time, two-year LDS mission. The mission requirement was in lieu of 60 of the required 90 hours of graduate study—though it had not been listed as a prerequisite in the *Deseret News* item I'd read back in February.

The Army, Thomas said, had to deny me an appointment in order to maintain the quality of chaplains and to keep the chaplaincies from being swamped with unqualified clergy. Thomas added that the Servicemen Committee had received notification of my rejection by telephone and had been assured my application was in the mail, marked *"disapproved."*

Never in my life had I felt so low, so dejected. Words

can't describe how I dreaded to face Helga with this news—our dream was dashed for sure this time. Still, I approached home with this faint glimmer of hope that she, with her unshakable faith, would again restore my spirits.

I gave Helga the disappointing news while we stood by the wall telephone in the kitchen, in the same spot where months before we had heard that we had been selected as candidates for the Army chaplaincy. This time, for the first time, Helga cried, but only for a moment. Then, leaning her head and shoulders away from my embrace, she said, "Claude, I don't know what will happen. But we've done our best, and now it is God's problem. He will cause things to work out for us, somehow."

Then, in an instant, Helga's grieved, anxious demeanor changed. She went silent and seemed to stare through me for a moment, dry-eyed and deep. "Besides," she said, "I still believe *we* will be chaplains." I believed her, though reason shouted that the dream was over, that the chaplaincy was out of the question for us. Her faith and confidence rang louder though, stronger and infectious. The dreaded rejection letter from the Army never came.

November arrived. I was substitute teaching in a science class—trying to explain the *big bang theory of creation*—at the Brigham City Indian School. The principal or his assistant stuck his head in the classroom. "You must call your wife during the next break. It is very important."

Helga's excitement radiated from the telephone as she informed me I was to return a call to Chaplain (Lieutenant Colonel) Will Hyatt through Operator Two in Washington, D.C.

I called Washington. Chaplain Hyatt opened with, "First of all, Reverend Newby, don't get excited. Everything is all right." He explained I was approved for the chaplaincy and asked if I accepted the appointment. I accepted.

"A letter is on the way," Chaplain Hyatt said, "instructing you to report immediately to Fort Ord, California. Please ignore those instructions and wait for orders directing you to report to Fort Hamilton, New York, for the

Chaplain Officer Basic Course . . . on or about 3 January 1966, en route to your assignment at Fort Ord, California." Helga was ecstatic, but not very surprised!

A few days later, resplendent in my new Army uniform with silver first lieutenant bars on each shoulder, I reported with my family, unannounced, to the Servicemen Committee. Surprise was all over H. Robert Thomas' face, like *what is Newby, the reject, doing in uniform?* Thomas' surprise turned to consternation when I produced official orders. "I'm here to be set apart, according to instructions," I said.

Shocked now, Thomas studied my orders. "This cannot be. You were rejected. The Army told me so, personally. Something is wrong here."

He stared at the orders in silence, trying, I presumed, to make sense of the incongruence between what he knew and what he saw. Finally, with, "I don't know what to do," he called Elder Gordon B. Hinckley, his superior on the committee.

Thomas' side of the telephone conversation went pretty much this way. "Newby is here with Army orders to active duty, to be set apart. . . . Yes, I have the orders in my hands. . . . Yes, they appear to be in order. . . . Yes . . . Yes sir." He hung up and said, "Elder Hinckley knows this can't be. We are to come to his office."

Helga and the children waited with Elder Hinckley's secretary while I entered his office with Thomas, confidently at first because I knew my orders were all right. Soon, though, my confidence wavered because, apparently, one whom I believed to be one of the Lord's anointed thought something about me wasn't *kosher*.

With reserved demeanor, Elder Hinckley acknowledged my presence as he took the orders from Thomas. After a moment he repeated Thomas' earlier denial. "This just can't be. He was rejected."

"Are you certain these are in order?" Elder Hinckley asked me.

"Yes," I responded and explained the telephone call from Chaplain Hyatt. "I've already been sworn in by a duly qualified U.S. Army officer. I'm a commissioned first lieutenant."

Elder Hinckley hesitated. To Thomas, he said in essence, "This can't be. I'm not sure what to do. I'd better ask President Lee."

Elder Hinckley dialed Harold B. Lee, his superior in the leadership of the church. After explaining the purpose of the call, Elder Hinckley continued in essence with, "Yes . . . They appear in order. . . . Yes sir."

Hanging up the telephone, Elder Hinckley said to Thomas, "President Lee said to set Newby apart. I know it isn't right, but that's what we will do."

Elder Hinckley invited my family in. Helga and the children took seats on the northwest side of his office. Elder Hinckley turned a chair around and I sat in it.

With reluctance obvious in his countenance, Elder Hinckley placed his hands on my head, and everything changed. In a voice flowing with warmth and acceptance, he pronounced a wonderful blessing upon me and through me upon my family. I knew all his earlier doubts were gone, which he confirmed publicly less than a year later in far-off Saigon and again six months after that in Fujiyama, Japan; but those stories come later. The impossible had happened. We were in!

For the first three months of 1966, I trained at Fort Hamilton, Brooklyn, New York, where I had served as a military policeman 10 years previously. Following training I reported with my family to Fort Ord, California. There I served from late April to mid-August, first as a chaplain to basic trainees and then as chaplain to the Reception Station, where draftees from Berkeley and other exotic—often vocally antiwar—places were processed into the Army prior to beginning basic training. In August, I volunteered for Vietnam.

*   *   *

I was ill when we left Fort Ord for Utah and for most of the trip there, I believed due to one or more of several shots I received the day before we departed—injections for plague, typhus, tetanus, all sorts of shots. Fortunately, I felt much better by the time we reached Ogden, Utah, though my arms and shoulders were still sore.

We drove straight through Ogden to the home of the Dallas and Joan Murdoch family in Grace, Idaho. There we left the children, and Helga and I returned to Ogden to find a temporary home. Soon we were settled in a rented home, had received our household goods and brought the children down from Idaho. The next priority was to reexamine our personal affairs, insurance, wills and such. I intended to make sure Helga and the children could get along without me, if necessary. I wanted her to feel free to remarry if I should die, yet free from marrying out of fiscal necessity.

To create good family memories, we played, fished, and water-skied with the Murdochs in Idaho and visited Yellowstone National Park for the first time.

As my departure drew near I became increasingly contemplative—not that I had premonitions or was scared. But I couldn't help thinking what the future might be like for Helga and the children should I be killed or dismembered, which were distinct possibilities if I served with the infantry as I hoped to do.

I especially wanted to serve with the 1st Air Cavalry Division, a new-type division much in the news, which I figured needed a chaplain who was infantry at heart, who wanted to be with the soldiers who had it hardest and hurt the most.

Many members of the LDS Church place great trust in blessings by the laying on of hands. Several Vietnam-bound LDS servicemen of my acquaintance each sought a promise of a safe return from war via this medium. Though I appreciated this practice and approved of soldiers seeking special blessings on the eve of war, I sought no such blessing and assurance for myself for valid spiritual reasons, I thought.

I reasoned that only by sharing the soldier's existence and sense of uncertainty about survival could I fully comprehend and appreciate his immediate and urgent needs. Only in this way could I understand how to reach him. In other words, I believed that to be effective as a chaplain I must voluntarily share the danger, discomfort, and uncertainty the infantryman endured. I reasoned he would, because I was beside him, respond with increased faith in what I represented and with deeper trust in my words, actions, and counsel. Thus, I hoped to better provide the spiritual comfort the soldier would so desperately need. Only Dallas and Joan Murdoch, Helga and two other officers knew how I felt about a personal "pre-combat" blessing.

The children would grow and develop in my absence. Milestones would pass. Joyful "firsts" and "once onlys" would come and go. One such passage would be the twelfth birthday of James, my oldest. With his birthday two months hence would come eligibility for a religious ordination, a special rite of passage. Another would ordain him in my stead.

Helga and I clung to each other emotionally and spiritually as "D-day" approached. We yearned to block out all but each other, while giving the children the attention they also needed. From such fleeting moments as a picnic for two on our last Saturday together, I increased my reserves of courage for what lay ahead, and I think Helga did also. On September 11 we attended church together, not for the last time, we hoped.

Mom, Dad and my sister Beulah called Sunday evening. I gathered from their emotional comments that they expected me to die in Vietnam. My reassurances were less than convincing because I couldn't promise what was beyond my control—things like life and death.

As our last social act together, Helga and I called on the wife of Air Force Captain Layne. Mrs. Layne elicited my promise, freely given, to try to visit her husband, who was already in Vietnam. This promise I wanted to keep because I understood the value of intermediary contacts between a soldier and his loved ones.

September 13 had passed in a blur, hastened on by our efforts to wring every ounce of joy and hope from each moment. Mostly, I remember the day for overwhelming feelings of melancholy and homesickness—even before we departed for the airport.

I had gathered my family around me after dinner and blessed them one by one, from the eldest to the youngest, and Helga last of all. I'm sure the blessings contained a mixture of assurance, promise, admonition and love, according to my perception of each individual's special needs. As I recall, this was a tearful occasion. With the blessings attended to, Melvin Lunt, a friend from my days on the police force, and his wife, Carol, drove us to the airport.

At the airport, Helga and I tried to reassure one another without violating our covenant of honesty—to not promise outcomes beyond our ability to deliver. I promised Helga I would keep no secrets from her; she promised to do likewise. We were but confirming a long-established compact to share everything so there would be no cause to worry about bad things being held back. The children handled their emotions well, or concealed them. Helga, James and Jeannie were focused and affectionate. John controlled his emotions by focusing his attention on airport activities. Laura maintained an extreme quiet, an almost stone-faced demeanor. Two-year-old Brenda knew something was happening, something she didn't like, and expressed her concern with anxious eyes and tight, clinging hugs.

The dreaded moment arrived, so slowly and all too soon—time seemingly dragging and contracting the way it can only in those rare moments when every nerve and emotion is at peak stimulation. I kissed each child one last time, squeezed James' shoulder, and said to him in effect: "You have the manly responsibilities now. I'm depending on you to look out for the family while I'm gone."

I hugged Jeannie especially tight because I was concerned most for her. She would enter puberty during this year of separation, and Daddy might be especially missed.

After hugging and kissing Helga one last time, I climbed up the ramp and boarded a Boeing 727. It was 9:25 p.m. My dear family waved until the plane had taxied from sight. My somber face stayed glued to the tiny, oval-shaped window long after she and the children were left behind.

At 1:30 a.m., I arrived at Travis Air Force Base by bus from San Francisco and checked into a room at the BOQ (Bachelor Officers' Quarters), which I shared for two hours with a Vietnam-bound helicopter pilot. He kept me awake while he searched for a clock he'd forgotten to pack and awakened me an hour or so later when he left to catch his flight.

At 9 a.m., I had checked in at the passenger terminal where I spent the next five hours getting more injections, being ill, writing letters and waiting. A medic jabbed two needles into my left shoulder simultaneously, one-handed. One or more of the shots probably accounted for my feeling sick. In a letter to Helga I tried to convey my love for her, to describe my misery, and to apologize for putting us through all this. Momentarily, I repented for having volunteered for the chaplaincy and for duty in Vietnam. *If I feel so awful, how must the "lowly" privates and draftees feel? They have no choice about going to Vietnam.*

two

Hoping for a Cav Assignment

The sun set at 12:45 a.m. September 15 (California time), as we flew west from Anchorage, Alaska, toward the International Dateline. At 2:30 a.m. September 16, following a stop in Japan, we landed at Tan San Nut Air Base in Saigon. After a brief delay to hear a welcome speech, we replacements got off the airplane, collected our luggage and boarded an old U.S. Army bus. A grease gun–armed enlisted airman rode shotgun for the short bus ride to the replacement in-processing center at Camp Alpha. The grease gun and chicken wire–covered bus windows (to deflect grenades) were the only immediate indicators this was a combat zone.

Vietnam impressed itself indelibly on my memory and olfactory nerves with that first glimpse and whiff. The night was hot and muggy, even at 0300 hours. Strange, yet vaguely familiar aromas assaulted my nose—decaying garbage and vegetation and human waste, all mingled with the essences unique to military bases—tents, latrines, machines, oil and disinfectant.

At Camp Alpha, I went exploring in the night. I was too intrigued with my surroundings and pumped up with anticipation to sleep.

Puddles of dirty, stinking water, evidence of a recent downpour, dotted the walkways between and around the hooches we replacements were billeted in. Just beyond the replacement center fence was a small cluster of makeshift shacks. I got a better appreciation of the natives' burden in this war when someone said, "Those are family housing for Vietnamese Air Force officers."

At dawn I cleaned up, dressed and ate my first in-country meal at the air-conditioned Tan San Nut Officers Club—pretty fancy place. I thought it amazing that rear-echelon troops and officers, while living like this, received the same combat pay as infantry.

My assignment came right after breakfast. I had my wish. I was going to the Cav—1st Cavalry Division (Airmobile)—in the central highlands to serve with infantrymen, I assumed, as I *knew* I should. After all, I had grown up in the hills of Tennessee, where the ideal of serving where one could serve best was instilled in me. I had fed on the lives and exploits of the likes of Sergeant Alvin York during World War I and other heroes such as my uncles and Audie Murphy of World War II and Korea. I honestly believed I was a natural to serve the grunt and that many other chaplains could better serve rear-area support troops because of their pastoral experience and "come to chapel" focus. Well, I was going to the Cav. Now all I had to sweat was where in the Cav I would serve. Later in the morning, in company with two other chaplains, I got a pep talk and a headquarters perspective of the war from the senior USARV (US Army Vietnam) Chaplain.

I slept lightly during my first full night in country, despite the soothing rhythm of a driving rain on the tin roof a few feet above the top bunk on which I lay—the sheets were clammy in the high humidity, and the required mosquito netting blocked any refreshing breeze.

The next day I teamed up with another chaplain for a bus trip to Long Binh, a major American base northeast of Saigon. On the way we passed palm trees, rice paddies, small businesses, hamlets and the first real signs of war: a civilian compound filled with burned-out vehicles that the Vietcong (VC) had destroyed three days earlier. We also passed the burned-out shell of an Army truck that had been destroyed by a direct hit from a recoilless rifle.

At the 93rd Evacuation Hospital, the resident chaplain took us to visit a 25th Division (Tropical Lightning) soldier who had just been brought in. The day before, while I explored my new surroundings, he was getting both legs blown off by the mine that destroyed his Armored Personnel Carrier (APC) and killed some of his crew.

Back at Camp Alpha, at about 3 p.m., I wrote to Helga and tried to express my feelings, impressions and experiences. She kept this and all my letters from Vietnam for several years, only to lose them during one of our many Army transfers.

At 2:30 p.m. September 18, after attending services with the LDS Group in Saigon, I boarded a C-130 cargo airplane for the two-hour flight to An Khe. My fellow passengers included about 65 American soldiers and two very attractive Vietnamese women, wives of ARVN soldiers. In flight, I casually examined the women. They each had beautiful eyes and features and appeared quite serene. Traditional Vietnamese dresses enhanced their beauty. Upon closer examination, though, the ladies' eyes belied their composed demeanor—stress was there and tension and fear. This was as I expected. These women and their husbands were engaged in a long, bloody war without the hope American soldiers shared, of leaving the war behind after a year.

The Vietnamese women and several soldiers off-loaded at Pleiku. Other soldiers took their places, and we continued on to An Khe, flying at treetop level with the rear-loading ramp open, which gave me a bird's-eye view of the jungles I anticipated spending the next twelve months in. Naturally, I was all eyes.

We landed about 5:30 p.m. on an airstrip called the Golf Course, at Camp Radcliff, the 1st Cav base camp. The camp, which supported some 20,000 soldiers, was named after the first American to be killed there. The airstrip was called the Golf Course because the general in charge of replacing the jungle with it had ordered that it be made "as smooth as a golf course." Some said the VC "named" the airstrip by placing eighteen holes in it—mortar craters, that is.

The weather here, unlike the heat and high humidity of

Saigon, was hot and dry. A two-hour flight had carried me from a hot, wet monsoon to a hot, dry one.

Despite tangled emotions—homesickness, relief at having arrived and anticipation of what awaited me—I had the presence of mind to note that the air terminal, such as it was, sat about midway on the westerly side of the Golf Course. The Golf Course appeared to be about 200 meters wide and two kilometers long and was paved down its center with perforated sheets of steel, called PSP. Several types of aircraft and buildings were visible across the runway from the terminal, mostly Huey helicopters and aircraft support facilities. Jungle-shrouded mountains stood out in sharp contrast to the east and southeast. The nearest mountain, Hon Cong, appeared to be about a kilometer southwest of the easterly end of the Golf Course.

Hon Cong Mountain sported a gigantic replica of the shoulder patch worn by soldiers of the 1st Cavalry Division. The patch depicted a black horse's head in the upper right corner of a shield-shaped, black-bordered patch of yellow, with a black stripe running diagonally across the yellow from the upper left to the lower right. This brazen symbol of air-cavalry presence reminded me of a novel about a legendary frontiersman and Indian fighter, Bigfoot Spencer, who wore his hair long as a challenge to Indians to take his scalp if they dared. No doubt, the 1st Cav patch up on Hon Cong had something to do with *esprit de corps* and morale, but I think my first impression was nearer the truth. That patch was sort of like the "I-double-dog-dare-you" flaunt I'd heard so often in my youth.

three

Assigned to the Medical Battalion

An enlisted representative of the Division Chaplain met me at the airstrip with the unwelcome news that I would be assigned to the 15th Medical Battalion, rather than to an infantry unit. This news so disappointed me that I recall nothing further about my first day with the Cav, except for writing a letter to Helga. According to my journal, I spent the night in the hooch of the Support Command Chaplain—he was away somewhere. I met him the next day.

During the morning of September 19, I in-processed and chatted with Chaplain (Lieutenant Colonel) Webb. He was the Deputy Division Chaplain, and he seemed pleased with my vision of duty—to soldiers, whatever their religious affiliation, preferably infantry soldiers in my case. He hinted that the assignment to the medical battalion would not likely be for my whole tour.

Resigned to my fate, I began searching for ways to make the best of it, to use my assignment to get nearer to the infantry, to go forward. To this end, with little more than in-processing to occupy my time, I spent most of the next two days orienting myself to the structure, mission and operational area of the 1st Cav and to the layout of base camp. Also, I read a lot and wrote several letters to Helga and the children.

On September 19 at about 10 p.m., 2200 hrs in military time, I met my new supervisory chaplain, Major Clinton E. Browne, a supportive, fatherly Baptist. The next day I met Chaplain (Colonel) McGraff, pronounced McGraw, and attended a steak cookout with the officers of Support Command, after which I spent my last night in Chaplain Browne's hooch.

Wednesday, September 21, I moved to the 15th Medical Battalion, commanded by Lieutenant Colonel (Doctor) Henry A. Leighton. I was assigned temporary accommodations in a hooch with one Captain Sparanio and was assured this arrangement was very temporary, as it was understood I required privacy for counseling. Sparanio, who looked like a Mohawk Indian, denied any Indian lineage. He apparently loved and missed his family, and he read the Bible a lot. He was easy to like and get along with.

Headquarters and Headquarters Company of the medical battalion occupied a narrow strip of land between the east-southeast end of the Golf Course and a small stream. The stream was about five feet across at the widest point in the medics' area. Heavy vegetation covered every spot that was not occupied or used as road or walkway, and this more than a year after the Cav arrived and started clearing away the jungle. I would soon discover that the little stream could be quite threatening during the rainy season.

The medics had built enough solid hooches on concrete slabs to house most of the officers. The hooches had tin roofs and were screened all around with heavy shutters, hinged at the top, so they could be swung out for ventilation or closed to keep out the rain.

Some officers and the enlisted men lived in twelve-man Army tents. One tent was designated as the unit chapel. It was furnished with logs for pews, a simple pulpit, and a foot-powered field organ. A wooden mess (dining) building also served as the battalion staff room. Battalion operations were directed out of a tactical operations center (TOC) in a well-sandbagged bunker.

Medical Companies A, B and C were each co-located with one of the combat maneuver brigades in the division. The brigades further broke down each medical company by assigning a platoon to each infantry battalion. Each company operated a medical clearing station at brigade level, and each platoon operated an aid station at battalion level. Individual medics (medical aidmen) were assigned to infantry units in support of grunts, up close and personal.

The Medical Battalion staff and Headquarter Company (HHC) operated a four- or five-ward hospital for ill and lightly wounded troopers, in addition to commanding and controlling the rest of the battalion. These wards were housed in Quonset huts and provided backup for the 2nd Surgical Hospital, which was located half a kilometer—half-klick—away, at the base of Hon Cong Mountain.

Each medical company, HHC included, had a Medical Evacuation (medevac) platoon. These platoons conducted helicopter operations to rescue and evacuate wounded and seriously ill soldiers. Medevac helicopters in the Cav mounted two M-60 machine guns, unlike the unarmed "Dust-Off" medevac choppers that supported other units in Vietnam.

The Division Chaplain expected me to coordinate and ensure division-wide support for soldiers of my own faith, in addition to supporting the medics. His expectations provided legitimacy to my intentions. I quickly realized that my assignment allowed me to get away from base camp and move almost at will across the 1st Cav AO. I could roam almost to Saigon to support a 7th Cav—Garry Owens—battalion on the coast at Phan Thiet. Another medical company operated west of Pleiku near the Cambodian border and Idrang Valley, the site of battles in November 1965 where more men of the 5th Cavalry and 7th Cavalry had died than were killed at the Battle of Little Bighorn under Brevet-General George Armstrong Custer. A third medical company operated at Landing Zone (LZ) Hammond, over the mountains to the east and to the northwest of the major port city of Qui Nhon and of Phu Cat Air Base.

For the remainder of my first week with the Cav, I visited patients in the battalion medical ward, wrote letters, read, scouted out the base camp and visited An Khe for a closer look at how the natives in the area lived. I also got ready to conduct and preach my first in-country general Christian worship service. My chaplain assistant, Pfc. David Berg, prepared to play the field organ for me, which welcome support was not in his job description.

That first Saturday I spoke by invitation in a service for members of the Seventh-Day Adventist faith. Most SDAs were assigned to the medical battalion because members of that faith were also conscientious objectors. That was also the day I first suffered stomach miseries in consequence of taking a large anti-malaria tablet. To lessen our chances of getting malaria, we took a small pill each day and a big one each week. The big pill frequently left me with an upset stomach and diarrhea. To make matters worse, I suffered severely from mail deprivation during the first week or two, or what infantrymen called a shortage of "sugar rations."

The war loomed closer on September 23. We were alerted to prepare to receive 27 wounded soldiers, the expected overflow from the 2nd Surgical Hospital. The wounded troopers arrived, and all of them (10, not 27) were treated at the 2nd Surgical Hospital.

Chaplain Browne attended my first Sunday service to support me—he insisted he'd not come to inspect or evaluate my performance. That afternoon, I attended and spoke at an LDS service in the 2nd Surgical Hospital Chapel, at the invitation of Major Harper, the group leader. I immediately felt a special bond with these young men, many of whom were very valiant in spirit. Friendships developed that continue today, 30 years later. Apparently, these feelings were mutual, considering what some of those men said of me on occasion.

It was during that first LDS service that I became aware of the bane of worship services in rear areas—the diesel-powered electric generator. This noisy contraption made it almost impossible to hear myself speak, and usually it was placed next to wherever worship services were conducted.

* * *

With the first week and my Sunday duties behind me, I began taking advantage of the dispersion of the medics across the whole divisional areas of operation and making good use of the organic medevac elements. It quickly dawned on me that I probably had about as good a combination of freedom to set my agenda and mobility to follow it as any officer in the division. I was more free to move about than most commanders were, because I did not have to limit my focus to a company, battalion or brigade area of operations.

To maintain this freedom, I made certain my priorities and agenda were based on doing the right things for the right reasons, and for me this meant effectively supporting American soldiers, first and last. The Sunday morning worship service for headquarters was the only regular external constraint on my movements. And since I had to be in the area anyhow each Sunday, I usually stayed around and attended LDS meetings in the afternoon.

From the start, I got along well with the battalion leaders. Colonel Leighton frequently attended my Sunday worship services. He always treated me cordially and respectfully gave me free rein to operate as I thought best. Only once did he suggest censure or anything less than satisfaction with my performance, and even then he veiled his dissatisfaction.

It happened following the Sunday worship service on October 10, I think it was, as I rode somewhere with Colonel Leighton in his jeep. Earlier during my sermon, I had sensed someone's displeasure with my simple message. As we rode, Leighton referred casually to a less than flattering portrayal of Mormons in Zane Grey's *Riders of the Purple Sage.* "I prefer more profound preaching," he added. *So you are the displeased soul I sensed.*

I took Leighton's veiled criticism as a statement of personal taste and neither rejection nor a personal attack. Never again during 27 years in the chaplaincy did another commander (or chaplain) imply criticism of my sermons.

By the way, I found nothing about Mormons in the one volume of *Riders of the Purple Sage* that I read.

I could have used some of Leighton's tact in criticizing his executive officer. It was during a staff meeting that the XO, a major, threw out God's name in vain in reaction to something. "Sorry about that, Chaplain," he quickly added.

"Why apologize to me? It wasn't my name you used," I replied.

Silence.

Though my retort was accurate, it was thoughtless, and I immediately regretted having upbraided the XO before the staff and commander. The XO was cool toward me after that, but not vindictive.

Routinely, I visited dispersed medical units, staying a night or two at each clearing station to counsel soldiers, take part in helicopter medevac missions, and generally be available to staffs and patients. Between trips among the dispersed medical companies, I visited the medical wards at headquarters and the hospitals on base and in Qui Nhon and Cam Ranh Bay. Of course, I also attended to the ever-present staff and administrative duties and meetings and scrounged building materials for a combination chaplain's hooch and office.

At least weekly, I reminded Chaplains McGraff and Webb that I was ready for an infantry battalion. Persistence bore fruit after two and a half months. But before telling that tale, I shall here highlight some actions and events that occurred during my 80 days with the medics.

Though it may seem of little significance, my homesickness evolved after about a month from feelings of constant, seemingly unbearable misery into a bearable, low-intensity ache that was interspersed with occasional bouts of acute heart pain.

On September 30, I flew via helicopter to LZ Hammond and joined with some Army doctors and medics to visit a civilian hospital in Phu Cat. At the hospital, I wandered around the area while the docs attended to the wounded and ill. Behind the little facility, near the northeast corner, I came upon a mature Vietnamese woman. She was bare to the waist and engaged in bathing herself by drawing well water in a bucket and pouring it over her head. The woman, engrossed in her personal hygiene efforts, seemed to be unaffected by my presence. Still, I hurried on, intent on giving the woman a degree of privacy, which may have meant more to me than it did to her.

Turning west as I hurried around the southeast corner of the hospital, I came upon the bodies of two infants. They lay unattended on a stretcher between two trees. At first, I thought the bodies were dolls because of the waxy, taut appearance of their skin. The infants had been smothered to death by a smoke bomb the previous night.

Inside the hospital were several female Vietnamese patients, including several new mothers. The patients were lying about on Army cots or atop bloody newspapers on the floor. They shared their beds, pads and newspapers with family members who stayed with them around the clock. Little children played happily in the midst of this scene. I was at once depressed by the conditions of treatment and impressed by the support each patient got from her family.

American medics brought a young woman in for treatment while we were there. She had serious shrapnel (mortar) wounds to her legs and arms.

Later, back at the Medical Clearing Company at LZ Hammond, a little girl was carried in with multiple fragmentation wounds. Her father, a VC, had used the girl and her mother to shield himself from a hand grenade. The blast wounded the little girl and killed her mother. The Americans promptly killed the girl's father and evacuated the newly created orphan.

On October 1 near Phan Thiet, I found myself aboard a medevac chopper, in the right-door seat behind an M-60 machine gun. The trip had started as an administrative run, a non-tactical flight, or ash and trash sortie, in Army jargon.

We had a routine flight until an urgent call diverted us to pick up some wounded infantrymen.

This turn of events placed me in a delicate position as a chaplain. Normally a door gunner would sit where I sat, but he had stayed behind, probably because of the intended nature of this flight. Now we were going into an area where infantry troops were fighting and where the VC might fire on the medevac chopper. We'd been warned the pickup zone was hot, meaning it was still receiving enemy fire. I locked and loaded the M-60 machine gun.

We flew about twenty minutes to reach the contact area (jargon for the place where friendly and enemy forces are engaged in battle), came in fast, flared and hovered for a moment, and settled into a muddy rice paddy on the edge of thick jungle.

Several mud-covered, soaked grunts—the label "grunt" was respectfully reserved for the infantryman—crouched near the tree line beside a buddy who appeared to be dead or unconscious. Quickly, the four grunts placed their buddy on the chopper. Two walking-wounded climbed aboard and we headed for Phan Thiet.

The LZ hadn't been hot, after all, but had we taken fire, I would have returned it. Officially a combatant or not, I couldn't have, wouldn't have, sat on my hands while wounded grunts and the chopper crew were shot at with impunity. In part, my reaction behind the machine gun—as would be the case often in combat—represented a triumph of training over education. My training and experience during years as a police officer and as a former infantryman and medic often won out over my *education* as a chaplain. Oh yes, the unconscious grunt reached the doctors in very bad shape, but alive.

Back during the Chaplain Basic Officer Course in early 1966, we were apprised of an applicable clause in the Geneva Conventions: "Chaplains shall not be *required* to bear arms." (Italics added.) A chaplain, by bearing arms, we were instructed, might endanger the noncombatant, detainee (as opposed to prisoner-of-war) status of any chaplain who falls into the hands of the Vietcong or North Vietnamese forces.

Risks that sounded significant in theory paled in the face of the reality. No American chaplain had survived capture by communist forces during the Korean War, perhaps because the closest thing communist forces had to a chaplain was the party political officer. Perhaps this statistic helps explain why many chaplains on the line in Vietnam placed little stock in the protection spelled out in the Geneva Conventions. Lacking regulatory or statutory prohibitions, each chaplain dealt with the decision whether to take up arms, even in extreme situations, according to his own values, conscience, and the dictates and tenets of his faith or church. Consequently, some chaplains in Vietnam kept a concealed weapon on their persons or kept one near at hand. Occasionally a chaplain was seen carrying a weapon openly—more on that later.

I wrestled with myself before writing of chaplains and weapons. Should I mention the issue at all and risk bringing harm to chaplains on some future battlefield? Should I risk offense to someone's expectations? Or should I be true to things as they were in Vietnam? I chose to write about the issue, to break my 30 years of silence because it is an integral part of the true story of what chaplains wrestled with in a confusing war without front lines or a clear and effective national strategy. Also, I write about the issue because I believe chaplains will, on some future battlefield, have to deal with self-defense issues not considered in the policy-making process, regardless of peacetime theorizing.

In Vietnam, some chaplains refused to keep a personal weapon close at hand, but had no problem with chaplains who did, provided those who did were discreet. Chaplains in this group saw no conflict between chaplains bearing arms and the Geneva Conventions and were often heard to say: "If ever I am in a situation that requires me to fight to defend myself or others, plenty of weapons will be laying around for my use." By this, chaplains implied they might use the weapon of a fallen soldier during a dire emergency.

Some chaplains insisted both the Geneva Conventions and tenets of faith forbade chaplains to take up arms under any provocation. Chaplains in this group generally looked askance upon chaplains of the other groups.

Other chaplains, believing God helps him who helps himself, strictly interpreted the Geneva Conventions to wit: Chaplains shall not be required to bear arms; neither shall chaplains be prohibited from bearing arms.

Several chaplains in the 1st Cav, even some senior ones, kept a personal weapon. One concealed a grease gun in his pack, and another carried a concealed nickel-plated revolver—though privately owned weapons were against regulation for any soldier.

Most field commanders, in my experience, smiled on the chaplain carrying a weapon for his own protection, and some of them on occasion allowed or forbade a chaplain to go into a hot situation, depending on whether the chaplain was prepared to "take care of himself."

While most chaplains dealt privately with the issue of personal weapons, on occasion a chaplain was less than tactful. For example, a national magazine published photographs of a young chaplain as he came "armed to the teeth" out of the jungle onto a firebase. In private conversation, the chaplain insisted he was but helping the grunts carry the many weapons of fallen comrades, lightening the grunts' loads. Whatever the real story, the Army Chief of Chaplains gave the young chaplain a written reprimand, which could have been a career stopper. However, the young chaplain was promoted ahead of his contemporaries, all the way to colonel (0–6). I thought that some of my leaders spoke with a forked tongue on this issue.

What did I do? I carried what I jokingly called my .45-caliber *camera*—for close-up shots. This item of equipment remained discreetly out of sight in my left-front trouser pocket, except on those occasions when none present objected to my possession of it. "Spare film" I kept in an ammo pouch on my pistol belt, naturally.

The issue of chaplains taking up arms would be discussed often following the Vietnam War. Eventually, the Army chaplaincy declared clear policy: Chaplains shall not bear arms. If placed again in Vietnam-like conditions, I would prefer the less restrictive, "Chaplains shall not be required to bear arms."

My first mail from home arrived October 3 and included letters from Helga, James, Jeannie, Laura and my mother. These were items recently touched by my loved ones—a modern miracle, almost too good to believe. Suddenly, the world seemed all right again. The pain of homesickness began to be bearable, almost. Mail!

The rainy monsoon came in earnest to central and northeast Vietnam, bringing the promise of cooler days and seemingly frigid nights in the highlands. Continual torrential rain turned the camp to muck. Low, moisture-laden clouds socked the camp in. Hon Cong Mountain was invisible at times from a hundred feet away.

At about 1630 hours October 4, all available medevac helicopters and all available doctors and medics were scrambled and headed for the top of Hon Cong Mountain. A CV-2 Caribou, laden with sky troopers, including several wounded grunts, had crashed head-on into the side of the mountain. It had crashed while trying to land on the Golf Course runway, despite redundant on-board and ground-based safety guidance systems. Fortunately, the Caribou could fly at the amazingly slow air speed of 40 miles per hour, which made the difference between life and death for several grunts, but not for the crew of the Caribou.

The mountainside was too steep for the rescue choppers to land at the crash site. So from the man-made flat top of Hon Cong, scores of rescuers, including medical personnel and medevac crews, tore their way slipping and sliding down the very rugged, jungle-covered slope to the crash site. There, to their amazement, they found more of the crash victims were alive than were dead.

All the survivors were injured, and many of them required immediate, operating room–quality medical attention. So the rescuers formed a human chain and moved the injured up the mountain to the waiting helicopters. Exerting superhuman strength, the rescuers defied gravity to keep each casualty-laden stretcher approximately level on the 50-to-80 degree incline of the mountainside. Though there was nothing funny about the situation, humor appeared, and from an unlikely source.

One of the rescuers on the human-chain wondered aloud why the doctors had bothered sending up one grunt. An M-16 rifle stuck straight upward out of the man's abdomen. The violence of the crash had driven the barrel of another grunt's rifle all the way through him.

Looking up at his benefactors from the litter, the soldier said, "They can't accuse me of not taking my weapon with me, can they?"

Based on a medic's description of this trooper's wounds, I expected him to die, despite his sense of humor. But I learned differently in 1969. A sergeant, who was on a second or third tour with the 1st Cav, told me the rest of the story. "Yeah, that was Sergeant [forgot the name]. He was wounded earlier that day during a 'blue-team' operation . . . He's stationed now at Fort. . . ." Perhaps *Readers Digest* had it right, that *Laughter Is the Best Medicine*.

The commander or executive officer had directed me to remain behind to help medical ward personnel attend to incoming survivors, if any. This order came in response to me asking where I could best help—a mistake I'd not make again. In the future, I would do what I thought best and repent later, if necessary. As it turned out, no crash survivors were brought to our facility.

By evening, routines were continuing as if little or nothing had happened. It's hard to imagine how individuals and units can so quickly fall back into and onto routine following tragedy. This ability, I suppose, is essential to maintaining one's sanity in war.

The next day, I learned that 15 men survived the Caribou

crash. A day or so later, another survivor showed up. This was probably Pfc. Henry L. Creek, who had been listed as MIA. He had pulled himself from the wreckage before rescuers reached the scene, and despite combat wounds and subsequent crash injuries, had climbed down the mountain. The surprised members of a patrol found him when he staggered from the jungle.

I wondered how prepared or unprepared for eternity those who died had been.

Meanwhile, the rains brought relief from the constant dust—of which we got our share, positioned as we were at the end of the airstrip and right next to an active helipad.

The morning of October 6, I struggled with intense yearnings to be with Helga. Then I considered all she meant to me, and my emotions soared. Suddenly, I appreciated my misery, an attitude some soldiers didn't share. Rather, some of them, officer and enlisted alike, saw separation from wife and children as an opportunity to fornicate and "adulterate" without fear of being found out or held accountable. This debasing philosophy was evident by the constant stream of soldiers to Sin City—and to the medics for penicillin.

Sin City was a military-controlled collection of brothels in An Khe, where soldiers could have all their lusts attended to at low prices and with lessened risk of catching a venereal disease. American military police guarded the brothels, and American medics examined the prostitutes weekly, so we were told. *I thank God for the misery I feel when separated from Helga. Thank God Sin City holds no attraction for me.*

These thoughts and feelings I tried to convey to Helga, to assure her of my love and my determination to maintain our high-fidelity marriage.

That evening something occurred that I must relate because it led to many other significant events. While visiting the sick and lightly wounded in the Quonset huts, I noticed a patient was watching me closely. Catching my eye, he asked where I was from. "Tennessee," I answered, though I might have said Utah, my adopted home state.

"Oh," said the slender, dark-haired patient and went silent.

I shrugged the incident off, little suspecting the chain of events that this soldier was about to bring into my life.

Notes

5 October 1969, 1st Cav. Div., G-1 Journal: 2115 Hours, "MIA: Pfc. Henry L. Creek . . . passenger on CV-2 on flight from fwd area . . . crashed into mountainside coming in for a landing . . . 1/12 Cav [then follows others, same crash]; SFC Armando Ramos, 13 Sig. Bn; Capt. Johnnie L. Daniel, Hq. 1st Bde; 1LT Kenneth W. West, Sp4 John T. Bird, Pfc. Donald A. Smith Jr., A 5/7 Cav; SSG Richard M. Prociv, Hq 1st Bde; Pfc. James G. Litts, 8th Eng; Pfc. Donald E. Lewis, B 1/5; Sgt. Homer L. Pickett, B 1/21.

four

"We Are Going to Crash!"

On October 7, during another visit to the medical wards, I greeted the patient who the night before had asked where I was from. After exchanging pleasantries and names—his was David Lillywhite—I asked, "Where are you from?"

"Snowflake, Arizona," he answered.

"That's Mormon country. Are you a Mormon?"

"Yes sir, I am."

"A good Mormon?" I asked.

"I try my best to be."

"I'm LDS, too," I said.

Smiling broadly, Lillywhite said, "I thought you were last night, but I didn't think the Army had LDS chaplains. And when you said you're from Tennessee, I figured you couldn't be a Mormon."

Lillywhite was a draftee, an infantryman, a longtime member of his faith and fairly new member of Bravo Company, 2nd Battalion, 8th Cavalry (2–8 Cav). He was being treated for boils, the results in part of living conditions in the field. Lillywhite told me of a buddy and fellow member of his faith, Pfc. Danny Hyde. He said Hyde had recently vowed to put his life in spiritual order. "Would you visit Danny?" Lillywhite asked me. I promised to visit Hyde, assuming I could easily keep the promise because I knew my way around the AO and how to deal with the gatekeepers to units, the sergeants major and first sergeants.

Besides what was about to happen with Danny Hyde, my association with Lillywhite soon involved me in another tragedy. This tragedy, actually an atrocity, led to a chain of events that years later would be written up in the *New*

Yorker magazine, published in a book, plagiarized into an award-winning underground film titled *Mao*, and produced as a major Hollywood movie titled *Casualties of War*. This incident would also get me a few lines of favorable mention in a seven-volume history of the U.S. Army Chaplaincy.

At 1645 hours October 9, following Sunday duties at base camp, I flew through driving rain to LZ Hammond. There I spent the night with the medevac pilots, one of whom I almost decked when he came up behind me unannounced.

The next morning I braved especially sticky, deep, vehicle-churned red mud to reach the 2–8 Cav field trains on the west side of LZ Hammond. There, the battalion Sergeant Major agreed to let me visit Danny Hyde out in Bravo Company, but I'd have to wait until the company got out of a firefight. He wouldn't promise when conditions in Bravo Company would be secure enough to receive a chaplain from another unit. I decided to try again the next day.

To make good use of what was left of the day, I returned to the medical company on Hammond in time to accompany a medical team on a visit to a prisoner of war (POW) camp at Phu Cat.

At the POW camp I saw two confirmed VC, a seventeen-year-old female and a VC Master Sergeant (or equivalent rank). The VC sergeant had surrendered to American forces on the condition that he could bring along his family and plow.

While the medics treated enemy patients, I wandered about the camp, but soon wished I hadn't. While passing a building, I looked through a window into an almost empty room. Inside, two ARVN soldiers were interrogating a VC or native suspected of being VC. Wires ran from a hand-cranked generator to the suspect's bare genitals. The Vietnamese interrogators seemed unconcerned about me watching them, which led me to conclude this type of interrogation might be a common practice. One of my great regrets is that I didn't interfere with this interrogation, though I didn't know what to do as it involved natives on a native compound. Apparently, the officer in charge of the medical detail did not know what to do either.

About 2100 hours, back at the An Khe base camp, I sat on a bunker during an alert—the enemy was probing the northwest perimeter. Unknown to me, Chaplain Browne had minutes earlier received a call from the division chaplain: "LDS man critically injured, being evacuated to 85th Hospital. Request Chaplain Newby, LDS chaplain, to proceed."

In the TOC, Colonel Leighton gave me the message from Chaplain Browne and said a chopper would pick me up momentarily at the medevac pad. Because of the weather, only emergency flights were authorized. The urgent call for a chaplain constituted an emergency.

Before the chopper took off at 2100 hours, I strapped myself into the right-door seat (machine gun position) of a fully loaded Huey (UH-1D). The other passengers were soldiers going on emergency leave or heading home after completing their tour. They'd been waiting, perhaps praying, for an emergency like this so they could fly out of An Khe. The crew chief checked my safety belt before we took off, the only safety check ever given to me during two Vietnam tours.

We'd just cleared the medevac pad when I realized I'd left my consecrated oil in the hooch. I took seriously the scriptural admonition to, when any are sick, "call the elders . . . let them pray . . . anointing with oil" (James 5:14). *Never mind*, logic whispered, *the power is not in the oil. Besides, I can probably find some olive oil at the hospital in Qui Nhon.*

Conscience whispered, *yes, but I am supposed to always be ready to do the Lord's work in the Lord's way.*

We were into the clouds and approaching the Deo Mang Pass (often called the An Khe Pass by Americans) at 5000 feet altitude by the time I'd wrestled through all this. Just then, the engine of the chopper began making odd noises, and we went into a sudden dropping U-turn to the left, almost a dive. The crew chief shouted excitedly into my left ear, "We're losing RPM and going down. We'll try to crash inside the perimeter!"

This is my fault. We're crashing because I am not prepared, I thought.

Closing my eyes, I prayed, "Heavenly Father, please don't let these others be hurt or killed because of my failings." A moment later, my prayer completed, I saw the tops of tall, almost bare trees whipping diagonally upward, left to right, past my window.

At just the right moment, the pilot pulled pitch or whatever it was that the emergency called for. The chopper autorotated in a controlled crash, hit the ground hard, and came to rest facing uphill on an incline, in the middle of an ammunition dump. The impact crumpled the landing skids on the chopper and caused serious structural damage.

In a flash, the crew chief had my door open and was in my face, inquiring if I were all right. Answering, "I'm okay," I jumped from the chopper and moved away, ducking low to avoid the main rotor blade that continued to spin and was skimming within a few feet of stacked boxes of artillery rounds.

Rescuers located us after about 15 minutes, and one of my medevac choppers landed to evacuate casualties. There were none, thanks to good fortune, a skilled crew and, perhaps, sincere prayers.

I was the only taker of a proffered lift on the medevac chopper. The crew of the downed chopper insisted on staying with their ship. "We'll wait for ground transportation, thank you," said the other passengers.

The medevac chopper dropped me off at my battalion, where I grabbed my consecrated oil, telephoned a report of the crash to Chaplain Browne, and stood by. At 2300 hours, Chaplain Browne called. Captain Dubois, 15th Transportation was providing me another chopper—I'd be the only passenger.

We approached Qui Nhon from the sea, which allowed

us to drop from the clouds without risking a crash into a hill, several of which were near the city. Once out of the clouds, I watched green tracer rounds reach upward at us from several points in the Qui Nhon waters. A moment later we landed safely at the airfield, and from there I hitched a ride to the 85th Evac Hospital.

At about 0200 hours October 11, a medic directed me to the bedside of a "black" soldier in the intensive care ward. The nurse who accompanied me said the patient had no chance of survival. A card on the patient's bed identified him as Pfc. Hyde, Danny, Company B 2–8, 1st Air Cavalry Division, Negro; religious preference: LDS. Before me lay the young trooper I'd been called to see. He was also the same trooper I had tried unsuccessfully to visit in the field the previous day.

Immediately, guilt and self-censure inundated me. *I should have stuck around Danny's battalion. Perhaps he wouldn't be here if I had reached him. Not likely, but maybe.*

At 1905 hours the previous evening, a claymore mine had traumatically amputated Danny Hyde's left leg and arm, damaged his other appendages, destroyed one eye and severely injured the other one. The blast also burned away all his hair and blackened the front of what was left of his body; thus, he appeared to be a black man.

After the nurse withdrew to give me privacy, I prayed mightily for the spirit to guide me that I might administer to Danny Hyde and convey to him whatever blessing the Lord wanted him to have. Next, I found an undamaged spot on Danny's head, anointed him with oil, sealed the anointing, and blessed him to live and return home to his loved ones. Even as I blessed Danny, I doubted the spiritual source of the promises I gave him.

The ministration completed, the nurse returned and noted on Danny's chart that he was *Caucasian* rather than *Negro*, according to me. Still, she insisted he was obviously a Negro. My feelings of guilt calmed somewhat as I returned to the airfield and during the flight to An Khe.

We departed Qui Nhon at 0400 hours with a send-off of green tracer bullets to match the welcome the VC had given us earlier. Upon landing on the Golf Course, my pilot, a major, said, "Young man, if you want an Army career, you'd better never again demand a helicopter to fly under conditions like this."

"It wasn't me demanding anything," I explained and told him about the urgent message I'd received.

Upon learning the nature of the mission and that I had willingly boarded two other helicopters within minutes of falling from the sky in one, the major said, "You've got more guts than I've got," and walked away.

The previous evening as we were about to crash, I'd felt as the Biblical Jonah must have when he advised the crew of a ship to throw him overboard, lest they all die. And that was before I knew I'd been called to the bedside of Danny Hyde, whom I'd failed to reach a few hours earlier.

In retrospect, it didn't seem reasonable for God to strike down a helicopter just to teach me a lesson, and from this new perspective my intense guilt seemed excessive. Sure, I could have waited all day in the unlikely event I could reach Hyde, but lacking the vision and foreknowledge of God, I had decided, reasonably so, to attend to other duties and try again the next day.

Thus, my feelings of guilt lessened even as I increasingly questioned the source and inspiration for the blessing I had given Danny Hyde. Had I been inspired when I blessed him to live, or had I spoken from misplaced guilt? The latter, I feared.

At 0730 the same morning, I learned from the Division Casualty Office which tracked sick, dead and wounded soldiers, that Danny yet lived and his condition was unchanged. With this news in hand, I visited the sick ward and told Lillywhite what had befallen his friend. At 0900 hours, I flew to LZ Hammond to get more information about what happened to Hyde.

From the medics and battalion chaplain, Charles Lockie,

I learned this. The previous evening, following a battle and while he dug in for the night, Hyde went forward of his fox-hole to place a claymore mine. Already, he'd inserted a detonator into the mine and connected the detonating cap by wire to the "klacker" (a hand-held device used to set off the mine, making it a "command-detonated mine"). A buddy had accidentally stepped on the klacker back in the foxhole as Hyde bent over to place the mine.

The medics at the clearing company on LZ Hammond said that though Hyde's were the worst wounds they'd ever seen on a living grunt, he was awake and alert when evacuated to Qui Nhon. He'd asked his buddies to send to his parents the cash he had on hand. I visited Danny at noon. His condition had worsened.

At 1430 hours, after visiting Danny Hyde, I flew to Nha Trang via a C-123 to attend a retreat for chaplains. Two 1st Cav chaplains paled when I walked in and one declared, "You're supposed to be dead!" Someone had concluded I died of injuries suffered in the chopper crash. After all, I had departed the crash site in a medevac helicopter, been flown to Qui Nhon, but wasn't listed as a living patient in any hospital there.

On October 13, I swung by on the way to An Khe and visited Danny Hyde. His condition was unchanged. By then, I'd almost concluded Hyde's original blessing had come of my guilt, rather than from God, that my administration might be causing Danny unnecessary suffering.

The next day, some Seventh Day Adventist troopers, in a fine Christian gesture, voluntarily poured concrete and prepared a pad for my hooch and office. Later that day I went on two medevac missions, and at 2000 hours I returned to Qui Nhon and Danny Hyde. He lingered on, barely clinging to life, too badly wounded for evacuation to Japan or the states.

Finding a quiet, private spot, I prayed for understanding

and inspiration on Danny's behalf. Then I returned to the ward, pulled the curtains around his bed and placed my hands again upon Danny's comatose head. This time, after waiting for inspiration, I petitioned for Danny's release from the effects of the previous blessing and commended him to God, to live or die according to God's will, not mine. Danny Hyde died at 0400 hours, October 21, 1966. I was thankful I could write to his parents about his recent vow to get his spiritual life in order.

A year later, Danny's parents would approach me as I walked about in uniform on a public square in Salt Lake City and request my help in finding someone who could tell them more about their beloved son's last days and circumstances.

Meanwhile back home my children suffered as much, probably more, than I, which became clearer in a letter I received on October 23. Helga wrote of James having become very agitated recently when he discovered his model airplane in the middle of the bedroom floor, crushed. Somehow, knowing Laura Jane was the culprit, he angrily demanded she be punished and that she replace the model. Helga sought motive. "Because the airplane took my Daddy away," Laura confessed. She wasn't punished.

Back in Vietnam, two days later, a young Vietnamese woman "propositioned" me. Approaching me with an infant on her hip at a market in An Khe where I bartered for materials for my office and hooch, she offered herself to me for ten piasters—a dollar or two as I recall. Instantly, an older woman jumped between us and, pointing at my chaplain insignia, chided the younger woman in very harsh tones. The young woman slunk away, eyes downcast, the image of shame. Obviously, the young mother felt shame, though her standards and circumstances differed greatly from mine. The incident brought to mind the Biblical account of Jesus' response when a woman taken in adultery was brought before him. I wished I could emulate the Savior and admonish

the woman in Vietnamese to "go thy way and sin no more
[cease prostituting yourself]."

Notes
10 October 1966, 1st Cav Chaplain Section Journal: 2040 Hrs,
    request from Hammond. LDS soldier critically injured ...
    request Chaplain Newby ... to proceed to 85th as soon as
    possible. 2200 Hrs: Major Brandt called to notify that Chaplain
    Newby's helicopter crash-landed in Song Be. 2300 Hrs: Notified
    by Cpt. Dubois that 15th TC is providing a plane and Chaplain
    Newby will be airborne shortly.

five

Friendly Fire

Occasionally, one religious denomination or another would hold a conference for its military chaplains. At noon on October 24, I received word that an LDS conference would be held in Nha Trang the following Sunday. This would be for all members, not just chaplains. General church authorities Elders Gordon B. Hinckley and Marion D. Hanks would be attending. This was great news for most LDS troopers, the importance of which other chaplains had difficulty comprehending until I explained just who these were in the hierarchy of the church.

The conference offered a great opportunity for the grunts and support troopers, leaders and privates to worship and learn at the feet of great spiritual leaders. But how, I wondered, do I arrange it in five short days? I'd need several layers of command and staff approval, the cooperation of the Air Force for transportation, and to contact LDS men throughout the division AO. And I must convince scores of small-unit leaders it would be in the best interest of each of their respective units to release each LDS soldier for two days. And I must do all this without experience or after-action reports for reference.

Well, being confident I could cause it to happen, I spent the rest of the day staffing my idea through technical (chaplain) and command channels. To my pleasant surprise, division-level approval came easily, and the U.S. Air Force agreed to provide transportation. By early evening, several others and I were out hunting for troopers who were LDS, which search I continued at LZ Hammond on October 25.

The plan developed quickly: On October 26, a 25-passenger CV-2 Caribou was "laid on" for the conference. By October 27, we had confirmation of 26 attendees, one more than the dedicated airplane could carry. In the next two days, the list of committed attendees grew to 37, 11 too many for the airplane seats available. Major Denver Harper of Salt Lake City came to the rescue; he would fly his Huey helicopter to the conference. We prayed our flights would not be canceled because of bad weather or increased combat activity.

At 0600, October 30, 34 troopers departed for the conference in Nha Trang. Two hours and 30 minutes later, I sat in a meeting with hundreds of soldiers, airmen and a sprinkling of sailors and civilians. Before the meeting, I had visited with Elder Hinckley and was pleased that he remembered me from when he set me apart almost a year earlier. I also became acquainted with Elder Marion D. Hanks; he and I developed a life-long friendship.

Following the conference, after getting the troopers in the air en route back to An Khe, I flew to Saigon aboard an Air Force C-47 in company with Elders Hinckley and Hanks and a few others. Elder Hanks took advantage of the flight to teach us military passengers from the scriptures.

After the conference in Saigon I linked up with a Captain Layne, USAF, thus keeping a promise to his wife to visit him in Vietnam. That evening I rode behind Layne on his Honda motorbike through the chaotic streets of Saigon—a scary, exhilarating experience.

Layne was expected to attend an evening meeting with Elders Hinckley and Hanks in the Brinks Hotel (which served as accommodations for American Officers). As Layne's guest for the night, I accompanied him to the leadership meeting.

The meeting began with about 12 men present, including the general and local church leaders. Elder Hinckley began the meeting by announcing there would be no business conducted. Instead, we were invited to share our thoughts and feelings in turn, beginning on his right and going around the room.

Each impromptu testimony was moving and some were amazing. Layne, for example, told of spending a long, lonely night in his downed jet fighter and of how he sang gospel hymns all night to "keep the VC away."

When my turn came, I told about Danny Hyde, David Lillywhite and grunts like them. In conclusion, I related the events leading up to and during the blessing in Elder Hinckley's office in 1965.

Speaking last, Elder Hinckley apologized to me for having questioned the validity of my orders to active duty. He said, in effect: "I did not mean to question you, Brother Newby, but I knew it was not possible for you to have valid orders. The Army had informed us you, specifically, were not acceptable in the chaplaincy. I knew something was wrong, and I would not have set you apart had President Lee not said, 'If he has orders, set him apart.'"

Continuing, Elder Hinckley said, "I'm sorry I doubted you, Brother Newby, for when I placed my hands on your head, the Lord revealed to me it was right, that you were in the chaplaincy because the Lord wanted you there ... which just goes to show, brethren, what the Lord wants to happen will happen, military regulations notwithstanding."

Elder Hinckley may never appreciate in mortality how supportive his words were to me there in that crowded room in the Brinks Hotel. So often over the next quarter of a century, his words reinforced and comforted me during dark hours and influenced me to continue in the chaplaincy for 13 years beyond when I could have retired.

The next day I used faked flight orders, provided by Layne, to return to the Cav. I was glad to escape from rear-area trappings and conditions, which I thought were silly and out of place in a combat zone—air conditioning, dress uniforms for Air Force personnel, spit and polish for the Army, and clubs and parties. It seemed wrong somehow when I compared these conditions with what the grunt endured.

This experience helped me remember how grateful I'd been to go to the 1st Cav in the first place.

I was promoted to captain sometime in October. At the time I had completed 10 months of active commissioned service and had been in Vietnam less than two months. The new rank changed nothing so far as my duties and operations were concerned.

The evening of October 25, I flew to LZ Oasis (near the Cambodian border) and spent most of the night debating various philosophies with doctors and pilots. About noon the next day, I headed for An Khe aboard a Caribou. We stopped en route at Duc Co Special Forces Camp and then headed east over the Mang Yang Pass, flying just above the treetops because of the weather and cloud cover. A trooper said later that he kept repeating every Catholic prayer he knew and had expected that any minute we would crash into the trees. I understood, because that was the scariest fixed-wing flight I ever had.

During November 1966, I continued to move almost constantly around the 1st Cav AO and conduct Sunday services for the Medical Battalion, except on the first Sunday of each month, when I had a visiting chaplain conduct a communion service, a practice I'd begun at Fort Ord, California. Overall, November was much quieter for me than October had been, though I was probably busier, knowing by then how best to use the systems.

On November 7, I moved into my hooch and office, a fine building under the circumstances and one I truly hoped would soon be occupied by someone else. The hooch was ready, except for lighting, and medic Keith L. Hardy kindly donated the materials and installed it. While installing the lights, Hardy mentioned that he was LDS—he requested and got a Book of Mormon.

Chaplain Garadella visited me on November 8. He had been honor-graduate in our basic chaplain course class and had given me a free ride from New York City to Chicago. After lunch Garadella and I visited Sin City so he could see what it was like. This was my one and only trip past the MP station at the entrance.

Later in the afternoon, while Garadella and I traveled in his jeep to Qui Nhon, he confessed a wish to ride in a helicopter, an experience denied him thus far in his Vietnam tour. I, being a 1st Cav chaplain, could hardly imagine chaplains and troops in Vietnam who didn't regularly ride in choppers.

On November 9, I delivered to Chaplain McClements a collection of food for the refugee camp he supported. I appreciated McClements' work with refugees, but avoided becoming heavily involved in such projects because I believed my time and energies as a chaplain belonged to American soldiers, especially infantry.

Major General John Norton, 1st Cav. Division Commander, gave me a compliment. A meeting between the chaplains and General Norton had just broken up. I stood talking with Chaplains McGraff, Webb and Browne. General Norton approached the group and said, "Excuse me, Chaplain Newby. I mean no offense, but you look more like an infantryman than a chaplain." He made my day.

I was especially lonely on November 18, James' twelfth birthday. The loneliness was bearable, though, mostly because this far into my tour the mail flowed in both directions, if spastic on occasion.

Sp4 David Lillywhite visited me on November 20. His battalion sergeant major, upon learning Lillywhite was a carpenter in civilian life, had kept him in the rear on R&U Detail (repair and upkeep). In this capacity Lillywhite helped build billets in the battalion rear area (a foolish practice—rear-area accommodations for troops who seldom saw the rear area). Anyhow, Lillywhite was back in my life and about to involve me in another situation.

* * *

On Thanksgiving Day, I conducted a worship service at 0930 hours for the Medical Battalion. Eleven men attended. I also offered Thanksgiving blessings in both the officer and enlisted messes (dining tents) at about 1300 hours. After lunch, I visited with the sick and with several troopers in their tents and then flew to LZ Hammond on a medevac chopper.

At Landing Zone Hammond I visited medical personnel and patients at the medical clearing company and was there when medevac and other ships brought in 20 wounded troopers and the remains of two KIAs. One of the KIAs had been part of the crew of a 1–9 Cav H-13 scout chopper when it was shot down in flames. His remains were almost unrecognizable as having been human; the blackened skull had exploded. All the wounded were in very bad condition.

Questions haunted me as I moved among the wounded and dead: *What of the families of those killed and maimed on Thanksgiving?* Probably a family sorely missed each killed and wounded trooper. And, probably, each trooper's loved ones were readying the traditional Thanksgiving meal even as he fell in battle. Thanksgiving would come hours later in the states. Over the land families would soon be offering Thanksgiving prayers for the safety of those who had already fallen, only to have hope dashed to pieces in a few days when a messenger of death arrived at the door. What would happen to hope in days ahead, when each family received word that a loved one—a son, husband or father—fell on Thanksgiving, despite their hopes and prayers? Would these tragic sacrifices mar all future Thanksgivings, or would time dull the memories and pain and allow hope and joy to return on some future holiday?

I was at Phan Thiet when November 1966 gave way to December. There in the medical clearing company mess I enjoyed the best meal I'd eaten since arriving in Vietnam. That evening, back at An Khe Base Camp, I became soaked as I hitchhiked (mostly hiked) to my hooch from a secondary airstrip, one well away from the center of the camp. By bedtime, chills and fever wracked my body. *Malaria*, I wondered.

A phone call at 2334 hours interrupted a night spent alternating between chills and fever. It was about a badly wounded LDS patient at the 67th Evac Hospital in Qui Nhon. Later in the night, the sound of gunfire infringed on my suffering. The shots remained a temporary mystery because I was too sick to investigate. They had been fired during a drinking party in the battalion area, I'd learn later.

At 0930 hours the next day in no-fly weather, still weak and chilled, I went by cold, open jeep to Qui Nhon, 45 miles across the mountains to the east. At the 67th Evacuation Hospital, I administered and gave spiritual counsel to John Martin, the trooper I had been called about the previous evening. Martin had sustained very serious gunshot wounds to the shoulder, chest, groin and leg. After seeing Martin, I visited other grunts from the 5–7 Cav and 1–9 Cav, each of whom had been wounded in the same fight as Martin.

On December 4, while making rounds of the medical wards, I saw a dry blood-encrusted flak vest lying behind a Quonset hut. An hour earlier the vest had been on Military Policeman (Sp4) Richard Grumberg, who was guarding the commanding general's quarters. A 105mm-howitzer shell exploded near Grumberg's guard post, killing him and wounding his partner, Sp4 Robert Simon. A "friendly" unit, American or ARVN, had fired the shell from a nearby base. This was, I think, my first exposure to so-called short rounds or "friendly fire" incidents.

I found it very curious that just one artillery round hit near the commanding general's quarters, in the middle of our very large base camp—the general wasn't in at the time. This is curious because artillery was usually fired in barrages, three or more tubes in unison, all with identical aiming settings. I wondered if this so-called friendly fire was all that friendly or if perhaps the shell actually landed where someone intended it to hit.

Of course, the phrase *friendly fire* as used by soldiers in the field had everything to do with the source of the fire and nothing to do with qualities or relationships. The phrase was very utilitarian in an us-versus-them (allies or "friendlies" and enemies or "bad guys") environment where quick recognition often spelled the difference between living and dying.

About December 5, I visited David Lillywhite on a building construction site in his battalion rear area. After visiting a few minutes with Lillywhite and his companions, I went my way, unaware I had left behind a special impression on a very troubled member of the building crew, which impression would soon draw me into the aftermath of a heinous war crime.

six

An Atrocity:
"Casualties of War"*

After dark on December 9, David Lillywhite and another soldier appeared at my door, at 1900 hours by my journal and 2200 hours according to the soldier's later court testimony. I looked into the eyes of the man with Lillywhite and quickly dismissed my initial impression that this was a social call.

The man's countenance and demeanor broadcast a heavy weight on mind and soul, and he was nervous about being in my office.

I welcomed the two troopers into the sleeping area of my combination office and hooch. The troopers took the two available folding chairs, and I sat on my mosquito net-draped bunk. After brief pleasantries, Lillywhite explained his purpose in coming. His companion, Sven (part of his alias in a future *New Yorker* magazine piece), had requested an introduction to me.

Sven began by hinting he was aware of a horrible crime and wanted help in dealing with it. Interrupting Sven, I advised him he forfeited privileged communication by talking in front of Lillywhite. Sven insisted he wanted Lillywhite to hear what he had to tell me. This is his story as I remember him telling it, and it agrees in most details with what he later testified to in court and with what he told magazine writer and author Daniel Lang. For convenience in telling, I shall

The temptation is great to omit the events in this chapter because they smear so many great men and mar the record of an outstanding unit. But to omit this would defeat my objective of giving an honest portrayal of those who served.

assign the key characters the aliases that author Daniel Lang gave them in his *New Yorker* magazine piece and book, both titled "Casualties of War."

The previous month, about November 16 or 17, Sven's platoon leader, Lieutenant Reilly, assigned him and four others to a five-man pony team mission under the leadership of Sergeant Meserve, with Corporal Clark as second-in-command. Two cousins, Rafe and Manuel Diaz, completed the makeup of the pony team. Meserve was respected by troopers, officers and fellow sergeants for his courage and combat feats.

The 1st Cav used five-man *pony teams* for missions of several days' duration, during which time the teams watched and searched a specified area, in this case in the vicinity of a hill designated as "Hill 192," to gather intelligence on the enemy. As I recall, the teams were called pony teams because they were too small and too lightly armed for serious fighting—not "stallions."

The evening of November 17, Meserve briefed Pony Team Three—called "Pony 3"—which was scheduled to begin its mission about dawn the next morning. He concluded his briefing by announcing the team would leave earlier than usual to allow them time to snatch a young woman from a local village. The team would take her along on the mission to *boost morale*. Hoping Meserve was joking, but fearing he wasn't, Sven immediately reported Meserve's words to a friend in his squad. His buddy shrugged off Meserve's stated intentions as a joke. But Meserve wasn't joking.

Sven became very anxious the next morning when under cover of darkness Meserve moved the team out and headed east toward the hamlet of Cat Toung, opposite from the direction of Hill 192, their assigned surveillance area. Sven, fearing the worst, cursed himself for not reporting Meserve's mission *briefing* to an officer.

* * *

In the village, after Meserve and Clark had entered and exited empty-handed from several huts, Rafe pointed out a hooch where he'd occasionally seen a pretty young woman. This time Meserve and Clark came out with a young woman in tow. Her real name was Mao. She was in her late teens and pregnant. They had snatched her from her home while her mother and younger sister, Phan Thi Loc (from court-martial records), cried and pleaded for mercy. Departing the hamlet, the team pushed hard to be clear of open and populated areas and into their jungle AO before dawn. Cover under the jungle would decrease the risks of being spotted by other Americans with the kidnapped female in their custody. Risk of discovery remained high until they reached thick jungle, especially because the 1–9 Cav routinely flew "first light" sweeps of the AO, with very impressive results.

Manuel hit on a bright idea for lightening his combat load by making their hostage, frail, pregnant Mao, carry his heavy rucksack during much of the climb up into the hills.

After a while, well out of sight of any villages and concealed from the air by heavy jungle, Pony 3 stopped and ate chow, but gave Mao nothing to eat, though they removed her gag. Soon after the chow break, the team came upon an abandoned native hut near the center of their assigned AO. Meserve ordered the team to clean out the hut; it would be the team's base of operations and become the scene of the crimes they yet intended.

Leaving Mao inside the hut, Meserve announced it was time for fun. Perhaps because he suspected Sven's dismay at what was going on, Meserve asked Sven to take his turn first in the hut. When Sven declared he would not take part in raping the young woman, Meserve warned him that he risked becoming a *friendly casualty*, unless he took his turn with Mao. Clark enthusiastically seconded Meserve's threat.

To press their threats home, for several minutes, Meserve and Clark berated Sven's courage and manhood and accused him of being homosexual and disloyal to the team.

Torn by conflicting loyalties and uncertain what to do, Sven moved a few yards away from the others and set a watch for the VC. He said the others would not allow him to move far enough away for his weapon, an M-79 grenade launcher, to be effective against them—rounds, once fired from these weapons, must travel some twenty-five yards, as I recall, before becoming armed.

Led by Meserve, each of the other team members entered the hut, in turn. During each visit, rising and falling screams pierced Sven's soul. Between these visits, Mao's screams were interspersed with moans and sobs. Clark, the second to enter the hut, came out bragging he had raped Mao with a knife to her throat, while her hands were tied behind her back.

During the gang raping and for hours afterwards, Sven endured his teammates' boasts about "how good" Mao had been and how she compared to other women they had "had." Sickened to his heart, Sven spent these hours wrestling with himself, torn between his searing conscience and that unexplainable loyalty that develops between fellow grunts in combat.

In the quiet of the evening, Meserve announced his intentions to keep Mao alive overnight to provide more fun the next morning, Sven said. Mao, having been kidnapped, used as a beast of burden, repeatedly raped, terrorized, and growing increasingly ill, was tied up and left alone, moaning and bleeding through the night.

The next morning, as if everything were as normal as things can be in combat, Meserve set the team to accomplishing the mission assigned to it. Shortly after dawn, Pony 3 spotted enemy troops nearby, and Meserve dutifully reported the sightings. In response to his report, higher echelons ordered an air assault into the area of additional ground troops and sent in the ever-alert 1–9 Air Cav Scouts. Apparently, a decision was also made to pull Pony 3 out before the arrival of nightfall, for at 1145 hours Meserve requested permission to remain out an additional night.

Though this request was denied, Pony 3 was ordered into a blocking position on a streambed.

Concerned about increased risks of discovery by approaching reinforcements, Meserve decided it was time to kill Mao, toss her body off a cliff. "Kill her," he ordered Sven, "or we report you as KIA," he threatened.

Sven refused to kill Mao and braced himself for the violent death he expected—knowing full well by now what Meserve and the others were capable of doing. But instead of shooting Sven, Meserve ordered first one and then the other of the Diaz cousins to kill Mao—they each refused. Clark volunteered.

Dragging Mao's abused, sick body from the hut, Clark shoved her into the nearby bushes. A moment later Sven heard what sounded to him like a knife being plunged into Mao's body. Clark returned alone from the bushes, wiping blood from the ten-inch blade of his civilian hunting knife. "She's dead," he declared.

Moments later, preparations to depart the area were interrupted when the heavily bleeding Mao crawled from the bushes, staggered to her feet and ran across a small clearing away from Pony 3. Clark and Meserve let go a stream of obscenities, and the latter ordered, "Kill the bitch!"

Everyone opened fire, including Sven, though he aimed an M-79 grenade to the side of Mao's direction of flight. Immediately, he cursed himself for having even pretended to fire at Mao, either for his own safety or in the heat of the moment.

Mao, her body riddled with bullets, made it across the clearing and disappeared into the bush. One of the Diaz cousins pointed to where he thought he saw a bush move, and Clark approached the spot and sprayed it point-blank with automatic fire. This time he made sure Mao was dead. Half her face and head were shot away.

Charlie Company received this message at 2015 hours, almost eight hours after Mao was murdered: "[Pony 3] reports that at 1230 hours killed one VC woman, fleeing from

Hill 192 . . . shot warning shots, but she did not stop, so they shot to kill . . . at grid-coordinate 978736."

"Well done," radioed Lieutenant Reilly to Pony 3.

At 1440 hours, a member of Pony 3 was medevaced from the field with a possible broken shoulder; unsure which member of the team it was. While these things were going on with Pony 3, Charlie Company sustained three WIAs that day during a long day of continual contact with the enemy. The war went on, situation *normal*, except for Sven.

Sven believes he survived the day on Hill 192 only because Pony 3 expended all its ammunition against the VC in the subsequent fighting.

Thankful to be alive, Sven vowed to himself to see justice done for Mao and her family, no matter what. Hoping for advice about how to proceed, Sven told his buddy everything immediately upon arriving back in his platoon area. The buddy relayed Sven's accusations to Lieutenant Reilly.

According to Sven, Lieutenant Reilly discouraged him from making an issue of the matter with, "After all, this is war, and she was a gook." At least Reilly replaced Sven on the pony team when it returned to the jungle to continue its mission—Pony 3 had come in temporarily to repair its radio. Reilly reportedly said he had replaced Sven, knowing he "would not come back alive."

Assuming no action was being taken on his report, Sven went directly to his company commander, Captain Vorst (an alias), during another operation. After talking with Captain Vorst three times, Sven concluded his accusations were being swept under the rug.

Meserve, Clark and the Diaz cousins had been split into different platoons, and each busted one grade for sleeping without mosquito net—a joke, as few nets were even carried by grunts in the field.

Manuel Diaz remained in Sven's platoon, in a different squad. Immediately, Sven became the focus of intense animosity by his fellow soldiers and former buddies. "The animosity reached its limit," Sven decided, a few days after the pony team members were dispersed.

Sven's squad came "accidentally" under friendly fire by the squad to which Manuel had been reassigned. Sven said, "Most of the incoming fire was cracking and impacting around me, while the rest of my squad gave me plenty of space."

Sven added in essence, "After the shooting stopped, I looked into Manuel's cold, hard eyes and decided I'd had enough." Upon returning from the patrol, Sven formally refused to remain any longer in the field with Charlie Company. Captain Vorst sent Sven to Division Base Camp at An Khe to await transfer to a helicopter door gunner position.

Sven continued to wrestle with his conscience at An Khe. By December 1, he was convinced command was not investigating his accusations. Meanwhile, he worked on the battalion Repair and Utilities (R&U) detail with David Lillywhite. While he worked on the detail, Sven witnessed a visit between David Lillywhite and me.

As he watched Lillywhite and me together, Sven suddenly "knew" a chaplain was the answer to his problem, but not just any chaplain. It had to be the one talking with Lillywhite.

For the next few days, Sven questioned others about Lillywhite's reputation, hoping to find in him someone who would not turn on him. Tentatively satisfied about Lillywhite's trustworthiness and having learned he was from Arizona (presumably a cowboy), Sven approached Lillywhite and asked him to go for a walk. After walking for a few minutes, Sven explained his reason for asking Lillywhite to walk with him, that he wanted Lillywhite to arrange a meeting for him with the chaplain who had visited him a few days before. Without hesitation, Lillywhite brought Sven directly to my hooch.

With years of law enforcement experience, I tended not to accept things as they first appeared. So I listened with a policeman's ear to Sven's strange story, not doubting serious crimes had been committed, for Sven's demeanor convinced me of this from the start. Rather, I listened to detect the depth of Sven's involvement in the incident he unfolded.

Soon, though, my suspicious policeman's nature yielded to the more compassionate and trusting chaplain. In Sven, I discerned a soul wracked with guilt, not for crimes committed, but for having failed to prevent atrocities against Mao, or die trying.

Before me was a man immersed in remorse, self-recrimination and shame because fear had immobilized him until it was too late for Mao. Here was a man torn by conflicting loyalties to buddies in combat—one of the strongest of human bonds—and to what is right, a coward in his own eyes whose behavior dishonored his own dear wife.

About midnight, I called in the Criminal Investigation Detachment, having satisfied myself Sven was for real. Within minutes, two investigators arrived. After listening with cool professionalism to Sven's brief synopsis of the crimes, the investigators explained to Sven his rights—just in case, though I think they also believed him—and took him off into the night. In parting, the investigators ordered me to talk to no one except my commander about Sven's allegations.

The next morning I wrote to inform Elder Hinckley of what I was involved in. The Brethren would keep confidences, and I believed they should be alerted in case the incident became public—which seemed probable considering the growing antiwar, pro-enemy movements back in the "world."

At 0900 hours the morning following Sven's visit to my hooch, I briefed Lt. Col. Leighton about the Mao incident. Then I attended a meeting of chaplains, where I learned I was being transferred—to Sven's battalion!

With the infantry at last! I should have been elated, but this transfer was rife with potential complications. Chaplain McGraff was understandably perplexed by my lack of enthusiasm, after all the lobbying I'd done to get an infantry battalion.

I explained to Chaplain McGraff my part in putting the Mao incident into criminal investigative channels, how I was violating CID instructions by telling him, and that the alleged incident occurred in the unit to which I was being assigned. Yes, I still wanted an infantry unit, but wanted him to know about the potential for conflicts of interest.

Chaplain McGraff said I should take the transfer, for he knew I could do the job, despite the secret I carried. I appreciated his attitude because I wasn't about to turn down an infantry assignment—I might not get another chance at one. So I went to the 2–8 Cav and kept my secret for about three months, but it wasn't easy.

The chaplain of a unit is required by Army regulation to interview any soldier charged with a capital crime. But how was I, as chaplain and confidant, to counsel the four accused soldiers, about whom I knew stuff they did not know I knew? I couldn't even explain to my new commander why a month passed before I visited the prisoners in their makeshift, Conex-container stockade. During the prisoner interviews, once I finally got around to them, I focused on spiritual aspects of the prisoners' lives. I carefully steered discussion away from their alleged crimes. One or more of the prisoners might, I feared, confess what I already knew, and that might somehow, under their right to privileged communication with a chaplain, tangle up the legal process and prevent it from taking its course, wherever it might lead.

Sven's company commander, Captain Vorst, was relieved of command of his infantry company in combat—presumably death to an Army officer's career—and sent to the rear to be the Battalion S-1 personnel officer—also not a great career move. I got to know Vorst and liked him. Neither of us brought up the Mao case until he learned of my involvement in bringing it to light.

Upon learning I had linked Sven with the CID, Vorst approached me, and my worst fears were not realized. Though

I'd fully expected Vorst, other battalion leaders and even troopers to angrily condemn me once my part became known, no such reaction materialized.

Captain Vorst seemed open and honest as he shared with me his part in the matter. He was appalled and momentarily incredulous when Sven reported the crimes to him, he said, and couldn't believe any of his men, especially Sergeant Meserve, could commit such horrendous acts as Sven alleged. Vorst said he promised Sven immediate action and tried to keep his promise.

According to Vorst, he personally reported Sven's allegations to the battalion commander. The colonel responded, according to Vorst, "We can't have a stain like this on our unit record. . . . Split the members of the team up into different platoons and bust (demote) Sergeant Meserve, Corporal Clark and each of the Diazes, for sleeping without mosquito nets." These demotions under Article 15 (non-judicial punishment) of the Uniform Code of Military Justice, if they were in fact administered, could have left the accused men free of criminal records and the unit record free of a horrible stain.

I never heard the battalion commander's side of the matter. He was reassigned out of the battalion before my orders of secrecy were lifted. Perhaps I could have gotten his side by attending the court-martial proceedings, but I was there only once, having stopped by on my way to R&R in Hawaii with Helga.

According to the *New Yorker* magazine, Sergeant Meserve, Corporal Clark and the Diaz cousins were each convicted. All the accused were dishonorably discharged; Sergeant Meserve was found not guilty of rape, but guilty of premeditated murder and given ten years in military prison; Clark got life for rape and premeditated murder; Manuel Diaz got fifteen years for rape, and Rafe eight years for rape and unpremeditated murder.

Mao's mother disappeared before the original trial, presumably kidnapped by VC. Two weeks after the trial, a

Vietnamese teacher told Sven Mao's sister was missing. Sven later said to Daniel Lang of *New Yorker* magazine, "Charlie kidnapped her, just as he did Mao's mother. So now it's only the father who's left—or is he? Who says we don't get along with Charlie? Between us, we've taken care of that whole family."

The Diaz cousins were retried, separately, at Fort Leavenworth. Manuel Diaz was set free because the CID had, allegedly, slipped up and not informed him he could have a civilian lawyer at *no expense* to himself. Rafe Diaz was convicted again, but his sentence was later reduced to 24 months, resulting in his immediate release from military prison. Clark drew a life sentence, later reduced to 20 and then to eight years, as was Meserve's. None of the four accused men spent a dime in his own defense.

The Mao incident appeared to hurt neither the battalion commander's nor Captain Vorst's careers. They each went on to achieve general officer rank.

My predictions about the Mao incident, officially "The Incident on Hill 192," were born out only gradually—in a magazine article, a book and two movies.

In 1969, the incident was published in the *New Yorker* magazine, under the title "Casualties of War." A major American movie company bought movie rights to the incident, as reported in the *New Yorker*. About 1970, a Berlin, Germany–based underground, counterculture group apparently plagiarized the *New Yorker* and produced the movie "Mao," which reportedly won honors at the *Cannes Film Festival*. The Hollywood film company sued the producers of *Mao* for film-rights violations. The World Court ruled in favor of *Mao*'s producers, presumably because *Mao* was based on official records, though *Mao*'s producers lifted aliases for the main characters from the *New Yorker* magazine, not official records.

In 1969 McGraw-Hill republished *Casualties of War* in a 115-page book. About 1990, the American film company that owned the movie rights released *Casualties of War*, starring Michael J. Fox, rated R. This movie, while it remained true to the gist of the Mao incident, took license with some details, misrepresenting how Sven met me and representing me as a Methodist, though Sven in his interview with Daniel Lang had made a great point of my being a Mormon.

The Mao incident was overshadowed by another war-crime incident on a much larger scale, the infamous My Lai incident, from which the chaplaincy came away looking less than good. Chaplain involvement in My Lai was given almost three unflattering pages in the seven-volume *History of the U.S. Army Chaplaincy*. Its authors, seeking something to place the chaplaincy in a better light, added a paragraph about the Mao incident—thus I attained a tiny mention in history.

Three weeks passed between the Mao incident and Sven's getting to the CID, through me. However, Chaplain Carl E. Creswell passed allegations of the My Lai incident to the Americal Division Chaplain shortly after it occurred, but more than a year passed before it came to light.

Nearly five years after My Lai became known, Chaplain Creswell commented:

"I felt . . . betrayed by the Chaplains [to] whom I had entrusted my knowledge of the My Lai event. If a history of a fumble enables future Chaplains to hang onto the ball, this exercise will be worth . . . our troubles . . . God forbid that in a similar situation, any Chaplain should ever be content with the actions I took."

This from the *New York Times*:

"Such incidents, along with general frustration about the conduct of the war, have served to revive the old 'two masters' problem concerning chaplains in the armed forces."

The Chaplaincy History account added:

"My Lai certainly did not enhance the image of the chaplaincy. . . . At least one author strongly insinuated that the chaplains' ministry was virtually ineffectual. . . . While the terrible circumstances at My Lai received more publicity, another situation of a similar, though less complex [nature] involved the kidnap, rape, and murder of a Vietnamese girl by a small group of U.S. soldiers. Though little credit was given to him for it, Chaplain Claude D. Newby, Latter-day Saints, was the first to properly respond to the report when a troubled soldier related the incident as he had heard it. Newby, a former military and civilian policeman, took the report to the Army's Criminal Investigation Division (CID) and the responsible individuals were eventually arrested and tried."

One of the authors of the seven-volume history, Chaplain "Smoky" Stover, saw the book *Casualties of War*. Wondering if it reported a true incident, he checked it out. Logically, Stover first contacted Chaplain (then captain) Wayne Kuehne. Kuehne was at the time (1972) co-located with Stover at the U.S. Army Chaplain Center and School at Fort Hamilton. Stover was on the staff and faculty, and Kuehne was a student in the Chaplain Advanced Officer Course.

Besides being in the same building at the school with Stover, Kuehne fit the description of Chaplain (Captain) Gerald Kirk—my alias in *Casualties of War*—better than I did. Kuehne in real life, like Kirk in the book, is six-foot, blond, long-nosed, and a Mormon who was once a Salt Lake City police officer. (He might challenge the long-nosed part). I, on the other hand, have brown hair (now streaked with gray) and was a police officer for Ogden City, Utah.

Anyhow, Kuehne denied any knowledge of the Mao incident. Stover almost wrote the matter off as a work of fiction, until Kuehne suggested he contact me, as I had been with the 1st Cav in Vietnam about the time the Mao incident allegedly occurred. Smoky Stover wrote to me, and the rest is, as they say, history.

Well, I'm glad my actions helped place the chaplaincy in better historical light and am pleased over its inclusion in the Chaplaincy History.

I'm sorry this horrible incident happened. I'm especially sorry for the victims and for the stain it placed on us all.

I saw Sven twice more after the night he came to my

hooch. A few days later, we were both passengers on a
Caribou headed to LZ Hammond, me to join his battalion
and Sven to return to the scene of the crime in company
with the CID. Sven thanked me for getting the investigation
started and told me what had occurred after he left my
hooch with the CID agents. He'd spent the first night locked
in a Conex container—metal shipping box—in "protective
custody." Then he was reassigned as a military policeman.
Obviously, his allegations were being taken seriously. I saw
him for the last time during one of the court-martials in
April 1967.

Notes
19 November 1966, 2015 Hrs: "Pony Soldier 3 reports that at 1230
    hrs. killed 1 VC woman, fleeing from Hill 193. They shot
    warning shots, but she did not stop, so they shot to kill."

seven

Infantry Assignment at Last!

An Army unit belongs to its commander, but I quickly developed a special, possessive relationship with the 2–8 Cav, as I would with subsequent units in which I served in combat. Sunday, December 11, I conducted my last general Christian worship service for the 15th Medical Battalion. In the afternoon, I attended LDS services at the 2nd Surgical Hospital for the last time on a regular basis. I'd grown very close to the men of this little congregation, most of whom were valiant and true, a tribute to their roots. I formed life-long friendships with some of them.

A recent letter from a member of the group touched me deeply:

Dear Brother Newby:

Your letter arrived and suddenly time seemed to stand still. Within the chambers of my mind I suddenly saw you again as the man I deeply loved and admired while in Vietnam many years ago. I can never forget the experience I had the first time I met you. Of course your unique voice had the quality to capture the attention and respect of everyone. Your stature was tall, lean, energetic and captivating. But, above all, I felt the whispering of the Spirit confirm your spiritual assignment as a servant of the Lord. On that particular day, you had a majestic spiritual glow around you. I immediately recognized it as a spiritual shield given as a gift of protection by the host of heaven. . . . There was no doubt that you were truly on an errand for the Lord . . . always prayed that I would someday be allowed to become a friend to

*you. . . . It was my observation that most everyone
wanted to be your friend. . . . You did a phenomenal job
of helping them feel better about themselves. . . . You
were an angel in mortal clothing.*

Sincerely,
Lanny Owens
(signed and dated June 16, 1994)

I was touched by this tribute, a tribute I believe many
soldiers would like to have paid to their own chaplain because of what the chaplains represented to them.

Transfer orders arrived on December 14, 1966. These orders assigned me to the Headquarters, 1st Brigade for duty
with the 2nd Battalion, Eighth Cavalry (2–8 Cav). The 2–8
Cav was unique among the battalions in the division in that
it was the first to have all its line companies use distingush-
ing call signs for their platoons, a practice that was subsequently adopted across the whole division.
Even with the Mao incident in mind, I gladly left my
self-made hooch and reported to Captain Vorst, S-1 in the
2–8 Cav. I went eagerly, but with a hint of reluctance at giving up the freedom I had to range across the division AO. I
was on the way to join the grunts—*where I belonged.*
I moved my belongings into the battalion chaplain's rear-
area accommodations, a leaky, dank, dark, mildew-smelling,
gloomy, spider-infested small-wall tent. The tent sat off by
itself on a flat spot above a road in the battalion area, in
front of a vine- and vegetation-covered cliff, and beside a
Conex and a makeshift shower—a barrel on stilts. By
lantern light, I explored the tent. It wouldn't do. I slept in it
twice, December 14 and 15, during which time I drew gear
and negotiated to get David Lillywhite as my chaplain assistant.

On December 16, I flew to the battalion combat trains area
on the west perimeter of LZ Hammond. There, I reintroduced

myself to the same sergeant major I had called on in October, the day I attempted to visit Danny Hyde just hours before Hyde was blown up by a claymore. Already, I felt that my destiny was linked with this battalion and had been from the time that I arrived in country.

Sp4 David Lillywhite, combat infantryman-turned-unit-carpenter, gladly left the security of the rear area and joined me in the field—he arrived at LZ Hammond later in the day, having come in a ground convoy. We set up a small tent about 30 yards from and 10 feet above the west perimeter. We dug a trench around the tent—rainwater frequently poured in torrents off the steep volcano-like mount in the center of LZ Hammond. Next we filled and stacked sandbags three feet high around the tent. Finally, we dug two foxholes inside the tent, one by each stretcher—Lillywhite's idea, based on experience.

Lillywhite and I, officer and enlisted, would share a tent in the forward-rear area, just as we would share ponchos in the field. I was very glad to start with an experienced infantryman, especially with Lillywhite. I thought we needed overhead protection from incoming rockets and mortars, but such preparations were not then common on LZs, except for TOCs and commanders' accommodations.

In the absence of Army doctrine for religious support in combat and having never heard of battlefield analysis, I intuitively assessed the situation during the first week of 1967 and established a general outline of how I wanted to operate—my operational concept.

METT-T is the Army principle of continuous battlefield analysis. The acronym, METT-T, stands for the Mission; Enemy force capabilities, deployment, actions and presumed intentions; friendly Troops deployment, current and anticipated operations and needs; Terrain and weather as these affect everything else; and Time and energy constraints.

Without applying my version of METT-T, I would have had to sacrifice the mission for personal safety, or wasted

time, energy and perhaps life, with little effect on the soldiers and unit.

In the Battalion rear area—usually on a base camp—I
kept a stretcher to sleep on and a place to store my duffel
bag, dress uniforms and so forth. My base of operations was
a sandbagged tent or bunker co-located with Battalion operations on its firebase—combat trains.

I operated forward of, not at, my base—my rucksack
and the field were home. Occasionally I returned to the rear
to change clothes, read my mail, mail letters, restock supplies, gather tactical information, obtain transportation to
hospitals or another unit in the AO, and sometimes to rest
overnight. By remaining flexible, carefully analyzing the
key situation, and using the assets of the unit to support
the unit, I usually managed to successfully rotate between
the infantry companies and to also work in frequent hospital visits.

My goal was to spend two or three nights in 10 with each
infantry company, during which visits I conducted worship
services at every reasonable opportunity, usually at the platoon or squad level. My 10-day worship cycle occasionally
caused tension between me and those chaplains whose theological focus was on the worship service as opposed to being with the troops. Some chaplains disapproved of operating
forward with the grunts more than was necessary to conduct
services.

For best results, I synchronized religious support with the
battalion mission and operations. Thus the places and frequency of worship services were driven by situations and
circumstances, rather than day of the week. Consequently,
though I observed the Lord's day personally, Sunday was
just another day in the hell of war, excepting the occasional
holiday truces and respite at base camp.

Other considerations being equal among units—similar
levels of stress and activity—I went to the company most
overdue for a visit, traveling usually on resupply flights or the
commander's Charlie-Charlie chopper. Other considerations

being unequal, which was usually the case, I focused my attention where the hurting was greatest, in consequence of recent events, current action, or because imminent action had high casualty-producing potential.

In practice, only rarely did a company wait longer than two weeks for a visit. On those rare occasions, weather was usually the culprit—I wasn't about to get people killed by placing my schedule above the situation.

In the field I attempted to divide each visit between the company command group and its platoons, and to conduct worship services at platoon level, as it was seldom secure enough to bunch up for a company-size service. Usually, I spent nights with whichever platoon or element I was with at the end of the day. My three-day-visits objective meshed well with the companies' practice of "logging"—being resupplied—every three days, barring heavy casualties and contacts and so forth.

Regularly I went along on platoon and company-size operations, which I considered maneuvers, not patrols, where the chaplain belonged. Seldom did I intentionally accompany squads, in deference to unwritten, unofficial chaplaincy "doctrine," because it was usually unnecessary to do so. Unintentionally, I accompanied many a squad-size operation because I'd be accompanying a platoon when it split into smaller elements, leaving me no choice but to go with a squad on a patrol or occasional ambush.

My on-loan infantry chaplain assistant usually accompanied me in the field; not so with school-trained assistants—the former was always an asset and the latter were often a liability. The chaplain assistant's primary duty in combat is to protect the chaplain. With school-trained assistants, I usually had to protect them. For example, one school-trained assistant couldn't keep his M-16 rifle in operational condition—I unjammed it for him in the midst of two firefights. In fairness to school-trained chaplains and assistants, lacking any Army doctrine for religious support in combat, each assistant had to feel his way along as I had to, but usually without my infantry tactical training and experience to fall back on.

Notes

7 December 1966, 1st Cav Div G-1 Journal: Pfc. Jesus Salalas, gsw, D 2/8; Pfc. Gregory Collon, frag, legs, A 2–8.

8 December 1966, 1st Cav Div G-1 Journal: Sp4 Robert T. Daugherty, swept away to sea, HHC 2–8.

eight

Holidays of Horror

In anticipation of lonely troopers at Christmastime, Helga sent to me some songs she got primary children to record on reel-to-reel tapes. There wasn't much else for me to prepare for Christmas celebrations in the field.

On December 17, I helped at the medical clearing company on LZ Hammond because 36 (my journal says 40) dead American grunts were hauled from the battlefield. A Chinook helicopter brought in the dead, which were slung beneath it in a cargo net.

These troopers gave their lives in the 506 Valley (though my journal says Happy Valley, I remember it, and have confirmed it was the 506 Valley). Charlie Company, 1–12 Cav had been decimated, according to Shelby L. Stanton (*Anatomy of a Division*). In fact, the casualties were in A, B, C and D companies of 1–12 Cav and in the 1–8 and 1–9 Cav, with the largest number being 1–9 Cav, according to the G-1 casualty list.

At Hammond, Graves Registration personnel had laid each of these 36 bodies—America's sons, dads, husbands and sweethearts—on his back with his head to the west. Seventy-two eyes, less the occasional empty socket or missing face, stared vacantly into the rain-laden heavens.

I moved among the bodies and looked deeply into those staring, glazed-over eyes, letting the strange images burn indelibly into my mind. Every body was contorted. Many rigor mortis–stiffened arms reached upward to ward off some horrible evil, as it were, while other arms stretched heavenward as if to grasp solace or rescue from some source visible only to the spirit, which had so recently departed the body.

I prayed for the souls of these men who gave their all in terrible, mortal combat, and for their loved ones. I prayed for each soldier as he stood about the dead in solemn contemplation of his own mortality. I even prayed for the news photographer, who in my mind greatly offended the memory of the dead and the senses of the living. And I prayed for the politicians and leaders who rightly or wrongly had placed these men here to die so horribly at Christmastime.

During these moments with the dead at LZ Hammond, I became convinced that a just and merciful God will requite these soldiers for their sacrifice in the 506 Valley. I was convinced this was so, even though many of them may have ended their short lives with profanity on their lips, as was so often the case during heavy fighting in Vietnam. I would soon discover in battle after battle that obscene and profane babbling frequently punctuated the horrible sounds, sights and smells of close combat. Sadly, profanity against the deity and obscenities involving motherhood were the most frequently heard expletives during times of such extreme stresses. These foul utterances were commonly used to emphasize urgency, orders and to express the terrors the men endured.

Even so, as I walked slowly among the massed dead, all laid out in military formation, I kept remembering Christ's declaration: "Greater love hath no man than this, that a man lay down his life for his friends" (John 15:13). These men had lain down their lives, reluctantly in most cases, but they'd done it. They'd chosen the risks of service to country, squad and buddy over the personal security offered by fleeing to Sweden, Canada or onto the college campus. These grunts "fought the good fight" (1 Timothy 6:12).

Those minutes there with the dead uniquely prepared me, I believe, to bring some hope to the hopeless in the months and battles ahead.

After attending to the dead, Lillywhite and I went forward for the first time together. We joined Bravo Company

2–8, which was securing LZ Strip somewhere east of LZ Hammond, named Strip because it was in the sand dunes by the seashore.

That evening we began our field ministry. In the darkness we crept from position to position and visited and played Christmas music on very low volume. The next morning I held a worship service with 17 attending—puny numbers for a unit in the field. Later I met Sergeant Wade, a black NCO who loved his men. His platoon had no lieutenant, so Sergeant Wade was also the platoon leader.

When I first saw Wade he was running his platoon through training maneuvers to improve their fire and maneuver tactical skills. Rarely did I witness such training drills in Vietnam because mostly there was no time, and when time and security were adequate the grunts were usually too exhausted.

Wade told me proudly and gratefully, "Chaplain, I've been with this platoon for eight months and never lost a man KIA." With Charlie 1–12 fresh in my mind, I prayed for Wade's success in sending all his men home alive. His noble, great hope would be dashed before Christmas.

Back at LZ Hammond at 1100 hours, I held a worship service for the 2–13 Artillery Battery. Fifty-seven troopers attended, about 50 percent of the unit—a small percentage compared to future service for infantry elements. From this day forward, every day was a day for worship and every bomb crater a potential worship site—I held services whenever and wherever I could for squads, platoons, companies, firebases, even two-man foxholes if necessary. For example, this same afternoon I held a second service at LZ Strip, just before the battalion moved to a new firebase farther inland, LZ Santa.

December 20 was a rare sunny day during the rainy season on LZ Santa. Around the perimeter, grunts struggled and sweated to sink foxholes into very rocky soil.

A trooper with his back to me as I approached cursed the

rocks, the sun, his entrenching tool, sergeants and so forth with generous use of God's title. Upon looking up and recognizing me as a chaplain, though he didn't know I was his new chaplain, he mumbled a weak apology for his language.

Seriously, but with a touch of tactful humor, I said, "You've got to quit talking like that, else you may die and go to hell."

Said he, "Promises, promises. I never get promoted." He left no doubt about his opinion of what and where he was.

One might feel to censure me for allowing any degree of humor in the face of profanity. But without being told, I knew appropriate humor, in combat, would reinforce parental training and past and subsequent teachings and admonitions—provided my actions supported my words, humorous or solemn.

For the most part, I dealt not with spiritually motivated Mormons and Baptists nor with devout Catholics, but with soldiers of multiple faiths, men who frequently lacked any significant spiritual and religious foundation. To support these men of such diverse backgrounds, I prayed hard for discernment to match each situation, person and moment.

For example, while on a patrol soon after our first meeting, I watched Sergeant Wade become irate at some troopers who bunched up (got too close to one another), making themselves inviting targets of opportunity to a VC or NVA sniper. Later, in a more secure area, Wade gathered the careless troopers around him and tore into them, using God's name liberally. Slowly, Sergeant Wade realized his troops were looking at something behind him. Turning, Wade saw me and dropped his eyes ashamedly. "Sorry Chaplain Newby, but you know what I mean."

"Yes, I know what you mean, Sergeant Wade. You love your men and want to keep them alive. But God knows what you said. Remember, God will not hold him guiltless who takes His name in vain."

Nothing else needed to be said. Sergeant Wade accepted

my gentle admonishment, and he and his troopers were impressed with both the brevity and content of my sermonette, some said.

Later in the day on December 20, after the aforementioned conversation with the trooper at his foxhole, Lillywhite and I took a little patrol of our own. Our destination was a stream that flowed west to east about 200 meters north of the LZ Santa perimeter. Our objective was cleanliness.

The fresh, clear water in the little stream invited us in, never mind that it was less than three feet wide and no more than three inches deep. Soon we found a small, secluded, sunlit clearing. After checking for booby traps and making sure as best we could that we were not being observed by hostile eyes, we went into action.

While I guarded against marauding VC, Lillywhite stripped down and washed out his undergarments. Then he dammed up the stream by lying on his back in it, head upstream. Soon the water backed up enough to flow soothingly over his shoulders and chest. We switched roles after he had enough of the deliciously cold water. What a break this was!

Under Lillywhite's mentorship, I quickly picked up several tricks for taking advantage of the environment and enhancing my chances of survival. The new assignment was going well, except for one tiny problem—I felt vaguely unfaithful to Helga and the children because I was so pleased to be with the infantry. These mixed emotions made little sense; I can't describe or explain them now. Well, Helga and I had both wanted the chaplaincy, and I had a mission there—here. It helped to believe deeply that I was finally at the core of our mission.

About this time, in response to receiving word of the wounding of a lieutenant and a sergeant in Alpha Company, I visited them at the Medical Clearing Company on LZ Hammond. The pair had gotten themselves ambushed while attempting to travel by jeep to LZ Hammond from the

Alpha Company AO. I should have learned from their mistake.

In another incident that occurred just before I joined the battalion—I don't recall which company—a platoon came upon a booby-trapped butterfly bomb. These were antipersonnel devices dropped by the American Air Force to saturate enemy-held areas. Well, the platoon leader gathered his men about him and showed them how to disarm the bomb. His lesson completed, so he thought, the lieutenant stood and said something like, "There, it is harmless now," and tossed the device over his shoulder. He awakened a few days later in a hospital in Japan and moaned, "I killed my platoon." A slight exaggeration—he only decimated his platoon.

This lieutenant's tragic mistake helps to emphasize the fallacy of the Army policy in Vietnam of replacing experienced leaders after six months. Extrapolating from my experiences, I'm convinced that thousands of U.S. deaths and untold maiming of our men can be chalked up to this policy.

From the start of my tour in Vietnam, I considered the six-month rotation policy almost as criminal as our civilian leaders' policies of "business as usual" for American society, limited war objectives and the strategy of gradual escalation against an oriental foe. Consequently, like generals-in-the-making Colin Powell and H. Norman Schwarzkopf, I promised myself to remember the errors of Vietnam and, if ever I got the chance, do something for grunts in future wars.

On the other side of the six-month command issue, the fighting is almost always done by soldiers and leaders who possess excellent, adrenaline-reinforced reflexes, but whose bodies and mental faculties are exhausted almost beyond imagination by the demands for constant vigilance and existence on the battlefield. This combination, given the frequent need in combat for instantaneous decisions and actions, makes for mistakes, deadly mistakes. For this reason, perhaps six-month commands could have been partially justified at the company and platoon level in Vietnam.

* * *

At the end of the day, December 20, on LZ Santa, Lillywhite and I dug a foxhole and set up a one-poncho shelter for the night. The next day, I returned to Qui Nhon via LZ Hammond. At Qui Nhon I visited wounded troopers in the 67th and 85th Evacuation Hospitals, ate a hamburger at the PX and spent the night with a Dust Off unit.

December 22 began in gloom and ended in blood. About 0730 hours, Bravo Company air assaulted into a small clearing in the thickly jungle-covered foothills to the west-northwest of LZ Hammond. I saw the company off. Had this combat assault happened a week or two later, I would have gone with them. But at this point I questioned if I'd be welcome and not in the way.

Bravo Company, commanded by Captain Charles R. Getz, landed without taking fire, and everything appeared quiet for a few minutes. At about 0800 hours, heavy automatic and assault weapon fire shattered the quiet of the jungle, as Bravo Company moved into it and away from the insertion LZ. An estimated platoon of NVA forces, dressed in khaki, had opened fire on the advancing troopers from well-dug-in and concealed fighting positions. During the next two hours Bravo Company suffered five soldiers killed and three wounded—most of the casualties were from Sergeant Wade's platoon.

Finally, a heroic or angry corporal broke the attack almost single-handedly—I can't remember his name. He, upon finding himself surrounded by dead and wounded buddies, leaped to his feet and charged the enemy positions, yelling and shooting from the hip. Apparently, he so unnerved the NVA that they fled their well-prepared fighting positions to escape his wrath. The corporal killed several of the fleeing enemies before breaking off the chase some 50 yards beyond their original fighting positions. The enemy sustained eleven KIA. Blood trails leading away from their positions suggested at least five more NVA were seriously wounded.

Meanwhile, from the air in the commander's Charlie-Charlie chopper, I could hardly tell a battle was raging and men were dying—the only evidence I had was the muffled explosions of artillery shells and wisps of smoke trickling up through the trees.

A few days later, that same courageous corporal learned how it felt to be chased by armed, angry foes. He and his pony team were chased for about two kilometers—a downhill race, fortunately.

Bravo Company, by the way, was the first unit in the division to earn a Valorous Unit Citation in Vietnam. The citation was for its performance on May 16, 1966 in an action that kicked off Operation Crazy Horse.

On December 23, I flew via a Caribou through very bad weather from Qui Nhon to LZ Hammond, then to An Khe. I returned to LZ Hammond on Christmas Eve, having been weathered in at An Khe the day before. That was just as well because my tent at LZ Hammond washed away during the night. Lillywhite and I spent the rest of the morning clearing the area and putting up a new tent.

At 1300 hours, Christmas Eve, I reported to Chaplain (Major) Dowd for special duty as escort officer for evangelist Billy Graham. The famed evangelist was appearing at LZ Hammond, as was Bob Hope. I've no idea why I was selected for this duty; it surely seemed odd to pick me, a Mormon, what with all the Baptist and other chaplains who were available.

Platoons of infantry were flown in from the jungles and rice paddies to attend, as a group, either Billy Graham's Christmas service or the Bob Hope Show. By this arrangement a trooper got to attend one of the events only if his platoon was chosen, and the choice of which event he attended was decided by whomever selected his platoon in the first place. Of course, things got mixed up on occasion. For example, a platoon of Alpha Company came for the Bob Hope Show, but got deposited at Billy Graham's service, instead.

My escort duties amounted to nothing. At the appointed time a CV-2 dropped from the overcast skies and deposited Billy Graham and an entourage of chaplains and media people, with a sprinkling of commanders and division staffers. Billy Graham moved from the aircraft into a press of chaplains. This group engulfed him and stuck so close on the way to the site selected for his service that I couldn't get near enough to him to introduce myself as his escort, much less to actually escort him.

Despite doctrinal differences between Billy Graham and me, I taped his sermon and subsequently shared it with all my grunts over the next month. I did this because Graham's visit and words meant a lot to many of them.

On Christmas day, after conducting a service for the 2–13 Artillery Battalion, I joined Bravo Company at the site of its tragic battle three days earlier. There I found Sergeant Wade understandably downcast over the dead and wounded members of his platoon. Wade was a very caring, even spiritual man, despite his occasional bouts of foul language.

For a few hours, I mingled with the troops and leaders, offering what support I could. Sixty-two men attended the Christmas service that followed.

After leaving Bravo Company, I held two services at LZ Santa, two more for Alpha Company in the hamlet of Nha Tuo, and finished the day with two services at LZ Hammond, my sixth and seventh on Christmas day. Merry Christmas!

Following the heavy casualties it had sustained on December 17, Charlie Company 1–12 had been lifted to LZ Bird, an isolated firebase near an area known as the Crow's Foot, to rebuild as a fighting unit and to, incidentally, spend Christmas. The company was hardly combat-ready when the NVA overran LZ Bird the night of December 26.

An urgent call brought me to the medical clearing company on LZ Hammond early on December 27, my 30th birthday. There I witnessed a horrible replay of December

17 as casualties poured in from LZ Bird, most of them from Charlie 1–12 Cav, part of the same unit that had been mauled in the 506 Valley fight 10 days earlier.

And from LZ Bird came another Chinook, this time with the bodies of 27 troopers swinging underneath it, piled atop each other in a cargo net. Again, the troopers' bodies were laid out in formation, each with its glassed-over, terror-filled eyes staring blankly at the sky, each face frozen in the terror it endured at the moment of a horrible death, and every body mangled.

Following half an hour with the dead, I ministered to the 65 wounded troopers inside and around the medical tents. The wounded, too, were mostly from Charlie 1–12 Cav. Back at LZ Bird, about 50 lightly injured Americans moved about in shock among the 49 NVA bodies scattered in and around the perimeter.

At the aid station, a wounded sergeant told me of lying in the dark during the attack, while within arm's reach two enemy soldiers whispered and gestured in the manner American commanders might in the midst of a fight. The sergeant, out of ammo except for a hand grenade, let these enemies move on without attacking them because the grenade would probably have killed him too at such close range.

A lieutenant related how a trooper, on his first night in the field, died behind a machine gun after stacking up a dozen NVA bodies in front of his position. Military historian S. L. A. Marshall wrote extensively about the December 27 attack on LZ Bird.

After attending to my duties among the dead and wounded, I returned to our newly erected tent and packed much of our gear and equipment for Lillywhite to take back to An Khe. After a week in the field and once having my tent washed away, I had a better idea of just what I needed to operate, which wasn't much. I came to Vietnam with but little luggage and to LZ Hammond with little more than personal clothing, essential field gear and some office stuff. I'd found that most of the office stuff and some of the personal clothing was in excess of my needs.

Our lightened load included a tent, two medical litters to occasionally sleep on, a field desk, a chaplain's combat kit, a lantern and a few office supplies. This stuff remained at my base of operations. For operations forward, I wore jungle fatigues, jungle boots, socks and undergarments. I also wore a steel helmet with camouflage cover and band and a bottle of insect repellent in the band at the back, web gear (load-bearing equipment—pistol belt and suspenders). On the belt and suspenders hung a first aid kit, two one-quart canteens, two ammo pouches, a much-too-small rump pack, a flashlight and a hunting knife. A gas mask was ever present on my left hip beneath a canteen. In my left front pocket I carried what I dubbed my *.45-caliber camera* for close-up shots. On my left arm I wore a wrist compass, and tied to the rump pack—until Helga sent me a rucksack—was a poncho, poncho liner (a wonderful item in the jungle) and air mattress. Inside the pack were the real essentials: a can opener with handles, Tabasco sauce and my scriptures. For the first few months I humped a chaplain kit, in which I had replaced liturgical items I didn't use with field hymnals and a battery-powered reel-to-reel tape player/recorder.

During my early days in the field, besides the canteens on my belt, one over each hip, I carried two canteens attached to the rump pack. Later, I got a civilian rucksack from home and hung two half-gallon canteens on it, one on each side. Oh yes, I eventually replaced the 32 field hymnals with selected hymns, which I had printed out and laminated to protect them from the weather—these I rotated biweekly.

When I first arrived in country, I was outraged to discover grunts in the field sometimes had to wait for items of clothing and equipment that were found in abundance in the rear, items designed for waging combat in the jungle— jungle boots and fatigues, poncho liners and air mattresses.

On good authority, I heard that during 1965 and early

1966, grunts in the field wore water-retaining fatigues and combat boots until these rotted off their rash-covered bodies, while many rear-area troops and commanders sported spit-shined jungle boots while working and living on dry wooden floors. All U.S. Army personnel in Vietnam wore jungle fatigues and boots when I arrived in country.

Still, some disregard for the grunt was evident. For example, in the 2–8 Cav, our grunts were issued little, almost useless rump packs, while the U.S. Army supplied fine American rucksacks to ARVN soldiers. The ARVN soldier, in turn, sold his rucksack to an American grunt, reported it lost in combat and got issued a new one, no questions asked. Thus, American grunts helped finance their participation in the war by buying American rucksacks (or "rucks") from ARVN soldiers with their own money. Adding insult to injury, many ARVN units in our AO could easily have gotten by with the little rump packs for the short forays they made into the field.

Other rear-area soldiers reflected disdain for the grunts by how they treated the personal possessions the grunts left in the rear. Each trooper arrived in country with a full duffel bag and usually some sort of suitcase and an AWOL bag. These contained the soldiers' issue of dress uniforms, and personal items such as tape players, radios, wedding albums, saved love letters, and so forth. The grunts' excess luggage was stored in unguarded tents. Grunts, upon returning to the rear, found duffel bags cut open; locks broken; suitcases, radios and cameras gone; and love letters and photo albums strewn about and tramped into the mud. Still, these long-suffering troopers returned to the jungle and fought to protect the rear. Surely, these grunts were America's best and brightest sons in the ways that count most.

Not wanting to be foolish, I reasoned that in the field it was prudent to not be easily recognized as an officer—a prime target. Consequently, I took pains to enhance survival by looking at myself from the perspective of an enemy sniper: I'd expect an officer to be empty-handed if anyone was, to have distinctive uniform markings, to always have someone nearby with a radio antenna sticking up. Within the bounds of regulations, I did what I could to lower my profile.

Chaplaincy policy required the chaplain insignia to be worn on the helmet—for easy identification by the troops. I reasoned my troops would recognize me after a few days, else I wasn't doing my job. To comply with the insignia-on-helmet policy, I drew a green cross on my green helmet camouflage cover—invisible in good light beyond 10 feet.

The brownish-green Army towel served three important survival functions: It padded pained shoulders under ruck-sack straps; it sopped sweat from my brow so I could distin-guish between friend and enemy; and it hid my officer insignia from hostile eyes.

As added camouflage, I usually carried a pick or shovel, later, when many platoons began humping (carrying) these tools to augment individual entrenching tools. This practice relieved a grunt of the extra weight, while it allowed me to avoid standing out as the only man in a column with empty hands.

Initially I questioned whether these self-defense methods increased the odds of someone else catching a bullet meant for me. *No*, I reasoned, *an experienced sniper will allow any number of soldiers to pass while he waits for a leader or someone with an antenna sprouting from his back. An inex-perienced sniper will probably fire on point elements, be-fore I even come into sight.*

In combat I was relieved, temporarily, of a problem that plagued me since the age of 12—a tendency to gain weight. Here in combat, for the first time in my youth and adult life, I lost weight without dieting, heavy exercise or a combina-tion of the two, and I did this while subsisting mostly on high-calorie Army C-rations. This serendipitous blessing I attributed to heightened body metabolism that was brought on by living continually on the thin edge between life and death, in a sphere of existence found only in close, personal combat. It certainly was not due to running, which activity would have gotten me shot by one side or the other. Now, back to the action.

On December 29, Lillywhite and I flew to the village of Nha Tuo near the coast east of LZ Hammond. Alpha Company, commanded by Captain Frank Yon, had remained behind after the Battalion Combat Trains moved northwest of LZ Hammond to LZ Santa. Alpha Company continued daytime patrols and night ambushes, with almost no contact during the days leading up to and right after Christmas. Conditions were about to change.

It was another welcome sunny day when I landed and introduced myself to Captain Yon. Yon, a Catholic, was in his late twenties or early thirties, old for a company commander in Vietnam. His background was in Special Forces and Military Intelligence—he was getting his chance at a combat command, and he was very good at his profession. I'd hardly finished introducing myself when a patrol came up on the horn—called in on the radio. The patrol had just been fired on by an unknown size force and suffered three friendly casualties. Pfc. Robert Petrimoulx died of gunshot wound (GSW) to the chest, and Sp4 Joseph Terrel and Pfc. Terrence Bishop were shot in the left arm and right hand, respectively. The enemy had immediately broken contact and headed into the nearby hills.

Captain Yon, obviously affected and frustrated, ordered most of the company to "saddle up" and moved out to try to overtake or block the enemy element. This time, I decided to go along and not ask. Still uncertain of the kind of reception my presence would receive, I took a position toward the rear of the two-column reaction force.

Frank Yon led the reaction force almost at a run to the north for about a mile. Then, while Yon coordinated with the patrol, I visited troopers as I moved forward in the column and met Sp4 Kenneth Steel. Though most of the men carried the lighter M-16 assault rifle because of its advantages in close-up firefights, Steel and a few others carried the M-14 because with its greater effective killing range and heavier punch, it filled a gap between the M-16 assault rifle and M-60 machine gun. Of course, a few men carried Light Anti-tank Weapons (LAW) for "busting" bunkers or shotguns loaded with buckshot or slugs. Steel was a very likable, open young man who seemed mismatched with his weapon. He and I became close during the last months of his short life.

After the delay, during which I'd worked my way to the forward half of the column, we moved into the hills in pursuit of the elusive VC. Chasing the VC like this was futile, but I understood why Captain Yon had to try.

Pretty soon I knew Yon had spotted me and half-expected him to accuse me of burdening his troops with the extra risk of protecting me. However, Yon surprised me by assuring me that the troops were grateful for my company and that I would always be welcome. "Your voluntary presence works wonders for morale and morals," he said.

On December 30, Helga's birthday, Lillywhite and I met Sergeant Ralph Jensen, a grunt from Idaho, one of two LDS men in the 3rd Platoon of Alpha Company. Jensen's humorous grin and down-to-earth attention to his duties made it hard to tell at first glance just how serious he was about his faith. He was the only grunt I knew who refused to use an air mattress, no matter how muddy, rocky, cold or wet he became. He could sleep anywhere, not that he was inclined to do so at inappropriate moments.

Lillywhite and I spent most of December 30 with the 3rd Platoon of Alpha Company. There we remained on full alert throughout the night because 200 VC were reported to be within two klicks of the platoon's ambush position.

We were told a temporary truce was in effect for New Year's Eve, and didn't care for the idea. Troops in the field commonly believed these frequent cease-fires gave the enemy opportunities to get in better position and condition to do them harm. According to reports we received in the battalion, an NVA regiment had used the Christmas truce to move into position to attack LZ Bird, which it did the following night and cost us dearly in life and blood. It was understood at battalion and below that we would engage the enemy if the enemy acted in any way hostile toward us, truce or no truce. Thus, in practice, if the VC bumped into our security patrols and ambushes, the fight was on.

Back at LZ Hammond, on New Year's Eve, we happily found our tent and laundry dry. Unhappily, there was no mail from Helga. I had spent a lot of the past two days yearning to be with and hold Helga in my arms. Already, I was nearing the mid-point in my tour, the preferred time for a six-day R&R with Helga in Hawaii.

To begin the New Year, the year I would go home, I had my most discouraging experience. At 0930 hours I conducted a worship service for an artillery battery. Just two men attended, which wasn't the discouraging part. To that point, I assumed music was essential in every service. Trouble was, I neither sang, played a musical instrument nor even hummed in tune. Well, for the first time, no one present could help me with the music, and my efforts to lead in singing were a total failure. I left the service after it was finished convinced I could never go through such an experience again, and very much in doubt that I had what it took to be a chaplain.

For the rest of the day I wrestled with discouragement and prayed for strength. By day's end I understood I could have services and influence men toward God without music. I felt spiritually assured I would never again feel so discouraged, provided I remained adaptable, ever ready to take advantage of available talent and willing to dispense with music, if necessary. The next day I remounted the *bucking horse*, so to speak, by conducting a worship service, a very successful one, and I resolved to obtain taped music from home to augment my services. My worship services went much better from then on.

Around New Year's several grunts developed a very painful condition similar to immersion foot, in consequence of being constantly wet. The troopers with bad feet were evacuated to the battalion field trains area at LZ Hammond for treatment and recuperation. Soon afterward, the battalion AO shifted to the Crow's Foot region—so named because of the pattern of a network of rivers and valleys—in the rugged mountains west of LZ Bird and the 506 Valley.

Our mission was to search out and engage the NVA regiment that had overrun LZ Bird on my birthday. I first learned of the operation from several barefoot grunts that waited at LZ Hammond for flights to the field. The Battalion Commander was committing them to provide perimeter security on one of three LZs we would open in the Crow's Foot area—LZs Ho, Chi and Minh. The battalion TOC and attached artillery battery would be on LZ Minh.

About 0929 hours January 4, I combat assaulted from LZ Hammond with A Company, the lead assault element. A few minutes later, we leaped from the choppers onto a ridgeline to open LZ Minh. My helicopter, about the fifth one in the combat assault gaggle, hovered in above tall elephant grass. The prop wash from the chopper flattened the grass in waving patterns outward in all directions from beneath it.

Standing on the landing skid of the hovering chopper, I hesitated a moment, estimated the distance to the ground, picked what I thought was a soft landing spot, and jumped, expecting to drop three to five feet onto a soft mattress of grass. To my surprise, I fell about 10 feet and impacted with my right hip on a protruding rock. Naturally, I came to a sudden stop, but inertia, my body and 40 pounds of gear tried to drive my right hip into the stone.

A sharp pain shot down my leg and spread throughout the hip area. I struggled to my feet and went limping about the business of helping check out and clear the area for the battalion main party. Over the next few hours the pain subsided into heavy numbness and I shrugged the incident off. After all, I was young and used to bruising. The pain gave way to soreness, then to tenderness and finally faded away as my tour drew to an end, leaving only a lingering numbness, in my big toe—which numbness hampered my gait for about two years. I wouldn't suspect my injury was more serious until I returned to the states and started running again, and even then I never immediately connected my problem to this injury—more on that later.

The rain was falling hard when we jumped onto the hilltop, as it had for days and would continue to do all day. A barrage of mixed artillery shells—high explosive and white phosphorus—had burst all about the hill just before we arrived. Immediately, my senses were assaulted by the nauseating, distinct, unpleasant stench of mingled white phosphorus and traumatized vegetation. Of all the remembered smells of war, the aroma of white phosphorus and vegetation mixed with human blood and flesh is the most vivid.

Enemy action against LZ Minh during the short time it was open consisted of just three incoming mortar rounds, all of which exploded outside the perimeter. Exposed as Minh was, it would have been much easier for the NVA to attack than LZ Bird had been and harder to support with artillery from other bases and LZs. However, the enemy forces were inconvenienced because they were deprived of a holiday cease-fire during which they could move up attack forces around LZ Minh.

Late on an overcast, wet afternoon I stood by the battalion TOC on LZ Minh in company with a visiting general and several officers. The commander of the artillery battery on the LZ, to show his stuff for the general, called a fire mission—two HE shells from LZ Bird—onto some vacant huts in the valley below us. The huts were on a direct line between LZ Bird and us.

Moments later we heard the radioed message from LZ Bird. "On the way, wait," meaning the two artillery rounds were in the air. Seconds later a single shell exploded in a bright flash, exactly on target. But before the sound of the explosion reached us, the second shell screeched past some 30 to 50 meters above our heads and exploded some 300 meters behind us—a very close call. The general wasn't impressed. Short rounds kill people.

On January 7, 1967, Lillywhite and I visited several wounded troopers in Qui Nhon. Lillywhite became ill while we were there and was admitted to the hospital. He rejoined me two days later, just in time to share a memorable, quite unusual small-unit action, and to become infected with malaria.

Notes

17 December (Military Index) KIAs, 506 Valley Battle: Sgt. Cesar Bryant, Deland, A 1–9 Cav [unit, when shown, comes from G-1 Journal]: Pfc. Richard Lee Carothers, Franklin, TN; Sp4 Howard Chisholm, A 1–12; Sgt. William Donald Cook Jr., San Jose, CA; 1LT Chester Garvis Cox, Lawrenceburg, KY; Cpl. Jack Joe Deaton, Indianapolis, IN; Pfc. Michael Earl Dent, C 1–12, Evansville, IN; PSgt. Willie Lee Earnest, Sunflower, Miss; Sp4 Dennis Keith, Erdos, Athens, OH; Sfc. Ellis Casiano Espinosa, A 1–12, Chicago, IL; Pfc. Timothy David Ewing [Dwing in G-1 Journal], D 1–12, Exeter, CA; Sgt. Antonio Garcia, Chicago, IL; Sgt. Jesse Yutze Gomez, C 1–8, Tempe, AZ; SSGT Julius Greathouse Jr., Corpus Christi, TX; Pfc. Eddie Dean Hollandsworth, Big Spring, TX; Pfc. John Elia Horn, A 1–9, Honolulu, HI; Pfc. Arnold Melvin, Hull, Oak Hill, NY; Sp4 Ronald Joe Johnson [Donald in G-1 Journal], A 1–9, Santa Cruz, CA; Cpl. Alton Ray Kennedy, Norfolk, VA; PSgt. Donald J. Leemhuis, Clinton, OK; Sp4 Joe Lee Lemon, Guy, Arkansas; Pfc. Angel Rafael, Luna, D 1–12, New York, NY; Pfc. Charles Henry McClennahan, New York, NY; Sp4 Henry J. Nelson, New Haven, CN; Pfc. Raymond Dennis Olzak [Obyak in G-1 Journal, where listed as MIA], Pittsburg, PA; PSgt. Roque Perpetua Jr., A 1–12, Kauia, HI; Pfc. Harry Turner Poland, Tompkinsville, KY; Pfc. Kennedy Eugene Schultz, D 1–9, Creve Doeur, IL; Sgt. Stephen Joseph Szijjarto, Wamego, KS; Pfc. Reginald Michael Thomas, Chicago, IL; Pfc. Raymond Delano Torry Jr., New York, NY; Pfc. Jimmy Vasquez [Vasquig in G-1 Journal], D 1–9, Pico Rivera, CA; Sp4 Jack LeRoy Wilbur, D 1–12, Dayton, OH.

Note: Only 11 of the above KIAs and the MIA are listed in the G-1 Journal for 18 Dec 66, plus Sp4 Mark L. English, US

55838617, B 1–8. Another 56 soldiers from all units are listed as WIA in the same fight.

22 December 1966, Bravo Company casualties, KIAs: Pfc. Gerald F. Gooden, home town unknown, gunshot wounds (GSW), chest and right arm; Pfc. James S. Hollis of Sacramento, California, GSW head; Pfc. George W. Jones of Los Angeles, GSW head; Pfc. Renold W. Peterson of Minneapolis, GSW neck and right arm and burns; and Sp4 John L. Schmecker of Shelton, Connecticut, GSW chest. WIAs Sp4 Thomas L. Thompson, GSW right thigh; Pfc. Dennis P. O'Brady, GSW chest; and Sp4 Israel V. Martinez, GSW thigh, broken. In addition, three medevac crew members were wounded while attempting to pick up Bravo Company casualties: 1LT Robert Richards, frags in neck; SSG Jack Craichen, frag in arm; and Pfc. James Clifford, frags both arms.

27 December (Military Index) KIAs, LZ Bird: Pfc. Samuel Quenton Asher, Milford, OH; Sp4 Freddie Lee Burnette, Durham, NC; Pfc. Anthony Charles Coffaro, New Brunswick, NJ; Pfc. Alfred Lee Davis, Long Beach, CA; Sp4 Gregory James Fischer, San Bernardino, CA; Pfc. Herbert Aaron Erwin, Jonesville, LA; Pfc. Howard Stanley Goldberg, Saddle Brook, NJ; Pfc. Armand Roy Graham, Long Beach, NY; Sp4 Robert Joe Hardesty, Lafayette, IN; Pfc. Randall Lee Hixson, Chattanooga, TN; SFC Paul Gray Jackson, Fayetteville, NC; Pfc. Richard A. Knaus, Cheektowaga, NY; Cpl. Robert Dennis Lajko, New Boston, MI; Pfc. Donald Herman Lederhaus, Milwaukee, WI; Sgt. Daniel L. Miracle, Williamstown, WV; Pfc. Ronnie Eugene Norris, Greer, SC; Sp4 James E. Nunley, Gary, IN; Pfc. Jerry E. Schmeltz, Chicago, IL; Sp4 Ronald J. Sheehy, Derby, CN; Sgt. Hugh G. Skipper, Paramount, CA; SSgt. Rodney Dale Staton, Guyan, WV; 1LT Jerald D. Wallace, Cisco, TX; Pfc. Roger Duwaine White, Battle Creek, MI; Sp4 Larry Joe Willis, White Heath, IL; Cpl. Roscoe Wright Jr., Wynnewood, OK; Pfc. Ronald Jerome Zitiello, Cleveland, OH.

Note: One source said that some 90 of the 140 soldiers on LZ Bird were killed or wounded. However, Stanton gives the figure as 58 KIAs and 77 WIAs as against 266 NVA KIAs (*Anatomy of a Division*, p. 89).

29 December 1966, 1540 Hrs: A 2–8 casualties, KIA, Pfc. Robert Petrimoulx; WIAs, Pfc. Terrence Bishop and Sp4 Joseph Terrel—all gunshot wounds.

nine

Lost Patrol

Early on January 9, Lillywhite returned from the hospital, alleging that he felt fine again, and we flew to Alpha Company, which was operating near the head of a southern valley in the Crow's Foot, near a north-running river. We landed in hip-deep water about 300 meters from the company position. We came upon three grunts as we waded toward the CP. One of the grunts, with his back to us, was cursing the situation, generously using divine titles. A grunt whispered, "Watch it, the chaplain." The offending grunt, Pfc. Theodore Lysak, pleaded, "Forgive me, Father."

Recognizing Lysak as a practicing Catholic, I said, without premeditation, "My son, do three rosaries, two Hails Mary and stop using God's name in vain."

Though I then confessed I was not a Catholic priest, Lysak assured me it made no difference, and he would obey my instructions. I never heard Lysak curse again, and henceforth he couldn't do enough for me—always trying to carry items for me, besides his gear and heavy M-60 machine gun, to dig my foxhole and so forth.

Minutes later in the CP area, 1st Sergeant Waley L. Watson invited me along on a patrol. The makeup of the nine-man patrol included Watson, Sergeant Theberge, the Mortar Sergeant and his radioman, Sp4 Kenneth Steel, three other grunts, Lillywhite and me. At 1100 hours, we moved out. Our objective was to reconnoiter—recon—a valley 300 meters to the west, beyond the flooding river, for a better location for a forward operating base (FOB) for the company.

We fell in with Watson's provisional—nonstandard—squad, and headed for the river. Everyone except Watson kept his feet while fording the swift current. About halfway across, Watson lost his footing and the current carried him away. Quickly, I ran down the bank, and leaping into the river below Watson and catching him as he passed, I pulled him to the west shore. Then I retrieved a tactical map—it had floated from Watson's pocket. We continued the mission as if nothing unusual had happened. Nothing had, really, as emergencies are the norm in combat.

A brief recon convinced the sergeants the FOB should stay where it was. But instead of turning back, Watson led us up a mountainside—perhaps to delay re-crossing the frightening river—to search for sign of enemy movement and activity.

Leaving the valley floor, we started up the mountain at the point of its nearest approach to the river, 50 meters southwest of where we'd crossed the river. I wondered, *Is this trip necessary or wise? Why hasn't the mountainside already been reconnoitered? Is this patrol just to test my willingness to share the grunts' life?*

The weather continued rainy, overcast and cold most of the day, which kept us soaked, cold and miserable, and hampered recon and navigation. We crossed a well-used north-to-south running trail about two-thirds of the way up the mountain. Because of the heavy rains, any sign of recent usage was washed away, if it were there in the first place. Watson called in a Situation Report—sitrep—and we moved to the top of the mountain.

There, Watson decided to follow a different route back to the company FOB, and we moved out in single file along a well-used, distinct foot path. Several minutes later the clouds broke momentarily and gave us a distant glimpse of a valley and river. Taking advantage of the increased visibility, Watson and Theberge oriented a map with the mountainsides and peaks and the river and valley below—or so they thought. Seeing the scene differently, I opined we were not where Watson and Theberge thought we were, that the valley visible below was not our valley. "You can tell by the pattern of the white water; the river is flowing from our left to right. Our river should flow from our right to our left," I pointed out.

After a moment of hesitation, Watson and Theberge rejected my opinion. "The course of the river is deceptive because it twists and turns so much," said one of them.

"A river has to be mighty crooked to flow upstream," I said, then held my peace.

We continued down the leech-infested trail in the direction the sergeants said we should go, naturally. Soon the clouds closed in again. And leeches attacked us, tiny leeches two or three inches long and only a little thicker than a coarse human hair—until they dined on our blood and swelled to the size of a man's finger. Not only did the leeches come out of the ground whenever we stopped, they even dropped on us from the trees. Frequently we paused and plucked leeches from one another's body and uniform—except that none were picked off me. While everyone else attracted several leeches, I found but one on me and pulled it off my neck before it attached itself to dine. This leech had the dubious distinction of being the only leech I found on my person during two years in Vietnam. According to my theory, leeches, like mosquitoes, prefer warm blood, so the bloodsuckers naturally gravitate toward other bodies, given an option, as my body temperature averages two degrees below normal.

Sp4 Kenneth Steel took the point moving down the trail, with his M-14 set on full automatic. As I recollect, the overcast lifted again at about 1400 hours, as we moved northerly past a clearing on the downhill side of the trail. My suspicions were confirmed. We weren't where the sergeants thought we were, for 50 meters below us, two flooding rivers converged, but only one river flowed in the Alpha Company area. I knew for sure that we were near a different valley, one I'd seen before from a different angle. A hill some 600 meters across the valley seemed vaguely familiar. I was on my way forward to discuss our position with

Watson, and was halfway past the clearing when Steel's M-14 shattered the quiet.

Steel, at the point, had let loose a 20-rounds magazine with one pull of the trigger. Returning bursts of AK-47 fire echoed his fire.

I dashed off the path and stopped in the tree line on the downhill side of the clearing. My reactions were intended to get me out of the open area and to a point where I could provide a lookout on our right flank. Meanwhile, several M-16 rifles joined Steel's M-14, and the AK-47 bursts ceased almost as soon as they began.

Fortunately for us, the enemy ambush was focused downhill—I suppose the NVA squad figured everything up the hill belonged to them, which would account for their having no security to their rear. A fatal mistake.

Steel said he came up on seven NVA soldiers near the trail, all facing downhill, and opened fire the instant one of them spotted him and started swinging a weapon around. He insisted his initial M-14 burst downed two NVA. The evidence supported Steel's word. Several fresh blood trails led from the ambush site, in the direction we needed to go. Days later, a captured, wounded NVA soldier said that two of his comrades were killed and the others all wounded—by Steel's assault.

The sergeants checked their maps, agreed between themselves about where we were, and called in artillery, first round smoke, to clear the area ahead.

"On the way, wait," came over the horn (radio). And we waited. Nothing. Not even the distant sound of a bursting smoke round.

The battalion sent a chopper to search for us near the grid coordinates Theberge provided. Meanwhile, recognition flashed on for me when a chopper arose from the hill to the northwest, across the valley—LZ Minh, the battalion firebase. After grunts secured my side of the clearing, I went to Watson and Theberge and told them where we were. Again the sergeants rejected my opinion, until events confirmed it, which confirmation we received when we glimpsed the search helicopter above the mountain. It was searching for us on the other side of the mountain and had flicked into sight during a turn.

"We spotted you for a moment above the mountain. Fly north and I'll guide you in by sight," Theberge radioed to the search chopper. Soon help arrived and aerial rockets were clearing our route into the valley.

In defense of Watson and Theberge, I had the navigational advantage on them because their perspective was limited to a ground level, jungle-limited view of the Alpha Company AO, while I frequently saw the bigger AO from the air. Perhaps Watson and Theberge were also handicapped by a stereotype of chaplains, that none could read a tactical map.

We moved out into the valley carrying three AK-47s, two Chinese Communist—chicom—rifles and lots of enemy gear that the NVA had left behind in their hurry to escape Steel's deadly fire. In the valley we followed the river to its juncture with the river we'd crossed that morning. There we turned south toward the Alpha Company FOB.

Just before dark, an Alpha Company platoon got into a firefight and killed two or three NVA right along the route we'd have to pass. That platoon was pulled back to the company ahead of us to preclude our accidentally shooting each other in the darkness. In consequence of the possibilities, I carried a captured weapon the rest of the way, loaded. We waded the last kilometer without further incident and arrived at the FOB well after dark, having humped, fought, swam and waded about 15 grueling kilometers since morning.

Arriving at the Alpha Company FOB well after dark, Lillywhite and I found our packs and opted to forgo setting up a rain shelter because we didn't want to violate noise discipline. Instead we each blew an air mattress partway up, folded about a foot of it under so it wouldn't stick out from under the poncho, drove an entrenching tool into the ground between the mattresses, and spread a poncho over both bags. Then we wrapped up in poncho liners and settled

down under the driving rain to try to sleep. To capture an illusion of warmth, we placed a single lit candle on the
ground between our faces. Lillywhite, showing his tough-
ness and infantryman skills, went promptly to sleep on his
left side, his face toward me.

Moments later in the dim light from the candle, I
watched a red leech rise out of the ground between our two
faces and raise up on its tail like a cobra. After quivering its
head toward the candle and me, the leech headed for
Lillywhite's nose. For my last heroic act of the day, I killed
the leech with a burst of insect repellent, just in time.

The relative importance of our incident in the events of
the day was reflected in a battalion journal entry: "Item 27,
1505, A/2–8: Patrol made contact w/ 7 VC, VC BE 735758.
VC fled, leaving behind 3 wpns (2 AK-47, 1 Mauser)."
Command was more interested in Lillywhite later, after the
medics estimated he caught malaria sometime during this
eventful day.

On Wednesday, January 11, I returned to An Khe to draw
pay and attend to personal matters and found I'd been charged
for $500 pay I had not received. The error corrected, I drew
$450 dollars and returned to LZ Hammond, where a tape
from Helga awaited me. After listening to the tape, I recorded
my answer and sent it off along with a money order for $398.

In early January, the remainder of the First Brigade returned to operate near the relative comfort and light-combat
area around the 1st Cav base camp at An Khe. However, the
2–8 Cav stayed in place under the operational control (OP-
CON) of another brigade. According to unconfirmed rumor,
our battalion commander volunteered his battalion to remain in the field so he could acquire more glory for himself.
Mysteriously, our malaria infection rate shot upward.

One cold, dismal morning, the battalion commander
asked me, in effect, "Why do the men let themselves catch
malaria? Don't they realize malaria can lead to blackwater
fever and permanent brain damage?"

"Yes, sir," I responded. "The troops know that, but they know permanent brain damage from an AK-47 round is much more likely." Tactfully I told the battalion commander some of the men believed he had let them down by volunteering them for another month in a very hostile AO.

Actually, the increase in malaria cases in the battalion—a real threat to a commander's tenure—came too soon after the brigade left us behind for the cause of the malaria to have been the result of lessened loyalty to the commander.

We spent January 12 and 13 with Bravo Company. On Friday the 13th we joined Bravo on an air assault into a blocking position on a hill to the northeast of LZ Minh. The blocking action resulted in nothing, so we swept down a rock- and jungle-choked canyon to the valley floor. Our point element killed two VC during the descent. Back in the valley, we had a worship service and spent the night without foxholes in an abandoned hamlet among dead palm trees. The area had been defoliated by Agent Orange to deny concealment to the enemy.

On January 14, I learned a school-trained chaplain assistant was being assigned to me. This was sad news for me but good for David Lillywhite; he would return to the relative safety of the R&U detail at An Khe. After receiving this message, I escorted Lillywhite to An Khe, where I stayed to attend church meetings with him the next day. At the airfield Sunday afternoon I cooled my heels for four wet, cold hours awaiting a flight to LZ Hammond. This allowed me plenty of time to consider how I would miss Lillywhite's spiritual strength, courage, savvy of the field, and comradeship.

Meanwhile, Alpha Company continued to operate in high mountains among rain-laden clouds and skilled enemy snipers. The company AO was somewhere east of LZ Hammond between the Crow's Foot to the north and Happy Valley to the south. Happy Valley had seen many recent battles and heavy 1st Cav casualties.

I finally got a flight to LZ Hammond, and from there I hopped a ride on the resupply chopper to Alpha Company. Upon reaching our destination, the chopper landed in a clearing on a rugged hillside where a platoon of infantry secured the LZ.

A high-powered rifle shot rang out as I leaped from the chopper. A grunt fell wounded about 30 feet from me. Ignoring the threat, we hurriedly loaded the WIA on the chopper, leaving his wound for the chopper crew to treat en route to the 15th Med.

At the FOB, Captain Frank Yon requested an immediate worship service. The men were very edgy and frustrated because of the snipers. They were eager to worship, to seek spiritual refuge. To deprive the snipers of a large target, I conducted three small services. Almost every man who could attend did attend a service, without regard to his religious preference. During singing in one of the services, done at a whisper, I noted a beautiful voice. It was Lieutenant Miller, the artillery forward observer. Miller willingly sang a solo during the three services that day and during many services to come.

I was talking with Captain Yon after the services when a burst of M-16 shots shattered the quiet. Yon and I dashed off toward the sound of the shooting and found Sergeant James C. Reeves, 1st Platoon. He stood over the bullet-riddled body of a VC. There was no doubt he was VC, for no farmers inhabited these high mountains. Up here it was just them and us. Apparently, the VC snipers were having it rough too, for this one was killed during broad daylight while he rummaged through our garbage.

To clear the trail, Reeves and a trooper dragged the body 20 feet from the trail and dumped it. Feeling compassion for the VC and wondering if his loved ones would ever know how he died, I prayed for him and for the troopers. But there was no sympathy in the troopers' eyes, just relief—one less sniper to worry about.

On January 17, I conducted another worship service for Alpha Company, and then left it to deal with the snipers without me. Later at Qui Nhon I purchased a Canon half-frame camera, which I selected for its size and economy. It fit well into an ammo pouch and gave me twice as many shots for each roll of film. Subsequently, I carried the camera encased in one of those plastic bags that PRC-25 radio batteries came in.

Oh yes, Battalion Operations called while I was on the mountain with Alpha Company to remind me I had four prisoners to visit at An Khe—the Mao case. I couldn't put it off any longer.

On January 18, I flew to An Khe via Qui Nhon, but I arrived too late to visit with the prisoners in their Conex prison. The delay came as a relief because I still had no idea how to go about counseling the prisoners. How could I counsel them and at the same time keep silent about what I knew while avoiding legal pitfalls?

The visits with the prisoners the next day were as bad as I anticipated, not between the prisoners and me, but within myself. In an attempt to minister to them, I approached each one with the attitude that he was my man and a son of God. I tried to blank from my mind the gruesome details of the crimes they were accused of committing against the young, pregnant Vietnamese woman, Mao. But foreknowledge was a difficult barrier to overcome, made more difficult because the prisoners were upset at chaplains. They'd been informed that the actions of a chaplain had led to their arrests. Perhaps they assumed their chaplain at the time of the crime, Charles Lockie, had caused them to be arrested and charged. I couldn't tell them otherwise.

All along I had believed another chaplain should counsel these men. Following the visit, I was more convinced than ever that it was a mistake for me to counsel them. But I had no choice, I thought, as I was their unit chaplain.

To rectify my predicament, I convinced the CID agents of the negative aspects of my position and got their permission to break my silence. Immediately I told Captain Vorst everything. He seemed surprised and relieved, not resentful or vindictive. With my part out in the open Vorst confided in me that, upon learning of Sven's allegations he had gone straight to his superior, the same who had since been reassigned to Division Headquarters. This individual had offered to take Vorst with him, but Vorst thought it in his best interest to decline the offer.

Over the next three days I divided my time between visits and services in the field and on LZ Minh. During a field service for Bravo Company, I took pictures of grunts gathered to worship in "Death Valley," the name I gave the place because of the spooky feel of a hamlet of vacant huts and the dead palm trees. I especially remember the night in Death Valley because of a whispered discussion with the company medic, a Seventh-Day Adventist, about the "proper" day for the Sabbath.

Word came on January 24 that Dave Lillywhite was in the hospital with malaria. That same day the battalion was ordered to An Khe for green line duty. The next day I returned to An Khe and worked on my office and living area. I wanted to be ready to meet the troops the next day when they arrived from the jungle. My efforts were premature.

The next day the brigade commander ordered my battalion to continue operations where it was. Realizing how down most of the grunts would be feeling, I returned to the field taking with me a new Army hammock. It had an A-frame-shaped rain cover and all-around mosquito netting. I'd never slept in a hammock and would field test it. I hadn't yet gained the respect I would eventually have for bursting mortar shells, how their deadly shrapnel sliced across the ground at just the right height to maim anyone just above the ground—in a hammock, for instance.

Well, with the hammock in my pack, I collected Sp4 Allen Kirkpatrick, my new school-trained and airborne-qualified chaplain assistant, and rejoined the demoralized troopers of Alpha Company in a valley near LZ Minh. Having run out of food and being unable to receive supplies by air, the company had humped off the mountain for extraction to An Khe and a month of base security. Instead, the company was ordered back up the mountain on foot, a real letdown. Orders to return to the sniper-infested mountain angered the troops, but they grumbled and did their duty.

At 1200 hours, before moving out, we had a company-size worship service (Kirkpatrick's first in the field) with 52 troopers attending. Being concerned that in their discouragement the troops and leaders might become careless, Kirkpatrick and I climbed the mountain with Alpha Company for whatever morale and spiritual support our presence might give. All afternoon we struggled upward through the dripping jungle. We climbed grades so steep we could reach straight out in front and touch the ground. It was so muddy and slick, we made progress only by grabbing onto whatever was available, as we slipped back a foot for every two we advanced. Kirkpatrick became ill from the exertion. He was not in true airborne condition and not acclimated. Fortunately for him, the normally hot weather was cold and damp for his first in-country hump.

Finally at the top of whatever hill we had been ordered to climb, we found punji stakes everywhere—sharpened slithers of bamboo that had been hardened in fire, smeared with human feces and placed in the ground and in pits to impale unwary grunts. A well-used trail came up the hill opposite of where we climbed. Well-concealed enemy fighting positions were placed strategically along the trail. There had been a lot of recent movement through the area.

While the men dug in and Kirkpatrick recuperated, I made the rounds and met Lieutenant Michael E. Berdy for the first time. Berdy was just beginning his tour in Vietnam. He was about six feet tall with the build of a weight lifter. He had light blond hair and was Jewish. When I first saw Berdy, a West Point graduate, he was engaged in the foolish, all too common error of new lieutenants—trying to set up night positions and ambushes in disregard of the advice of his more experienced platoon sergeant.

I introduced myself to Lieutenant Berdy and asked him to come with me and examine some enemy fighting positions on the trail. Out of earshot of his men, I shared with Berdy some lore about sergeants and lieutenants and suggested he have more respect for his platoon sergeant's experience. I never saw Berdy make the same type of mistake again. Unlike some officers and sergeants, Berdy considered my advice and acted on it without discounting it because it came from a chaplain. This marked him in my eyes as an officer destined for greatness in the Army.

Meanwhile, later in the afternoon on January 25, back on the mountain with Alpha Company, I cleared away the punji stakes between two trees and set up my new hammock. What a disappointment. First of all, I could lie only on my back in the hammock. Second, I could hardly wiggle. Third, after about half an hour, my knees were locked and on fire from the unusual stress generated by the curvature of an occupied hammock. After an hour, fed up with hammocks, I dropped to the ground, wrapped my poncho liner tight about me and slept the sleep of the restless. I returned the hammock to the supply sergeant the first chance I got. None in the field wanted it.

The morning following my one and only attempt at hammock sleeping, Alpha Company was ordered back to the sniper-infested area it had vacated two days before. All day we humped up and down ridgelines along rain-slicked hillsides, and by evening we came within smelling distance of the decaying VC Sergeant Reeves had killed on January 16. There was no sign that other VC had attempted to recover the body, though the snipers took little time making their presence known. The weather broke before dark, allowing choppers to bring in supplies, at which time the snipers recommenced their deadly, demoralizing work. Kirkpatrick missed the excitement, having departed with me on a log bird.

We left Alpha Company intent on visiting troops in the hospitals at Qui Nhon. However, we got stranded at LZ Minh for a cold, clear night, the first moonlit night in months. Perhaps the rainy season was about to let up, I hoped. It was.

On January 27, I flew to An Khe via LZ Hammond, having been unable to catch a flight to Qui Nhon. After showering and changing clothes, I flew on to Qui Nhon to visit Lillywhite, but he'd already been evacuated to Cam Ranh Bay, farther south on the coast.

Tragedy struck Brigade Headquarters on January 28. Grunts had killed an NVA officer who had in his possession an ammo box full of official-looking documents. The ammo box eventually arrived at the Brigade TOC at LZ Uplift. There several people gathered around the S-2 (Intelligence) officer as he separated the documents, which were booby trapped. The exploding booby trap killed two people, one of which was probably Vincent J. Weedo Jr. of Hackensack, New Jersey. Chaplain Dowd conducted a memorial service for the booby trap casualties, at which I offered a prayer. Following the memorial service, I flew around the AO for four hours with the battalion commander, then to An Khe for the night. The next day I reunited with the LDS troopers and attended meetings. That same day Corporals Donald Yates and Peter Keller were killed in some engagement that Delta Company was involved in.

I learned something about dealing with the news media on January 30. The chaplains had been called to LZ Hammond to meet with General Norton. Also in attendance was a correspondent who allegedly worked for a major American magazine. During the meeting we received encouragement to talk candidly with the reporter because he promised to write about the fine work of the chaplains in combat.

Several chaplains thronged around the reporter and eagerly expounded about their individual duties and philosophies. With two other chaplains, I held back from talking with the reporter. I'd become suspicious because of some of his subtle questions. Events confirmed my suspicions, as it turned out.

The reporter's true intentions would become clear when his piece was published. It focused on perceived conflicts of interest between a chaplain's avocation to God and his serving under a mortal commander—the old "two masters" straw man. The article was but one of a growing number of media attacks on the Army, the fighting soldier and the chaplains who served him. The article quoted, not too accurately, several chaplains who'd eagerly shared their views and philosophies. None of the quotes, misquotes or twists favored chaplains, nor were they complimentary of the service we provided the soldier.

During the meeting with the general and reporter, I arranged for Chaplain Marvin Wasink to provide a communion service for my headquarters element on LZ Hammond. From the meeting I headed for Alpha Company back up into the mountains because snipers were again giving the grunts a hard time. Troopers were being hit daily. One died to snipers on January 27, Pfc. Jose T. Boyless of Taylor, Michigan, I believe.

The chopper dropped from the clouds toward a steep mountainside, flared briefly and came to a hover in a small clearing. The terrain was so steep that with the right landing skid about two feet off the ground, the main rotor blade skimmed within inches of the ground on the uphill side. We made a perfect target for the snipers in the area. Appreciating that fact, the crew chief began pushing supplies out the open door even before the chopper had leveled out and hovered.

Taking the actions of the crew chief as my signal to dismount, I jumped to the ground from the left skid. This caused a sudden shift of balance on the chopper that caught the pilot by surprise. Barely, he avoided overcorrecting, which would have driven the rotor blades into the hillside and into many of the grunts in the clearing. Had the pilot been less skilled, the carnage would have been beyond description. Naturally, I was very grateful for the pilot's skills and because no one was hurt or killed by my tactical error. I was also relieved that no one ever mentioned my mistake, though the look the co-pilot gave me spoke volumes.

*   *   *

We loaded the one dead and four wounded (grim testimonials to the effectiveness of disciplined snipers) troopers onto the chopper. A moment later the chopper disappeared into the relative safety of the lowering clouds. Disappearing from the snipers seemed like a good idea, so we hoisted the supplies and moved quickly into heavy foliage in a draw about 40 yards downhill. Under the relative cover of the jungle, we redistributed the C-rations, ammunition and such. We moved up the other side of the draw some 150 meters toward the Alpha Company FOB, east of and higher than the LZ. I was fourth in line as we cautiously moved up a well-defined path. Ahead of me were 1st Lt. William H. Thompson, his RTO and the point man.

A single high-powered rifle round cracked past our heads when we were about 50 meters from the company position. I saw the muzzle flash of the sniper's weapon and glimpsed the sniper for an instant as he disappeared behind a tree by the path directly ahead of us. Reflexively, our point man sprayed the area with M-16 fire. Thompson joined in with a magazine of his own a split-second later. But it was too late. The sniper had withdrawn, leaving not even a blood drop for our satisfaction. Looking back, I suspect the sniper was trying to get our detail and the guys in the perimeter to open up on each other; a smart move, but it didn't work.

This gave me but a small sample of what the men of Alpha Company had endured from the moment they returned to this hill. Under constant harassment from snipers, they saw a steadily growing list of friendly casualties and were frustrated over their seemingly ineffectual efforts to hurt the enemy in return. Each trooper was vividly aware that at any moment he might feel, rather than hear, a sniper's bullet. Captain Yon had his emotions in tight control, despite his frustrations over a search-and-engage mission that had degenerated into one of trying to find individual snipers before they hurt any more of his men. Understandably, the men were jumpy, and none smiled in greeting.

Throughout my military career, I had heard that the

sniper is the most cost-effective weapon on the battlefield and the most destructive of troop morale. The situation seemed to confirm the sniper's effectiveness against morale. The snipers were Montagnard VC, I suspected, because of their American Indian–like stealth and effectiveness. This effectiveness was matched, in my experience, only by sappers.

On January 31, following a very wet, cold night, Alpha Company continued defensive operations. This included perimeter defense, small patrols and *counter-sniper* ambushes (I coined the phrase; at least I'd never heard it before). The sniper or snipers kept shooting, but with less success than the day before.

Three different times during the day a sniper round cracked near me—cracked past, not whined like in the movies. Many more shots were fired at other targets.

Good and bad news came early on January 31. The good news: Alpha Company was alerted to prepare for pickup and movement to An Khe! The bad news: first Alpha Company had to hump off the mountain because its LZ was too rough for a pickup. Then the bad bad news: higher headquarters cancelled the move of the battalion to An Khe.

Intending to fly out, at about 1800 hours I joined the patrol to secure the LZ so a chopper could bring in hot chow and a scout dog with its handler. We moved onto the hillside LZ, where I'd arrived the day before, as the chopper made its final approach.

The chopper dropped fast and steeply through the overcast sky and came to a hover. We'd barely begun offloading supplies when a shot rang out. A grunt on security fell wounded, a little below and in front of the chopper. The helicopter took off posthaste without the wounded trooper or passengers and with part of the supplies Alpha Company desperately needed.

We stayed near the LZ until full darkness in case the chopper—any chopper—came for the wounded trooper.

Finally, well after dark, a very brave medevac crew snatched out our WIA, despite the darkness, low clouds, worsening weather, and snipers. The medevac chopper dived through the clouds, flared and hovered. Almost instantly the chopper departed with our wounded. I'd decided to stay with Alpha Company. The night was wet and cold, but quiet.

Notes

28 January 1967, D 2–8 Honor Roll, Internet: KIAs Cpl. Donald Francis Yates, Round Lake, New York; Cpl. Peter Joseph Keller Jr. Detroit, MI.

ten

Close Contact

On February 1, Alpha Company was ordered off the mountain to replace Delta Company in the valley; Delta Company was heading to An Khe. With the scout dog team—the handler and his beautiful German shepherd—in the lead, we moved out at 1015 hours. I joined the lead platoon and took position in the middle of the point squad.

The scout dogs alerted the first time when we'd moved no more than 25 meters beyond the FOB perimeter—most of the company was still inside it. Squads fanned out downhill on both sides of the trail and swept forward. Nothing. We moved another few yards and the dog alerted again. Another sweep with the same negative results.

After we maneuvered through several dog alerts, Captain Yon, under orders to reach the valley during daylight, told the point platoon to disregard further alerting by the dog and keep moving, carefully. So we moved on with the dog's behavior working on our nerves.

"Take 10," we were told, about an hour after we first started moving. We were still within 200 meters of our starting point. About a minute into the break, the platoon leader radioed the point to move out. Captain Yon had countermanded the break order.

Just as I started forward, I saw the dog handler jerk his M-16 45 degrees left and let loose a 20-round magazine. Then, still standing, he grabbed into a pouch for another magazine. Pfc. Martinez, the handler's backup, made a flying tackle and took him to the ground under a hail of AK-47 fire. The beautiful point dog was hit in the left rear hip, but Martinez and the handler were unhurt. Next, the lead squad (sweeping me along with it) dispersed to both sides of the path and swept forward.

A dead VC or NVA officer lay in his own blood, just around the bend from where the handler had opened fire, about 40 feet from the spot where I'd sat for the aborted break. Upon reaching the dead officer, the troopers in the lead squad sprayed the surrounding jungle with M-16 and M-60 machine gun fire. Captain Yon and Lieutenant Miller rushed forward. We in the point element pushed on some 20 meters, past the excellent, wounded scout dog; then we held up for artillery support.

We were ordered to hug the ground. Lieutenant Miller had called in a barrage of 8-inch artillery 200 meters to our front. (We were almost out of range of our usual 105mm artillery support.) The 8-inch artillery had longer range and legendary accuracy, not to mention a heavier punch.

Well, this time the artillery was off about 150 meters, due either to the 8-inch tubes' inaccuracy (which I doubt), to the cannoneers' aim or to Lieutenant Miller's fire control coordinates (which I also doubt). In any event, the incoming artillery exploded in the triple canopy jungle 40 or 50 meters to our front, beyond the crest of our hill. Protected by the little crest, we were shaken and shocked, but otherwise unhurt by the blasts and shrapnel. Fortunately, Lieutenant Miller's frantic call stopped the incoming after the first volley.

Looking back on the scene, I imagined lying there with the earth pounding me in the chest and trying to crawl under my brass belt buckle for overhead protection.

Between the brief firefight and the artillery barrage, the dog handler explained what had happened. When the anticipated 10-minute break was interrupted, the dog handler arose with his dog and took about three steps forward into the curve in the trail. There sat five enemy soldiers about 20 feet beyond the curve, also taking a break. The enemy and handler saw each other at the same instant, but the handler reacted a fraction faster and killed the NVA officer. Then as he scrambled for a full magazine, four weapons tracked toward him. *"I'm a dead man!"* the handler thought. And he would have been dead but for Pfc. Martinez's quick thinking. The handler heaped praise on Martinez for his better combat skills and reflexes.

On reflection, I believe the enemy squad had been intentionally "stalking" us from the front, perhaps to delay our movement or withdrawal from the area. I think the VC accurately interpreted our obvious preparations for a break and decided to have one of their own—a fatal error on their part. Before we moved out, I noticed the dead officer's right ear was missing. I was saddened for the dead and for whoever had desecrated his remains.

We continued humping and sliding down the mountain without further enemy interference. We were leaving the snipers behind, the anticipation of which was dampened by neither the rain and mud, nor our aching and chafed shoulders and backs; I carried more than 40 pounds, about half of what most grunts carried.

By 1830 hours we were in place to relieve Delta Company. Our first order of business was to fill our canteens from a stream that flowed through the valley from the north. The floodwaters had receded and the water was crystal clear. Of course, we added water purification tablets to our canteens. Despite being constantly soaked, we'd been hard pressed for drinking water. Most of us waited the required 15 minutes before sating thirsts and soothing parched mouths and throats.

I spent the night at LZ Hammond and got to An Khe the next morning, ready for operations in a quieter AO, I hoped. Alpha Company joined the battalion at base camp a day or so later.

During the move from the jungle to the base-camp perimeter, one of my companies was hit by yet another of the all-too-common tragedies of war. Still in the jungle, a platoon leader, upon receiving word we were going to An

Khe, foolishly formed his platoon into formation to inspect
the grunts' appearance. The matter would have ended there,
but just then a machine gunner in another platoon, hidden
from the formation by light ground vegetation, succeeded in
clearing a jammed machine gun. Several of the grunts in the
formation fell wounded, friendly "casualties of war."

Beginning February 2, I entered what was probably the
quietest 20 days of this tour in Vietnam, excepting the first
83 days. Best of all, battalion casualties were low for the
whole period.

I enjoyed attending LDS services at Camp Radcliff
two weeks in a row and had fun some days patrolling the
vast base-camp perimeter on an unreliable two-wheel
scooter or tote goat. Another time I visited Lillywhite in
the hospital at Cam Ranh Bay. He was better and in high
spirits.

During a lighter moment the afternoon of February 17,
Lieutenant Frazer of Delta Company challenged me to show
my skills with my "camera." This occurred at one of the
bridges being defended by Delta Company along Highway
19 between An Khe and the Mang Yang Pass to the west.

"What shall I use for a target?" I asked.

"I'll walk down the road 10 feet, and you use me for a
target, ha-ha. Nobody can hit anything with that damn
thing," answered Frazer.

"Okay, but let me zero in on something else first."

So a sergeant paced off 50 meters and placed an empty
90-recoilless casing on the stump of a burned-out tree.

Casually, I raised the .45, left-handed, pointed and fired,
all in a single, seeming nonstop movement. Frazer and the
troopers were impressed by the distinct ring of brass hitting
brass. Calmly, I said to Frazer, "I'm ready. Pace off 10."
Frazer declined to pace, and I declined to repeat the performance. I, too, had been impressed by my *lucky* shot.

At evening chow, the adjutant informed me I had been
put in for a Bronze Star for Valor for an action in January—

the recommendation would get lost. Oh well, my actions hadn't rated a hero's medal, anyhow.

At base camp the grunts, after five uninterrupted months in jungle and paddies, spent each day filling sandbags and patrolling beyond the perimeter. They spent each night guarding the perimeter or on ambush beyond it. Base security, though it was generally safer, offered little rest for the infantrymen.

During this period I attended an LDS conference at Nha Trang, along with 15 troopers from the 1st Cav. I spoke during the conference, as did Sp4 Paul Moody, a grunt from a 7th Cav battalion. We received inspiring talks and counsel by Keith Garner, head of the Southern Far East Mission, and Colonel Rojsa, the leader of LDS personnel in the III Corps area of Vietnam. Master Sergeant Fanoimoana, with whom I had served briefly at Fort Ord, California, led the music.

My pleasure in the conference was lessened when Fanoimoana informed me Captain Stephen A. Childers of Alton, Illinois, a friend from the recent Fort Ord days, had been killed when he hesitated to fire on a VC who shielded himself behind a child. More sad news awaited me the next day back at Camp Radcliff. Pfc. Gerald W. Gannon of Poughkeepsie, New York, had been killed during my absence.

An old Army saying goes like this, referring to breaks: Take 10. Expect five. Get two and a half. Well, the saying applied to our promised one-month break.

On February 21 we headed back to the field, this time a few klicks (kilometers) farther north to the Bong Son Plain and surrounding mountains and coastal areas. LZ Hammond was closing down. The new battalion forward base would be on LZ English, a klick or two north of the town of Bong Son.

At LZ English, I set up a tent for temporary accommodations and sandbagged around it. Then I put Kirkpatrick to work constructing a more weather- and shrapnel-proof hooch of sand-filled ammo boxes—good thing for him, too, as events would prove.

On February 23 I linked with Bravo Company in our new AO on the Bong Son Plain where we would operate for most of the remaining six-plus months of my tour. The company AO was generally flat with palm tree–shaded hamlets dispersed on raised plats of ground among flooded rice paddies. Late in the day, the company split its AO into sectors for platoon-size operations. I joined the Second Platoon. The first night we patrolled. Night patrol was a rare tactic for American infantry units.

Moving in three columns through a rice paddy, we spotted, fired at and chased two shadowy figures. The enemy had been moving casually along a rice paddy dike, mistakenly confident the night belonged to them.

While some troops chased the two VC, the platoon leader, medic, RTOs and I dropped behind the rice-paddy dike we had been moving on, and just in time. We were barely behind the dike when enemy machine-gun fire commenced raking it. Simultaneously or perhaps a moment after, nine dark forms rose from a position about 30 meters to our south and fled to the northwest, straight into a Bravo company OP. The troopers on the OP killed one VC and wounded at least one other.

Sometime after midnight, we moved into a hamlet and set up a platoon-size ambush. I waited in the predawn behind the stump of a long-dead giant tree, cold and clammy in the morning dew and air.

At 0530 hours, February 24, we moved out toward the company CP. Minutes later, as we started around the outskirts of a hamlet along our route, I spotted and called attention to three dark figures fleeing across our front from the hamlet. The grunts opened fire, but the shadows escaped, possibly unhurt. We made it through the night without taking friendly casualties. *Welcome back to the war!*

About noon, in company with the second platoon, I rejoined the rest of Bravo Company. From there I flew to An

Khe, met with attorneys concerning the Mao case and drew some pay.

First Lieutenant Nathaniel Ward wrote in his personal journal: On February 25 Delta Company troopers, while securing LZ Santana, cornered four VC in a cave that was snuggled so close to the LZ that artillery could not reach it. Two VC were captured immediately and one was killed as he tried to flee. A fourth VC, deeper in the cave, refused to come out. A trooper crawled in as far as he could and "was able to reach him only by knife. Knew Cong wasn't dead as he kept emitting cries . . . Several .45 cal. rounds finally killed him."

To get the dead VC out, Ward added, "The men tied a rope to his feet, threaded it over a tree limb, hoisted the body up, and left it hanging until a 1–9 Cav scout spotted it from the air. Lt. Col. John C. Dashiell, our new battalion commander, chewed me out. I sent a squad back to take down the hanging remains."

Meanwhile, that day or the next I arranged a six-day (only five nights) Hawaiian relaxation and recuperation (R&R) leave for Helga and me. The Armed Services were committed to giving an R&R to every American military member in Vietnam during each one-year tour. Many married soldiers opted for R&R with their wives in Hawaii, as opposed to exotic places of easy access to prostitutes like Bangkok, Kuala Lampur, Hong Kong, Japan and even Brisbane, Australia.

On February 27 I visited hospitals in Qui Nhon, where I purchased an airplane ticket for Helga to come to Hawaii. I arrived back at LZ English at 2200 hours. Back in the battalion AO, things had heated up while I was in Qui Nhon.

Upon arriving at the battalion late in the day, I learned it was engaged in heavy combat. A platoon of Delta Company had met heavy resistance as it attempted to enter a village. The situation had developed rapidly and the whole battalion was involved. Bravo Company had already sustained one killed and several wounded, and Charlie Company had three or four friendly KIA and 9 WIA.

Upon learning of the battle, I immediately visited our wounded grunts at the 15th Medical Clearing Company, and the dead at the Graves Registration point next door. Following these ministrations, I tried until just before dawn the next day to catch a flight to Bravo or Charlie Company, which supposedly had an NVA force of about 300 surrounded in a hamlet. Lt. Ward wrote in his journal that during the wee hours of the morning one of his squads reported seeing a small element of NVA sneaking from the village. Thinking smartly, the squad leader let the NVA pass, assuming it to be an enemy recon team seeking an exfiltration route for a larger body of NVA. "Squad leader allowed recon team to pass [back in]. . . . When the VC started back out, it was merely a matter of killing them as they filed past. Excellent thinking. . . . I probably would have fired on the first figure I saw," wrote Ward. "My soldiers have more guts and strength than I could ever conceive. They are unhesitant and brave beyond belief. Some of our U.S. 'citizens' should actually witness them work."

Just after dawn February 28, I reached Charlie Company on the cordon line, at the south side of the village. Shortly after that we entered An Do. Though fighting had ended in the hamlet, the scars of battle were all about. An elderly man poked through the ashes of a hut, probably for personal valuables or the remains of family members—which, I wondered. Meanwhile, the artillery continued to pound a larger village about 200 meters north of us.

At 0745 hours Charlie Company was ordered to back off into the open rice paddies so more artillery could be placed on the village north of An Do—An Noy, I think it was. Moments later, a combination of naval gun and 8-inch field artillery shells nearly drowned out the 105mm and 155mm explosions, which had been continual for several hours. I took advantage of the wait to move along the line of troops and visit some very weary grunts and leaders.

The artillery stopped at exactly 0900 hours and Bravo Company assaulted, sweeping on line from the west across a large rice paddy. From my vantage point in the Charlie Company blocking position, I saw the muzzle flashes from the Bravo Company grunts' weapons as they advanced into enemy fire amid geysers of water being kicked up around them by return fire. No trooper faltered or lagged behind his place in the assault line—each marched ahead as if he were unaware of the enemy small-arms fire cracking about him. Bravo Company would take heavy casualties during the assault, I feared—it didn't.

Coming into the village behind Bravo Company I saw five dead NVA, each missing a right ear. I also saw a dead man and woman, whom I assumed were husband and wife. The body parts of several children were strewn about, none large enough to tell which body it belonged to.

We searched the village through the early afternoon for intelligence, enemy equipment and bodies. At 1330 hours my troops cornered a small element of VC and killed one. They captured two wounded and promptly killed them.

Officially Companies B and C sustained seven friendlies killed and 10 wounded. Alpha Company sustained two KIAs after it arrived to search and secure the larger village (actually two villages divided by a deep, heavily vegetated streambed).

The Alpha Company CP settled along the south bank of the riverbed, between the villages of An Do and An Noy. A few minutes later, an NVA sniper round fired from the south riverbank caught Kenneth Steel under the chin, killing him instantly. The shot came from below, from the riverbank he had been standing on. Steel fell back and a medic, probably Sp4 Peter P. Malacznik of Los Angeles, scrambled to his aid—too late. A moment later, two chicom grenades sailed upward from below and landed by Steel. One of them hit the foot of the medic who was trying to treat him. Both grenades were duds.

Lieutenant Thompson (the same who had escorted me

among the snipers back in January) went after the sniper, backed by Pfc. Herbert A. Fralix. Contrary to Yon's orders, the two sneaked down into the riverbed at a point several meters to the east and worked their way toward the sniper's hiding place on the bank. A single shot rang out, followed almost instantly by a burst of M-16 fire. Thompson lay dead, shot through the head from above. The NVA also lay dead, his body mangled by fire from Fralix's weapon.

Pfc. Kenneth L. Steel of Fremont, Nebraska, was the first trooper I got to know in Alpha Company. It was he who thwarted the NVA ambush back on January 9.

Before leaving the village, I stood where Steel fell, and there I grieved and prayed for Steel, for 1st Lt. William H. Thompson of Belleville, Illinois, and for all who fell that day, on both sides.

Someone awakened me with a low whisper at 0200 hours on March 1. A Delta Company squad on ambush had sustained five friendly wounded and two killed—seven out of eight men—when it was counter-ambushed.

A few minutes later at the 15th Med I saw to the dead, Sgt. William Hopkin and Cpl. Robert Johnson, and to the wounded one whose thigh muscle was torn loose above the knee and peeled back over his abdomen, looking just like a good-sized prime roast awaiting the pot.

I accompanied the wounded to Qui Nhon. There I also visited troopers who had been wounded during the previous two nights and the day before.

Writing of the counter-ambush action the next day, Lt. Ward described what happened this way: "Engineers had scooped out positions for the perimeter guard. . . . About midnight I awoke to . . . tracers pouring into the engineer command post. . . . I crawled to the CP when I heard the cries from the wounded out beyond the perimeter—one of our ambushes had been hit. . . . The patrol [ambush] leader panicked . . . ran back through our positions. . . . It's amazing that he wasn't killed trying to cross back in. . . . He suffered a head wound. . . . We had communication with someone in the ambush—he was afraid to use his radio for fear of being overheard by the Cong. I could hear the cries over the phone. . . . It was imperative to send out a recovery team, and I had an idea the VC were waiting for such foolishness. But there were wounded. . . . Thank God my platoon sergeant volunteered—it is difficult to write of the fear one has when men have been killed, and suddenly it's one man's responsibility to direct others—or go himself—out into the unknown darkness to confront a killing opposition. Sergeant Wilson and five others made contact with the ambushed and fortunately encountered no fire. Impossible to move wounded so we secured a landing zone. . . . Those eight men hit were torn all up from grenades and rifle fire . . . tore open heads, back, blew web gear right off of the bodies, ripped off arms and legs. Sickening—one man begged to be killed, and he probably would have been better off . . . a buck sergeant due to leave the field in a few days. Yesterday he threatened a suspect with a .45 pistol—I remember thinking how one bad turn someday might deserve another.

"I knelt down by one of the wounded—his knee bent as if resting. The wind blew sand across his face and into his eyes—I brushed away the silent cover and attempted to elicit a response from him. I put my hand behind his head to hold him up . . . then I realized he was quite dead, for the entire back of his skull had been blown away. Even my shock couldn't prevent the wind from slowly, methodically, drawing cover over his face.

"1 March. This morning we returned to look back over the ambush site. The men had set up in a small patch of sugarcane about 100 meters from the engineer perimeter—not in the area that had been designated. . . . Don't know why the patrol leader selected this area—cane provides good concealment but no protection while every movement can be heard. They fell asleep about 2200 hours when the VC began moving in on them . . . from three directions . . . the men must really have been asleep for enemy didn't crawl along the rows but across them . . . exposing themselves

over each mound. But knowing how well the Cong can infil-
trate undetected. . . .

"They had moved to within five meters of the machine-
gun position . . . only one of the ambushed returned fire. . . .
Obviously the Cong wasn't aware of the severity of their
damage . . . three Americans killed and five wounded . . . in
the background the Buddhist temple. . . . Recommend my
platoon sergeant be considered for a decoration" (From Lt.
Ward's personal journal, pp. 24–26).

Notes

Lieutenant Nathaniel Ward's personal journal, which he kept
    during his almost four months in Delta and Charlie Companies,
    2–8 Cav. I quote from it often because his entries often
    correspond with my own.
1 March 1967, D 2–8 Honor Roll, Internet: KIAs Sgt. William
    Burton Jr., Hopkins, SC and Cpl. Robert Edward Johnson,
    Highland, NY.

eleven

Left Behind in "Indian Country"

At 0900 hours, March 1, back at LZ English, Kirkpatrick and I joined Chaplain (Catholic) Phil Lucid—the same who to help me get home had pressed 40 dollars into my hand a year before upon graduating from the chaplain basic officer course—for his first trip to the field. Lucid had recently joined the 1st Cav. He was going with us to provide Catholic services to my units.

Before boarding the chopper to fly to the field, I briefed Lucid on a few points of survival and conducting austere religious support operations. Then we flew to Bravo Company, near the scene of the previous two days of fighting.

Instead of getting off at the Bravo Company *location*, my destination, I asked the pilot to fly us to the other company, stand by while I introduced Lucid, and then return Kirkpatrick and me to Bravo Company. He agreed. In 10 minutes or less we were back, feeling confident all was in order, as an infantry company usually took at least 30 minutes to break down supplies and move out.

Upon arriving at the Bravo Company location, Kirkpatrick and I jumped off the chopper into the cloud of dust cast up by the downwash of the chopper rotors. The chopper took off the moment we hit the ground, and the dust quickly settled. That's when we knew we might be in trouble!

This was no longer the Bravo Company location. No friendly, familiar faces greeted us. We'd been dropped in enemy territory—just two of us, in a clearing surrounded by battle-scarred huts and palm trees, where two days of battle had probably left the locals feeling extremely hostile. The clearing we were in joined two others, one which stretched to the southeast and one that angled westward toward the jungle.

"Naked and exposed" hardly describes how I felt. For a moment, amazement distracted me from the immediate danger. How could the chopper pilot have dropped us off without first assuring American forces were still present? But he had, and here we were. It took little imagination to appreciate the dangers we faced.

Between us, we had but two weapons, and one of them tended to jam—a chaplain and his assistant smack in the middle of NVA- and VC-infested territory. To make matters worse, we had neither radio nor other means to call for help, nor could we expect to be missed for several days; the commanders and staff didn't keep track of my movements. Several kilometers lay between us and LZ Santana and there was little chance we could evade all the enemy and enemy sympathizer eyes between us and there. There were too many open areas on the plain, and most of what wasn't open was heavily booby-trapped. *We have little chance of avoiding capture or death by any number of means* was my assessment of our situation.

Reflexively, I headed us out of the open toward one of the lines of palm trees leading westward toward the jungle. The jungle, I figured, would be less heavily booby-trapped, and it offered us the best chance of concealing ourselves. In the jungle I could keep us alive, I believed. We could overcome the obstacles and drawbacks, despite the odds against us . . . unless the enemy had us spotted already, or unless an enemy patrol literally stepped on us in our hiding place, unless random friendly harassment and interdiction (H&I) artillery got us, unless a strategic bomb strike blew us up, or unless one of a thousand other vagaries of war worked against us.

Our most urgent need was to avoid immediate death or capture, for the VC and NVA habitually searched American resupply sites after the companies vacated them. In this manner, the enemy took advantage of the grunt's tendency to lighten his load by tossing aside an occasional stick of C-4 explosives and the less tasty C-ration items.

Barring the vagaries of war, we would hide in the jungle, I figured, and pray a 1–9 Cav aerial scout patrol spotted us first or that another American unit entered the area. But even these possibilities were fraught with risks. Likely, aerial scouts would appear first. However, being prime targets themselves, feared and hated by the enemy, these aerial scouts tended to shoot first and count bodies when they spotted soldiers in places "friendlies" weren't supposed to be.

And should another ground unit be sent into the area, the area might be prepped first with tube and aerial artillery— which would also be very bad for us. Still, we much preferred these and other risks to being discovered by the enemy. Yes, the situation looked bad, despite the confidence I had in my escape and evasion (E&E) capabilities, untested under fire though they were.

While I assessed our situation and moved us toward the jungle, the Bravo Company Commander, Captain Getz, wondered why the supply chopper had returned only to depart the area without making radio contact with him. To be on the safe side, Getz ordered the rear platoon to send a patrol back and investigate, which was very fortunate for us. Also fortunate for us, we were still in the open when the point man of the patrol reached the edge of the clearing. This gave him plenty of time to positively identify us from within the shadows of the jungle.

I've little doubt, based on experience, that the point man would have blown us away had we reached the jungle before he saw us. His natural, proper reaction would have been to blast away at any noise or movement on the company's back trail.

In hindsight, which the Army calls an After Action Review or AAR, several factors combined to almost kill us or see us captured. The Army had no effective doctrine for religious support operations in combat, nothing for the chaplain and assistant to train to. No standard procedures or checks existed to trigger prompt concern for the chaplain and his assistant's whereabouts. Nor did the chaplains have radios or other means of independent communication. Besides these drawbacks, I made matters worse by assuming the pilot would communicate our intentions to Bravo Company and that Bravo Company would remain at the logging site longer than it did. I assumed too much.

After a quiet night in the jungle with Bravo Company, I held a worship service at 0830 hours, March 2. Then I humped with the company back to the villages where the fighting had raged February 27 and 28.

Back in the village we received orders to destroy all structures still standing, including the coconut log bunkers beside the ashes of former native hooches. A bulldozer was being sling-loaded to us beneath an Army flying crane—the biggest chopper on the battlefield.

While we waited for the dozer, I conducted another worship service for those who couldn't attend the earlier one. Later, during the bunker-razing operation, there occurred a touching scene that revealed the complex makeup of the American soldier.

Pfc. Harry E. Kerrpash arrived with his bulldozer and began knocking over bunkers, working northward from the south side of the village. These bunkers were above ground and consisted of an A-frame of coconut logs covered with halved coconut shells, with two or more feet of hard-packed soil over those. The bunkers typically were closed all around except for a crawl-through opening on one end. The almost enclosed bunkers provided adequate protection from all but direct hits by heavy artillery, by bursts directly in front of the tiny entrance, or by near-misses by air-dropped bombs.

Considering the strong enemy resistance we'd met here, destruction of the bunkers seemed a reasonable precaution. The Vietnamese, though, had a different perspective—the bunkers were all they had left.

The demolition operation went smoothly until we came upon two Vietnamese women and several children, lined up in front of a bunker. One of the women cried hysterically as the dozer approached. Our Kit Carson Scout—a former VC—said the woman pleaded for us to spare the bunker because it was all the home the two families had. I suspected the bunker concealed her VC husband or one or more NVA soldiers. The second woman, with a child on her hip, stood stone-faced, as we'd come to expect of the Vietnamese, especially the VC.

Well, Kerrpash, intent on doing his duty, revved his engine threateningly and moved resolutely forward, only to hesitate 20 feet in front of the women and children. After hesitating, Kerrpash inched the dozer blade closer to the civilians, only to stop again. Turning off the dozer engine, Kerrpash dismounted and told the platoon sergeant, "I can't do it. I have children that age."

The platoon sergeant turned the matter over to the lieutenant. The lieutenant called the company commander. Breathing fire, Captain Getz rushed to the scene, but once there, he hesitated to stare at the women and children and declared, "That bunker is one foot outside my company AO. Let it stand."

Next, a grunt approached the bunker with a grenade in hand. The crying woman became hysterical, and "stoneface" even showed alarm, thus convincing me one or more husbands hid in the bunker. The grunt never threw the hand grenade, despite his suspicion that the bunker concealed one or more NVA, foes who had so recently tried to kill him and had killed his buddies, probably with the help of these women.

I held my peace, amazed at the compassion of troops who had lost buddies in the last days and (some of whom) had in the heat of battle probably killed wounded NVA or removed ears from the dead. Now, these same hardened grunts couldn't ignore the crying families, perhaps part of the enemy. Every trooper on the scene admitted, after the fact, that he was convinced an NVA hid inside the bunker. I understood the dozer driver, the captain, and the troops and was relieved at the outcome, but haunted by the recollection of Childers' recent death when he hesitated in the face of a

VC behind a human shield. I'd see the dozer operator again, in a hospital in Japan.

The two Vietnamese families lined up for pictures. (I'd already taken several of them.) The bulldozer moved on, and the grunts and I took a break in the shade of a palm tree. A few minutes later the stone-faced woman delivered to us two green coconuts (the natives favored green coconuts), opened and ready to eat, a thanks offering, I thought.

I spent the night of March 2 with Delta Company, which had sustained two KIAs and five WIAs at 0151 hours. The next morning, after conducting worship services, I returned to LZ English and to the first day in the last 10 without combat—for me, but not my unit.

On March 3, I covered the 15th Medical Clearing Company at LZ English. The day was quiet, so I played chess and discussed matters spiritual with Kirkpatrick and Paul Moody.

On March 4 I received orders to testify March 11 in general courts martial in connection with the Mao incident—smack in the middle of my scheduled R&R with Helga. I hurried to An Khe in the highest state of anxiety I'd experienced in a long time. But good things happened there the next day. First, I was excused from appearing in court so I could go on R&R. And second, I took part in the baptism of Sp4 Deloyd (Dee) Bailey.

With Boring and Bailey dressed in borrowed white cook's clothing, we gathered on the south bank of the cool, deep Song Be River that ran through Camp Radcliff. Lieutenant Scott B. Thereur conducted the service, and Boring baptized Bailey.

After the war, Bailey became a very successful Texas lawyer, published a book on the scriptures, and retired quite wealthy before age 50. In 1994, Helga and I would ride to Arizona with Bailey to attend a funeral for Wayne Boring's son, Wayne.

twelve

Illusion: R&R vs. Reality of War

After a few days of low-intensity combat, I returned to An Khe on March 8 to prepare for R&R. Preparing for R&R brought me in conflict with some despicable rear-area policies.

At Camp Radcliff, I accompanied two grunts to a small Post Exchange (PX). They were also going on R&R. The PX was situated on the inner side of the belt road that circled Division Headquarters and the Golf Course or airfield. We were shopping for ribbons and other items we needed for our uniforms.

An overweight sergeant in clean, pressed jungle fatigues blocked our entrance to the PX. The dialogue went like this, in essence: "What's your unit?" asked the sergeant.

"Second of the Eight," I answered for the group.

"Well, you can't shop here."

"Why not? This is an Army PX, isn't it?"

"You can't shop here because your battalion doesn't help with police call," the sergeant stated, with finality.

I controlled my rising ire and quietly said, "Army PXs are open to ALL soldiers. Our battalion doesn't help with police call because it is out in the jungle fighting. We are coming in, and we shall take what we need. Whether you accept our money is up to you, but it will require at least a general officer to stop us."

Having had my say, we pushed past the sergeant and did our shopping. Meanwhile, the sergeant ran to the rear and cranked up his field telephone to call for reinforcements.

After a few minutes, we went to pay for our selections.

The sergeant rang up our purchases and took our military script in scowling silence. I reported this matter to Major Harold E. Iverson, battalion executive officer, but heard no more about it.

Meanwhile, our shopping complications were not over. The PX had few of the items we needed. Perhaps we could do better in town.

Accompanied by the same two grunts and Wayne Boring, I headed for the main gate and An Khe. The military policeman at the gate had his own ideas and orders though. He demanded we each show him a condom. I said I didn't have a condom and didn't intend to have one. "Then, by the commanding general's orders, you can't go into town," the MP insisted.

This was too much, coming on top of the incident at the PX. In the same careful voice I'd used on the PX sergeant, I addressed the MP. "Neither Specialist Boring nor I will show a condom. We are not about to have such an item in our personal effects should we be killed. And we are going through the gate. You'll have to shoot us to stop us, either that or get a colonel or general here to order us not to pass."

We passed. I protested the condom policy through command channels, probably to no effect.

I departed An Khe for Cam Ranh Bay on March 9, headed for Hawaii. At 0400 hours, March 10, after 15 hours and a fuel stop on Guam, I was hugging Helga at the Honolulu Airport.

Our five nights and six days in Hawaii were wonderful. After resting and becoming reacquainted for a day and a night at the Fort DeRussy Hotel, we rented a Honda motorbike and toured the Waikiki area. The first evening, we attended a luau at the invitation of the wife of Sergeant Fanoimoana. After the luau we moved into a cabin in Haaula for our remaining four nights.

Our extracurricular activities included attending the temple and church meetings, snorkel fishing at night with a couple we met at the luau, visiting the Polynesian Cultural Center, and shopping. I think we also ate a few meals and took in the movie *Doctor Zhivago*. Our R&R was marred in only two ways—Helga became ill and required treatment at the Tripler Army Hospital, and time flew as if it were on wings of lightning. Leaving Helga at the airport was harder even than it had been to leave her at home. Parting was such sorrow—nothing sweet about it.

I was dreadfully torn during the return flights to my unit. Part of me flew eastward with my darling Helga while part of me reached anxiously ahead to my grunts in the field. *Which of them died while I was away? How many?*

Of course, given any choice in the matter, I wouldn't have missed R&R with Helga—none in the field would have wanted me to. But the guilt, unreasonable though it was, was very real. One trooper died in my absence—Pfc. Robert L. Van Gieson of Van Nuys, California, gave his life on March 12.

I landed at Cam Ranh Bay at 1545 hours on March 17, my mind already adjusted to returning and intent on reaching the field as quickly as possible. But it took until afternoon the next day to reach An Khe via Qui Nhon and Pleiku—each about 45 miles from An Khe, one to the east and the other to the west.

That night, while I worked my way "home," Lt. Ward took his platoon into an ambush position not far from the Buddhist Temple on the Bong Son Plain. "In the distance we saw a group of men collected . . . so deployed in pursuit until I realized the threat—they wore the khaki uniforms of the North Vietnamese Regulars. They were . . . obviously drawing us into something. . . . Decided the wisest course was to move into a defensive perimeter until nightfall. . . . After SSgt. Wilson reconned our ambush position, we . . . moved into the site by pairs. Set up around an isolated house

that was bordered by a natural tree-line defense. Did not dig
in for fear of disclosing our location. . . . At five minutes after midnight they hit us on four sides. . . . Threw it [assault]
back and my machine guns finally neutralized their fire after
20 minutes—could have been much longer. . . . From time
to time we could see the khaki uniforms as they took up new
positions. I was sure we would be overrun as the rest of the
company was too far away. . . . NVA hugged our perimeter
knowing they would be safer from artillery. I decided that if
it came to being overrun I would bring the HE . . . on our
position—Wilson agreed . . . changed the gun's [M-60's]
positions. Moments later they attempted to storm the southern end, only to run directly into a repositioned machine
gun. I felt great.

"An artillery round struck dangerously close, showering
us with fragments . . . scared the hell out of us but the NVA
also backed off. Guess they believed we would sacrifice our
position for them. . . . I had two dead and five wounded.
One of the men, Pfc. Michael Neal Johnson, lay there snoring through the entire fight—we kept kicking him trying to
wake him up. Later we realized his head wound . . . Johnson
just kept snoring and never regained consciousness. . . . I
called for 'dust off' in the midst of the battle because of the
seriousness of the wounds . . . warned pilot it would be a hot
pickup—then it becomes his discretion as to whether to go
in or not. He sounded so cool and merely requested suppressive fires . . . enemy ceased firing until wounded had been
evacuated—then resumed firing. Could it have been a gesture of honorable warfare? I feel sick—why must our people die like this? How many more fights can we emerge
from? . . . As I look back on last night, I see my mistake
was . . ."

The light NVA company that attacked Ward's platoon
sustained six killed and 11 wounded. It had "repeatedly attempted to overrun the position, but heavy fire had forced
them back," according to Ward's journal for March 26.

"The enemy backed off in several directions. . . . SSgt.
Bohannen took off with two squads in chase . . . I heard a

heavy firefight ensue, but sergeant indicated over the radio that he needed no help . . . returning several hours later with six VC hamlet guards. . . . Sergeant claimed he had dropped approximately 20 suspects fleeing towards Tam Quan. . . . Battalion commander wanted accurate body count . . . he personally flew over . . . no evidence—bodies or footprints—was visible. Either suspect had played dead, carrying off those who were hit, or my sergeant manufactured the kill . . . several men said they had personally killed and physically checked the dead. Battalion commander wasn't satisfied . . . by now was more than displeased with me. Platoon sergeant gave . . . call sign of an observation chopper that had assisted during the chase by scouting overhead . . . pilot not only confirmed a count of 18 bodies but indicated that the troops on the ground had employed outstanding tactics."

One of Ward's men had fallen into a punji pit a week earlier but had not been hurt because he fell just right. Moments later a grunt was severely wounded about the face and chest when he tried to pull one of the punji stakes from the pit—booby trapped.

It being Saturday when I reached An Khe, I delayed going forward so I could attend LDS services the next morning, after which I went to LZ English, arriving there at 1520 hours. The good news when I arrived was that none of my companies was engaged in battle. That changed, though, before twilight, and the frequency and intensity of combat and our casualty rates heated way up.

Alpha Company got into a fierce battle minutes after I reached LZ English. During the fight, which continued through the night, the company sustained two friendlies killed and 14 wounded. Delta Company sustained three seriously wounded in a separate action.

At 0230 hours, March 20, I visited the three wounded Delta Company troopers at the 15th Med—they'd been ambushed.

At 0730 hours, I returned to the 15th Med and visited three wounded troopers from Alpha Company and one from Bravo Company. I don't recall anything about the Bravo Company action but assume the company was engaged beside Alpha Company.

Finally, at 0830 hours, I got a flight to Alpha Company, which was engaged in an ongoing fight with a strong, tough combined VC and NVA force. A grunt killed a VC just as I joined the CP group. The company was spread out along a steep, muddy bank between two terraced levels of rice paddies. The CP group hunkered behind a berm (mound of protective earth) on the east side of a village.

One of Captain Yon's lieutenants updated me. The company had been ambushed the evening before as its lead element crossed the berm at the point where we now crouched. Under intense enemy fire, Alpha Company withdrew behind the berm and spread out. Pfc. Donald E. Jones of Kewanee, Illinois, had been left behind, presumed dead.

After the company had pulled back, another trooper was shot in the forehead when he raised his helmet-covered head above the berm, probably in an attempt to see Jones. As the lieutenant briefed me, the dead trooper's bloody helmet lay at my side, a bullet hole centered about an inch above the front brim. I believe but haven't proven that the trooper shot through the helmet was Pfc. James Curran.

At 0930 hours, we assaulted across the berm and into the trees and village on the other side. Light, sporadic, ineffective small-arms fire greeted us from deeper in the village— the NVA and VC had exfiltrated the scene, leaving some of their buried dead and a few well-concealed snipers to delay us. They left Jones, too.

Pfc. Jones was dead. He had been disemboweled, mutilated and killed within 30 feet of the berm, a little to the left from the CP's night position. Thousand-meter stares and taut faces bore solemn witness to Yon and Jones' buddies' haunted, grieving souls.

At 1400 hours, an M-79 grenade wounded Pfc. Jonnie

Nickerson in the leg. The grenade was one of our duds. Nickerson was treated at the 15th Med and returned to duty.

Meanwhile, after Alpha Company searched the area where it had fought all night, we patrolled westward to a hill about two klicks distance. On the hillside, with security measures attended to, I conducted a worship service. The troopers were very attentive and quiet, more in-drawn than usual. It would require time for them to shake off the memory of Jones' treatment at the hand of the enemy. *Heavenly Father, please use my words of worship to comfort these men*, I prayed silently.

The morning of March 22 found me still trying to reach either Bravo or Delta Company. Having no success out of LZ English, I flew to LZ Santana, and there I languished the rest of the morning. About noon I got a lift and joined the men of Delta Company, which had spent the morning doing a battle-damage assessment of the village where a fight had occurred the day before. I joined in the search that continued most of the afternoon and included damming a stream so we could search along the banks for normally submerged cave and tunnel entrances. The afternoon action included several grunts shooting at and missing an armed VC as he fled from us across a rice paddy.

During the search, I shot the head off a King Cobra; the snake had threatened (at least it was a threat) us from the side of the trail. We had a very subdued worship service at twilight.

A burst of small-arms fire shocked me into instant wakefulness at 0610 hours the morning of March 23. Two VC or NVA soldiers had stumbled into the Bravo Company perimeter, which was fairly near to Delta Company, and paid for it with their lives. The NVA, one of whom had been humping a mortar base plate, came from the direction of nearby LZ Santana, which had been mortared a few hours earlier.

At 1050 hours, still on the 23rd, I held another worship

service. Troops came to attend from all over the village. We were very spread out because of the size of the village. A grenade exploded about 10 minutes after the service ended, followed almost immediately by a radioed call for medics.

The company medic and I dashed some 200 yards to the scene of the explosion. Six grunts lay scattered about a 30-foot-diameter clearing—all wounded. Five of the six wounded had been with me in a worship service just minutes before. Moments before, while the troops searched the area, one of them saw a dud 40-mm grenade. It lay near the edge of an approaching grass fire. Reflexively, the trooper kicked the grenade away from the grass fire. The resulting explosion took off half his foot and took out five buddies. One grunt had been searching a depression, bent over with his back to the blast. One of his wounds came close to castrating him.

Lieutenant Ward recorded this incident as follows: "23 March. During the search operation, I . . . recalled platoon back to original starting point adjacent to a bridge. Men began collecting, when someone saw a dud grenade round lying in a smoldering fire—remnant of a burned hooch. Fearing the heat would detonate the explosive, he attempted to kick it into the water—the result was six wounded. . . . One boy had his toes blown off. . . . Another soldier took multiple fragments in the face, chest, and groin."

Though the details differ somewhat, I'm pretty sure Ward and I wrote of the same incident, from our separate perspectives. "Captain McGowen, despite his 13 years of prior enlisted experience and being a great commander, found upon returning from R&R that he had been relieved of command for having too many accidental casualties—the dud incident and others," said Nathaniel Ward.

The crunch of time was hard to fathom. A week before I had been with my sweet wife in Hawaii. This week, while other troopers took my place in Hawaii and pretended Vietnam wasn't real, I sat among my grunts and agonized about Jones' cries of terror, now silent. After three days back in combat, Hawaii seemed the distant, unbelievable fantasy.

*   *   *

I accompanied the Delta Company wounded on the medevac chopper and did what I could for them while we were en route to the 15th Med. The next day I continued to Qui Nhon and visited our men in the hospitals. From there, I went to Nha Trang and met with Major Lord, U.S. Air Force and LDS. He called me to be a member of the LDS leadership for the Central District of Vietnam. Though the call seemed impractical, considering my assignment, I accepted on condition the call wouldn't detract from my battalion duties—in accord with guidance to all LDS chaplains.

I rejoined Alpha Company in the early evening because it was again engaged in a prolonged battle and had sustained casualties. My journal is blank for this evening and the next day, but I remember this fight in particular because it occurred on Good Friday, and because of what happened to the mortar sergeant.

Sergeant Theberge had been wounded earlier in the day and evacuated. A sniper had shot him in the back of the head, the shot passing through a light-colored bottle of insect repellent on the back of his helmet. Theberge returned to duty a few days later with his head swathed in white gauze—even better markings for an enemy sharpshooter.

That morning, moving from the helicopter after it dropped me off, I headed to the company CP. In passing, I asked Pfc. Smith, Smitty, a slender black soldier from St. Louis, to sing a solo in the worship service I intended to conduct as soon as conditions allowed, likely after nightfall.

Later, right after dark, those who wanted to and could do so gathered to worship near the center of the FOB. I commenced the service, held at a whisper, and at the appropriate moment I announced Smitty's solo. Strained silence met this announcement, and then from the dark came, "Chaplain, Smitty was medevaced, shot in the stomach."

Smitty had grasped a buddy's M-16 to help the buddy up a muddy bank, and the weapon discharged accidentally.

Smitty's former girlfriend wrote me sometime later. She said Smitty collapsed and fell dead while he danced with her, a month after he was released from the hospital.

Easter morning I joined with Chaplain Dowd, to provide concurrent Catholic and general worship services to all elements of my battalion. An ABC television crew accompanied us to film Chaplain Dowd in action for a television special, *The Combat Chaplain*. A helicopter was at our disposal for the whole day, as we were supposed to be in an Easter cease-fire.

Beginning at LZ Santana and going from company to company, we celebrated Easter, conducting services concurrently, usually within 50 feet of each other. The services were strikingly dissimilar.

Chaplain Dowd's masses, even in the field, were formal and traditional, with bright-colored alb and other priestly garments. My services, on the other hand, were informal and included more singing.

Before our third set of services, the television crew prepared to film my congregation. "We'll shoot your congregation singing and splice it into a mass to improve the show," the camera operator explained—a little journalistic license there.

This is a good point at which to insert a special note about my congregation's singing during Easter services. In each service we sang *The Battle Hymn of the Republic*, which in those days contained the phrase "as He died to make men holy, let us die to make men free." We changed this to "let us live to make men free," which set well with young men in the jaws of death. More recent LDS hymnbooks also read "live to make men free." Did we start something?

Our final joint Easter services occurred almost astride of Highway 1, the main north-south thoroughfare in Vietnam—a pitted asphalt road hardly wide enough for the jeeps to pass each other. After those final services, the reporter prevailed on the company commander to send out a mock patrol so he could film it *coming in*, for inclusion in the television special. A platoon leader drafted me to lead the patrol. "So they can see a real combat chaplain," he said. I accepted the honor, but took care to conceal my chaplain insignia from the camera. Chaplain Dowd went along with the ruse.

Notes

Lt. Ward's journal, diagram, 18 March 1967: "2 KIAs, Woodall; 2 WIAs, Johnson and Schmidt, (Ward's RTO).

D 2–8 Honor Roll, Internet: 18 March 1967: KIA Pfc. Ralph Traylor Woodall Jr., Jesup, Georgia; Pfc. Michael Neal Johnson, Breutwood, MD.

    Note: Lt. Ward says five of his men were killed in the action, and two others besides Woodall and Johnson are listed in the U.S. Army Casualty Information System as having died, but only Pfcs. Michael Johnson and Ralph T. Woodall's names appear on a page in Ward's Platoon leader memo book, and both names are scratched out.

thirteen

Hard Core VC

On March 27 or 28, I was with Charlie Company two klicks from the sea and three klicks from a small peninsula that jutted out into the sea. From our hilltop the peninsula appeared to be about 25 meters wide where it connected to the mainland, expanding to 100 meters long and the same distance wide. It rose from just above sea level at the neck to 20 to 25 meters high near its point. The jut of land ended in a cliff that extended half the length of the peninsula on both sides.

About midafternoon a platoon chased a squad of armed VC and cornered them on the peninsula. The platoon leader quickly deployed a squad to block off escape from the peninsula, and with the other squads he searched the peninsula. Nothing. The VC had disappeared, as it were, into thin air.

I accompanied another platoon to the peninsula and helped search for the VC. After an afternoon of turning over rocks, probing crevices, poking in every bit of vegetation, we concluded there must be a hidden cave entrance below the water line. Sure enough, near dark the lowering tide revealed a cave entrance on the southeast side, under a high cliff.

To reach the suspicious opening, we shimmied 12 feet down a crevice in the rock. Yes, it was a cave, with two side-by-side entrances, both partially concealed by an almost flat, slanted, 10-foot-wide rock.

Probing the darkness of the opening, we saw two areas of sandy bottom, above which were small ledges that slanted upwards and out of sight. Turning off the flashlights, we settled to wait. I spent part of the evening hours visiting in whispers with troopers in blocking positions. Just before midnight I descended quietly down the crevice and joined the lieutenant and men on watch before the openings.

Exactly at midnight, responding to some instinct or skill I could not detect, two troopers turned on their flashlights and focused their beams into two parts of the cave. Each beam illuminated a right foot. The feet were simultaneously, tentatively descending into the water from some place above and 10 feet in from the entrances.

Instantly, two right feet and ankles were shattered by bursts from four or five M-16 rifles. The two shattered appendages froze in place, dangling in the seawater. Neither wounded leg was withdrawn from exposure to more shots. For 45 minutes the mangled feet were immobile; then a foot descended beside the foot on our left, and a woman of about 30 years dropped slowly into the beam of the flashlights.

We quickly bandaged her mangled foot and ankle, and she joined the Kit Carson Scout in another 45 minutes of pleading for the other wounded VC (her husband) to surrender and receive medical attention. Then the VC couple and scout took another half hour to coax four more VC from the cave.

With six enemy prisoners in hand, we began moving them to the beach for evacuation to the rear, wounded first. I climbed up the crevice and, reaching down, helped hoist up the wounded VC male, whom I passed off to two troopers who were designated to carry him across the face of the cliff to the beach. As I turned back to the crevice to help with the female, I heard a whispered "We'll slip and drop him halfway across." Swinging around, I ordered the troopers to surrender the VC to me (I don't think the two had realized who I was in the darkness) and to keep the female safe until I returned for her.

Fortunately, the cliff face slanted away from the abyss just enough to allow me to cross the ledge upright, with my right hand against the cliff for balance. So with my left arm under the VC's legs and his left arm around my right shoulder, I crept across the cliff and placed him in the care of the troopers on the beach. Then I carried the female across. By then emotions seemed to have yielded to compassion.

On the beach I went to my knees, still holding the female VC in my arms. So far, she had remained stone faced and stiff as wood, cooperating only enough to allow me to carry her across the cliff.

To ease the wounded POWs' pain, the medic injected the male with morphine, but he seemed flustered about where to inject the female—not wishing to expose her body, perhaps because I was there. I helped the medic over his problem by pulling her black "pajamas" uniform top down over her right shoulder. The medic administered morphine to the woman just as the helicopter made its final approach to pick up the prisoners of war. The chopper swept in and hovered to a landing about 20 feet behind us, with its whirling rotor blades driving beach sand at us like a million stinging needles.

To protect the woman and her wounds from the blasting sand, I shielded her with my own body. Her hard core demeanor melted. The tension slipped from her body, and she cuddled her head willingly against my chest. I felt a momentary connection with the VC woman, a moment when kindness overcame her fears and hard core antagonism toward American soldiers, her deadly enemies.

Easier or not, April came, as all things do, given enough time. The first two weeks of April were very busy, though my unit engaged in fewer firefights and battles than in the previous month. On April 3, I worked with tanks for the first time and was not impressed.

At some level of command, it was decided we needed armor on the Bong Son Plain, so a battalion of tanks and armored personnel carriers of the 4th Infantry Division joined us. On April 3, accompanied by Chaplain Lucid, I joined Alpha Company for its first combat operation with tanks, a flop. Someone failed to give weather and terrain enough consideration. The rainy monsoon had recently ended, and the paddies and lowlands were still soft.

Alpha Company was operating about three klicks northwest of LZ English, just off the Bong Son Plain, behind a mountain ridge that jutted into the plains from the southwest. The lead tank approached our position from the east, crossed a dike into a solid-appearing paddy, and bogged down halfway across.

With the infantry providing a defensive perimeter, we spent the afternoon watching tank after tank bog down as they tried to extract the lead tank and then one another. Last of all, a tank retriever arrived; it got stuck, too. The tanks and retriever were still bogged down when I flew away the next morning.

Two days later I was again in the field with Alpha Company, this time with Lieutenant Berdy's 3rd Platoon. We were patrolling somewhere on the plains. Kirkpatrick was with me. To cover more ground, we dropped our rucksacks (I had a civilian one from home) in the company FOB. The action of the day was light—occasional sniper shots and light resistance as we entered a hamlet, with no casualties on either side. At one point we came upon a pagoda (a Buddhist religious structure) that had been riddled with gunfire and shrapnel, in front of which I took pictures of Kirkpatrick, grunts, and Lieutenant Berdy (my last picture of him).

Moving on, we came upon an armed VC who fired on us and fled toward the heavy foliage along a riverbank to the northeast. The crew of an Aerial Rocket Artillery (ARA) helicopter came on our frequency and volunteered to help. Hoping to avoid friendly casualties when we searched for the VC, we marked our position with smoke and Berdy directed the proffered ARA support into the foliage along the riverbank to our east. Already in a picture-taking mood, I squatted by a palm tree ready to snap shots of the rockets as they left the tubes and of the explosions when they hit 200 yards from our position. Not too smart.

The ARA ship attacked from south to north, diving from about a 2000-foot altitude. Timing my shots carefully, I snapped a picture as the rockets left their tubes on each side of the chopper. The shot snapped, I swung left while I advanced the film and snapped the rockets the instant they exploded. The last shot, though, was by reflex, not good timing; the rockets exploded 70 meters from us, not the 200-meter distance we expected. We escaped injury from the shrapnel that screeched by and rained down among us.

Night was almost upon us when Berdy's platoon finished its futile search for the VC along the riverbank. The decision was made for the platoon to stay the night in the area where we were, rather than shoulder the risks involved in moving through VC-infested country in the night to rejoin the company. So we settled in until full darkness; then, discretion being the better part, we moved to a new position, where we shivered away the night without poncho liners.

On April 6 at An Khe, I suffered temporary shock at the "blatant" behavior of a fellow chaplain and friend, Jack Keene. Keene was assigned to the 1–12 Cav, the battalion that took such heavy casualties before and after Christmas.

Keene's office was on the north end of a long building that had been intended for troop billets originally, though troops seldom saw the place. His office faced east, and an inside door led to his sleeping area. A curtain of macaroni-like beads screened his cot from the office.

Smiling, I dropped in on Keene and stopped dead in my tracks. A pair of dainty feet, obviously female, protruded beneath the beaded curtain. Now, such behavior as I suspected I would expect from many soldiers and officers, but not from Jack—a married man and chaplain.

After having his fun at my expense, Keene called the woman out and introduced me to his wife. Mrs. Keene, who had taken U.S. government employment in Thailand during Jack's tour, had wrangled permission to visit her husband in the combat zone, forward-rear area, of course. Jack was quite pleased with himself for the joke he'd played on me and for the surprise visit—hers, not mine.

*   *   *

On April 10, accompanied by Catholic chaplains Dowd and Lucid, I for the second time held services for all my companies in one day. Then I made my first visit to the Marine AO in southern I Corps. The 2nd Brigade of the 1st Cav was operating there, with Marines out of LZ Montezuma.

In late March or early April, LDS chaplains, leaders and members in Vietnam were invited to attend a conference in Japan. Hugh B. Brown, a member of the leading council of the LDS Church, and his immediate subordinate, Elder Gordon B. Hinckley, would be there.

Undaunted by tradition or policy and with command approval and the Division Chaplain's blessing, I went about getting LDS troopers to the conference. For my part, I had misgivings and mixed emotions about going to Japan. On the one hand I hungered for the spiritual opportunity, but on the other hand I begrudged every moment I was away from my grunts and battalion. Meanwhile, life, death and the war continued.

Notes

2 April 1967, Honor Roll. D 2–8, Internet: KIA Pfc. Vance George Williams, Dallas, TX.

fourteen

Blessed by a Dying Soldier

Sp4 Naylor returned to the field from R&R with his wife in Hawaii. While on patrol, mere hours later, he hit the ground when the point man for his squad tripped a wire and yelled "booby trap!"

"Dud," said the squad leader, rising to his feet after what seemed a safe interval.

Naylor climbed to his feet and, for some reason, turned to face the rear. At that instant, the booby trap—a butterfly bomb—exploded. Naylor fell mortally wounded by a BB-size shrapnel, which entered the nape of his neck.

Rushing to the 15th Medical Battalion Clearing Company at LZ English, I stood by Naylor's head while the medical team fought to save his life. Working without administering anesthetics to Naylor, the medics cut into Naylor's arms inside at the elbows, severed each main artery and inserted IVs. I thought Naylor flinched when the medics cut into his arms.

A few minutes later, with life signs restored and stabilized, the doctors turned to the tiny wound in Naylor's neck, by which time Naylor was paralyzed, his spinal cord severed by shrapnel. Whether paralysis occurred in the field, I don't know.

A day or so later in the hospital I found Naylor suspended, as it were, on a rack, one end of his body connected to the foot of the apparatus and his head, with clamps in his skull, to the other end. This contraption allowed the medics to turn Naylor as if he were on a spit. He was facedown, staring at the floor, when I arrived.

Lying on my back on the floor, I scooted under Naylor.

Looking up into his eyes, we visited. With eye movements and labored speech, Naylor struggled to acknowledge my efforts to comfort and reassure him. Soon, I prepared to leave because talking was too difficult for Naylor, and because it hurt so to see him as he was.

"Wait," Naylor gasped out, his eyes wide and beseeching.

I waited. "God . . . bless . . . you, . . . Chaplain . . . Newby," Naylor whispered.

I had been blessed before and I've been blessed since, but never did I feel more blessed than when Naylor—the grunt—blessed me.

Word came that Naylor—perhaps Eugene Naylor of Lancaster, Kentucky, though the date of death is wrong—died soon after my visit. His benediction upon me may have been his last words in mortality.

Following the visit with Naylor, I hitched flights to English. There, Kirkpatrick joined me and we flew to Bravo Company. Some background is necessary here.

The battalion leaders, with two exceptions, had received me well when I joined them in December 1966. The first sergeant of Headquarters Company was one of the exceptions. He was displeased at having a leg (non-paratrooper) chaplain in his battalion and, worse still, a leg chaplain who couldn't be buffaloed into a whitewall haircut—lots of skin over the ears, in the airborne tradition. Captain David Root was the other exception. Somehow, I thought for years that this individual was Jim Bell, until his XO gave me the correct name; then I remembered.

Captain Root resented my presence because he, an avowed atheist, considered chaplains to be bad for the troops. The first sergeant I could generally ignore and did, as he stayed on LZ Hammond or English, out of my way. Captain Root, I couldn't ignore. Root was the battalion S-3 Air Officer (scheduler of helicopter support), whose cooperation and support were essential to my mission.

Root didn't cooperate. During my first months in the battalion, he frequently, intentionally gave me false information about flight schedules. At first I chalked it up to the vagaries of combat, to hectic support operations, and to variables not in Root's control. My attitude changed the day Root attempted to bump me from a flight so doughnut dollies, Red Cross ladies, could fly someplace. I refused to be bumped, and confronted Captain Root the next time I was at LZ Hammond.

Root responded, "Chaplain Newby, I've been an atheist all my life. As far as I am concerned, you are a bad influence on the troops, and I'm duty-bound to protect them from you. I'll do everything I can to make you miss flights and otherwise hamper your activities."

After thanking Root for being candid, I responded in kind. "I will not be bumped. And if you give me false information about flights or interfere in any other way with religious support, you and I will be standing before the battalion commander." *Is Root a living contradiction of the maxim that there are no atheists in foxholes?* I wondered. Time would tell.

fifteen

A Long, Rough Day

Dave Root had become commander of Bravo Company early in April, I think. Surprisingly, I detected no hint of resentment during my visits to his company. *Perhaps he tolerates me because his men accept me.* The change in Root's attitude, obvious as it was, was nothing compared to what lay ahead.

When Kirkpatrick and I joined Bravo Company on April 14, it was operating with a company of armor that included several M-60 main battle tanks and some thin-skinned Sheridans. That morning the company had sustained two WIAs from sniper fire. This was a long, hard day and prelude to a longer one to follow.

April 15 dawned bright and hot. The first significant event occurred at 0630 hours. "Chieu hoi," cried a black pajama–clad male as he stepped carefully into the open from a line of palm trees, his hands in the air.

He was Bau, a VC soldier, age sixteen years. After a quick search for weapons, Bau led us into the trees to an American M-16 rifle (we paid any VC who brought a weapon along when he *chieu hoi*'d), two magazines of ammo and two hand grenades. He said the weapon, ammo and grenades had been there for a month, which I doubted.

Bau, as further proof of his intentions to desert the VC, he said he escaped during the previous night by killing 15 VC—eight in My Trung hamlet and seven in My Huong. He would guide us to the dead VC.

At 0940 hours, I arrived with a patrol to the hamlet Bau led us to, about two kilometers northwest of the Bravo

Company FOB. There we found five black pajama–clad casualties, mostly women, victims of hand grenade blasts and multiple shrapnel wounds. Bau identified one of the women as the leader of the group and a VC political officer. Another was a teacher and another the chief of local rice carriers. I took pictures of the wounded VC. Four of the VC were alive, but in very bad condition.

Naturally, the intelligence people at division were excited about Bau and wanted to visit the scene. So the patrol and I attended Bau's VC casualties while we waited for helicopters to deliver intelligence officers and evacuate them. Soon, most of Bravo Company joined us. After we evacuated the wounded VC, we took blocking positions 200 meters to the west, across draws that ascended westward from the plain and upward on the mountain. Division Intelligence believed a large NVA element was using the draws to withdraw from a just-ended battle.

By then, Bau had been extracted to the rear for more intense interrogation. Apparently he satisfied the intelligence officers at division, for soon he was made a Kit Carson Scout and assigned to Delta Company 2–8. Obviously, the VC knew Bau's deeds and movements. Almost immediately, his name started appearing in captured documents. The VC, it seemed, were tracking Bau's every move, which continued until they got Bau months later.

Back in the field, a few minutes after we took a blocking position near the draw, we saw a pair of hands extend into the air from a clump of bushes 50 meters south of our position. A squad leader approached the bushes and challenged, "Chieu hoi." An NVA sergeant arose and moved slowly into the open, a foe who had endured enough.

This enemy prisoner of war was the only result of our blocking operation. After an hour or so, we rejoined the tanks for a sweep to the north. Moving on foot with armor was hot, exhausting and nerve wracking. It required increased, constant vigilance for booby traps and punji pits, combined with the struggle to keep up with tanks. Tank commanders tended to show little appreciation for the grunts' limitations and concerns. During this recon-in-force with the tanks, an incident occurred that lowered my already low esteem for the American news media.

As we passed through a sandy area dotted here and there by Vietnamese graves, a news photographer asked a tank commander to provide him a photo opportunity by running a tank tread over some graves. The tanker told the reporter what he could do with his camera. He wasn't about to provide a staged demonstration of callous disregard for sacred Vietnamese things.

At about noon, after parting ways with the tanks, we patrolled to the south. On the way, as I moved along a trail east of a village, I spied a Vietnamese female who seemed out of place among several civilians who worked in a rice paddy on our right. The lieutenant with whose platoon I moved shrugged off my suspicion.

An hour or so later and farther south, we came under sniper fire from a village on our right. In response, Captain Root positioned a reinforced machine-gun team in a hedgerow just north of the village and then maneuvered the rest of the company around the village and swept it south to north.

At 1605 hours, after we'd swept about halfway through the village, two military-age men dashed from a hooch and fled northward with troopers in hot pursuit. One of the fleeing men ran straight into one of our machine-gun positions. He died in a hail of M-60 machine gun bullets. The other man escaped.

A few minutes later, while Bravo Company waited to move on, I saw the suspicious female I'd seen earlier. This time she was hurrying east along a dike toward a village—very unusual activity for a civilian under these circumstances. I suspected her of tailing us and being a spotter for VC snipers and mortar teams. This time, Captain Root, taking my suspicions seriously, sent a platoon to capture the woman. She escaped.

Next, Bravo Company regained the trail, and we moved south another kilometer. There we set up a company FOB and sent out patrols. Sporadic sniper fire continued, but so far no American had been hit. At 1650 hours, 1st Platoon captured a VC suspect. Fifteen minutes later, 2nd Platoon discovered fresh bunkers and foxholes, well concealed and laid out for aggressive action. A green lieutenant who had joined the company that morning found a punji pit the hard way, by falling into it. Amazingly, the lieutenant fell between the stakes without receiving a scratch.

While the lieutenant was *discovering* his first punji pit, 3rd Platoon was attempting to capture a uniformed VC, which the troopers accomplished by shooting and wounding him.

Five minutes later, one of the sergeants in the 3rd Platoon tripped a booby-trap wire as he passed through a hedgerow. The booby trap, a nasty butterfly bomb, was a dud.

After a day like this, Root was certain the enemy knew exactly where we were and expected us to be attacked during the night, with good reason. During the last minutes of daylight, he had us going through the motions of preparing an FOB. Then, after full dark, we moved quietly to a vacant hamlet 300 meters south. There we set up for the night, for real.

The hamlet was laid out in an oval pattern, north to south, and surrounded by white sand. Fifty feet north of the hamlet, a heavily vegetated streambed angled past from east-northeast to west-southwest.

In the dark, two light-infantry platoons established the defensive perimeter around the hamlet and the night defensive position (NDP). The platoons also put two-man listening posts out about 50 meters in front of the perimeter, one of them being to the west about 20 feet from the vegetation along the streambed. Meanwhile the last light-infantry platoon prepared to go on ambush, and the mortar platoon planned defensive and offensive fires for the night. What happened next never made it into the battalion journal.

The plan called for the platoon going on ambush to exit the perimeter near the north side, through an element of the platoon guarding the northwest part of the perimeter. After leaving the perimeter, the platoon was to enter the streambed, follow it a kilometer to the west-southwest, and there set an ambush.

As sometimes happens, plans went awry. The lieutenant led his platoon from the perimeter through an element of the wrong platoon, on the northeast. Consequently, those who needed to know never got the word.

Meanwhile, I was recovering from mild shock. Captain Root, the atheist, had asked me to join him on an inspection of the perimeter fighting positions. Root and I had worked along the west perimeter to the southernmost point, when out beyond the northwest perimeter four grenades exploded in rapid succession. The grenade blasts were followed immediately by withering M-16 and machine-gun fire, outgoing from the northwest perimeter. Simultaneously, heavy fire poured into the perimeter from the northwest. Naturally, the troopers on the east side of the perimeter opened fire too—better safe than sorry.

Root and I rushed back to his CP group and radios through the hail of incoming fire, with flying bullets cracking around us as only near misses can, interspersed with bursting grenades.

We reached the CP group unscratched, where within the meager protection offered by a hooch on one side and a bunker on the other, Root quickly sorted the situation out. This was easy to do because all the gunfire sounded distinctly American. "Cease firing!" Root radioed.

Gradually at first and then quickly, the gunfire slackened and ceased, like applause ending in a theater.

"Give me an up on casualties," Root radioed, meaning each element was to report the number and nature of friendly casualties so he could request adequate medevac support.

By the light of the moon, I watched Root's face as, one by one, the platoons radioed in. "Negative on casualties."

Piecing together the chain of events, this is what happened:
"We have heavy movement in the streambed; sounds like a company-size element," came in a whisper over the radio

from the two-man listening post. "They're coming right at us! We're throwing grenades and coming in. Give us cover!" The squad nearest the LP, knowing the ambush platoon had not departed the perimeter where it was supposed to, confirmed the frantic message and got ready.

Meanwhile, in the streambed, the members of the ambush platoon were trying to move quietly westward along the riverbed, past the LP. Suddenly the grunts hit the ground, their hearts in their throats, when the LP's four hand grenades began bouncing off trees.

From the perspective of the men in the streambed, three things happened simultaneously. While the troopers cringed in the midst of bouncing and exploding hand grenades, some saw two shadowy figures rise from the sand and flee eastward, from which direction a withering hail of bullets from automatic weapons suddenly erupted. "VC!" the grunts yelled and opened fire at the fleeing LP. Reflexively, the rest of the platoon opened fire with machine guns, M-16s and M-79 grenade launchers. It had been amid this barrage of cracking bullets and exploding M-79 grenades that Root and I dashed to the CP radios.

The shooting over and no one hurt, Root dropped the radio handset and walked to the other side of a bunker, out of sight of his RTOs. There he dropped to his knees with his forehead on the barrel of his weapon, as though he were about to either pray or blow his brains out. Coming around the bunker, this scene greeted me—I'd followed Root out of concern for how he might react.

By the light of the moon, I kept an eye on Root's trigger finger, which wasn't inside the trigger guard, and waited. While I waited, I wondered which was greater, Root's relief because no one was hurt or killed or his chagrin because with all the shooting, the troops hit nothing.

After what seemed like five minutes, I tentatively placed my right hand on Root's left shoulder and said, "Don't feel too bad, Dave. It's over. Be thankful no one was hurt."

It was a different Dave Root who responded. "Oh, I'm not feeling bad. You know, Chaplain, I've been an atheist all my life, but now I'm beginning to doubt." Root added, "It is your presence which accounts for Bravo Company going through all we did today without sustaining a single friendly casualty." Thus ended April 15, 1967, a long, rough day punctuated by the old question: Are there atheists in foxholes?

Out of the infamous Bataan Death March in World War II came the saying "There are no atheists in foxholes." Well, Root had declared himself an atheist previously. Was he? Are there atheists in foxholes? I suppose so, but it's surely harder to be one there. I never met another soldier who professed to be an atheist in the midst of combat.

That Dave Root's atheism had been shaken, that he believed what he said to me the night of April 15 became evident in the days ahead. From then on, Root was on the horn requesting a visit by One-Niner, my call sign, if more than five days elapsed since my last visit to Bravo Company. And Captain Root started attending worship services when his duties allowed.

The rest of the battalion was busy that long day, too. At 0300 hours, April 15, the troops in Delta Company, which was set up in a grove of palm trees, had gone to full alert upon hearing a series of piercing screams come from a village nearby. While the screaming slowly died away and for the rest of the night, the Delta Company perimeter was probed from all directions. With the dawn, Delta Company moved into the village and found two small children. Someone had cut off their legs and arms and left them to scream away the last pitiful minutes of their short lives (Ward, p. 66).

Notes

2–8 Battalion Journal, 15 April 1969, Item 34, 1805: "1755, B 2–8 . . . found punji stake pit, well concealed, approx. 2'×2'×2', destroyed."

sixteen

Hero Declines a
Medal of Honor

In 1967, Air Force Chaplain (Major) Jim Palmer organized an LDS servicemen conference at Fujiyama, Japan, near Mount Fuji. He invited the LDS soldiers who were in Vietnam to attend.

I left for the conference on April 18, accompanied by seven LDS troopers and my chaplain assistant, Allen Kirkpatrick. At Cam Ranh Bay, Wayne Boring and Kirkpatrick surrendered their R&R seats to troopers who were bumped from the flight to make room for senior officers. We really appreciated them for giving up their seats so others would have this opportunity.

Leaving Boring and Kirkpatrick behind, we departed Cam Ranh Bay at 1730 hours, April 21, and arrived at Camp Zama R&R Center, near Tokyo, Japan, at 2200 hours. By 0200 hours the next morning, I had arranged a bus to take us to Fujiyama. I'd also borrowed civilian pants, a shirt and, most importantly, a sweater—April in Japan was frigid after Vietnam.

We arrived at the Fujiyama Hotel conference site at 0900 hours, where I was assigned a room with Chaplain Arnold T. Ellsworth, my former seminary supervisor.

The conference began at 1000 hours with an invitation to anyone in attendance to speak. Lieutenant Scott B. Thereur, one of those who spoke and the then current An Khe LDS Group Leader, related stories about me and the VC, stories he had heard from men of Charlie Company 2–8, stories I hardly recognized.

I shared the pulpit Sunday morning with one of our two visiting general authorities. Earlier in the day, during a picture-taking opportunity session with majestic Mount Fuji in the background, Elder Hinckley had whispered, "What are you speaking about this morning?"

"Don't know, yet," I replied.

"Share with the conference the story you shared with us in the Brinks Hotel in Saigon," he instructed.

"Yes sir," I answered.

I spoke next to last in the morning session, followed by Elder Hinckley. He took the occasion to again publicly apologize to me for having "doubted" the validity of the military orders calling me into the Army Chaplaincy. Again, he related how the Lord had revealed to him that I was in the chaplaincy, though it was impossible for me to be, because it's what the Lord wanted. Again he concluded with, "which goes to show, what the Lord wants to happen will happen, military regulations notwithstanding."

Hugh B. Brown spoke in the afternoon, and I thrilled at his first-person recounting of the "currant bush" story, a very effective, instructive saga that affected his career in the British military during World War I and changed his life forever.

During one session, a Naval officer told of a sailor who tried but failed to attend the conference. The sailor, part of the crew of a river-patrol boat, was coming into base, intent on attending the conference, when a grenade came hurtling into the boat. "Grenade!" someone yelled.

The sailor threw himself onto the grenade. He awakened much later in the hospital to the praise of an Admiral who informed him he was being recommended for the Medal of Honor because he had selflessly thrown himself on the grenade to save his buddies. "But you can't do that, sir. Someone yelled grenade and I hit the deck, in the wrong place," exclaimed the wounded sailor. I salute that unnamed sailor for his courage and honesty. I also salute those parents and leaders who trained him so well in his youth that highly developed moral reflexes overrode false glory.

After lunch I attended the baptism of a Japanese lady. The ordinance took place in the icy waters of the hotel swimming pool. Following her baptism, still dripping water and shivering, the lady asked me through an interpreter to confirm her. This honor I gladly accepted.

Between the conference's conclusion and the flight to Vietnam on April 28, I wandered around Tokyo with Cav troopers, spending one pleasant night with Air Force Chaplain Jim Palmer and his family and another with the Price family. In company with the Prices, I visited with Elder Hinckley in Tokyo for a few more pleasant hours.

On the Ginza I attended a Japanese stage show with an all-male cast, including the female roles. The colors were fantastic. This experience saddened me because I couldn't share it with Helga or the children. Another time troopers Griffin and Clement and I attended the movie *What's Up, Tiger Lilly?* We walked out because of off-color content.

Notes

23 April, Ward's journal, with Charlie Company: "set up defenses around a large beautiful home. In one room was a magnificent four poster bed, which I promptly took over. At 2300 hours, an early warning post was grenaded as the enemy took the entire company under fire. . . . I smacked the hell out of my eye getting out of bed, got entangled in my mosquito net and couldn't find my boots. . . . Should have known they would choose to hit us about the time I got settled in a real four poster."

seventeen

False Promises and Hopes

During a staff meeting sometime near early May, Lt. Col. Dashiell announced, "Because of the 1st Cav's effectiveness, we can expect lighter action and fewer casualties in the Bong Son Plain area. Military intelligence predicts we will see fewer set-place battles, but more enemy antiaircraft fire, and more frequent and fiercer rocket and mortar attacks on our bases." However, contrary to military intelligence expectations, the NVA seemed more determined than ever to maintain their influence on and around the Bong Son Plain.

Soon after the announcement, a company in a sister battalion hit an NVA unit that was holed up in a village on the plain. The American battalion sustained about 28 killed in action. For two days, the NVA held out against continual field and naval artillery and returned fire at whatever came within range of their weapons. NVA resistance ceased only after air strikes turned the village into a maze of shattered trees and overlapping bomb craters. NVA casualties could only be estimated—the bombs rendered an accurate count impossible.

On May 2, I joined Alpha Company atop the first mountain range west of the plains. This would be my next-to-last visit while Frank Yon was in command. Conditions were nicer here than on a different mountain back in January. Here, elephant grass covered large sections of the mountaintop, and punji stakes and snipers were not in evidence.

Under a double-poncho shelter, I spent the night with Sp4 (medic) Peter P. Malacznik and two other members of the company CP group. "Chaplain, I'm uptight with God," declared Malacznik during a spiritual discussion. This slang being new to me, I thought Doc was declaring closeness with God, not anger, which was what he really meant.

Early May 3, a patrol bumped into an NVA unit, but the enemy retreated after a short firefight, with the Americans in pursuit and attempting to maintain contact. Meanwhile, the rest of Alpha Company air assaulted beyond the contact area to entrap—fix—the NVA and force a battle. But the NVA, choosing not to be fixed and fought, disappeared downslope into the jungle. Later, back at the FOB, I conducted two worship services.

At 1130 hours, May 4, a booby trap wounded Pfc. Buddy Smith of Charlie Company. The VC had rigged a booby trap using a C-ration can, fishing line and a cartridge. The device, when Smith triggered it, sent a bullet through both his legs and blasted fragments into his face.

On May 8, I was back with Alpha Company. In the afternoon we air assaulted from the mountain into a rice paddy on the plains, at which point I left to visit hospitals in Qui Nhon. After I departed, Yon moved his CP into a nearby village, intent on taking advantage of the shade. At about 1800 hours, a booby trap wounded Malacznik and five others. Someone told me Malacznik lost a foot—goodbye Los Angeles police career. The other wounded were 1st Lt. Michael Berdy, right eye and both legs; SSG Tony McCray, right leg; Pfc. James Loftis, chest and abdomen; Sp4 Ronald Guy, chest and right leg; and Sp4 Harry K. Stackhouse Jr., right hand. Among the wounded were the other two grunts with which Malacznik and I shared shelter the night of May 3.

Yon, fearing more booby-trap casualties, moved the company FOB into the rice paddy for the night. About twilight the troopers began knocking down shocks of straw. According to one account, a trooper in the CP knocked over a shock of straw located inside the perimeter and out slithered several very upset king cobras. Though the troopers killed eight of the deadly serpents in the fading daylight, they feared some had escaped. Sp4 Fralix said his squad killed two of the cobras. Lt. Robert Wilkerson of Salinas, California, said the cobras began to appear after a trooper set fire to a shock of straw and that the appearance of the snakes put an end to any of the troopers who were lying around on the ground. Wilkerson believes there was more likely three or four cobras in the perimeter, rather than eight, including two the he located by flashlight and killed. Shortly after the incident, a trooper told me that he stood all night on one foot atop his helmet (an exaggeration, of course).

Meanwhile, Kirkpatrick and I were with Charlie Company on a bare plateau of red clay a few meters southwest of the paddies and villages on the plains. We had received sniper fire as we moved into our night position. At 2030 hours, I saw a flash of light on the mountain about 300 meters to our southwest. Seconds later an M-79 grenade exploded on the mound of dirt before a machine-gun position, also on the southeast side. No one was hurt. I thought the M-79 round had come from where I saw the light on the hillside, but the troopers returned fire in a different direction—shooting probably at the sound of the firing launcher, which sound I missed.

The VC and ARVN forces, according to common belief, kept hostilities out of the port city of Qui Nhon because both Vietnamese forces used the city for R&R. Whether the *common knowledge* was true, I knew not. However, to my knowledge, Qui Nhon was attacked only once during my tour of duty, and I just happened to be in town for the occasion.

The attack on May 9 wasn't much as attacks go, but I'd never have guessed it by how those rear-echelon folks responded. At the 85th Evacuation Hospital, sirens were blasting, most lights were turned off, and people were running excitedly in all directions, like in the movies. A sergeant was quite a sight to behold as he ran about, clad only in boxer shorts, pistol belt and helmet, waving a .45-caliber pistol and shouting orders at no one in particular.

On May 10 I tried to call Helga via the MARS system. No luck. I spent the night of May 12 on ambush with Alpha Company. For the next few days I visited troopers, held services, accompanied large patrols, and hopped from company to company. Come to think of it, hostilities did taper off some in May. Even so, besides those mentioned elsewhere, Alpha, Bravo and Charlie Companies each sustained at least one friendly KIA and several WIAs. Delta Company amassed several casualties too, in addition to those at the end of the month.

On May 16 Charlie Company began taking serious sniper fire from a ridge simultaneously with a number of grenades incoming from close up. Battalion ordered the company extracted—it was working near the coast in support of American Marines and an ARVN unit. Ward's platoon secured a PZ.

While artillery suppressed sniper fire from the high ground, aerial rockets and machine-gun fire were called in to suppress the enemy, which was near enough to toss grenades. 1st Lt. Ward, who had transferred from Delta Company, described what happened next: "The gunships flying escort raced over first with the outside door gunners firing wide open. The fools skillfully managed to strafe the entire length of two sides of the LZ . . . don't know how many men they wounded. . . . Fire [enemy] became more accurate as Cong must have been firing from maximum range and began moving closer. Directed two ARA ships in. . . . Company commander took his CP out in the initial lift—such a brave leader. Second lift made their approach from the east as others had taken hits from the north . . . supporting gunships got excited again . . . ship on southern flank came in low and fast. His first rocket went over our position and low into the village we had departed. There was a pause, the ship's nose dipped and I saw the second round strike directly on line but short of our perimeter. Something reacted within telling me to run away (perpendicular to his sheath.) . . . The concussion from the third rocket lifted me off the ground, throwing me forward into a hole. The blast kept me down until the second lift had passed on . . . dirt and dust filled the air with the sickening smell of the explosion. My radioman was lying on the ground where I had been standing. Blood was gushing from his nose and mouth. The rest of the men hit must have lain down but the rocket came in right on top of them—they had no cover. Tried to see if my RTO was alive as Sgt. Draper helped drag him to the waiting helicopter as the third lift came in for my platoon. I tried to keep his head from hitting a rock—all the while dragging his radio. The metal [shrapnel] had severed his handset, blowing away his ear and the side of his head. I ran back to police up what weapons I could. By now intense fire was coming in . . . only hope the other dead and wounded were loaded . . . in the air I suddenly realized my RTO might be alive as his mouth was moving—he was choking on his blood. Hung his head across me so as to drain the blood away and stuffed the hole in his head with a large compress. . . . Final count was four killed and eight wounded. . . . Sickening feeling as I remember the flash, heat and blast. . . . All I could do was keep running away—impossible to warn anyone else. . . . The RTO who was killed by the friendly rocket fire, was a nice, clean Christian kid who said his prayers every day. That death I will never understand. . . . That's three RTOs in three months . . . just learned my RTO died on the operating table—what else can I write to his parents?" (Ward's journal, pp. 84–86).

I returned to An Khe on May 20 to prepare for a conference in Nha Trang the next day. There I met eight replacements, all going to my battalion. We nine discussed religion and spiritual matters until 0300 hours the next morning.

With 31 men I departed An Khe on a CV-2 Caribou at 0730 hours. Two men had stayed behind because there was no more space on the plane. Had I not been in charge of the group, I would have given up my seat on the airplane.

At 0900 hours I sat in a leadership meeting with Elder Marion D. Hanks. I also spoke in the conference, as did Sp4 Paul Moody, Keith Garner (an ecclesiastical leader stationed in Hong Kong) and Elder Hanks. The gist of my talk was spiritual booby traps. Later at lunch, Elder Hanks questioned me in a friendly and encouraging manner about my experiences, and a lifelong friendship that had begun months earlier grew from the occasion. At 1930 hours I attended an LDS meeting at An Khe.

By reading my journal one might assume all was quiet on the Bong Son front between May 22 and 29. Tell that to Lieutenant Nathaniel Ward and Sergeant Oscar Draper of Charlie Company. Ward lost his foot to a mine on May 22. The same mine wounded Draper in the back. From Ward's journal, "Early this morning ... Mission ... Combat assault consisted of 46 ships—the largest one [combat assault] I've witnessed ... landed in tall grass ... in the center of my area and overlooking the ocean were a series of large rocks—natural lookout points. One of my men was crawling up the western face on a most difficult path. Seeing a somewhat natural path of rocks, I started out, leaping from rock to rock. There was a blast, confusion, blackness, nothingness and suddenly awareness. My first thought was that a mortar round had landed nearby, and I felt a multitude of sharp pains all over. Suddenly the stench of cordite and explosive penetrated, and I looked at my right foot only to see it wasn't. Instead I saw a splintered stump of bone, burned flesh and torn pants where a boot had once been. The realization was 'instamatic,' and I believe I accepted it at once. Immediately I began to feel myself over—to stick my fingers through the gaping absence in the palm of my left hand. Foolishly I tried to rise, unable to move my left leg which I could feel was shattered. . . . I laid back. . . . The thoughts of my army career, my wife, running, my traumatic loss, my life. . . . Far away I could hear the medevac chopper slowly approaching, working its way in to me. It had been a laborious four months only to discover a land mine at seven in the morning" (Ward's journal, pp. 88–89). Ward signed off his last journal entry, "Good Morning Vietnam," because he was wounded in the morning.

Retelling the story to me in 1997, Ward said, "I made a little run, intent on springing onto a large boulder to check it out. Apparently, I was almost in the air, reaching with my left foot, when a mine exploded beneath my right foot. The first thing I thought, as I lay there, much of my right leg gone and my left leg and hand mangled, was *how am I going to run marathons now*?" Draper, who had been hit six days earlier, was wounded again by the same blast that got Ward.

Ward stayed on active duty for several years, then became an attorney and made several trips back to Vietnam. Later he said that he'd been informed that a command-detonated 105mm artillery round had gotten him and that the enemy blew up that hill that day.

In the life-is-stranger-than-fiction catagory, Ward, who spent two years of his youth in Indochina, said he was stranded in 1960 by a temporarily misplaced car key on the same little hill on which he lost his foot in 1967. He had been there during a nicer time in company with his sister and her friend.

About 0130 hours the next day, May 23, an enemy mortar killed Pfc. Clifford E. Kelsey and wounded Sgt. Albert C. Smith, Sp4 Harry M. Winnie, and Privates first class Kenneth Westmoreland and L. D. White, all of Charlie Company. Later the same day Sp4 John F. McGuthrey of Alpha Company fell from a chopper and broke his arm, and a mine wounded Pfc. Vincent K. Zummo of Delta Company—so went a quiet day in the battalion.

Alpha Company was again on the mountaintop west of the plain. After I joined the company, we swept down the east side of the mountain, under extremely hot and humid conditions. On the way, we discovered a VC medical aid station. The station was dug into the hillside.

In the heat, our water went fast. Fortunately we found a stagnant puddle of water near the bottom of the mountain, from which we filled our canteens with high-protein water—lots of microbes, polliwogs and such. Of course, we killed the little critters using water purification pills before consuming them.

A chopper came in the midafternoon laden with mermite cans full of hot food and cool liquids, plus essential supplies, of course. While the mermac cans were being lined up, I backed off into the trees on the south side of the clearing to wait until the enlisted men were all fed, and to take advantage of the shade.

Three of the cans contained something very cold, ice tea as I later discovered. Obviously those cans would be most welcome to the grunts.

One by one the troopers filed from the trees, keeping about 15 feet between themselves. Eventually, Sergeant Ralph Jensen appeared in the chow line—I don't think he knew I was with the company.

Well, I watched Jensen approach the last three cans, the cold ones, with a food-laden paper plate in one hand and an empty canteen cup in the other. At each can, he paused, looked in and moved on. Finally, Jensen hooked the empty canteen cup on his belt and disappeared into the trees. No doubt he washed his chow down with tepid, high-protein ditch water while watching his squad members down liquid so cold it formed condensation on their cups.

Jensen made me proud the way he obeyed the health code of his faith, even in these circumstances. Perhaps his behavior with the tea was no big deal to non-LDS folks—and to some LDS, those who called him foolish for passing up ice tea under the extreme circumstances we were in. But in my eyes Jensen, far from being foolish, was a giant of faith.

By the way, Ralph Jensen had spent a month in hospitals in Japan since I first met him, recovering from being

shot in the lower back and buttock by a helicopter door
gunner.

May 29 was but the first of three very rough days, especially for Delta Company. I joined with Delta Company at
about noon, conducted a worship service and started min-
gling and visiting. A trooper, Neil K. Thomas, borrowed an
Army field hymnal to learn songs so he could recall them
for spiritual strength. I complimented Thomas for his spiritual maturity.

We set up for another night on the plain, with OPs all
about and hunter-killer teams operating to our east. These
teams, being free to move about a specified area, differed
from ambushes. Ambushes stayed in place and covered a
point within an area. Full darkness was barely upon us when
the observation posts and hunter-killer teams began hearing
movement on all sides. We went to full alert.

Reports of movement around our positions continued for
an hour or so, but no attacks came. Then a hunter-killer
team reported 15 to 20 enemy coming toward its position.
Each member of the hunter-killer, on signal, tossed two
grenades, fired a magazine of M-16 rounds, and dashed toward the nearest OP, assuming the OP was alerted to the arrival of incoming friendlies. But a trooper on the OP, out of
fear, confusion, or because he didn't get the word, blew a
claymore mine when the herd of shadowy figures came
charging out of the night. Amazingly, the blast or hail of
steel balls injured none of the team.

Reports of movement continued to come in, so we remained on full alert until dawn to the accompaniment of
bursting artillery and the flickering light of parachute flares.
For a first-time experience, I stood a watch in the night with
a starlight scope and was quite impressed with how clear
objects appeared in its pale green glow.

We swept the area around the FOB at dawn on May 30
and found but a blood trail where our ambush had fired on a
single VC during the night. No bodies, nothing to account
for all the noises in the night. At 1040 hours, Delta Company

air assaulted to an area south of LZ English. We met no resistance, so I remained on the chopper and returned to English and to mail from Helga.

Meanwhile, at 1206 hours one of the Delta Company squads, led by Sgt. Robert M. Eason, sustained six WIAs from an explosion, probably a claymore mine. Eason himself was wounded in both legs, the right wrist, the jaw and testicles.

Choppers extracted Delta Company at 1653 hours for another air assault, as soon as it finished evacuating the wounded. The company combat-assaulted into an area to the north of the central area of the plain at 1708 hours. The stage was set for more heroics and tragedy.

As Delta Company approached its objective in choppers, the battalion received a classified message: "G-2, DTOC, from local civ. that there is a VC Battalion at coord, above . . ." Sixteen minutes later, Delta Company, now on the ground in a rice paddy, took several rounds of small arms fire as it entered a hamlet several hundred meters north of where the enemy battalion was reported to be.

Two troopers were wounded as the company scrambled up the bank into the village. In the hamlet the troopers spread out for an orderly search and to establish a defensive perimeter. The enemy that fired on them moments before had apparently faded away.

This hamlet, the troopers discovered, was laid out in an east-to-west oval shape, about 40 yards wide and twice as long. It contained several huts, aboveground bunkers, palm trees and other ground vegetation, and a well.

It being near the end of a hot, humid and frightening day, the troops were low on water. The native well was very tempting, and shortly a trooper yielded to temptation. With the canteens of some of his squad members in hand, he went to draw water from the well, which he no doubt approached cautiously, but not cautiously enough. The NVA had removed the delay-fuse from an American fragmentation grenade, left the safety pin barely in place, and hid the grenade three feet from the well. An almost invisible fishing line connected the grenade's pin to a bucket on the rim of the well. The blast and sizzling, slashing shrapnel snuffed out the trooper's life almost instantly. This incident and casualty did not make it into the day's battalion or G-1 journals.

After 1800 hours, I was at the 15th Med with the remains of the grunt killed at the booby-trapped well, Pfc. Daniel Nelson, I believe, when medevac scrambled for another mission. A doctor, knowing the mission was to one of my companies, alerted me, and I accompanied the medevac chopper to Delta Company. The time was 1830 hours.

As the medevac chopper flew north, a smoke-enshrouded village came into view to the northwest; I saw that ARA rockets and heavier artillery rounds were exploding all around the village, except to the north. Moments later, approaching from the north, the medevac chopper swept in fast at ground level, nosed up, halted in midair, hovered a moment and settled on its skids. Grunts laden with their wounded buddies rushed the 50 feet from the village to the chopper. Hurriedly, I helped load the casualties onto the chopper, men I knew and with whom I'd spent the previous day and night. Moments later, the chopper skimmed the ground for a few hundred meters to the northeast, then gained altitude and headed for LZ English, giving the area to the east and south a wide berth.

The company commander updated me. At 1800 hours Delta Company had received orders to check out a village almost a klick to the south, where an NVA battalion was supposed to be holed up, according to military intelligence. Lieutenant Frazer's platoon got the mission. Without delay, Frazer moved his men from the village into the rice paddy and headed south across the rice paddy with two squads leading in a V-shaped or wedge formation. As the platoon crossed the rice paddy, Pfc. George A. Sutt, the last man in the right wing of the wedge, had to choose between veering left or going straight ahead, climbing a bank and passing through the edge of a village. He chose to go straight ahead up the bank and directly into the muzzle of an NVA 30-caliber machine gun.

From about 10 feet, machine-gun bullets stitched Sutt at chest level, slinging him backward into the rice paddy. Sutt had been in the field less than a month, according to Pfc. Michael Dougherty. Instantly, bullets from other automatic weapons, interspersed with green-tracer rounds, began sweeping the remainder of Frazer's platoon, while other enemy elements took the company FOB under intense fire.

Quickly, the troopers dragged into the FOB three grunts who had fallen toward the rear of the platoon formation.

Lieutenant Frazer and most of his platoon were still pinned down in the rice paddy. Those troopers who could continued to low crawl back to the FOB under a rain of bursting artillery shells and shrapnel.

By the arrival of twilight, all but three of Frazer's men were back inside the FOB. The exceptions included a trooper who appeared dead and two grunts intent on recovering a buddy's remains.

Squad leaders Michael Dougherty and Frank LaBletta slithered forward when the last of the platoon broke for the perimeter. The two heroic grunts reached their buddy's body, almost under the barrel of the machine gun that had killed him.

Back in the company, aware of Dougherty and LaBletta's intentions, the company commander called in "Snoopy," an aircraft bristling with mini-guns, to keep NVA heads down. The grunts got ready, needing no orders, to give covering fire.

With daylight almost gone, Dougherty and LaBletta each grabbed the dead trooper near a shoulder. On signal, the pair leaped to their feet, raced across the rice paddy and delivered their buddy into waiting, willing hands, having dragged the body a hundred yards with NVA bullets kicking up dust at their heels and green tracers cracking all around. Dougherty sprained his ankle during the run; otherwise neither was hurt.

With the two troopers and the body inside the perimeter, we thought all the living were out of the rice paddy. Not so. After full darkness, a yell came from the paddy, "Give me cover. I'm coming in!" A shadowy figure charged the perimeter and collapsed among his buddies. It was Pfc. Neal Thomas, he who had recently borrowed a hymnbook from me.

Earlier, when the NVA machine guns first opened up, Thomas dived to the ground and buried his face in the soil, only to find himself the focus of unwelcome, undivided NVA attention. "The gooks shot at me every time I so much as twitched," he said.

Thomas tried to inch backward on his stomach toward the company perimeter, but a bullet tore through his helmet and another one tore a large chunk from one of his buttocks, from just below the waist. He played dead and waited for nightfall.

Thomas' tour of duty ended early. He kept the field hymnal. His Dad answered my letter and asked for his son's bullet-riddled helmet, but it was long since lost in the system.

All night the darkness was dispelled by flares and fires in the village across the paddy, and the night was shattered by continuous artillery bursts and the ripping sound of mini-gun bursts as Snoopy reached its fiery hands of death from the sky into the NVA positions. For a second or third night I had no sleep, though I tried off and on, protected and concealed, I thought, by a small palm tree near the south perimeter.

Notes

6 May 1967, G-1 Journal: 0600, C 2–8 WIA—Pfc. James Willis, frag hostile grenade. 0700, B 2–8 WIA—Pfc. Clifford R. Lundy, mulit-frag, both legs, booby trap. 1600, D 2–8 WIA—Sp4 Jerry H. Blond, gsw, left ankle, combat assault.

8 May 1967, ibid: 1800, Pfc. James C. Loftis, frag chest and abdomen; Sp4 Peter Malacznik (medic, HHC), frag both legs, arm, buttock.

12 May 1967, ibid: 2045 (11 May), B 2–8 WIA—Pfc. Donald B. England, frag head.

15 May 1967, ibid: 2330 (14 May), B 2–8 WIAs—Sp4 Mirley J. Esprit, frag chest, hostile grenade; Sp4 Johnny R. Maze, same, chest and left leg; SSG R. Bernard, same.

16 May 1967, ibid: 2150, B 2–8 WIA—Pfc. George L. Jones, right hand, ps (punji stake). C 2–8 KIA—Sp4 George R. Arnos, frag neck, friendly fire, ARA, hostile action; Pfc. Brizzoli (A Co?), back of head and right leg (same as above). WIAs (same circumstances)—Sgt. William H. Anderson, frag from ARA, hostile action, contusion both feet; Sgt. Oscar Draper, frag neck; Pfc. Don H. Burrell, frag under left eye; Pfc. Willis W. White, frag. 2200, A 2–8 WIA—Sp4 Norbert Kuhle, frag right foot, hostile grenade.

17 May 1967, ibid: 0220, B 2–8 (0220 hrs) WIA—Ramond J. Cumba, frag back, hostile M79; 0245, Sgt. Riley Cleveland, gsw left arm, sniper; Sp4 Pascel Harrell, VC grenade hit shoulder, dud; 1200, Pfc. Frank M. Cordello, frag right eye, hostile grenade; 1400, Sp4 James J. Waters, hostile grenade.

19 May 1967, ibid: 1130, B 2–8 WIA—Sgt. Kenneth L. Stager, frag neck, hostile grenade; 1630, A 2–8 WIA—SSG Gnel (?). Burdett, frag, right thigh, hostile grenade; Pfc. James McGuire, left thigh (same).

22 May 1967, ibid: 0715, 1LT Nathaniel Ward, traumatic amputation leg, hostile booby trap; Sgt. Oscar Draper, frag back (same).

23 May 1967, ibid: 1159, A–8 WIA—Pfc. Jack L. Brammer, gsw, both feet, w/.45 pistol while drawing on VC suspects. 1700, D 2–8 KIA—Sp4 Robert J. Bohmer, gsw chest, ambushed while patrolling river; WIA, Pfc. Willie P. Smalls, frag slight (same).

27 May 1967, ibid: D 2–8 WIA—Pfc. Vincent K. Zummo, frag left hand and arm, stepped on mine.

30 May 1967, Newby journal: 1200 hrs, 6 booby casualties brought in from D Co. Claymore? WIAs from Sgt. Eason's squad: Eason hit in testicles; Pfc. Francis P. Pepka Jr. hit in right arm; Sp4 Terry K. McComb multi frag wounds, left leg and hand, and face, died 5 June at Clark AB, Philippines; Pfc. Leland R. Pato, abdomen; Pfc. Freddie M. Ray Jr., abdomen; and Pfc. Michael A. Attrado, was hit in both legs. D 2–8 KIA—1800, Pfc. Lonny L. Ehlers, gsw head. WIAs—Sp5 Wallace C. Dunn, gsw leg; Sp4 Emmett Doe (HHC, medic?), frag both legs, hostile grenade.

30 May 1967, Honor Roll, D 2–8: KIAs. Pfc. Daniel Ivan Nelson of Rutledge, MN and Pfc. George Steven Sutt of Indianapolis, IN.

Note: Veterans of the fight insist it was Sutt who was killed by the machine gun, leaving Nelson as the booby trap casualty.

Stars and Stripes newspaper, May or June 1967: Day was growing short on the Bong Son Plain. The men of A, 2nd Battalion, 8th

Cavalry had set up a perimeter . . . and were making necessary preparations for nightfall. Suddenly, shots rang out . . . troopers hit the ground. . . . Capt. Frank B. Yon rushed immediately to the radio and demanded to know what was going on. "Well," came the response, "we had five unfriendlies roaming around our area. Now we have four KIAs and one WIA." "What is their description and do they have any weapons," asked Yon. "Each enemy casualty has two deadly weapons, approximately one inch long; the heads are shaped in sort of a flat triangle . . . they are about four feet and of brownish color—I believe they are called cobras."

eighteen

Close Calls

During the hours before dawn on May 31, Charlie Company 1–12 Cav air assaulted to our north. At dawn it passed our lines on the east and took a position in the village east of the rice paddy in which Frazer's platoon had been hit. The NVA stopped shooting before dawn and our artillery ceased firing at daylight.

Immediately, Frazer's platoon swept the paddy to recover equipment—the dead and wounded were already off the field. During the sweep, a trooper made a chilling discovery. He kicked up a barely concealed double strand of black electric wire. One end of the double-strand wire led to a detonator or klacker in the enemy machine-gun position, the gunner that had started the fighting the evening before. The other end of the wire was plugged into an American claymore mine that was hidden in the clump of bush I had used for concealment during the night. The mine was well placed. Had it been set off it would have decapitated me or wiped out the company CP group—the CP was set up well within the effective kill zone of the claymore.

In awe and amazement, I stared at the claymore. *Surely, I've received divine protection. Why? Heavenly Father, I pray it is because my efforts to serve are acceptable unto Thee.*

The vagaries of war, how strange and unpredictable they are. Dougherty, with his sprained ankle, had sat just inches from the hidden, deadly claymore while I took his picture. Why had the claymore not been used against us? Because the detonator had been rendered ineffective when a strand of the

buried wire was severed by shrapnel. The claymore mine, of
such intense and emotional interest to me, merited this simple
note in the battalion journal: "0630, D 2–8 found booby trap
claymore type. Wire ran abt. 100 meters away. Destroyed."

Orders came to saddle up and be ready to move out. I
turned away from the claymore and started toward my rucksack, but turned aside to join some new guys huddled with
some veterans about 30 feet away. The replacements looked
very out of place and very scared in their fresh uniforms and
bewildering loads of weapons and gear. Approaching the
group, I introduced myself and tried to ease the new guys'
obvious anxieties. Pfc. Charles W. Kreuger of Menasha,
Wisconsin stood about 18 inches to my left while we visited. His slender body appeared especially overloaded. He
carried an M-79 grenade launcher and a bag of M-79
grenades, in addition to his other gear. We'd visited only a
couple of minutes, when hunger pains attacked me—very
unusual, to feel hungry when we're getting ready to assault
an enemy position. Always before, hunger had evaporated
in anticipation of battle as the body automatically shifted
into "fight or flight" mode.

Well, this time was different, so I excused myself and
went to get some C-rations from my pack. The group with
whom I had just visited literally exploded after I'd gone 25
feet from it and rounded the corner of a Vietnamese hut.

Dashing into dissipating smoke under a rain of body
parts and equipment, I found seven troopers sprawled on the
ground. Kreuger's upper torso and lower body remained
connected only by a small strand of muscle in his left side.
Another trooper's right eye hung down to his chin. All but
one of the casualties were in very bad shape, some of them
having been in combat for less than an hour.

Assuming Kreuger was dead, we tended the other six
men while we waited for the medevac chopper to arrive.
Later, the medics and I were disturbed because Kreuger was
still alive upon arrival at the 15th Med, but not for long. The

doctors sent reassurances. Kreuger couldn't have lived no matter what we did, and he felt no pain. Still, logical or not, we wondered.

Wounded with Kreuger were Pfc. Roger L. Kennedy, arm and back; Pfc. Daniel H. Broetzmann, left eye and right side (right eye, as I recall); Sp4 James E. Taylor, back; Pfc. Ronald D. Ball, back; Pfc. Edward Tucker, back; and Pfc. Howard D. Jackson, back. Division G-1 incorrectly listed the casualties as having been hit by a grenade at 0700 hours while on a recon patrol. As M-79 grenades are quite stable until fired from a launcher, there being no pin to dislodge accidentally, we surmised a sniper's bullet exploded them in Kreuger's pouch—the crack of the shot would have been muffled by the exploding grenades.

The company moved out as soon as the wounded were in the air, and minutes later we passed lines—the Army term for moving one unit through another—with Charlie 1–12. As I passed through Charlie 1–12, I snapped a picture of a trooper in a telling position. In true infantry style he napped at the ready, lying on his right side in the depression between rows of some crop, his feet on one row and his helmet-covered head resting on his right shoulder on the other row. He held a hand grenade loosely in his right hand, and his left hand was in position to pull the pin if necessary. A .45-caliber pistol lay at the ready balanced on his left thigh. I wondered if all his precautions helped when Charlie 1–12 sustained from 25 to 35 percent casualties before the sun sat again.

Delta Company moved south another 500 meters after passing Charlie 1–12. There we stopped in and around a clearing that was obviously prepared for defense against American forces attacking along our route of approach; well-camouflaged punji stakes were strategically placed to impale all who threw themselves behind graves, tree trunks and in depressions for protection from cracking bullets.

From the sky came Lt. Col. Dashiell, the battalion commander, followed by the 1st Cav commanding general. I listened in while Lt. Col. Dashiell and General John Tolson discussed tactics with the company commander. Delta Company would take a blocking position along the southeast side and lower end of the village into which the NVA had retreated and dug in. Charlie 1–12 would sweep through the village from the north. Delta Company wouldn't sustain casualties for a while, I guessed—correctly as it turned out. So, by hitchhiking on the general's chopper, I went to LZ English and from there to the hospitals at Qui Nhon.

While I was away, Charlie 1–12 sustained five killed and 22 wounded during unsuccessful assaults on the village. At 1800 hours, I rejoined Delta Company in its blocking position and trooped the line during the remaining daylight to update the men on the condition of their wounded buddies. With mixed emotions, I was saddened by the Charlie 1–12 casualties and relieved because Delta Company had sustained none during my brief absence.

I picked a spot on the line near the company CP and dug my foxhole in the gathering darkness. I intended to catch a little sleep within the protective embrace of the earth. But my plans changed immediately when I discovered I had dug into a termite nest.

Above ground, next to my termite-infested foxhole, I watched and listened for hours to the overhead rush, flash and blast of artillery as it rained on the village. The incoming ordnance included field and aerial rocket artillery and big naval guns, all targeted about 200 yards across a clearing from my position.

Like the men of Delta Company, I'd gone three nights without sleep. By midnight the tumultuous noise had lost its power over my groggy mind. The continuous crash of artillery actually took on a lulling effect similar to the pattern of rain on a tin roof. Soon I was sleeping so soundly that even a short round of artillery failed to awaken me. Minutes later, though, I jerked full awake at the gentle sound of cloth scraping against vegetation as a sergeant crept to my position. "Chaplain, McMillan is dead. Short-round," he said. A 105mm shell had exploded about 50 meters in front of our line and about the same distance from my position.

Battalion Journal, 0005 hours, 1 June: "2345, D 2–8 . . . 1 US EM KIA by [frag, scratched out] GSW wound in head and body. Serious. Medevac completed 0008." Though I wrote McMillan in my journal, the Division G-1 journal listed Sp4 James Taylor as the man wounded by the short round. However, G-1 also listed Taylor among those wounded with Kreuger, earlier. It is quite probable that Taylor, whose condition was listed as good on the earlier report, was treated and returned to duty. Whatever, I find no record of a McMillan being killed then. Nor do the records list Taylor as being KIA. So I keep looking for McMillan and anyone else who died then—one official source says the short round killed two troopers.

At 0335 hours, another sergeant captured an NVA lieutenant as he attempted to exfiltrate the enemy position. The sergeant got the NVA officer's pistol for his efforts.

The U.S. Air Force air-dropped HE and napalm on the enemy position at 0730 hours, June 1, which strike I observed and photographed from a bomb crater. We assaulted the NVA position in the village at 0930 hours and met no enemy resistance. Then, hoping to overtake the evading NVA, we linked up with tanks and pressed on to the north, but we saw nothing more of the NVA that day.

After six hours of humping and hustling to keep up with the tanks, during which another Delta Company trooper was killed by a booby trap at 1010 hours, we left the tanks and moved south about two klicks. Being exhausted, out of water and very thirsty, we set up for the night. At 1700 hours, I returned to LZ English and found a tape from Helga waiting to rejuvenate my shell-shocked body and soul. I recorded for Helga an answering tape before crashing for the night.

*   *   *

I arose refreshed after sleeping until 0800 hours on June 2 to allow my bodily systems to adjust to less stressful conditions. Then I attended to administrative matters and wrote letters to the children. Later in the day, I attempted to recruit Sp4 Paul Moody of Delta 2–12 for my chaplain assistant—no luck. I sought a replacement because Kirkpatrick was being transferred to the 173rd Airborne Brigade to fill a critical shortage of airborne-qualified chaplain assistants. I never heard from Kirkpatrick again.

A month or so later an armored personnel carrier turned over and pinned Moody's legs into the ground. He was bruised, but not seriously injured. Still later, after I left Vietnam, Moody was seriously wounded by AK-47 fire. He survived to become a seminary teacher—that had been my old job for a year.

At 1630 hours, June 2, I joined Alpha Company for the night. I'd been unsuccessful in reaching Charlie Company. During a one-hour period, beginning at 2000 hours, Charlie Company received 80 to 90 incoming M-79 grenades and some small arms fire—results, five lightly wounded. The M-79 fire came, we suspected, from the same individual who had been firing on our night positions for weeks. So far he had caused only minor damage to us for the most part. I nicknamed him *mad blooper*, mad for his determination and blooper for the sound an M-79 grenade launcher creates when fired.

Eventually my troopers killed the mad blooper. At least they killed a VC who behaved like the blooper. At the time of his death the VC carried an American M-79 weapon and ammunition bearing the same lot number as that which we carried. The nightly attacks ended.

At 0730 on June 3, I accompanied Alpha Company on an air assault into the Quang Nhi Province in I Corps or War Zone I. That day the battalion also entered a rare nine-day period of very low casualties. This was my first time in I

Corps, and after a few quiet hours of humping around, I flew back to LZ English.

Between the time I returned to LZ English and that evening, when I joined Charlie Company in the field, I wrote several official and personal letters. I also read in the *Stars and Stripes* about Bau, the 16-year-old VC who surrendered to Bravo Company on April 15. The article about Bau bore a fair resemblance to facts as I knew them and added that he was serving as a Kit Carson Scout for an unnamed American unit (my Delta Company). Bau continued to get frequent mention in captured enemy documents. His former comrades tracked his every move, seeking revenge.

At 1830 hours I returned to Charlie Company, where the next morning I held a worship service. Following the service, the company moved to the west side of the plains. There a VC surrendered to us, and we captured two VC women who had hidden in a cane field. On June 5, I returned to the division base camp at An Khe, where I spent the night.

Ammunition dumps, essential though they were, increased the hazards of life on firebases, as they had to be within the limited confines of the perimeter.

At 0940 hours, the day before the ammo dump explosion at LZ English, Pfc. James P. Burns of Bravo Company sat in hiding on a slight rise, almost invisible in thick vegetation. From below, 200 meters away, a sharp-eyed trooper spotted him and, thinking him an enemy sniper, killed him with a single shot to the head. Subsequently, Burns' body was evacuated to LZ English and placed overnight in a refrigerator truck—the truck was parked by Graves Registration and the 15th Medical Clearing Company.

Near midnight an enemy mortar shell or one of our own flares landed in the main ammunition dump at LZ English. The initial explosion created a fireball, followed by a chain reaction of explosions. Artillery and mortar shells were strewn all over the base and airfield—many had exploded on impact, while others lay about laden with potential death for the unwary. Some 500 meters from the ammunition dump, Kirkpatrick had huddled through the night beneath a stretcher and air mattress—small comfort in more ways than one.

Personnel and wounded troopers at the 15th Medical Clearing Company, less than 200 meters from the dump, hustled into culverts and bunkers. Two of my WIAs, who were being held there overnight, endured several hours of horror in an open-ended culvert. Unprotected medevac choppers and the refrigerator truck melted in the fervent heat, along with Burns' remains.

At noon the next day I arrived at LZ English, the engineers having cleared the airstrip. From the airplane I went by jeep, weaving around unexploded ordnance past the 15th Med area to my battalion area. Nothing but black spots and bunkers gave evidence that the 15th Medical Clearing Company had ever been there. The black spots marked where medevac choppers and the refrigerator truck melted down. Except for the two troopers in the culvert, the men of my battalion came through the ammo dump episode shaken, but unhurt. The battalion trains area was a mess, though.

On June 7, I accompanied Alpha Company on an air assault to the top of the east-west running ridge that divides the Bong Son Plain from I Corps to the north. We landed without opposition and set up a larger than usual FOB.

After sunset, the troops gathered for a worship service in a clearing on the hillside, the congregation facing south. We worshiped with the troopers watching over my shoulder as twilight descended on the Bong Son Plain—the place of so many terrible memories. In the fading light, Lieutenant Miller, the artillery FO, stood forth and sang *How Great Thou Art*. Our souls vibrated and our bodies tingled—the hairs on the back of my neck snapped to attention. Under Miller's majestic voice, we were at peace. Even the plain seemed peaceful for just a flicker of time. Never had the song touched me so. "Oh Lord, my God, when I, in awesome wonder, consider all. . . ." The special feelings and memories of this sacred moment in hell spring unbidden to my mind and lips whenever I feel especially worshipful and in awe of my God and his Christ.

The next day, I patrolled with the 1st Platoon into the Quang Nhi Valley in lower I Corps. En route the patrol fired on heavy movement in the bush, across a draw from the trail we were on. Out charged an angry, possibly wounded water buffalo. Fortunately, the beast charged away from us. Water buffalo generally didn't like American troops, perhaps because we didn't smell like their humans.

Except for the buffalo, nothing noteworthy occurred until we were about halfway back to the FOB, at which point we were ordered to secure an LZ so ice cream could be delivered to us! Eagerly we obeyed, but to no avail. "Disregard," said a second message. I assumed someone at LZ English or higher had decreed ice cream would be delivered no lower than the company. Suddenly, the troopers with me became upset and careless in their anger. Fortunately, the enemy forces we engaged minutes later were just as careless. In a recent e-mail, Ray Bluhm said, "I . . . decided not to deliver the ice cream to the platoon you were with, as I recall. . . . even more serious was the real danger that the choppers . . . would have given away the platoon's position and direction of movement back to the company. Bumping into the VC squad shortly thereafter was a clear confirmation. . . ."

Upon receiving Bluhm's message I reflected on what could have, probably would have, been. The enemy squad was near enough that a chopper would certainly have given the enemy our exact location. They could have attacked us while we were diverted—to our deaths—by the ice cream. In their place, I would have laid a hasty ambush for us and annihilated the platoon as it moved out, its members relaxed with their stomachs full of ice cream.

Instead, we bumped head-on into a squad-size element of VC and after a short, fierce firefight, the enemy faded into the jungle, leaving behind two rucksacks and assorted documents. We sustained no casualties and saw no sign that the enemy had. I stayed a second night with Alpha Company because we reached the FOB too late for me to fly out. Thanks, Ray Bluhm, for our lives.

On June 10 and 11, I accompanied a chaplain, whom I shall call Fred, so he could provide communion services for all my companies. However, I came to regret using this chaplain because, following a service for Alpha Company, he embarrassed the troopers with his vile language—the men expected more from the chaplain than they did of themselves. I think this chaplain's disregard for sacred matters caused some troopers to be less certain about eternal things and, consequently, to be more scared about their fragile mortality.

Our casualty rates picked up briefly beginning on June 12. Delta Company moved into an area near the beach and at the base of a small, cone-shaped, single-canopy-covered hill. The hill was infested by VC and sown with mines and booby traps.

Within minutes of arriving in the area, Delta Company moved toward the hill and sustained a friendly KIA at its base, the first of several casualties the hill cost them—mostly to mines and booby traps.

Delta Company pulled back and I joined it for a quiet night—fortunately, mines and booby traps don't move about in the dark. At 1035 hours the next day, while I visited hospitals in Qui Nhon, a mine blew off Sp4 Richard O'Brien's foot. At 1550 hours a grenade wounded 1st Lt. Thomas M. Mancini of Alpha Company as he was engaged in destroying a VC complex.

The night of June 14, being unable to return to Delta Company, I remained on LZ English and visited with Captain (LDS) Tilton, commander of a 1–7 Cav company. While Tilton and I visited in the relative security of LZ English, the enemy probed the Delta Company FOB, wounding one trooper.

At 1300, June 15, I flew to Delta Company. At 1500 hours we crossed the beach and humped about two klicks northward, hugging the surf in hopes that fewer mines were there. Eventually we came to a rocky hill. The hill jutted a few meters beyond the beach and ended as a cliff.

Atop the hill we established an FOB. Soon two engineers arrived to check for surprises. They found and disarmed nine mines and booby traps before dark and four more the next morning. Amazingly, we set no mines off accidentally.

The next morning I had fun with a squad of grunts, searching cliffs along the shore. The surf below us was fantastically beautiful—almost made me forget where we were.

Later in the day, at LZ English, I learned the battalion was returning to An Khe with the promise of a month of easier and safer duty. I tried to reach Charlie Company for the night, but it was weathered in.

Notes

31 May 1967, 2–8 Journal 0644, "At 0630 D 2–8 . . . found booby trap, claymore type. Wire ran about 100 meters away, destroyed."

0730, "D 2–8 . . . received 1 rd of s/a fire . . . hit grenade on 1 indiv webgear causing it to explode. 1 US KIA, 6 US WIA."

2215, "Friendly casualties as of this morning: D 2–8, 1 KIA, 6 WIA; C 1–12, 2 KIA, 16 WIA, 3 MIA (bodies recovered the next day); A 1–19, 1 KIA, 4 WIA; A–8 Eng, 5 WIA."

2255, "D 2–8 1 EM wounded by frag hand . . . HE arty."

31 May 1967, G-1 Journal: 0700, D 2–8, WIA Pfc. Edward Tucker, Arty (short round), back; 2240, Sp4 James Taylor, (same), right hand.

1 June 1967, 2–8 Journal, 0005: "2350, D 2–8 1 US EM KIA by gsw (frag) wound in head and body, serious . . ."

0350 "2–6 D 2–8 obsv 2 indiv, engaged, 1 escaped, other captured . . . [a] 2nd Lt."

1019: "1010, D 2–8 has 1 EM KIA by an unknown type booby trap, he was on hill setting up OP . . . a B-3 can with M-2 grenade, no [fuse] delay."

2 June 1967, G-1 Journal: 2200, C 2–8 WIAs—1LT Chester Collins, frag, hostile M79 fire; Sp4 Victor Sherman, left wrist

(same); Pfc. Steven L. Leuga (?), frag left side (same); Pfc. Raymond J. Beckstead, frag chest (same).

5 June 1967, G-1 Journal: "0940, B 2–8 KIA—Pfc. James P. Burns, gsw head, mistaken for VC."

1000, D 2–8 WIA—Pfc. Mark J. Carnevale, left arm, eye foot, booby trap, amputation right foot.

5 June 1967, Honor Roll, D 2–8, Internet: KIA Sp4 Terry Russel McComb, Lapeer, MI.

6 June 1967, G-1 Journal: 0410, B 2–8 WIA, Pfc. Dan L. Tanner, ringing in ears (ammo dump went up).

13 June 1967, G-1 Journal: 1030, D 2–8, KIA—Pfc. Clyde R. Houser Jr., gsw chest, frag, booby trap.

1040, WIA—Pfc. Richard M. O'Brien, mine, trauma. amp, r. foot, left leg and hand frag.

1600, D 2–8 WIA; 1600 non-hostile, Pfc. Ronald C. Johnson, meningitis.

1600, A 2–8, 1LT Thomas M. Mancini, frag r. leg; Sp4 Michael S. Storey, frag, r. side and back.

14 June 1967, 2–8 Journal, 1052: "1035 D 2–8 received 1 US WIA from anti-personnel mine, lost foot . . ."

15 June 1967, G-1 Journal: 0400 D 2–8 WIA—Pfc. Charles L. Vance, frag r. hip . . . hostile fire while on perimeter guard.

nineteen

"Light Action"

By June 18, all the battalion less Alpha Company had moved to the division base camp at An Khe in anticipation of a month of light action and low casualties. Alpha Company arrived on the 19th.

It was great to consider the prospects of again regularly attending LDS meetings at An Khe for a month. It was during this period that I did something unbecoming of an officer, but fun. How it happened I forget, but Sp5 Wayne Boring and I got into a brief, friendly wrestling match, something a captain and sergeant shouldn't do. At least it was dark out.

For this indiscretion and violation of the solemnity of the Sabbath, I tried to excuse myself by making allowance for exuberance because of the fact that each day in the field, like every other, was the day to worship, given the chance. Besides, my hero, a prophet, liked to wrestle, too. Another besides, An Khe was much quieter than I was used to. Pretty lame excuses, but all I have.

On June 22, Alpha Company lent me Sp4 Walter Robiston Jr., nicknamed "Preacher" by his buddies. He would be my chaplain assistant for a week or until Division sent me a new one, whichever came first. He was a licensed Baptist preacher from South Carolina and a good infantryman too.

June 23 was a day for surprises. The first surprise was delivered by Lt. Col. Dashiell who called me in just as I was about to hit the road. He'd found a tape from Helga in his ice chest. We had no idea how the tape got delivered to Dashiell.

After retrieving the tape, I stowed it and picked up a jeep and driver from Battalion, for Preacher and I planned to spend the day visiting and conducting worship services for the troops of Alpha Company. We expected it to be an all-day task because the company was dispersed over several miles along Highway 19 between An Khe and the Mang Yang Pass to the west.

At 0900 hours, we headed out with Martinez driving and Preacher in the back seat. Obviously, my mind was somewhere other than on business, perhaps on the tape from Helga that I hadn't had time to listen to. For whatever reason, we were out the main gate and headed west before I noticed Martinez was unarmed and Preacher carried only a .45 caliber pistol. "I never draw a weapon for driving assignments," Martinez said.

"My M-14 is in for repairs, and this is all I could get," Preacher said.

Turn around and get weapons. Nah, not enough time. The troopers need services today. I ignored the prompting and we drove on.

Then came another ominous sign, which I also noted and discounted. The vehicle was so sluggish it barely made it up the first hill we came to—only three of its four cylinders were firing. *Oh well, there's plenty of traffic should we run into trouble.* On we went.

Our first worship service was at the farthest bridge to the west in the 1st Cav AO. At 1100 hours, a trooper was killed in Bravo Company, at another location. When the trooper died, I was preparing to start my third worship service of the morning, at Bridge 96.

Toward the end of my service at Bridge 96, a "Coca-Cola" girl arrived from the east—so called because she was one of several Vietnamese teenagers who each day peddled a bicycle laden with cold sodas to sell to the troops along the highway.

My combat senses set to tingling when the girl approached a rackety, beat-up civilian bus that had come from the west and stopped just short of the bridge. The girl aroused my suspicion by engaging in conversation with a military-aged male passenger on the bus, interspersed with frequent glances in my direction. Alas, for the third time that day I shrugged off the little warning voice. This time, though, I was distracted by an urgent message. A whole company of 173rd or 101st Airborne had been annihilated near Kontum. The 1st Cav was on alert to move to the Kontum and Dac To area.

So, shrugging off premonitions, we headed for Base Camp, intending to bypass the next Alpha Company position, which was co-located with an artillery unit some three miles to the east beyond a high ridge.

As we neared the top of the ridge, we passed through a dugway where clay banks arose above the road on both sides. Above the dugway the ground on both sides dropped below roadbed level. The road climbed and ran straight from the dugway for about 150 meters and then curved north and out of sight at the crest of the hill.

The jungle stood well back from the road on the north side and 50 to 100 meters on the south. Elephant grass grew from a few feet to 10 feet high wherever there was no jungle or roadway, the shorter grass being nearer the road.

I removed the .45 from my pocket as we approached the dugway, just in case, for I was still uneasy about the exchange between the Coca-Cola girl and the man on the bus. The jeep added to my concern. On three cylinders, we were doing no more than 20 miles per hour, and slowing. To a trained sharpshooter, we were almost as vulnerable as a sitting target.

Ambush! screamed my brain the instant geysers of dirt began sprouting up on the right shoulder of the road ahead of the jeep. A fraction of a second later, my ears confirmed what my eyes saw. An AK-47 on full automatic was kicking up those geysers. The enemy had hit us when we were about

200 feet from where the road curved left at the top of the hill.

One enemy gunner had opened up as we entered the kill zone, firing ahead of our jeep—leading us—and no doubt expecting us to try to speed away from the kill zone as quickly as possible. Had we sped up as expected, we would have driven straight into almost certain death. Martinez, however, reflexively slammed on the brakes and brought the chugging, laboring jeep to an instant halt, sparing our lives.

As Martinez hit the brakes, I leaped from the jeep and down a bank into the elephant grass. A fraction of a second later, Preacher landed almost on top of me. Almost simultaneously, Martinez threw himself down across the seat I'd just vacated, beating by a fraction of a second a burst of machine-gun fire from a second concealed position straight ahead, where the road curved to the left. Three bullets tore through the windshield and dash and passed on, missing Martinez. Other rounds punctured the radiator and a tire.

With the AK-47 and machine gun blazing away, Martinez slithered from the jeep and joined us in the grass. Hot lead cracked continually over our heads. My first thought was *the gunners will keep us pinned down while others sneak up and frag us. We've got to move away from the road!*

Ordering Preacher and Martinez to follow me and stay low, I crawled south into higher grass. We stopped about 70 feet from the road, though I wrote "50 to 70 meters" in my journal. Sitting back-to-back so we could watch for the enemy in all directions, we took stock of a bad situation.

"Let's run for the jeep," said Martinez, the driver.

"No, let's fade back into the jungle and work our way to bridge 96. We can do it," said Preacher, the infantryman.

"We'll stay here, because, barring a lucky shot, the VC can't reach us without maneuvering, and if the VC come for us, we'll capture the weapon of the first one who comes close," said I, the chaplain. I believed our best chance lay in avoiding our death or capture until better-armed Americans came along to rescue us.

The decision made, we waited with two relatively puny .45 pistols at the ready. While we waited, I considered the real odds, which weren't favorable. Our weapons—two pistols—were puny indeed against machine guns, and the traffic was too light for us to assume help would come in time. Sure, we could hurt the VC if they came for us, but we couldn't hold them off long if they were determined. I figured the VC were determined and would attack in the next few minutes, and we'd kill two enemies at the most before they killed or captured us. Preacher and I were unwilling to be captured. We remembered how Pfc. Jones died. And for a chaplain, capture by communist forces equaled death, I believed.

As I pondered our chances, peace and assurance suddenly flowed into my mind. Instantly, I *knew* we would escape. I shared this with Preacher and Martinez and assured them it was of the Lord.

For about 15 minutes we waited. The VC continually fired bursts into the grass in a criss-cross pattern, but the rounds no longer came close enough to crack the way near misses do.

Then we heard it—a truck was approaching from the east. Through the grass I saw an American five-quarter-ton truck come into view. Several well-armed soldiers were in the open truck bed. To my shock, the truck continued past where we'd left the jeep without giving the least indication of alarm or interest, neither slowing nor speeding up.

Thinking fast, I jumped up, fired a shot into the air to draw the Americans' attention, and yelled, "Americans over here. Ambush!"

In the back of the truck, heads swung our way and someone yelled. The truck screeched to a stop between the high banks where the road passed through the dugway. Soldiers leaped from the truck and formed a tight circle around it. *Oh no! The VC will frag them from the banks*. Leaping to my feet, I rushed toward the road, intent on securing the banks before it was too late. As I scrambled onto the road I saw why the truck had not slowed—our jeep wasn't there. *They stole our jeep!*

Angered at the thought, I raced toward the truck, yelling as I ran for the troopers to secure the banks. That's when I saw our jeep.

Martinez had left the jeep in neutral, and it had rolled backward off the road, down a four-foot bank into the elephant grass.

Preacher and Martinez had joined us by the time I got the security established on the banks. Then from the east came a deuce-and-a-half truck carrying an ARVN army band. Each band member was armed with an American M-16 rifle.

The truck stopped in front of the five-quarter-ton truck and the ARVN musicians leaped out. Immediately, and in good military order, they dashed up the banks and secured the area—I was impressed. An ARVN sergeant hurried up to me, saluted sharply, which I didn't particularly appreciate under the exposed circumstances. "Dai-ui," pronounced Diwee, "how can I help you?" he asked in pretty good English.

With the ARVN sergeant acting as my interpreter, I led about half the band in a sweep of the VC ambush positions. By then, of course, the enemy had faded away in the face of all our reinforcements and my valiant charge as leader of the band. Thus, I became the only American chaplain, probably the only American ever, to conduct an ARVN army band, not in making music, but during live combat maneuvers.

Soon after the sweep, troopers in another jeep stopped and traded a mounted spare tire for our shot-up one. We coasted the jeep down to Bridge 96, where we replaced the water in our radiator and radioed in our sitrep.

While we were being ambushed and so forth, the division stood down from alert. So, no longer pressed to hurry to camp, we followed a large, heavily armed convoy past the ambush site and stopped at the artillery position on the other side of the hill. The jeep ran as well as it had before, despite the punctured radiator.

At the artillery site, we worshiped with some impressed, respectful Alpha Company grunts and redlegs who'd heard about the ambush and could hardly believe we had escaped. Redleg is Army slang for an artilleryman.

Back at Battalion, Major Iverson complimented us about how we had reacted to the ambush and to subsequent events. He stood by while Martinez and I received treatment for our minor wounds, then said, "I want you in the future to travel Highway 19 with convoys."

An interesting exchange occurred during General Tolson's evening briefing, as related to me by someone, Iverson perhaps. The operations officer concluded his remarks about the ambush with "one of the enemy weapons was an AK-47."

"How in hell does a chaplain know if he's being shot at by an AK-47?" General Tolson snapped, implying chaplains live too safely to distinguish between weapons.

"The chaplain was Newby of the Second of the Eighth," someone answered.

"Oh," said General Tolson and dropped the subject.

Three days later, a civilian bus—Captain Ray Bluhm said it was a truck—was ambushed at the same spot where we had been; a woman passenger was killed. Preacher and I passed through the ambush site several times over the next month, with me driving so Preacher could ride shotgun. We tagged along with a convoy when it was convenient.

In retrospect, my suspicions about the Coca-Cola girl were well founded. She fingered me for ambush, I'm certain. She probably assumed I was someone very important, perhaps the equivalent of a VC political officer, because the troops listened so respectfully to me.

Long before I went to Vietnam, Helga and I agreed to share everything, good and bad. Neither of us would withhold bad news out of concern it might cause the other to worry. Better, we agreed, to be assured one knows everything and need not fret about bad news being held back.

Thus, I opted, upon arriving in Vietnam, for Helga to be

notified if I sustained wounds, no matter how serious. A few days after the ambush, before Helga got my account of the incident, a taxi driver delivered a telegram from the Department of the Army. The telegram caused Helga little concern because it described my wounds as minor and said I had returned to duty. However the telegram set the stage for a real scare two weeks later.

On June 24, I conducted a memorial service for our comrades who had died during the last operation. Representatives from each company marched into the 1st Brigade Chapel, which, like most chapels at base camp, gathered dust most of the time. I announced the purpose of the service, and an honor guard posted the national and unit colors (flags). Then, following airborne tradition—most of the fallen had been paratroopers—the company first sergeants, in turn, read the name and rank of each honored trooper. After each name was read, a trooper marched solemnly forward and placed a pair of jump-boots before the altar rail, highly shined toes toward the congregation.

Then, standing behind 29 pairs of boots, each representing someone I loved, I tried to honor those who gave their lives and to bolster the faith and hope of their surviving buddies. Chaplain Dowd followed me with a sermon; a prayer was offered, taps was played, and the colors were retired. This was a very moving tribute, but so inadequate compared to the sacrifices these troopers had made.

On June 25, besides general Christian and denominational services I arranged a Baptist service and allowed Preacher to live up to his nickname, which caused a fellow chaplain's eyebrows to arch—he opined that enlisted men shouldn't be permitted to perform functions reserved for ordained clergy.

Combat for the battalion remained light during late June and most of July, with a few exceptions: As for me, my biggest problem was arranging ground transportation—the tote goat or gamma goat I'd used in February was long dead. Some days I worked Highway 19, other days the perimeter and Y-ring (part of the patrol area outside the perimeter), and visited hospitals and troops on Muc Non Mountain. In between, I went with companies and platoons on special operations. Casualties were light, with one major exception.

On July 1, I wrote in my journal, "Going home month after next!" The first two days of July were quiet, but busy. We had an especially spiritual meeting on July 2. July 3 and 4 were notable exceptions to quiet duty around base camp.

I spent the morning of July 3 attending a farewell for chaplains who were near the end of their tours, those about to return to the "land of the big PX" or the "world." At 1300 Preacher and I accompanied Alpha Company minus its second platoon on an air assault and clandestine mission. We were to be inserted into the jungle several klicks from a suspected VC assembly area (where forces mass for battle). The VC unit, according to Intelligence, was preparing for an attack on the division base camp. Our mission was to find the enemy without being detected and then call in reinforcements, air strikes and artillery to wipe the enemy out.

For the mission, a tracker-dog team, two handlers and a black Labrador retriever, augmented Alpha Company. To extend our range, we carried several collapsible jugs of extra water. We were months into the dry season, and water would be hard to find.

We air assaulted about 15 klicks northwest of base camp and immediately set out under extreme heat, made worse by the necessity of traversing the first several hundred yards on hands and knees beneath bamboo. We humped until just before dark and then settled down for the night in and around a small grassy clearing (no digging in because of extra-stringent noise discipline).

Someone, a dog handler, I think, gave me a long-range patrol meal (LRRP ration)—dehydrated chili con carne, just add water. The LRRP meal was good, not as good as some C-rations, but many times better than the MREs (meals-ready-to-eat) that would replace C-rations in the late 1980s.

Most of the water we carried was gone, having been con-sumed to replace what we lost in heavy sweating. A little water yet sloshed about in my canteens and in a five-quart bladder in my pack, which water I shared with the troops.

Notes

23 June 1967, 2–8 Journal: "1100 B 2–8 reports 1 friendly KIA when he wandered [sic] off trail, wounded by friendly fire."

23 June 1967, 1st Cav Div Operational Summary: "At 1205, a 1/4 ton vehicle w/3 personnel from 2–8 HHC received automatic wpn fire, traveling east on Hwy 19, at BR333460. Fire not returned."

24 June 1967, Div Journal (AVDAGP): "HQ 2–8, Newby, Claude A02323895, Cpt, HHC/1st Bde, June 1205, laceration left forearm. Good. Bn. Medic. Vic An Khe. Passenger in jeep hit by small arms fire."

30 June 1967, G-1 Journal: 2030, A 2–8 WIA—Pfc. Gerald J. Roberts Jr., frag, l. leg, hostile grenade, point man.

twenty

Deadly Fourth of July

Dawn broke warm and muggy on July 4, with the promise of coming heat sufficient to rapidly sap our bodies dry unless we found water, quickly. But first, our mission objective awaited us, the suspected VC assembly area.

At 0700 hours we moved out toward the west along a distinct path through the jungle. The company CP and I were with the 1st Platoon in the lead. At the very front of the formation was perhaps the best point man in the whole battalion.

After moving about 500 meters, we came to a point where our path ended and intersected a well-used trail that ran generally north and south. I followed the column to the right on the new trail and had moved about 15 feet from the T-intersection when Herbert Fralix, the point man, called a halt.

While Fralix checked something out, I watched the unsecured trail behind us, south of the intersection. A trooper from the CP took it upon himself to back up and provide rear security. I relaxed when a trooper from farther back in the column moved forward to assist. But I didn't relax for long.

Three rifle rounds cracked above my head and snapped me from my reverie. The shots were answered with automatic fire by the two grunts at the intersection. Three unsuspecting VC had approached nonchalantly from the south and, upon seeing us, recovered from shock a shade faster than the two troopers did. One VC pumped off three shots as he back-pedaled up the trail and out of sight.

By the VC's casual manner, it was obvious Alpha Company had successfully accomplished its clandestine approach, but now we'd lost the element of surprise.

Captain Ray Bluhm ordered an infantry squad and the team with the dog to pursue the three fleeing VC, while the rest of the company moved into the VC assembly area (which is what the point man had spotted).

The black Labrador quickly picked up the scent of the VC, and we tracked them about 300 meters into an open field. There, their prints joined 18 other sets of "BF Goodrich" or "Ho Chi Minh" sandal tracks (nicknames the grunts gave footwear the enemy fashioned from car tires). A few meters farther on, all the tracks split, confusing the poor dog. We returned to the company empty-handed.

We found the rest of Alpha Company in the middle of an impressive base camp. Under the jungle, the VC had constructed scores of hooches and other structures, eating and working tables, even sanitation facilities—all with materials taken from the surrounding jungle and arranged with casual military precision. These structures covered a circular area about 300 meters across—plenty of room for a battalion to bivouac. But, except for the three VC on the trail and heavy signs, the VC remained invisible. It appeared the new compound yet waited for its first occupants. The Military Intelligence people were correct, it appeared, about the enemy massing for an attack on something—and our base camp at An Khe was the nearest, most likely target.

Captain Bluhm, in compliance with his initial orders, intended we not broadcast our presence in the area more than we already had. Consequently, we'd not call for choppers to resupply us with vitally needed drinking water.

After Bluhm studied the map with the lieutenants, the 1st Platoon, led by Lt. Richard Hostikka, went seeking ground water a kilometer to the northeast where there might be water, as indicated on the map by a line of blue dashes, the military symbol for intermittent streams. I accompanied the 1st

Platoon on the water mission while the remainder of Alpha Company remained to search and burn the complex.

We took nearly three hours to work our way the thousand meters to the blue line, with Fralix doing most of the chopping and thrashing through bamboo and dense jungle. Finally, exhausted and bone dry but for sweat-soaked fatigues, we reached our objective. Yes, there was water, a small, filthy, stagnant pool at the bottom of a 10-foot embankment—glorious water all the same!

A trail ran along the west bank about 10 feet above the streambed, which was dry except for the stagnant pool. Being older and perhaps a little wiser, I stayed on the trail while several thirst-crazed troopers threw caution to the wind and rushed down the bank to fill their canteens. More than one of the troopers filled bellies and soothed parched throats without waiting for water purification tablet to take effect—thirst makes people crazy.

Nothing happened at first. No shots interfered with the grunts' reckless water-gathering efforts. Meanwhile, I sat next to a tree and ritualistically opened C-ration beans and franks and crackers, then wrapped a little "snake" of C-4 explosive around the base of the can of beans, the grunt's preferred food-heating method, and lit it.

At this point, Sp4 Robert C. Boswell climbed the bank carrying several full canteens—he carried no weapon, as he'd left it laying about three feet from me, its barrel pointed in my general direction.

Engrossed in meal preparations, I barely noticed Boswell as he dropped the canteens and picked up his M-16. Reflexively, I hit the ground when the rifle went off in Boswell's hand, seemingly into my left ear. On the way down, my mind registered blood and body matter spattering on me and my beans and franks. "Medic!" Boswell screamed, and took off up the trail, holding his face.

Doc and I and a couple of grunts caught Boswell. We had to tackle him to the ground before we could administer first aid. He'd shot himself in the face, with the bullet entering under the chin, passing through tongue, teeth, gums and jaw-bone, and exiting near the left ear. The bullet had then slammed into the tree inches above my head.

Within a half-hour of the shooting, Boswell was being strapped into a sling and hoisted via cable from the stream-bed into a hovering medevac chopper. We never heard from him again.

Our canteens refilled with purification pill-treated water, with Boswell headed home and nothing pressing for a moment, four or five of us took a break and visited.

Like every soldier in Vietnam, I was aware of the passage of time, especially milestones like the halfway point, which had passed while I was in Hawaii. However, I never kept a short-timer's calendar—"362 days and a wake up" and so forth. I intended to count the days only after less than a month remained of my tour.

Fralix, Boswell and I had entered Vietnam about the same time the previous year. Fralix had six weeks left on his tour. So naturally, considering Boswell's fate and it being the Fourth of July, our thoughts and conversation turned to going home, to our chances of returning for another tour and to related topics of interest to short-timers.

"Man, I'm not coming back to 'Nam. I'll get up in them hills of West Virginia [or was it North Carolina?], and the Army will have to send itself after me to get me back over here," a grunt declared. The other grunts, except for Fralix, agreed with these sentiments.

"How do you feel about a second tour?" I asked Fralix.

"I don't want to come back, but I'm very grateful for what my country has given me. No, I don't want to come back, but if my country asks me to, I'll come," Fralix said.

Fralix's sentiments would probably have ended discussion of the subject anyhow, had not new orders punctuated his last comment. Lieutenant Hostikka sent Fralix and another trooper to lead the rest of Alpha Company to the watering hole. So while we rested and waited, Fralix spent several more hours tearing through the jungle—he was too combat savvy to use the same trail twice.

About an hour before dark, Fralix returned at the head of the rest of the company. Soon afterward, our canteens full, we moved out eastward along the dry streambed, Fralix on point, followed by five or six others, then me.

New orders came up the line. "Hold up and about-face." Captain Bluhm was backtracking 300 meters to a small clearing to dig in there for the night. So we turned around and, for the first time in my memory, Fralix was the last man in a column.

A few minutes later, I broke into the clearing after most of the grunts had already entered it and spread out to defensive positions. Captain Bluhm and the lieutenants were clustered near the southwest side of the clearing. First Sgt. James S. Catron, the tracker team and dog, plus a few others with no pressing duties, sat about the clearing, mostly leaning against their rucksacks.

I entered this scene, moved about halfway into the clearing, dropped my pack, sat and leaned against it, facing the direction I had come. A few seconds later, I had a strong, almost vocal impression to "get up and move."

Not knowing why I got the impression or if it applied to anyone else, I moved some 20 feet, entered the brush at the north edge of the clearing and turned. Fralix had entered and was crossing the clearing toward Captain Bluhm. He was almost to my rucksack when something exploded in a blinding flash about four feet in front of him, by my rucksack. Shrapnel hit me in the face and I went down.

Quickly looking across the clearing, through dissipating smoke, I saw a score of troopers sprawled about the clearing, some writhing in pain. Fralix's uniform was in tatters, his helmet gone. Blood poured from dozens of places between his ankles and his chin.

*   *   *

"Medic! Chaplain Newby's hit!" cried a trooper. I wasn't the only one. Nineteen others were too, in addition to Fralix and the dog. I felt only stinging and numbness in my right cheek. A medic slapped a bandage on me and I helped him treat the other wounded.

Sp4 Robert A. Woodrow had caught a BB-size fragment under his right eye, a quarter of an inch higher than the BB size fragment beneath my right eye—a quarter of an inch that was the difference between life and death. Woodrow's fragment passed through soft tissue and entered his brain. He died where he fell, despite all we could do. Cheekbone protected my brain and probably saved my life.

In heavy darkness a Chinook arrived to extract the casualties. Leaning into the rear-prop blast and hot exhaust thrown out by the chopper, we on-loaded the wounded, about a fourth of the present-for-duty strength of Alpha Company. The loading done, I backed to the edge of the clearing, intent on staying with Alpha Company as I felt no pain. "Hey, Chaplain Newby's not aboard," someone called from the darkness.

"Chaplain, get on the chopper," ordered Captain Bluhm, and I did, since it was his company.

Wonderful and sad events occurred later in the combination emergency/operating/triage area of 2nd Surgical Hospital at Camp Radcliff. First, a doctor confirmed what I already knew; my wound needed no further attention. So I went about visiting the wounded while the doctors and medics, some of whom wore flashy Hawaiian shirts and Bermuda shorts, plied their doctoring skills and griped because we had interrupted their Fourth of July celebration. "The booze and steaks will be gone," some moaned. It was easy to believe my ears—I'd become used to the disregard some support people held for the grunt.

Surrounded by doctors and nurses, Fralix was fully conscious and nude; the remnants of his jungle fatigues, boots and gear had been cut away. With my hand on his uninjured forehead—we'd just prayed together—I asked,

"Fralix, remember our conversation today about coming back to Vietnam if ordered to, how you said you'd come?"

"Yes."

"Well, considering this," I asked, casting a meaningful glance at a complainer. "How do you feel now?"

"I doubt they can fix me well enough. But if they can and if I'm asked to, I'll come back again," answered Fralix, in the best and briefest Fourth of July patriotic talk I ever heard—and the gripers never had a clue. To be fair, few of the attending medical people were griping, and those who were may have talked as they did, not out of disregard, but to rile Fralix up so he would fight harder to survive.

The VC, I concluded, had been trailing us when Captain Bluhm gave the company an about-face to return the way we had come. Accurately guessing Bluhm's intentions, the VC set a surprise for us, which surprise they detonated just as the last man in the column—Fralix—crossed the clearing. This is in essence what I told Major Iverson when, at the hospital, he asked me "what really happened out there?" It is possible I told Iverson wrong, based on something I later heard in confidence—that earlier on the Fourth of July a trooper threw a hand grenade into the clearing, and it failed to explode until we returned.

From Bluhm's perspective, the enemy had no way of guessing where we were going, nor did they have time to set up a command-detonated claymore mine. He is convinced the explosion was one of our own duds. Still, why would one have been thrown into the clearing earlier?

Later, a trooper brought me Fralix's pocketsize New Testament—Fralix wanted me to have it. Two shrapnel fragments had penetrated the little book before entering his body—the angle of the entry and exit holes showed Fralix was no more than four feet from the blast. The New Testament probably saved Fralix's life by slowing the fragments before they reached his heart. Recently I returned the New Testament to Fralix, to the joy of his wife, Delores, his mother, and her more than 60 grandchildren and great-grandchildren.

On the fifth of July I sported the only black eye I ever had, though many a boy and some men had tried to give me one.

A few days later, back in Ogden, Utah, Helga was returning home with all the children from visiting an acquaintance in Roy, Utah. All at once from the back seat, three-year-old Brenda began chanting, "Daddy is dead. Daddy is dead."

Naturally, Brenda's chanting bothered Helga. It is hard to imagine Helga's shock when, upon arriving home, she found another taxi driver and telegram on her doorstep—her shock magnified by Brenda's chanting. With fainting heart, Helga opened the telegram. Yes, her mate was wounded again—but not dead! A flood of relief washed away the dread.

Unbeknown to me until 1998, my parents also received telegrams from the Army. Carolyn Gothard, a friend of the family, described the first instance this way. "One summer afternoon my mother and I were visiting Beulah when a cab pulled up . . . The driver handed her a telegram . . . She began to cry and sat down on her door steps. She had trouble breathing. . . . I opened the buttons on her dress and massaged her back. She finally opened the telegram . . . read her son had been slightly wounded. . . . Your sister June finally convinced her that you were O.K."

Back in Vietnam on the Fourth of July, Alpha Company remained in the ill-fated clearing overnight and continued the mission the next day, with a 15-kilometer hump to the east through very rough terrain and foliage. Of this hump, Bluhm wrote, "We were tasked to march 12 ks [kilometers] east and be in position before 0300 the next morning around a village. . . . We moved all day through that thick brush and that night we made a night river crossing. . . . It was a horrendous march, but my men did it well, and I was very proud of them."

An enemy grenade wounded SSG Donald Langston in the leg on July 7, and Sp4 Sonny Youngblood, a tall, friendly black trooper, caught a VC spear through his upper thigh. The spear had been rigged to swing or strike when a trip wire (fishline) was released. A shorter trooper would have taken the spear in the groin or abdomen, with much more tragic consequences.

While Alpha Company and I were in most of the fighting that involved the battalion during early July, those nasty vagaries of war continued to take their toll in the other companies. For example, at 2200 hours on the evening of July 8, Pfc. George Potter died near his position on the base-camp perimeter. Potter had wandered off in the dark, probably looking to relieve himself. His buddy, hearing noises where they shouldn't be, blasted him in the stomach with an M-79 shotgun (double aught) round.

I spent July 8 trying to hold services along the highway, but threatening enemy actions limited me to just one, at Checkpoint 70. July 9 was a typical Sunday for me while the battalion was at Base Camp. Besides attending and participating in three LDS services, I held six general Christian worship services for the battalion. My most difficult duty of the day was counseling and consoling the trooper who killed Potter the night before. I reflected on how I was prepared for this kind of counseling when, back in January, I almost caused a helicopter to crash into my men.

On July 10, Chaplain Keene and I acted foolishly while trying to reach one of my units so he could provide communion. We exited the base-camp perimeter on the northeast side through a concealed, carefully marked route used by patrols. Then we crossed the cleared or field-of-fire area and went afoot into the jungle and tried to find an element of Alpha Company, which supposedly was set up about 800 meters from the perimeter wire.

Several factors contributed to making this a foolish endeavor. First, going and coming, we risked destruction by friendly duds that had been strewn about over two years by artillery and mortar barrages. Second, we might bump into a VC ambush or patrol. Third, without radio contact the Alpha Company element might blow us away as we approached, assuming we could find it, which we didn't. And finally, upon returning, we might have been blown away by the base-perimeter defenses, a high probability should we break out of the jungle at an unexpected point or if different troopers were on guard.

After an hour, we safely moved back across the kill-zone through the snares-and-flares zone and reentered the perimeter at the point we had exited earlier. I vowed to never again do such a foolish, unnecessary thing.

Back in March I had requested career status in the chaplaincy and an airborne assignment following this combat tour. In July, I was notified that career-conditional status had been granted me, and I was promised that an airborne assignment would follow my Vietnam tour. Consequently, on July 13, I combined a visit to the hospitals in Qui Nhon with an airborne physical examination.

The results of the hearing tests bode ill for an airborne assignment, and I was tempted to "doctor" my hand-carried medical records. Doctoring had worked once with a school report card when I flunked third grade, after all. But conscience prevailed, and I wrote a letter, instead, and spelled out why I thought high-frequency deafness need not interfere with jumping from airplanes.

I spent July 14–18 suffering and trying to recover from influenza and painfully swollen hemorrhoids. (The latter were a frequent problem for me during the years in Vietnam.)

On July 17, to start my blood circulating, I ran almost a mile to the shower point and then back. Most of the next day I spent in bed suffering the residual effects of the flu and my "home remedy," plus about the worst hemorrhoid symptoms of my whole tour.

At 1845 hours, having dragged myself from my sickbed

to conduct what I thought was to be a worship service for Alpha Company, I found the men expecting a memorial service. So we held one for Sp4 Woodrow, who was killed by the claymore on the Fourth of July.

After the memorial service I returned to bed. Meanwhile, on Highway 19, three troopers went AWOL from a bridge position and entered a village where one of them allegedly killed a woman, and for which all three were apprehended by the military police. They were rear-area troop, not grunts, as I recall.

To my knowledge, this was one of only two crimes against civilians committed by men in this battalion since I joined it. The other incident, which I couldn't confirm, allegedly occurred on the Bong Son plain. A trooper, during the interrogation of a female VC suspect, pulled down her black pajama top and bit off her right nipple. Of this alleged incident I heard disgusted comments, but no one admitted to seeing it happen or to seeing the injured woman.

On July 19 Captain Bluhm asked my advice on dealing with a trooper in Alpha Company, John Fontana, who had requested reclassification as a conscientious objector. "Should I require Fontana to bear arms, to go on ambush and so forth while he waits for a decision on his claim?" Bluhm needed to know. My advice was to relieve Fontana of any combat-related duties, immediately process his request, and send him to me for the required chaplain interview.

Later, I interviewed Fontana and reported that he was sincere and that the basis of his claim was well-founded and thought out.

After the interview, impressed with his sincerity, I asked on impulse, "John, how would you like to read the earliest known record of conscientious objectors?"

"Yes," Fontana eagerly responded.

So I marked the story of the Anti-Nephi-Lehies in the Book of Mormon and gave it to Fontana with the warning that it was a religious book, and if he read beyond the marked section, he did so at his own risk.

Notes

4 July 1967, G-1 Journal: Alpha Company 2–8 casualties, KIA: Sp4 Robert A. Woodrow. WIAs—Privates 1st Class Stephen Overstreet, buttock and stomach; Larry L. Gilpin, left leg; Raymond Jones, leg; Prentice D. LeClair, leg and face; Cornelius Birth, leg, side and arm; Richard W. Bryan, leg; Bobby Sexton, leg; Thomas Houghton, stomach, face and both arms and legs; James G. Chavez, thigh and side; Robert T. Scheffler, leg; Herbert Tipton, leg and arm; and Herbert A. Fralix, face to ankles. Also wounded were 1st Sgt. James S. Catron, knee and thigh; Sgt. James P. Moore, leg, side and arm; Johnathan Kinder, arm; Specialists Fourth Class Carl J. Webb, leg; William Thelman, leg; and Andrew Greer [Gerrier of Livermore Falls, Maine], arm. Sp5 Jeremiah White. Headquarters Company: Cpt. Claude D. Newby, face. [Also wounded, though not listed in the G-1 Journal, was Sp4 Lee Pippin, who wrote me, "All of a sudden a loud bang and my right side was on fire . . . saw Woody was down . . . the first time that I cried as a man."]

7 July 1967, G-1 Journal: Sp4 Sonny Youngblood, crossbow arrow through thigh; Sp4 Bernard Cosmoski [date, company?].

twenty-one

Premonitions

A few days before the twenty-fourth of July, Wayne Boring, Scott Thereur, and several other troopers began laying plans for a celebration. On that date each year Mormons celebrate the arrival of the pioneers in the Salt Lake Valley in 1847—it is an official holiday in Utah.

To add some pioneer, or at least Western authenticity to the occasion, Boring made a "bucking bronco" from a 50-gallon metal barrel. From somewhere, probably home, he came up with the necessary rodeo bareback rigging and plenty of rope to suspend the barrel between four trees to create the bucking effect. Boring shaped the sides of the barrel to resemble the back of a horse. Next he welded on eight metal eyehooks to which eight ropes would be attached, four for suspension and four to make the barrel "buck."

Administrative matters consumed Monday morning, July 24. After lunch Preacher and I joined several others for our rodeo. We met them in a grove of trees near the river, inside the base camp. I got good pictures of the event.

Next, we raced one another in rowboats at a recreation area of sorts. Then in the river we swam and conducted ducking battles for a couple of hours, after which we retired to my hooch/office and dined on tuna salad sandwiches and milk. For a finale to the great day, we held a chess tournament. Thus, the An Khe troopers and a Baptist preacher commemorated the 1847 entry of the Mormons into the valley of the Great Salt Lake.

Sometime during the festivities, one of the troopers told us a sad story about how his friend, whom I shall call Roger, had wrongfully and foully been shot by an Ogden police officer on this holiday a few years earlier. He was a little taken aback when I confessed that it was I who had shot his friend.

It was Wednesday, July 24, 1963, and I was on motor patrol in the central area of Ogden. I had spent most of the day on traffic control for the Pioneer Day Parade, followed by an evening of keeping the peace at the annual rodeo. We had expected trouble based on experiences the previous night, but were breathing easily because brawls, and perhaps a riot, had not occurred immediately following the rodeo. The quiet was deceptive.

The call came in at about 11:40 p.m. as I refueled my patrol car at the main fire station. A fire department dispatcher alerted me to fighting at Fowlers Drive-in on Washington Boulevard. I responded immediately, as the drive-in was in my patrol area.

At the scene, I parked by Bob's Bar B-Q, a half block south and on the same side of the street as the drive-in. Officer Richard DeVoe was already on the scene, and Officer Bill Stettler arrived about the same time I did. Other officers were nearby directing post-rodeo traffic. About 100 teenagers and young adults were milling about the parking area at Fowlers and on the boulevard. No one was fighting. The mood of the crowd was more rowdy than foul.

Trying to reinforce the light mood of the crowd, we moved through the area urging individuals and small clusters of people to keep calm and not linger too long.

For some reason DeVoe separated from Stettler and me before we reached Fowlers. Looking back along the path we had taken through the crowd, we saw DeVoe struggling with a white male and surrounded by several older, meaner males, the ones most apt to start trouble. I reached DeVoe, pulled a Hispanic male off his back and asked what was going on.

"He's under arrest," DeVoe said of the man he was holding.

We have to get him away before the crowd goes mad, I thought. No time to debate the merits or wisdom of the arrest.

We headed for my patrol car, with DeVoe and me each holding the prisoner, Roger (last name omitted), by the belt and an arm and Stettler protecting DeVoe's left flank.

The crowd moved in on us about halfway to my car; the mood had changed from rowdy to mean, like a rippling wave beginning where DeVoe arrested Roger. En masse, several adults jumped Stettler and DeVoe. Roger, suddenly freed from DeVoe's grip, swung across in front of me and tried to flee, with me holding on to him. So he turned and attacked me. Over Roger's shoulder I saw a swirling mob, kicking and shoving where I'd last seen DeVoe and Stettler.

Now more concerned for my fellow officers than with preventing Roger's escape, I tried to turn him loose so I could go to their aid. But Roger preferred fighting to fleeing. I knocked him backwards, but he barreled into me before I could get set. We went down with me on my back beneath him. Though I had my hands full, I had to help DeVoe and Stettler. So, still on my back and fighting Roger one-handed, I drew and fired a shot into the air, intent on drawing the officers on traffic duty to DeVoe and Stettler's aid.

Roger's continuing struggles prevented me from returning my weapon to the holster, so I switched the pistol to my right hand and knocked Roger off me with my left. Quickly I regained my feet and looked among the crowd for DeVoe and Stettler. Stettler was on his feet, pushing toward the sound of my gun. He was about five feet away when Roger came off the ground and charged me, head down.

Simultaneously, Rogers's shoulder struck my right forearm and my weapon exploded—the muzzle flash appeared to leap straight at Stettler's stomach. Stettler stopped like he'd been hit hard and looked down at his mid-section. Meanwhile, Roger dropped on his stomach. Without taking my eyes off Stettler, I dropped astraddle of Roger to hold him down.

After a moment, Stettler looked up and shook his head.

No, he wasn't shot. But in all that press of humanity someone had to have stopped my bullet. But no one was down or behaving as if he'd been shot.

Someone in the crowd said of Roger, "He's shot! Why did you have to shoot him?" *Who, me? Not possible. I know where my shots went, one into the air and the other into the crowd behind Stettler.*

Well, my eyes had deceived me. The gun is quicker than the eye. My second shot went downward, not outward, entering Roger's lumbar area and exiting through his buttock. No wonder he laid down.

The crowd had been momentarily cowed by the shooting, but quickly became a raging, riotous mob. After placing Roger in an ambulance, I returned and helped police of city, county and state break up the riot, helped by fire hoses. The rest of the night I spent answering questions and writing statements.

Reflecting back on the incident, certain elements in the crowd were intent on causing trouble, and there would have been some, even without the shooting. I thought DeVoe had used poor judgment in arresting Roger in the middle of the crowd. Firing my pistol would have been good judgment had DeVoe and Stettler been in as bad a situation as I thought they were, but was bad judgment in hindsight. To my mind, shooting Stettler would have been the worst possible outcome.

Having shot Roger accidentally, I was relieved his wounds weren't serious. I regretted shooting him, but I felt no guilt, despite bad judgment calls. Had Roger not resisted illegally, he would not have been shot. My actions were vindicated by my superiors, the community, local media and eventually by the courts.

The media were very kind to me. Headlines included, "Police Chief Thanks City Council for Endorsement of Riot Handling" (*Ogden Standard Examiner*), "Teen Brawl Results in Shooting Injury" (*Salt Lake Tribune*), and "Officer Injured, Youth Shot in Ogden Scuffle" (*Deseret News*). The media spun the story in my favor, generally, by emphasizing points favorable to me and phrasing reports to justify my actions. For example, one article described Roger's gunshot wound as "in the lumbar area of the shoulder," as opposed to the more negative-sounding "shot in the back." The *Salt Lake Tribune* featured a picture of me behind a table laden with knives taken off youths during the riot—actually, the largest of these weapons had been taken off a youth at the rodeo grounds earlier, not during the riot.

Darrell Renstrom, Weber County assistant district attorney, said "No evidence has been received to date to warrant a complaint against Officer Newby." I returned to patrol the evening after the incident.

About a month later, September 1963, I sat in a religion class at Weber State College while the instructor called the roll. He reached my name and called "Newby, Claude?"

"Here," I answered.

"Roger?"

"Here," answered the man I had shot a month earlier, from directly behind me. It was no coincidence that Roger and I frequently missed the same class periods during Fall Term, for whenever he appeared in court I was there to testify against him.

Roger was convicted of *Failure to Disperse and Resisting Arrest* and drew a monetary fine. About a year later, he invited me to attend his farewell when he was about to depart to fulfill a church mission.

This experience was, I believe, part of my preparation for Vietnam and the aftereffects of friendly fire casualties.

Back in Vietnam, the return of the battalion to "real" combat approached rapidly as July drew to a close. A month of low casualty rates had temporarily dulled leaders' and troopers' capabilities to shrug off the horrors and risks ahead. But the veterans couldn't shrug off the memories. We would deploy with many new, inexperienced troopers and a new battalion commander. Lt. Col. John E. Stannard replaced Lt. Col. Dashiell as battalion commander on or about July 27. Attendance at worship services improved as deployment drew near. Anxieties increased visibly in veterans and replacements alike, in veterans because we knew what was ahead, in replacements because they didn't know.

Anxiety among the leaders was heightened because we knew the battalion would enter unknown territory in the Marine AO, come early August. Reportedly, where we were going the enemy was too well entrenched for the Marines' resources, a situation suited for the 1st Cav.

Our combat trains would return to LZ English. The battalion would open a new firebase near the Song Re Valley, in lower I Corps. When we deployed, three companies of infantry would air assault into the mountains and valleys near the Song Re to find, fix and destroy enemy elements, while the other company secured the firebase. The risks would be high because we'd be almost out of range of supporting artillery, except for the 105mm-artillery battery, which would accompany us.

Sp4 Prentice Dale LeClair of Alpha Company came seeking help to get out of the field. This surprised me because LeClair, an American Indian from Tulsa, Oklahoma, was a fine, combat-tested infantryman, one of 21 that had been wounded with me on July 4.

"Chaplain Newby," LeClair said, "I'll be killed if I go on this mission. I know it."

My first impulse was to catalogue LeClair's concerns as normal pre-battle jitters, but, deep inside, I believed him. Perhaps LeClair's premonitions rang true because I'd grown up on stories of Indian warriors' uncanny mystic experiences and "visions."

However, I had few options. I might get LeClair out of the field, temporarily, for cause. But from the command perspective, premonitions did not equal cause. Oh yes, LeClair's wife was about to have a baby, but paternity wasn't sufficient cause to have him excused from the field, either.

Perhaps I could have convinced Captain Bluhm to find

LeClair a temporary detail at base camp. But I had to be judicious in my recommendations, for a chaplain's ability to speak for the troops grows or shrinks depending on his demonstrated judgment. And LeClair was but one of several troopers who sought my help in obtaining a rear-area job out of fear he would be killed otherwise.

I reasoned with LeClair and offered what spiritual and moral reassurances I could. For two hours LeClair and I discussed his concerns. We tried to convince each other the chances were favorable, despite his premonitions. "LeClair, your odds are better than most because of your experience, barring the vagaries of war."

LeClair departed my office to face his fears, resigned to whatever happened, believing nothing he did would change the outcome this time. I hoped LeClair was wrong, but felt he was going to his death, as he felt. Naturally, for the sake of my sanity, I tried with less than impressive success to shrug off my foreboding.

Sunday, July 30, I taught a Sunday School lesson in the morning, conducted a general worship service in the brigade chapel, provided services to the men around the Y-ring all afternoon. At 1945 hours, I attended the Sacrament Meeting and spoke on revelation—LeClair was still on my mind. I met Major Smith, who was being reassigned to base camp, and felt impressed he should replace Scott Thereur as LDS group leader; it was time for Thereur to go home.

At 0400 hours on July 31, I accompanied Alpha Company on a 23-ship combat assault into Happy Valley. This was a rare international operation in which we cordoned a large village, and the civilian national police entered and searched it. The operation was uneventful. Being part of a 23-ship night assault was exhilarating, all those infantry-laden choppers lifted as one off the airfield, followed by a synchronized assault into the rice paddies surrounding the target village. Of course, the assault would have been even more impressive in the daylight.

By noon we were back at base camp, where I trooped the perimeter until dark talking to troopers, most of whom like me were trying to prepare spiritually, emotionally and mentally to return to the field. Perhaps command had had the same idea, a shakeout operation in Happy Valley to hone our combat senses for the upcoming months.

I stayed close to the flagpole on August 2, intending to participate in an aerial reconnaissance of our about-to-become new area of operations. For reasons I can't remember, the recon was called off. We'd go into unknown territory relying on others' observations.

twenty-two

Battle of LZ Pat

By 0800 hours on August 3, the battalion was ready on the airstrip. We were to fly by fixed-wing aircraft into the Marines' AO, then air assault into the area of the Song Re Valley.

At 0830 hours, I held a worship service for Delta Company, with about 60 men attending—attendance always picked up the closer we got to combat. Almost all of Charlie Company, 125 men, attended a service at 0930 hours.

We lifted, mostly in C-130 cargo planes, at 1000 hours. My "seat" for the one-hour flight to Marine LZ Montezuma was the left caisson of a 105mm-artillery piece—not very comfortable. Riding with the artillery piece was more disquieting in some ways than the dangers on the ground. My imagination ran wild with images of what the heavy gun would do to my body in a crash.

At Montezuma I held a service for Alpha Company and then air assaulted with Charlie Company onto a mountain to the east of the Song Re Valley, a notorious NVA AO.

During the night I got acquainted with my new chaplain assistant, Sp4 Kenneth Willis. Willis had transferred from the Army Security Agency (ASA). He had completed a tour in Vietnam, performing electronic espionage, and had been permitted to extend with the 1st Cav only after writing to President Lyndon B. Johnson for an exception to ASA prohibitions against such extensions and transfers. Willis eagerly accepted the chance to join me and get nearer the infantry. I understood him. "The minute you and I met I knew I would respect you. Something told me I'd be OK if I were your shadow," Willis said of the occasion. Obviously, I'd have no trouble getting Willis to stay with me in the field.

With Willis' arrival, Robiston returned to Alpha Company. He had been a great assistant. I would miss Preacher.

After a few hours with Charlie Company, Willis and I flew to the new battalion LZ, Landing Zone Champs. There, stranded for the rest of the day, we appreciated a little humor to break the monotony.

Chaplain (Lt. Col.) Parker Thompson had recently replaced Chaplain McGraff as division chaplain. Thompson's new deputy was a recent transfer to the Army from the Navy—why and how, I don't know.

Well, soon someone discovered that the former sailor had date-of-rank on Parker Thompson. Just like that, the 1st Cav had a *Navy* division chaplain. Of course, he knew nothing of Army ways, much less about cav operations in combat.

About 1400 hours, Battalion Operations alerted me to the division chaplain's approach. I went to the pad to meet the chopper, expecting Chaplain Thompson. Instead, a stranger alit and quickly explained how he had so recently become the "boss." Then came the funny part. "Chaplain Newby, in one hour, I want to conduct a Catholic mass here on the LZ for the whole battalion."

Uncertain if he were joking or for real, I explained the situation. Though we had part of the battalion, the TOC people and an artillery battery on the hill, everyone was very busy digging in and probably would be unable to break away for a service before dark. "Most of the battalion," I explained, "are in the jungle, and the mass has to go to them."

"I want to have a mass for the whole battalion. In the Navy, when I wanted a service, I simply announced over the public address speakers, 'Now hear this. Now hear this.' Why can't you simply announce the mass and have everyone take a break for it?"

"Come with me, sir, please." I led him to the TOC and introduced him to the operations officer. The operations officer explained why preparing the LZ took precedence over everything, what with our being almost beyond the range of supporting artillery.

I pointed out the locations of the other infantry companies on the large operational map. The division chaplain pointed to the symbol for one of the companies on the map and asked how far the company was from the LZ.

. "Eleven hundred meters."

"That isn't far. Couldn't the company come in for a service?"

Patiently, before the amazed TOC personnel, I explained that while the company wasn't far from us as the crow flies, it would take about eight hours of steady chopping, climbing and slipping to reach us. That wasn't going to happen, I assured the chaplain, because it would create unacceptable interference with the unit mission and inflict undue hardship on the troops. Shaking his head, the chaplain got in his helicopter and departed.

I expect the new division chaplain was beginning to wonder what he'd gotten himself into by leaving the Navy.

The next morning, August 5, was scary, not because of what we ran into, but by evidence of how rapidly combat skills had deteriorated. All morning, the company I was with maneuvered through the jungle and occasional manmade clearings as we worked around the southern base of the mountain on which Alpha Company was helping establish our new fire base. By early afternoon we had patrolled around the base of a mountain, from the west side to the east side of LZ Champs. Along the way I mentioned to the company commander that the men in the lead platoon were bunching up dangerously in a clear area. Nothing changed.

Farther north, now east of LZ Champs, we patrolled up a sparsely vegetated valley, hugging the hill and jungle on our left. I didn't care for our position because the valley was less than 150 meters wide, which meant we were quite exposed and well within small arms range from both sides.

Again, I held a little session with the company commander. The platoons' flank security was sticking too close to the unit; it needed to be deeper into the tree lines, especially when we halted on occasion. The company commander, perhaps in part because of my observations, reprimanded the lieutenants. Dispersions and flank security improved immediately, at least in appearance.

With better flank security, we promptly discovered an enemy complex inside the tree line on the west side of the valley. These bunkers were unusually well-constructed and reinforced. Judging by the size, layout and extensive engineering that had gone into the complex, I guessed it had recently housed an NVA division headquarters.

Without our improved flank security, we might have walked right past those bunkers. I shuddered to think what would have happened had their builders occupied them. Others probably shuddered, too, as latent combat skills began to resurface.

The company was ordered the next morning to locate an NVA commissary and supply depot that reportedly sustained NVA operations for the whole area. We moved north about 500 meters to where our valley joined a river flowing from the east. The river was 100 feet wide and chest-deep on me at midstream. Several dead water buffalo were lying about and in the water—obviously, the 1–9th Cav had recently worked the area.

Leaving our packs with the company CP security, I accompanied a platoon across the river. We waded across just north of where the river curved from a west-northwest course to a northern direction. As I waded ashore on the east bank, I remembered I had replaced the camera in the ammo pouch without enclosing it in plastic—I had used the camera before crossing the river. Sure enough, the camera was soaked. I had Willis quickly snap two pictures—my last on this tour.

We patrolled east along the river for about a kilometer and came up dry. Again, I thought, *Military intelligence doesn't know what it is talking about.* There was just no sign on our side of the river to suggest we were anywhere near a major NVA commissary and supply depot. We recrossed the river and patrolled back to the west and found the NVA cache, on the side of the river we'd started from, 200 meters from where we'd first crossed to search on the wrong side.

The commissary contained 10 tons of salt in great, Conex-size blocks, stashed in open-sided sheds that reminded me of my grandpa's corncribs. Another shed was packed to the roof with strips of cinnamon. Nearby was evidence that an American LRRP team had recently operated in the area—which explained the dead water buffalo and why we'd been sent there. Obviously, the LRRP team had identified the target and had been extracted, and the 1–9 Cav killed the NVA's walking transportation and commissary, the water buffalo, on the way out of the area.

The salt we found was too hard and heavy for easy removal and redistribution to Vietnamese farmers. So the grunts soaked it in JP-4 fuel, packed in a hefty C-4 explosive charge—and hardly dented it.

Early in the evening, we retrieved our packs, and I had a good bath and shave in the river. Meanwhile, like the company I was with, the other companies in the battalion had now gone three days in the new AO without any significant contact with the NVA and without friendly casualties. Day by day LeClair's premonition of death haunted me less and less.

On August 7, at LZ English, the deputy division chaplain informed me I was selected to initiate a division policy of sending a chaplain to Japan each month to visit 1st Cav casualties. I was to go to Japan the following week.

Back to LZ Champs as quickly as I could go, I reported this development to Lt. Col. Stannard. "It is an honor to be selected for the trip, and I would love to see our men in the hospitals. But I'm concerned about leaving the unit just now," I explained. Stannard heard me out and said, "Go to Japan."

Right after I told division to cut me orders for Japan, the battalion got orders that made me wish I hadn't made the call. Alpha Company was to assault onto a grassy ridgeline overlooking the Song Re Valley. I *knew* this was a very bad place even before I saw it.

That evening Ken Willis announced he had quit smoking and wanted to discuss the LDS faith. My reaction was tempered by well-remembered counsel to LDS chaplains: never proselyte soldiers and their families unless specifically asked by them to do so, and when possible refer those who ask to missionaries or local leaders. We were instructed to never try to convert or participate in the conversion of other chaplains, under any circumstances. For me, chaplain assistants seemed too close, uncomfortably so, to this proscribed population.

At 1000 hours, August 8, I accompanied Major "Woody" Hayne, whom I remember as the Operations Officer—though Bluhm said a Major Olson held that position—and the battalion Artillery LNO on an aerial recon of the hills surrounding the Song Re Valley. Never before had I experienced so strongly what aviators called the *pucker factor*—a gross, but accurate description of those sensations one gets in anticipation of being shot at from beneath.

Later, on LZ Champs, I expressed to Major Iverson strong reservations about going to Japan and tried to enlist his help in convincing Lt. Col. Stannard to countermand the Tokyo trip. Iverson, though he understood my feelings, ordered, "Quit trying to get out of the trip. Go to Japan."

So I went to An Khe to get ready for the trip. Some of the Alpha Company troopers beat me to Japan—as WIAs. My combat senses had been very accurate.

About 0940 hours August 9, Alpha Company air assaulted onto a south-running grassy ridge—designated LZ Pat—overlooking the Song Re Valley. The lead platoon hit the objective—an objective that had received no artillery prep, according to several troopers, and probably no ARA prep, according to what a chopper pilot told Lt. Robert Wilkinson.

Sp4 Joe Gratz, who was among those leaping from the first hovering chopper to spread out and establish security for those still inbound, insists there was no shooting at first, as does Sp4 Joe Letarte, who arrived minutes later in the second wave. However, the shooting had begun when the second wave jumped from choppers, according to both Lt. Wilkinson and Sp4 Mark Y'Barra

Said Sp4 Lee Pippin, "Nothing was right that day . . . gunships never prepped LZ . . . lives lost that didn't need to be lost . . . We started taking fire as soon as we started getting off the choppers. I was shot in the back while covering for Zak who was trying to get his M-60 set up. The NVA were everywhere and the only cover was the bodies of our dead buddies."

From behind several anti-aircraft weapons and from numerous bunkers and spider holes, hostile eyes watched the arriving choppers and the company's defensive preparations. The anti-aircraft weapons dominated the LZ from two nearby high points, Hill 450 at its north end and Hill 625 to the west. Apparently the NVA gunners' priorities were gunships and command choppers, then the choppers bringing in the last platoon and the troopers on the ground, in that order.

The anti-aircraft guns unleashed their hellish fire just as the choppers approached the LZ with the last of Alpha Company, the heavy-weapons platoon. Almost immediately, the AAA guns downed two 1–9 Cav gunships and an H-13 scout chopper and disabled the brigade commander's command and control bird.

To the sound of anti-aircraft fire, troopers in the weapons platoon began jumping to the LZ, seeking whatever sparse cover was available and hoping the slick ships wouldn't be shot down on top of them.

Most of the slick ships made it away from the ridge before the enemy shifted its anti-aircraft fire to the LZ, and each lift ship left the area under its own power.

Already, from concealed spider holes and bunkers on and around the LZ, NVA infantry had opened fire at close range on the exposed, vulnerable troopers. Some were cut down even as they leaped from the choppers; someone said LeClair died that way. However, Shelby L. Stanton, in *Anatomy of a Division*, said LeClair was stitched across the chest by anti-aircraft fire as he ran into a more exposed area to retrieve ammunition for the heavy weapons. No matter which version of his death is closer to true, LeClair's premonitions had come true.

Joe Letarte said, "We in my position had almost no cover. If I moved even an inch I drew machine-gun fire." "It was the same where I was," said Gratz. "Then we started drawing fire from behind. I thought our guys were shooting over our head, too close, and yelled for them to stop. It was NVA shooting out of spider holes inside our perimeter."

The killing and maiming continued for about four hours, interspersed with miracles here and there, like Lt. Hostikka's narrow escape. Hostikka was hunkered low under intense enemy fire, trying to regroup his men, when a bullet killed his RTO and another bullet entered Hostikka's helmet and whirled around his head between helmet and helmet liner, said several grunts. Captain Bluhm said "I can still see Hostikka lying there with a grin on his face, wiggling his finger at me through the hole in the helmet."

"Kelly's ruck pack was hit and literally blew up on his back," said Gratz.

"Gratz didn't seem to be hurt too bad, but he never came back, though Roberts, who seemed in worse shape, returned in time to be killed before the month was out," said Letarte.

Jack Walton of Novato, California, jumped onto LZ Pat along with the Weapons Platoon. Moments after he jumped into hell, an NVA popped from a spider hole and shot him in the neck. The impact spun him about and flung him to the ground. After shooting Walton, the NVA soldier turned his fire elsewhere—a fatal error. Walton recovered and killed the man that had shot him, then fell again, his jaw shot away by yet another NVA who was inside the company perimeter.

Then, for about four hours, Walton, twice severely wounded and untreated, watched the battle rage. He said he saw a medevac chopper explode in the air, and a Navy fighter go down in flames. "I saw Jerry Hodson get shot while he helped 'Pop' Theberge, who'd been hit in the head. I heard an LDS man, a real nice guy, became a killing machine after Song Re," Walton told me in 1995.

After hours of excruciating pain and terror, Walton was medevaced. He didn't know the fate of some of his buddies until 1995, when he and I contacted each other.

Early in the battle, Alpha Company mortars and recoilless rifles were rendered ineffective because all remaining ammunition was out of reach and because these weapons made easy targets. SSG John Stipes, Weapons Platoon leader, tried to suppress the anti-aircraft guns with mortar shells, until the NVA guns zeroed in on him and forced him to take cover.

With the heavy weapons rendered useless, the M-60 machine guns were Alpha Company's main, almost only effective defense—and these were knocked out one by one.

At one machine gun, PSG Theberge, who had crawled to the position after breaking his ankle jumping from a chopper, was shot in the head and knocked unconscious (*Anatomy of a Division*).

From another precarious machine-gun position, Sp4 Michael Hotchkiss and his crew blasted away at the enemy. "Lysak was hit first, three times. Then Carl Gunter, assistant gunner, was shot in the head. After Carl was hit, a mortar round hit Hotchkiss in the back, killing him and wounding Mark Y'Barra, ammo bearer, who said, 'Then I lay there for four hours. It seemed like half an hour, looking back,'" said Walton.

Lt. Wilkinson said, "Gunter was one of the radio operators wounded on Pat. He was lying right beside me when he was hit in the head. Joel Findley was my other operator. We were laying side by side when Fendley was hit in the arm and chest. He died a short while later. The same mortar round wounded Lysak again, who returned to feed ammo for Hotchkiss's machine gun after getting his earlier wounds dressed."

Andrew Gerrier wrote: "The things that stick out about LZ Pat: flying over a footpath with commo wire running right down the middle of it and thinking *we are in trouble,* the sounds of bullets snapping all around us, being pinned there with Andy Zac in the saddle nearest to Hill 450 and being helpless, then thinking it was about over, only to see a hand come up and pull the weapon of a fallen trooper back into a spider hole. We threw in two grenades. One came right back out. I kicked it back in, and we heard one explosion. I think the one I kicked back in was a dud."

While most of the company was exposed to direct fire all through the fight, the platoon sergeant Ralph Jensen had been inserted on the south of the LZ where they were protected from most direct fire. Even there it was dangerous, as he explained: "After a while, my RTO and I moved up the hill about 20 meters so we could get a better idea of what was happening in the rest of the company. We'd just moved when a mortar exploded right at the spot we had just vacated." Such was the luck of the draw that awful day.

"The battle at Song Re Valley was the worst I ever experienced, not excepting my Korean War experiences nor a later battle in the Aschau Valley when the NVA shot down 128 Cav choppers in a single morning," said one senior sergeant.

All Captain Bluhm's platoon leaders had their hands full during the battle at LZ Pat. The platoon leaders were Lt. Hostikka, First Platoon; Lt. Robert Wilkinson (SSG Gerald Donnovan was platoon sergeant), Second Platoon; Lt. Joseph Petrovich, Third Platoon; and SSG John Stipes, Weapons Platoon. At one point in the fight, Bluhm and Petrovich ran a foot race to get a machine gun where it was needed. At another point, Petrovich, with his RTO, Pfc.

Edward F. Hayes, led a four-man attack on an enemy position. He came out unhurt. "Either I was lucky or because I'm smaller . . . I was able to move about without getting wounded," said Petrovich who stood just over five feet tall.

Captain Bluhm recommended Sgt. Theberge for the Distinguished Service Cross for his actions on LZ Pat. Bluhm heard that Theberge died in the hospital of secondary complications. Alpha Company received the Valorous Unit Award for its action on LZ Pat—the equivalent of a Silver Star. Five Silver Stars and numerous Bronze Stars for valor were also awarded to the men of Alpha 2–8 for their action on that day. While these tokens of well-deserved recognition are a source of great satisfaction and pride to many aging veterans of LZ Pat, there was little comfort for the survivors of LZ Pat that horrible day.

The next morning Ken Willis, in my absence, went to the Alpha Company field trains at LZ English, where troopers were sorting the gear of buddies who fell at LZ Pat. One tough, war-hardened grunt cried openly as he held a fallen buddy's unmailed letter in his hands. "Doc Conrad's bloody web belt was shredded, completely torn apart by shrapnel in the back," Willis said. The next day near LZ Pat, with Bravo Company Willis killed an NVA soldier. In the same fight, three civilians were caught between the battling forces; an old man, a woman and an infant died. "I can still see that dead baby attached in death to its mother's breast," Willis wrote in 1998.

LeClair's death hit me the hardest—and each death hurt sorely. My grief for LeClair was intensified because I hadn't gotten him out of the field. I didn't feel guilty, just deeply grieved, saddened and sobered.

The next day I was an emotional wreck during the flight to Hokado U.S. Air Base, Japan. Part of my turmoil resulted from intense awareness that in a month, barring death and injury, I'd be soaring from Vietnam again, not to Japan, but to my darling wife and adorable, *perfect* children.

My spirits should have soared at these thoughts, and they did, but only to limited heights. I was beginning to sense how difficult it would be to leave my grunts in combat for the last time—just how difficult it would be I couldn't imagine.

My orders to Japan included four days of R&R and five days of temporary duty. I went to Japan on an R&R flight and was to return to Vietnam via whatever transportation was available.

I'd received verbal instructions forbidding me to begin the hospital visits until after the R&R period, which I tried to obey, though I seldom enjoy sightseeing without someone special along to share the experience.

I arrived in Japan at 2330 hours August 11 and got to bed in the BOQ by early morning on the twelfth. Later in the morning, at the PX, I purchased a set of Nortaka china for Helga and a necklace for Lieutenant Howard's wife. For dinner, I experienced the culinary delights in a Navy Chef's Club, followed by a movie at 2030 hours. The Tiptons, an Army family I'd met in April, took me to church meetings the next day, in which I spoke three times—in Sunday School, Priesthood and Sacrament Meeting. I enjoyed the rest of a pleasant Sabbath day dining and visiting with the Tipton family.

On August 14, I visited Chaplain (LDS) Jim Palmer and his lovely family. Sometime during the R&R period, I went horseback riding and spent a night with the Tiptons.

Notes

Captain Bluhm's Alpha Company casualties on LZ Pat KIAs, G-1 List: Sgt. Robert Maxwell of Fresno, California; also KIA Sp4 John Michael Beyraud; Sp5 Andrew Conrad, company medic of Millington, Michigan (with whom I often visited); Cpl. Joel Findley of Richmond, Texas; Cpl. Joseph Harrison of Thomasville, Georgia; and Michael J. Hotchkiss of Anaheim, California; Sp4 Prentice D. LeClair of Tulsa, Oklahoma. WIAs, G-1 List: PSG Frank Theberge; SSG Artis Wallace, Sp4s John W. Smith, and Raymond Snaders, Pfc. Chris Swensen, Pfc. Clarence

Durham, Pfc. Kerry Holt, Pfc. James Collins, Pfc. Carroll Bartholomew, Pfc. James Bailey, Pfc. Dennis Kelly, Pfc. Mark Y'Barra, Pfc. Jack Walton, Pfc. Theodore Lysak [my self-appointed protector], Pfc. Carol Gunter, Pfc. Dwight Johns, Pfc. Edward Sammons, Sp4 Lee Pippin and three others whose names I don't have.

An incomplete list of non-Alpha Company casualties include Sp4 Ray E. Moran of Big Bear Lake, California; Pfc. Ceasar A. Pinto of New Bedford, Massachusetts (he may have been in Alpha Company); and pilot Francis A. Rochkes of Pana, Illinois.

twenty-three

The Last Month

I spent all day, August 21, visiting troopers in the 249th Station Hospital. Among those I visited were four men from Alpha Company, casualties of the battle at Song Re on August 9. Sergeant Theberge was there with another head wound—despite which he immediately and happily recognized me; Pfc. Swensen (LDS), who had taken a gunshot wound in the shoulder while he tried to protect the wounded Theberge; Sp4 Campbell, shot in the right shoulder, going home; and Pfc. Lysak, my Catholic protector, shot in the arm and hit by mortar fire and going home, alive at least! With these latest casualties, most of the Alpha Company troopers whom I had met during late 1966 and early 1967 were wounded or dead, and so many were the latter.

After a day of hospital visits, I traveled by train and subway to dine and spend the night with the Price family in Tokyo. Price, a civilian, worked at the American Embassy, as I recall.

On August 23, I flew via chopper (with a medevac pilot named Marks) and visited the troops in the 106th U.S. Army Hospital in Yokohama. There I found Pfc. Harry E. Kerrpash, the bulldozer operator who on March 1 couldn't destroy a bunker in the face of crying women and children. He'd lost a foot and perhaps an eye to a mine or booby trap. Kerrpash recognized me after I described our first meeting.

I found the 2–8 battalion signal NCO in another hospital where he was being treated for hepatitis. His story vividly shows the dangerous, destructive power in helicopter rotor blades. His weird, unusual accident happened like this.

It was a week before the sergeant came down with hepatitis. He sat on one hole of a two-seat latrine literally minding his own business. Fifty feet behind him, two choppers idled on the log pad, their rotor blades whirling. Beneath the sergeant was part of a steel barrel, partially filled with diesel fuel to better burn the human waste he and others deposited in the barrel.

Unfortunately, the pilots of the choppers didn't have their minds completely on their business, as slowly and unnoticed by them, the vibration of one or both of the choppers brought them nearer to each other.

With a crack of thunder the tips of the rotor blades met. About five inches of one of the blades broke loose and took off at supersonic speed straight for the latrine.

The sergeant's first hint of trouble came when the barrel beneath him took flight, knocking both his legs straight out in front and splashing diesel fuel and human waste all over his person.

The rotor blade, after passing through both sides of the steel barrel below the contents level and knocking it five feet forward, continued for another 50 feet.

The sergeant's only injuries were to his dignity and some nasty bruises on the back of each calf. He didn't think the incident led to his developing hepatitis, but I wondered.

Following hospital visits on August 23, I spent the night with the Marks family, grateful for the hospitality of the Saints in Japan. Next day, August 24, I shopped in Yokohama, traveled via military sedan to Tachikawa, and spent a short night with Chaplain James Palmer and his family.

At 0230 hours on August 25, I arrived at Tachikawa Air Field for a return flight to Vietnam. That is when I learned I was supposed to have arrived at 0130 hours. An enlisted airman heeded my plea and got me on the plane, anyhow. At 1200 hours I landed in Saigon, via stops in Okinawa and at Clark Air Base, the Philippines—where I visited for 30 minutes with Chaplain (LDS) Robert Cordner. Finally, at 1730 hours on August 25, via Cam Ranh Bay and Pleiku, I arrived at An Khe.

The next morning, August 26, I attended LDS services and visited with Sp4 Paul Moody. Before returning to the field, I reported on my trip to Chaplain Parker Thompson. Thompson said he and Lt. Col. Dashiell were writing a joint letter about me to the chief of chaplains, and together the two of them were working to ensure I received the awards for valor for which I had been recommended—nothing came of the promise, though I'm sure they did what they could.

As I arose to leave his office, Chaplain Thompson ordered me to "stay out of the field and relax for the remainder of your time in country." Oh yes, he added, "You were reported AWOL for failing to return to Vietnam with the same R&R group you went to Japan with. Not a good career move," he joked.

It was raining and cold when I arrived at LZ English at 1710 hours. Lacking a dry place to sleep, I wrapped up in my poncho for a miserable night.

While I was in Japan the 2–8 Battalion had returned to the Bong Son Plain and the surrounding mountains and shore. Because of the weather, it took until August 29 to reach any of my companies. Meanwhile, during the night of August 28, a booby-trapped artillery shell killed Sp4 Julian Mendez of Bravo Company. He died near the beach, as did several other grunts, killed by similar booby traps. For example, a mede-vac chopper landed about 70 feet from where several casualties were laid out. Each one of the casualties had been hit by the same booby-trapped artillery shell. The medic jumped off the chopper to help. Moments later, another booby-trapped 155mm shell exploded beneath the stretcher on which the medic and three grunts carried a casualty of the first explosion. The casualty and the four bearers were killed instantly and their remains were hardly recognizable as human.

Back at English, I checked on Mendez at the 15th Med. His lower body was mostly gone, including all but a bare strand of cartilage where his genitals had been.

On August 29, I accompanied Alpha Company on an air assault onto the mountain near the southwest sector of the plains. I'd tried very hard to reach Alpha Company, to pass on what I knew about the casualties in Japan. I also wanted to receive an update about the action on August 9, and to just be with the men again and to soothe the guilt I felt for having been away when the company took such heavy casualties.

After evening chow on August 30, Willis and I flew via LZ English to the 1st Platoon of Charlie Company. The company was operating along the north bank of a small river near the coast. A little later, the 2nd Platoon of Alpha Company arrived and became OPCON to Charlie Company. The reinforcements were because we expected a strong force of NVA to cross the river in the night. After dark, the platoon split into squads and spread out about 20 feet from the riverbank to cover a section of the river.

Once in position, Willis and I spread a poncho liner and laid down. At midnight I checked the squad I was with and found every trooper asleep. After awakening the squad leader, I decided to stay awake myself, just in case. Fifteen minutes later, we received sniper fire and M-79 grenades. The grenades missed our position by 30 feet. We didn't respond because we suspected the NVA were trying to draw our fire so they could pinpoint our position.

The platoon from Alpha Company wasn't so fortunate, scattered as it was in squad- and team-size blocking positions along the river to our west, facing south. About 0100 hours, NVA soldiers sneaked within striking distance of one of the positions, and tossed homemade hand grenades—beer or soda cans packed with C-4 explosive. Ralph Jensen sustained a shoulder wound that earned him another 10 days in the hospital. The grenades killed three Alpha Company troopers in a position near Jensen's: Marvin L. Franklin Jr. of Oklahoma City; Sp4 Lawrence G. Grass of Belleville, Illinois; and Cpl. Gerald J. Roberts Jr. of Torringtron, Connecticut.

In yet another of the 2nd Platoon (Alpha Company) positions, Joe Letarte and his exhausted squad succumbed to sleep. Letarte had earlier received a sedative for bad sunburn. Consequently, he had completed the first watch and was fast asleep in the wee hours.

"I awakened to the sound of the grenades and the shots that killed Grass, Franklin and Roberts, less than 20 feet away," said Letarte. "A moment later, I was sitting up when up the bank came a figure wearing a steel helmet, which detail I could make out from his silhouette. At first I thought the approaching figure was one of us, until he placed a hand on each of my shoulders and spoke in Vietnamese as though he were instructing someone. All the while I was feeling for my weapon. The figure fled when I swung my M-16 in his direction. A moment earlier, the figure had stabbed Buddy Braakefield in the shoulder in passing."

At 0900 hours on August 31, Willis and I attended to the three KIAs from Alpha Company and tried to visit Jensen, but he had already been evacuated to Qui Nhon. About 1000, back in the field, I held a worship service for the 2nd Platoons of Alpha and Charlie Companies. I intended to spend the night with these elements, but was recalled to LZ English, something about a GI prisoner.

"I go home to Helga this month!" This was my first waking thought the morning of September 1, at LZ English. But my tour wasn't over yet. Though I recall no details, the prisoner matter kept me at LZ English until 1700 hours, at which time I finally joined the 2nd Platoon of Charlie Company on a hill near the Bong Son River, nearer the coast. Soon after I arrived, we worshiped together, then started preparing for a platoon-size foray down the mountain.

At 2000 hours, well after full dark, we headed down the very steep north face of the mountain, slipping, sliding, holding on to limbs and whatever to maintain our place in formation and avoid falling into the abyss. Pfc. Michael McCord fell into a depression at 2130 hours, after we'd "progressed" perhaps a third of the distance toward the valley. The medics and I feared McCord's back or neck might be broken—he had no movement from the neck down.

A few minutes later the medevac chopper crept into the extremely narrow draw and performed one of the hairiest, most heroic extractions I ever witnessed—and I had an un-enviable bird's-eye view.

The pilot moved his chopper very carefully into the draw, until the main rotor was chopping grass a few feet above my head, to its front and on both sides of the draw. Hovering there, the pilot held the chopper steady in the air while the crew chief lowered a litter on a cable. Below, dis-regarding the whirling blades over their heads, the platoon medic and grunts immobilized McCord in the litter. After hoisting McCord up, the pilot eased his chopper backward until it had space to bank and drop toward the valley to pick up speed, almost too late.

Naturally, McCord's rescue operation required use of the chopper's landing lights, and these attracted the enemy. Fortunately, though, the rough terrain slowed the enemy's efforts to get into position to shoot down the hovering chop-per. Their first shots came just as the chopper banked and dived, at 2230 hours.

"That was the most incredible medevac I ever saw," said Willis, who witnessed it from his perch higher up the moun-tain.

Our presence given away, we climbed back up the moun-tain, assuming our mission was over for the night—not so.

We had barely regained the mountaintop when the platoon was ordered down the mountain by a different route. The lieutenant didn't like the orders and neither did I, but orders were orders.

At 2345 hours we began our descent, along a spur of the hill and down a trace of a trail through erosion washes.

A sniper opened fire on us 45 minutes into our descent. The incoming wasn't even close enough to crack around us in passing. Still, we called in artillery, which was as ineffective as the sniper's fire, exploding as it did far from his position. This time, the company commander aborted the patrol mission, having concluded we were not going to reach the valley undetected. At 0200 hours, I rolled into my poncho liner to sleep.

At 0700 on September 2, we humped down the mountain and took a position nearer the rest of Charlie Company, along an east to west running canal near the Bong Son River. Soon afterward, we got orders to recon across the canal. The first trooper into the water sunk instantly over his head—the bank went straight down. Quickly, I helped pull the trooper out and then did something very foolish, which I think I'd never do again. I swam across the canal with Willis right behind me, and after lending him a hand when he started to go under, we secured the opposite bank so the squad could cross over, floating their gear on inflated air mattresses.

Our search came up dry, but we didn't, having searched the riverbanks from a leaking boat, one weaved from palm fronds. A few minutes later, we rejoined the company to help search a village, and a chopper was hit by small arms fire as it came into the village. The enemy fire came from the banks we'd just searched.

On September 3, I held a worship service at 1000 hours, my last on LZ English. At 1330 hours I conducted a memorial service in the field for Mendez of Bravo Company. And at 1600 hours I conducted a hilltop memorial service for Grass, Franklin and Roberts of Alpha Company.

On September 4, I left the Bong Son battlegrounds for the last time, I thought. As part of my farewell efforts I traveled by jeep with Moody and Willis and visited wounded troopers in the hospitals in Qui Nhon. We stayed the night there.

About 1330 hours, September 5, I arrived back at LZ English, intending to retrieve my rucksack and say goodbye to the battalion commander and staff—which plans changed because of what had been happening in Bravo Company.

Five troopers had been wounded, including Sergeant Earl W. Fernandez (LDS), SSG Roosevelt Williams, Sp4 Lloyd Gabriel, Sp4 George Jones, Sp4 Jefferson Lewis and Sp4 Gary Stene.

In late afternoon, Willis and I joined Bravo Company on the rocky east side of a mountain spur, due west and over a hill from LZ English. I wasn't supposed to go, but I couldn't "*not* go."

Arriving at the Bravo Company position, I found the company CP radios atop a clear knoll about 50 feet above some cliffs. Troopers were all over the cliffs. Below the cliffs, a cave entrance slanted upward to where several VC had taken refuge. To the left of the cave opening stood a rock about the size of two Conex containers, and, strangely, much of the bottom of the rock stood a foot to three feet above the ground. Two crevices extended upward from the cavity under the cliff, one to the top and the other between the main cliff and the big rock. Another part of the cliff rose 20 feet above the big rock.

Captain David Decker, who had recently taken command of Bravo Company, updated me. So far, he'd failed to get all the cornered VC out of the cave. Five VC had come out, but one scooted back into the cave at the last moment and rolled out the fatal hand grenade that wounded Sergeant Fernandez and the other five troopers.

Consequently, Decker's men tried unsuccessfully to burn the remaining VC out with JP-4 fuel and to force them out with CS gas. When I arrived, the troopers were pushing

250 pounds of C-4 explosives into the cave—to blow the VC out.

Notes

1 September 1967, 2–8 Journal: "C 2–8, 2–6 element at 2130, 1 EM fell in hole . . . possible broken back . . . medevac complete. At 2220, received 3–5 rounds s/a fire."

2 September 1967, 2–8 Journal: "0115, C 2–8, 2–6 element received 4 rd s/a fire, came from w . . . neg assess."

5 September 1967, 2–8 Journal: "0923, B 2–8 fd cave complex while searching. 3 × VC threw 2× grenades, 1 was dud. Results, 5 US WIA, 1 serious, all medevaced . . . VC trapped in cave. Trying to get them out."

1030 "B 2–8 captured 5, 4 det from cave wearing shorts. Neg equipment. Believed to be more in cave. Trying to talk out."

1930 "B 2–8 Readout Detainees . . . Hamlet guerrillas. One states 2× guerrillas left in cave. Man who was killed was a guerrilla, also a secretary to the hamlet chief. No grenades left."

1830 "Cave blown at 1828, found 1 male, 1 female, found 6 enemy KIA . . . one of enemy WIA died on way to med."

twenty-four

The Last Day

To get out of the way of the anticipated explosion, I climbed above the cave and cliff and joined an RTO who was monitoring the company radios. I moved about 15 feet from the RTO, squatted down under rapidly darkening, rain-laden clouds, and waited for the blast in the cave, which I expected to be soft because of the earth and stone beneath me.

Suddenly there was a blinding flash accompanied instantly by a tremendously explosive clap of noise. *That was a lot more than 250 pounds of explosive* was my first rattled thought.

Then I saw the RTO standing in a daze several feet from his smoldering radio. Fortunate for him, he'd put down the radio handset and stepped toward the cliff for a better view of the action a moment before lightning struck his radio. We were both shaken and momentarily dazed, but unhurt. The blast from the cave, when it came, was very tame by comparison to our near miss.

Moments later, having descended to the cave entrance, I looked upward when a lieutenant at the top of the cliff yelled that someone was climbing up the larger crevice.

"He's American," yelled the lieutenant. "Those (expletives deleted) made a GI go through all that (another expletive)!"

Enraged beyond reason, the adrenaline-charged lieutenant and a sergeant pulled the man from the crevice, only to discover he wasn't American after all. Enraged anew at the VC because his unusually tall, "cave-pallored" body had deceived them, the two leaders rushed the VC to the edge of the cliff to fling him headlong to the rocks below, I thought. But upon seeing me looking up at them, the two hesitated. Slowly, the wildness drained from their eyes and countenances, and they turned and led their prisoner away from the precipice.

As the first VC was being hustled away, another soldier, situated on the rock by the other crevice, called, "One is coming up here!"

As I scrambled up the rock, I saw a female arm extend from the crevice to the soldier.

"Don't touch me, you bitch," the soldier snapped. Slapping the girl's hand aside, he lifted her from the crevice by the hair of her head.

"Stop it," I snapped, as I pulled the young woman away from him.

"I'm just trying to help her, Chaplain," he mumbled.

"She doesn't need that kind of help," I retorted, harsher than was necessary under the circumstances.

Turning from the soldier, I studied the young woman in my arms. She was 16 to 18 years old. Her clothes were partly burned away as was much of her skin—some of which came off on my hands and uniform.

Hoisting the girl as gently as I could across my left shoulder, taking off more skin and flesh in the process, I prepared to take her up the cliff to the medics, Doc Rehmer and Sp4 Edward O. Bilisie.

Bilisie tossed down a rope. Grabbing the rope in my right hand, I walked the cliff face with the girl on my shoulder, while the medic and two troopers pulled up the rope.

About halfway up the cliff, the girl emitted a sound, something between a grunt and a gasp. Coming over the top of the cliff, I laid her gently on her back.

"She's dead, Chaplain," said Rehmer after examining her.

"No, her heart's beating!" I insisted.

"It's your own pulse, Chaplain, from climbing the cliff with her on your shoulder." Yes, she was dead, probably since that last grunt halfway up the cliff.

"Sergeant Fernandez died at the aid station," someone whispered in my ear, as I knelt over the girl's body.

Fernandez had returned recently from R&R, or leave,

with his wife. I recall that he returned that day from leave, but Lt. Alfred E. Lehman says differently. According to him, Fernandez was a close friend of his and had been his platoon sergeant during infantry advanced training, prior to Lehman's going to officer candidate school and becoming an officer. "I bade my wife a final farewell when I left her to return to Vietnam because my Hawaiian kahuna told me I would be dead in three months," Fernandez told Lehman.

"Fernandez was killed three months to the day his kahuna told him that," said Lehman to me.

In the deepening twilight, I joined Captain Decker above the cliffs. While Decker expressed his regrets over Fernandez's death, a trooper pressed a quart-size container of ice cream into my hand. Choppers had brought ice cream in while I was beneath the cliff, and the trooper had set the portion aside for me.

A few days later, in a different world, it seemed unimaginable that I ate ice cream under those circumstances, reeking as I did of charred flesh and death, but I had. Sleep didn't follow, though.

For my last night in the field, I never bothered setting up a rain shelter. Instead, I inflated my air mattress about halfway, donned my poncho and slipped the back of it under the top of the air mattress, and settled down into a rock chute of sorts, facing downhill. Thus I spent my last, long, wet night in the field with the Bravo Company, 2–8 Cav.

All night long I pondered my mixed emotions about leaving the troopers and going home. I thought about the noble traits so common in these grunts, and regretted the flashes of cruelty like the ones I'd just witnessed. And I was awed that the RTO and I had escaped harm from the bolt of lightning. I loved these wonderful troopers, who in my opinion were the best and the brightest of young Americans. I wondered how I would be able to leave them come morning. I knew I had to leave; I just wasn't sure how.

Vague, unreasonable guilt is probably the most common trait among Vietnam veterans. So it was with me, only my

unreasonable guilt wasn't vague. I arose the morning of
September 6, cold, soaked to the skin and stinking of burned
human flesh. I was still torn between overwhelming desire
to go home to Helga and the children and almost overwhelming guilt—like I was deserting these men. My guilt
feelings were compounded because I also felt disloyal to
Helga and the children for feeling guilty about leaving here.
Such emotional chaos as I was going through can't be described, only experienced. *One year is all that's required* I
told myself, but it didn't help right at the moment.

My problem was settled for me. At 0700 hours, an H-13
helicopter landed. Colonel Stannard climbed out, marched
up to me and after brief greetings said, "Get in my Charlie-
Charlie and go home, Claude." He added a few words of appreciation for my services and promised to do everything he
could to see I got all the medals for valor I deserved, those
I'd been put in for and more.

I climbed in the right seat of the two-seat H-13 chopper
and began my homeward journey. Colonel Stannard stayed
on the ground with Bravo Company to be sure I got out, as
did Ken Willis.

After I departed, packs were pulled out of the cave. One
belonged to the girl who died on my shoulder. From letters
and documents in the pack, SSG Nang, the company interpreter, and Sp4 Barry Hannel determined that the girl was a
nurse recently arrived from Hanoi. The pack contained a
picture of the girl with her mother and also a knitted white
sweater that had been carefully wrapped in plastic. James L.
Russ Jr. and Barry Hannel scrapped out a shallow grave and
buried the girl with the white sweater over her face. To the
Vietnamese, white is the color of death and also the color
for young unmarried women, wrote Willis.

A real person died on my shoulder that day, complete
with past and dead hopes and dreams.

Willis wrote in 1999, "As you departed the field that last
time you removed an olive-drab bandanna from around
your neck and gave it to me. I wore it every day . . . and still

have it . . . the knot you created when you tied the ends together remains to this day."

Later, I learned mine was the first and only official chaplain visit to hospitals in Japan. An insider told me the whole Japan-visit thing had been a ruse, used by command and Chaplain Thompson to keep me out of the field during my last month, lest I be killed—I'd used all my numbers, they believed.

At An Khe, someone handed me an Army Commendation Medal with V device for valor. I headed home with this, the lowest of all combat decorations, plus the air medal, another purple heart, and the "general issue" bronze star for service.

A few days would yet pass before I left Vietnam behind, presumably for the last time. But for me, my tour of duty ended about 0704 hours on September 7 when I climbed into Colonel Stannard's Charlie-Charlie chopper and flew out from the Bravo Company AO.

On the trip to An Khe, before boarding the Caribou, in a symbolic act of finality, of closure, I took from my left front pocket an item of government equipment. After rendering it harmless, I placed it in my rucksack—an action that could have brought me considerable embarrassment and some expense. At base camp, I landed at the alternate airstrip nearer An Khe and hitched a ride in the back of a two-and-a-half-ton truck to the division administrative area. From there I walked to the battalion area.

Unknown to me, the item I'd placed in my pack fell out when I jumped from the truck, which fact I discovered about an hour later as I prepared to turn in my gear to the supply room. With great anxiety, expecting to miss my flight home, I reported the loss to the battalion adjutant.

I believe it was Captain Spiegelmeyer who, after calling the supply sergeant, informed me a trooper had found and turned in my lost item—quite a coincidence, if true.

By long odds, someone other than a member of my battalion found the lost item and kept it. *Was the lost item really found, or are the supply sergeant and Spiegelmeyer conspiring to protect me by writing the item off as a combat loss?* Being one who gives little credence to coincidence, I'm left with benevolent fellow soldiers, divine intervention, or both. I can live with that.

On September 10, I talked for the last time in an LDS Sacrament Service at Camp Radcliff. Two days later I flew eastward toward home from Cam Ranh Bay, two days short of a year from the day I left the states for Vietnam.

Notes

On 8 May, Berdy would earn his first purple heart when he and six other Alpha Company troopers were wounded in a firefight. Berdy sustained "frag" wounds to the right eye and both legs. Several months later, almost at the end of his one-year tour, Berdy—a new captain—would take command of one of the companies. Then on 26 December 1967—still Christmas in the states—he would die while returning with his men from a Bob Hope show in Qui Nhon. The rotor blades on the Chinook that was transporting them malfunctioned and slashed through the fuselage. Berdy and 11 others were slashed to death by the rotor blades or died in the subsequent crash. Berdy would be one of four 2–8 Cav commanders to die during a two month period in late 1967 and early 1968—a 100 percent "Killed" ratio for line company commanders in the battalion. Among the troopers killed with Captain Michael E. Berdy of New York City following the 1967 Bob Hope show were Sp4 William H. Campbell III of Burlington, Massachusetts; Sp4 Ronald D. Evans of Cincinnati, Ohio; SSG Allen D. Ford of Pueblo, Colorado; Sp4 Barry S. Kyle of Bradford, Massachusetts; Corporal Bernard F. Poblock of Detroit; Cpl. James L. Russ, Jr. of Youngstown, Ohio; 1LT Thomas M. Van Zandt, hometown unknown; and Sgt. Stephen M. Vuga of Pittsburgh, Pennsylvania.

On 19 November, 1967, Captain David Decker and his RTO Sp4 William H. Fowler III gave their lives at Dac To in Kontum Province, while attempting to reach a fallen platoon leader, Lt. Thomas Olearneick. Sp4 (Doc) Edward O. Bilisie died 11 days later in a plane crash as he was returning from the hospital where he'd been treated for a punji stake wound.

twenty-five

"But There Is No Peace"

I'm lying in a prone shelter. Suddenly, a chicom grenade—a potato-masher type—hurdles from the darkness and lands against me. Frantically, I grab the grenade in my left hand and fling it across my body to the right. The "grenade" emits a blood-curdling scream—I wake up lying in bed at home. It's Helga that I hurled toward the window, not a grenade.

At Cam Ranh Bay, Vietnam, that September day in 1967, I searched in vain for a familiar face among those waiting with me to return to the states. Then I boarded a civilian charter flight and headed home, leaving behind the dangers and faces of war, I thought.

In my baggage were military orders assigning me to Fort Bragg, North Carolina, and a written promise from the Office of the Chief of Army Chaplains that an airborne assignment awaited me. But on that long flight homeward bound, the war memories and faces behind me impinged considerably on the wonders and anticipation of what was ahead.

The word *world* means many things. To God, it is a degenerate human condition that we must be in, but not of; to scientists, a celestial sphere; and to some, a collection of possibilities. To soliders in Vietnam, the world was America, home, sweetheart and family, the land of plenty, the land of the big PX. For me, the world was Helga; James William, almost 13; Jeannie, 11; John Allan 8; Laura Jane, 5; and Brenda Lynette, 3.

These awaited me at the Salt Lake International Airport,

and at the first glimpse of them at the terminal gate, my mind, heart and spirit caught up with my body. In an instant the faces of war were behind me, beyond the greatest ocean in the world. At least, they were temporarily.

Helga got the first hug and kiss. A few moments later, following hugs and kisses all around and with emotions under the tight rein and my war-worn civilian rucksack on John's back, we went to our rented home in Ogden. There, immersed in family and home, the faces of war grew dimmer, and I feared I might forget those I'd left behind, especially the dead. But little did I know.

That I would not, could not leave Vietnam behind me became quite obvious during the two short weeks we lingered in Utah. This began to become apparent with a telephone call from a former seminary student of mine.

The call came just before noon on my second Sunday back. During a morning session of a conference in the Ogden, Utah, Tabernacle, Elder Gordon B. Hinckley had asked that anyone who knew how to locate me to please do so and invite me and my family to attend the afternoon session of conference. Naturally, we accepted the invitation.

We weren't surprised then when Elder Hinckley invited me to take a few minutes of his time to address the conference. I don't recall speaking especially well, but I vividly recall the reawakening of memories, faces and feelings about Vietnam—and ever since these have remained close to my consciousness.

The first week in October my son and I attended a session of a work-wide church conference in Salt Lake. I wore my dress-green uniform for the first time in more than a year. Backstage after the session in the world-famous Mormon Tabernacle, Elder Marion D. Hanks asked me, "What is your rank?"

"Captain," I answered, pointing to my left shoulder where the silver double bars of a captain *should* have been clearly visible, but weren't. Obviously, I'd become rusty at this dress uniform business, but to forget the insignia of rank? Elder Hanks smiled in good humor at my discomfort.

While speaking during a session of conference the next day, Elder Gordon B. Hinkley remarked, "In the congregation is Chaplain Claude Newby, who just returned from Vietnam," and went on to relate a spiritual anecdote from my life as an enlisted man back in 1958. I felt quite honored.

In anticipation of earning paratrooper pay to replace the combat pay I no longer drew, we deemed it proper to report to Fort Bragg, North Carolina, in a new car, rather than in the well-used Ford we owned. So we bought a 1967 Rambler Ambassador station wagon and shipped our household goods. We headed east, with stops in Idaho to visit Dallas and Joan Murdoch; and in Louisiana, Tennessee and Georgia to visit family.

Two disappointments awaited us at Fort Bragg. First, there would be a long wait for on-post housing. Second, despite a written commitment by the Office of the Chief of Chaplains, I'd not received the airborne assignment I'd wanted.

Colonel Jim Skelton, the XVIII Corps and Post Chaplain said, "I need chaplains in the training center more than in airborne units. I manage my assets, despite what Washington might have promised you." So it was back to a basic training center, this time under the technical supervision of Chaplain (Major) Virgil Wood, a Baptist as I recall, and an easy man to work for.

Chaplain Wood assigned me religious support responsibility for a training battalion in a brigade commanded by Colonel John P. Barker. Barker and his Executive Officer, Lieutenant Colonel O'Brien, would soon play parts in an effort to end my chaplaincy career. It was about to become clear that not all things dangerous had been left in Vietnam.

Chaplain Blanke (assigned alisa), the Training Center Chaplain, gave me a week to in-process and find civilian housing. Meanwhile, the family was assigned to temporary accommodations in an unhealthy, dismal, coal smoke–choked barracks. After a futile week of house hunting, Chaplain Blanke warned, "find a place right away, or else." So we looked farther afield and rented a barely affordable house, a nice home on ten acres near the village of Cameron, North Carolina, seventeen miles north of Fort Bragg.

The property included a stable and corral. Farms bordered it on three sides, and a commerical pine forest was across the dirt road to the south. The stable and corral would come in handy when Bishop Abe, a Hawaiian of Japanese descent, asked us to board two Shetland ponies. We took the ponies to be good neighbors, no charge, of course! I had grown up with horses and even served with a horse unit in the Army. The ponies would provide great fun and experience for our children.

There on the farm, I tried to show Helga that I loved her in deed, and strove to make up for time lost while I was in Vietnam. The children and I got in lots of shooting practice with shotgun, rifle and BB guns. Almost everyone who visited us was introduced to and became hooked on our homemade game of ambush.

One day the family was on the way to town when, from the back seat of the station wagon, Brenda Lynette suddenly threw her little arms around my neck and exclaimed, "My Daddy is as big as the sky!"

"What?"

"I mean my Daddy is as strong as the sky," she clarified, quickly tightening her little arms about my neck for emphasis. Not everyone felt so positive toward me.

While Chaplain Wood received me well, Chaplain Blanke's reception was something else. Soon after I arrived, Blanke called me into his office for a welcome speech, and said that he had had trouble with the LDS chaplain who preceded me at Fort Bragg. "Nothing personal," he added, "but I don't understand how your church has the audacity to place you men in the chaplaincy to compete with professional clergy." He strongly advised me to move the on-post

LDS meetings into his sphere of responsiblity so he could "be sure the Mormons are treated properly." I promised only to conduct weekly LDS services in the training center, to accommodate trainees during their quarantine period.

Chaplain Wood, on the other hand, appeared glad to have me in his brigade. He and several other chaplains were attending a Duke University class titled something like "Offbeat Religions in America." Each chaplain-student was assigned a written and oral report on a religion the professor considered offbeat. Wood chose the LDS religion so he could use me as a resource. First I got ecclesiastical approval, then agreed to help on condition that my participation be limited to a presentation followed by questions and answers, free of argument over points of doctrine.

At the appointed time Wood introduced me to the theology class: "I resent Chaplain Newby. When God was giving out vices, Baptists, who come alphabetically before the Mormons, chose coffee. The Mormons came along and chose plural wives." The class members approved Wood's humor. I accepted it in good nature.

Besides my primary support for two training battalions, I took a turn one evening each week counseling trainees on a first-come basis, without regard to each trainee's unit. Each night, 15 to 25 or more trainees lined up to see the chaplain. The trainees came seeking intervention over perceived unfair treatment, for personal and family concerns, for guidance on personal actions such as becoming a conscientious objector, and seeking relief from some fearful aspect of training like crawling beneath streams of live machine-gun fire on the infiltration course. They came to discuss the "advantages" of going AWOL, and seeking help getting out of the Army. Occasionally a trainee came seeking spiritual or moral guidance.

Due to heavy counseling demands, time was scarce for visiting the trainees and cadre in billets, work and training areas. Consequently, I implemeted the operational concept I'd developed at Fort Ord in 1966—making certain I was on hand during those times of greatest stress on the trainees and the cadre. This modus operandi helped save my career, as events would show.

Immediately after arriving at Fort Bragg I recommened training for the airborne assignment I hoped to get eventually, and for which I regularly pestered the Post Chaplain. But something was wrong. At Fort Ord in 1966 I could easily run a seven-minute mile wearing combat boots. Now, I barely made a mile in ten minutes, wearing running shoes. I discounted the hip injury I had sustained in early 1967, for the pain had subsided and eventually disappeared, leaving only a numb big toe. Though I could jog slowly for hours, I feared I'd be unable to pass the airborne physical when my chance came.

Airborne units had a mockup of an aircraft, built from the fuselage of a C-47 airplane. I often watched paratroopers and hopefuls, like me, make practice jumps from the mockup. After several months of watching, I had a night dream:

I'm standing in full paratooper gear in the open door of a C-47 aircraft, in flight. On the signal I leap out into space, but my main chute doesn't open! With the jumpmaster glaring disapproval at me as I fall, I pull the D-ring to deploy my reserve chute. It fails me too. As I plunge toward the ground, the jumpmaster yells, "Don't worry, Chaplain. It counts!" My imminent death would not prevent me from becoming jump-qualified.

I awoke before "hitting the ground" and lay awake pondering the dream and my motives for going airborne. Never again did I pester Chaplain Skelton for an airborne assignment.

twenty-six

Relieve Him for Cause

Early in December 1967, I answered my office telephone and heard, "Claude, this is Chaplain Blanke. Mrs. Blanke and I are planning a Christmas party for the chaplains and wives in the training center. How will 1300 to 1700 hours Sunday the nineteenth work for you?"

"That conflicts with my worship services at 1300 and 1500 hours and with another speaking assignment at 1700," I explained.

"It is seldom possible to find a time that fits everyone, but this time fits the other chaplains, so that is settled. You and Helga come by if you can, even if only for a few minutes between services, and we will appreciate it and understand," said Blanke, cheerfully.

On the day of the party, assuming Chaplain Blanke had been up front with us, Helga and I stopped in at his home for a few minutes. All seemed gracious and in good order. And things seemed to be going nicely at home and work. But unknown to me, Chaplain Blanke was building a case to rid the chaplaincy of me.

The plot thickened and came to a boil at the same time I became aware it existed, late in January. Earlier, I had gotten permission to take the LDS trainees to a meeting in Raleigh..On the Sunday of this event, I arranged for another chaplain to conduct my regular worship services, and posted notices of the change in the schedule for LDS services on the chapel doors and in the Daily Bulletin, required reading for all leaders.

Then came the ice storm. Cold rain commenced Thursday just as I started home from work and quickly changed to sleet. The roads had become ribbons of glare ice by the time I slid, literally, into our driveway about 6:30 p.m. We lost electricity and telephone service early in the evening. With the loss of electricity we also lost indoor cooking capability, heating, and culinary water, which all relied on an electric compressor and pump. By midnight the indoor temperature had plunged below freezing, where it remained for forty-eight hours.

Fortunately, our battery-powered radio worked well, and over it we heard orders, in the name of the commanding general: "Because of extremely hazardous conditions, all personnel will remain where you are, whether at home or at work . . . until further notice."

Bundled in sleeping bags and doubled up in our beds, we were reasonably warm through the night. Friday morning we awakened to clear skies and a white, crystal-like winter wonderland scene, a sparkling world of ice-encrusted, frigid beauty. The pine trees across the road bowed their tops to the ground like followers of Islam in prayer, without breaking off. Every wire, branch, and twig sported a coat of ice diamonds. The general's "stay put" order was still in effect, and just as well in my case. An ice-coated main power line drooped across the road just a few inches above the road surface, blocking our exit. I wasn't about to see if the wire was live.

For two days we melted ice for drinking and sanitation and cooked soup over an outside fire. Saturday morning the ice glaze remained, but was showing signs of melting. The "stay put" order was still in effect. By mid-afternoon the ice had dropped off the power line and it had sprung up, opening our way to the outside world. We headed for town, but thought better of it when the approaching headlights of a car suddenly switched sides with each other. We came very close to crashing into the upside-down car. Black ice, or glare ice, coated the hardtop rural highway. The unhurt driver of the overturned car slithered out on his back through the driver's window.

Back home a few minutes later our telephone rang—it

had still been out of order when we'd ventured out. Chaplain Bobby Moore, standing in for Wood, was on the line. He informed me Chaplain Blanke had written to Colonel Barker and recommended that I be relieved from duty "for cause."

Blanke accused me of gross dereliction of my duties. Specifically, he charged me with: (1) neglecting the trainees during the stressful period of the ice storm; (2) failing in my social obligations, to wit, coming late to his Christmas party and departing early; (3) neglecting my responsibilities to LDS soldiers; and two allegations that I no longer recall.

Reportedly, Colonel Barker reacted angrily to Blanke's charges and ordered me, through Moore, to report to him at 0800 hours Monday. Moore opined Barker would relieve me from duty and my career would be destroyed. Next day I went about my Sunday duties with a heavy heart.

Early Monday morning, I waited in my office for the moment of doom, with good reason to suspect this was the end of my career, though I believed myself to be innocent of any wrongdoing. Colonel Barker was notorious for relieving officers first and asking questions later, thus ending careers, so the rumors went.

While I waited for the appointed hour of judgment, there entered my mind Christ's admonition and promise to his apostles, applicable when they would be brought before the law for *righteousness sake*: "take no thought what you shall say . . . for the words will be given . . . what ye shall say." Perhaps this promise applied in my case. I prayed fervently for divine intervention, that my "calling" might be spared.

Lieutenant Colonel O'Brien, the Brigade Executive Officer, called just before 8:00 a.m. "I've convinced Colonel Barker to listen to your side regarding Chaplain Blanke's allegations. So instead of reporting to Colonel Barker, be in my office at 0900 hours," he instructed. This reprieve totally surprised me, especially because O'Brien was an enigma to the chaplains—the consensus was that he disliked them.

Yet another surprise came while I waited anxiously for 0900 hours to arrive. The surprise arrived in the form of a letter from the Office of the Army Chief of Chaplains. Normally the mail came after lunch. The letter said:

Dear Chaplain Newby:

"We have just received the efficiency report . . . for the period of 1 August to 10 September 1967. Although the report covered a very short period . . . it is a testimony to your dedication to your Calling, to your courage and capacity for work. It is an outstanding report. . . . Please accept our congratulations . . . prayers. . . ."

(Signed by G. W. Hyatt, 5 January 1968)

Feeling much better, I knocked on O'Brien's office door promptly at 0900 hours, entered on command, saluted sharply, and reported myself "present as ordered." O'Brien put me at ease (a semi-relaxed, half-at-attention standing position), read the allegations against me, and asked me what I had to say for myself.

In my defense, I first explained how I had but obeyed the commanding general's orders by remaining home during the ice-storm crisis. "Besides," I explained, "I really had no choice in the matter because a power line blocked my way."

Second, I related my conversation with Chaplain Blanke concerning the scheduling of his Christmas party. Third, I outlined the background and justification for all my actions related to the LDS services and trainees, and explained why I had declined to place all LDS services under my accuser's supervision. After responding to the remaining two allegations, which I no longer recall, I described Blanke's negative reception when I first arrived at the training center. Finally, I proffered the letter from the Office of the Chief of Chaplains. "This letter, which I received this morning, belies most of the things of which I stand accused," I said.

Lieutenant Colonel O'Brien studied the letter for a moment in silence and returned it: "I wish my branch would write letters like that. Go back to work. I'll handle Colonel

Barker." O'Brien called an hour later: "Everything is fine with Colonel Barker. However, he wants you to move into on-post quarters as soon as you can. He'll use command influence to help you get housing."

Henceforth, no one at Fort Bragg openly challenged my credentials or my duty performance. To the contrary, once Colonel Barker ordered other chaplains to emulate me, by name. Another day he singled me out for praise in the midst of a chewing out that he was administering to the Training Center Chaplain and my colleagues. Though the attempt to get me "fired" worked in my favor for the most part, I was marked down on my next efficiency report in the sociability category. Probably, the lower sociability rating was justified. Following Vietnam, I found it very difficult to be at ease amid the chatter and clatter of social gatherings while the war raged in vivid color on the nightly news.

As mentioned earlier, I tried always to be with the units in the field during times of highest tensions. Consequently, I was present and frequently took part when my trainees went through (crawled) the infiltration course under live machine-gun fire.

On the infiltration course the trainees, armed with M-14 rifles, entered a deep trench that was reminiscent of the trenches of World War I. Then, on a signal, the trainees scampered from the trench and belly-crawled or slid on their backs across a course crisscrossed with barbed wire and pocked with sandbagged pits. In several places, strands of the barbed wire were stretched tight and crisscrossed between stakes, just high enough to allow a man to slither beneath them on his back, using his weapon to hold the barbs up to keep them from snagging his uniform. From behind the objective or finish line, several machine guns fired bursts across the course. The guns were locked into position so they couldn't fire lower than 30 or 36 inches at the highest point of the course. But they were still dangerous. And those sandbagged pits offered no protection. Rather, each pit contained explosive charges sufficiently large to blow off an arm or leg, or even to kill a man. These charges were set off among the trainees to simulate exploding mortar rounds.

Occasionally, I crawled the infiltration course for fun or to provide emotional support to trainees. For example, a first sergeant sent a trainee to me who was petrified by fear and had refused to leave the trench for the first of two daylight crawls. The trainee agreed to attempt the night course (his last chance), provided I accompany him. I did, we made it, and he was graduated on time. Immediately following that crawl, I stood beneath a floodlight in my mud-spattered splendor, visiting with some members of the cadre. Colonel Barker appeared, glared at me for a moment, and walked off without saying a word. *He's perturbed by my appearance and wishes he'd relieved me when he started to,* I suspected.

Putting concerns about Colonel Barker aside, I turned my thoughts to what I saw around me. I reflected on the fear the trainee had demonstrated earlier. An idea flashed into my mind. *From now on, I'll hold a worship service right here for the trainees, just before they crawl the infiltration course. I'll have the trainees' full attention here! It will be great for them. Perhaps I can get the service added to the training schedule.*

For effect, I would conduct these unique services with the trainees seated in the bleachers and looking over my shoulders at the dreaded infiltration course, a great visual aid.

These special, simple services were an instant success. I began each service with us singing *The Battle Hymn of the Republic*, followed by prayer and a sermon by me, then another song and a closing prayer. In my "infiltration-course sermon" I compared the infiltration course to life and the drill sergeants' instructions to scripture—the sergeants liked the comparison. Birth I compared to leaving the trench, to leaving comparative security behind and going forth to face obstacles, uncertainty and danger. "In life, as with the infiltration course," I said, "there is—or should be—a clear objective, the reaching of which places one beyond the danger. Just as in life one has the scriptures to give him spiritual guidance, so on the infiltration course one has his drill sergeants telling him how to proceed. If one heeds his sergeants' instructions and keeps going, he will get past the obstacles and explosions and pass unharmed beneath the cracking bullets, reaching safe haven. And in life, one who heeds God's commandments and keeps going will be protected from the 'fiery darts' in life and will return back to God, from whence he came, through Christ." Almost all trainees attended these services voluntarily, as did most of the cadres.

Unknown to me, Colonel Barker observed one of these services. The next day he issued a written order: "Every chaplain in this brigade will conduct worship services at the infiltration course, and will include *The Battle Hymn of the Republic* in these services." Colonel Barker had no authority to dictate the contents of chaplains' worship services, but how could I object!

Some weeks after I began these special services, a trainee in another battalion was shot in the arm while crawling the night infiltration course (I suspected he stuck his arm up and got it shot on purpose to avoid going to Vietnam).

By coincidence, the next day all the Training Center chaplains, about ten of us, gathered in a headquarters building at Chaplain Blanke's call. We met Colonel Barker coming in as we were leaving the building. His face was livid and his teeth clenched, probably because he'd just come from trying to explain the shooting mishap to his own boss. Anyhow, Barker got in Chaplain Blanke's face and roared, "And where were you chaplains last night when my man was shot?" Then glancing at me, he said softly, "I don't mean you, Chaplain Newby. You're always there." After aiming a few more harsh words at Blanke, Barker stormed away without waiting for any response.

As previously mentioned, I tried to always be on the range when a company of trainees fired the rifle for record. These were high-stress occasions for the cadre, whose efficiency reports, even their careers, were on the line. Out of the blue one day a company commander challenged me to a shooting match. He was feeling great because his men had just fired for record and done very well. I accepted the challenge, though I'd never fired an M-14 rifle. The M1 Garand and M-1 and M-2 Carbine rifles had been the standard weapons back when I was infantry.

The company commander and I each loaded a 20-round magazine and took a shooting position. He knelt and rested his weapon on a sandbag. I stood to fire freehand, without a rest for the rifle. Our impromptu rules were simply to knock down a line of about twenty silhouette targets at maximum range, 300 yards as I recall, beginning with the target on our right and working left. We were free to fire when the pop-up line of targets appeared.

Feeling very relaxed, I took a left-handed stance and aimed where I expected the first target to appear. The target appeared. I fired instantly and shifted left as the target fell. Six times in rapid succession I dropped targets before the captain could get off a shot using his by-the-book method. Finally, he fired and hit his target, but he had to skip ahead to do so, in violation of the "rules of engagement." Quickly, I knocked down the targets the captain had skipped and passed him again. The referee, a sergeant, declared me the winner—a brave act, as he worked for the captain.

To ease the captain's embarrassment at being "bested" by a chaplain, I confessed my prior infantry experience, and how I'd grown up with weapons and shot competitively. The captain took defeat well and I didn't gloat.

twenty-seven

Below the Zone

It was about 9:00 p.m., October 1968. The children were preparing for bed. Helga and I were just beginning to relax when the telephone rang. "Hello Claude. Virgil here."

"Virgil. Virgil who?" I asked.

"Virgil Wood—Chaplain Wood, Claude." He caught me off guard, for while he usually called me by my first name, I had the impression Wood expected me to address him as "Chaplain" or "sir." I did that naturally because he was my superior officer.

Wood continued, "Claude, do you know you made the majors' list?" I didn't even know such a list existed. He explained he'd accidentally found my name on a list for promotion to major from "below the zone." Below the zone, he explained, meant I was selected for promotion ahead of my contemporaries, from among the top 10 percent of captains in the Army. This was quite a change from eight months earlier when it looked like my career was destroyed.

Normally, an officer was notified of selection for promotion by his chain of command when the promotion list was released, or sooner. But everyone in both chaplain and command channels had missed my name, and I hadn't known to check.

In late summer 1968, author Daniel Lang of *The New Yorker* magazine called me. He wanted my version of the story about the Mao incident in Vietnam in 1966. This incident is recounted in detail in chapter 6 in a piece titled "Casualties of War" in the September 1969 issue of *The*

New Yorker; and in a movie by the same title starring Michael J. Fox.

Lang had learned my identity and about my connection with the Mao incident during interviews with Sven (alias for one of the parties involved) at the latter's home in the Midwest. I told Lang what I knew, with the approval of the Fort Bragg Information Officer, of course. My account, Lang said, agreed in every important detail with Sven's. He promised me a copy of the article when it got published.

After January 1968, with Chaplain Blanke's attack behind me, life was quite good, except for the children's schooling. Our recent move to on-post housing had forced the children to change schools again, their fourth change of the school year.

Beginning with Jeannie's birthday on April 13, we made frequent overnight trips to the beaches about 110 miles east of Fort Bragg. Wayne Boring, who had followed me here from Vietnam, usually accompanied us on these fun trips, where we had great times playing ambush amid the sand dunes, surfing—body and air mattress—and "gigging" for flounder in the coastal tide pools.

We planned an April trip for Helga to visit her mother Martha Raasch in Berlin, Germany. To contain costs, we booked her flights in and out of the John F. Kennedy International Airport in New York, where I'd drive her and pick her up. The Borings agreed to stay with us so Carmen Boring could tend the children while I worked. The murder of Martin Luther King Jr. in Memphis, Tennessee significantly affected these plans, coming as it did a few days before Helga was scheduled to depart for Berlin.

That this trip would be different immediately became obvious. We knew Army and National Guard units were out in-force, but I expected they would be deployed in actual riot areas. Not so. As we passed in the dark through Raleigh, North Carolina, armed troops were visible on almost every corner and combined patrols of policemen and National

Guardsmen were everywhere. At several checkpoints, we had to "prove" our peaceful intentions to suspicious military and civilian officers. Several times we were advised, but never ordered, to turn back for our own safety. An eerie, familiar feeling, a heightened state of awareness and wariness, accompanied me through riot-torn cities. I felt as though I was in the jungles of Vietnam.

We felt better between Baltimore and Long Island, New York, because we saw no evidence of riots or troops on the freeways and turnpikes. Though New York City had experienced heavy rioting, we got to JFK, and I got out too, without interference from either rioters or the military or civilian police.

The boys and I took a canoe trip in July 1968, thanks to the willingness of a lieutenant to take a chance on us. He was the recreational officer at Pope Air Force Base. Our trip was down the Little River, which was in flood stage.

For the occasion I wore jungle fatigues, with pockets buttoned down. Helga delivered us to the river and we pushed off into the current just outside Fort Bragg, with me in the stern, James in front and John in the middle.

We made good time all morning, slipping easily between and around the snags and sunken logs that created few obstacles in the high water. About noon, we tied up near a bridge and purchased the fixings for lunch at a country store. That is when I forgot to button my pocket after returning my wallet to it.

An hour later, we hit a particularly rough stretch of water that was too muddy to be called white water, and the current pushed us into a sunken tree near the south bank. We would have made it, but John stood to dodge a limb and tipped the canoe. James easily pulled himself to the bank while I secured the canoe to a snag and turned to rescue John, who was being carried away by the current. Swimming hard, I caught John and pulled him to safety; life vests made the difference between rescue and tragedy.

A few minutes later with the boys safe on the bank, I got

the water out of the canoe and we were on the way again, re-freshed by the dip and exhilarated by the adventure.

About two hours later, we arrived ahead of schedule at the place where Helga was to pick us up. Storm clouds were threatening. After pulling the canoe up a steep bank to the roadside, I left the boys with it and went to call Helga from a farmhouse a quarter mile down the road.

Hard rain hit as I approached the farmhouse. The call completed, thanks to a friendly farm family, I waited on the porch for the rain to let up—it came down in sheets, like the heavy monsoon rains in Asia. Lightning flashed almost without letup, the strikes coming seconds apart and striking all around.

James and John were safe from the lightning beneath the concrete bridge, I thought. Then dimly through the driving rain, I saw two shapes dragging a canoe through a hail of lightning that hit like a heavy mortar barrage.

"Leave the canoe! Run!" I yelled, as I raced to meet the boys. A moment later, back safely on the porch, we watched the area where we'd abandoned the canoe. We could hardly see the road, much less the canoe in the driving rain. The lightning passed on after half an hour. We hurried through the slackening rain to retrieve the canoe, but someone—a pickup had passed during the storm—had stolen it.

While I waited for Helga to come for us, I reported the theft of the canoe to the county sheriff. That's when I dis-covered I'd lost my wallet with all my identification cards and meager funds; it had floated out of my unbuttoned pocket. And the worst was still ahead. I had to explain this to my Air Force lieutenant friend who had bent the rules to rent to Army personnel. Eventually a formal military proce-dure called a *report of survey* absolved me of responsibility for the loss of the canoe. I hope the incident didn't hurt my Air Force friend's career.

Family and military life was very busy, especially on Sundays. Each Sunday I conducted general services in the morning, an LDS service for trainees in the early afternoon, participated in a service for singles in the late afternoon, and attended civilian services with my family in Fayetteville in the evening.

The civilians at church seldom saw me out of uniform. One evening, I dressed in "civvies" (civilian clothes) and accompanied Jeannie to a daddy-daughter dinner date program. We arrived at the Fayetteville chapel a few minutes early and took our seats. One lady sitting behind us whispered to another, "Chaplain Newby looks funny with clothes on." Presumably, she referred to civilian clothes as opposed to my usual uniform.

Despite the busy schedule and satisfaction at home and work, I felt pulled back to Vietnam, an urging made stronger by the nightly war news and my surroundings. These rendered quite unpleasant many of the things about the peacetime, garrison environment. For example, it was very difficult to attend social functions, especially the formal ones. The crowds made me very tense, and I felt ashamed for basking in elegance while the grunts fought and died in far off Asia. Though I attended to my social duties as best I could, my unease must have shown through because the problem soon showed up on my efficiency reports.

The same nightly news that infuriated the populace and fueled the protestors increased my anger at my surroundings and at the "business as usual" attitude of the country in general. And anger and unrest turned to increasingly strong feelings of guilt for being safe in the world while our soldiers fought on.

One day during Tet 1968, I stood in for a battalion commander in the reviewing stand while his battalion of trainees—several hundred strong—practiced passing in review. It occurred to me there that before me was almost enough young men to replace those who were killed in Vietnam during the past week. This observation did not help me adjust. Then something happened that spurred me to action.

In September 1968, thinking back to occasions when I

had arranged for soldiers in the field to attend conferences in Vietnam, I decided to do the same for soldiers at Fort Bragg. If it could be arranged, I'd take a group two thousand miles to attend a stateside religious conference. My superiors in the chaplain line gave their blessings to the idea along with their collective opinion that it couldn't be done. Well, I did it anyhow.

By carefully coordinating with various Army and Air Force commanders and staffs, I got permission to take as many trainees and soldiers to Salt Lake City as a C-130 cargo aircraft would carry. A line colonel in my chain of command included with his endorsement of the plan his off-the-record warning the operation could ruin my career. "You can't expect to turn loose an airplane load of soldiers and trust them to stay out of trouble and all show up for the return flight." But I trusted that these soldiers would not let me down.

Well we went to Salt Lake City, and every soldier stayed out of trouble from Friday to Sunday. Each one of them showed up at the appointed time for the return flight, to my great relief.

During the conference, something else happened to bring the Vietnam War closer to home. It was Sunday afternoon, as I recall, and Helga and I were strolling around Temple Square. I was in uniform. A man and woman approached us, and the lady tentatively asked, "Are you in the Army."

"Yes, ma'am, I am."

"We wonder if you can tell us how to get information about our son? He was killed in Vietnam."

"Gladly. What is your son's name, his unit in Vietnam, and when did he die?" I asked, after expressing condolences.

Our son was Pfc. Danny Hyde," said Melba (Denney) Palmer. Her companoin was Marlow G. Palmer, Danny's stepfather.

It was easy to tell the couple about their son, and it required no research. I'd been intimately involved with him from the time he was wounded in October 1966 until his death eleven days later. What was hard was controlling a flood of emotions at the mention of Danny Hyde's name and the realization that Danny's parents stood before me. I shared with the couple all I knew of their son's last days, and how he'd declared his intention to David Lillywhite to quit smoking and get his life in order. I told of my futile attempt to visit Danny earlier on the day that he was wounded. I related his last words as I'd heard them from his buddies and the medics. Finally, I shared the details of my visits to Danny in the hospital and how I finally commended their son to God's will, holding back only the gruesome details about his wounds. After this encounter, the pull of Vietnam became increasingly difficult to resist.

On December 12, 1968, while in Washington, D.C., with a carload of soldiers for the groundbreaking for a temple there, I dropped into the office of the Army chief of chaplains. "I'm here to volunteer to return to Vietnam," I said. With those simple words, I was on my way back to Vietnam for a second tour that made the first one seem easy by comparison.

The next day, I arrived home to find Helga in the hospital suffering with pneumonia. At her bedside, I broke the news that I was returning to Vietnam—omitting that I was doing so voluntarily. She chose that moment to break the news that she was pregnant with our sixth child.

twenty-eight

"Haste to the Battle"

(From the hymn "We Are All Enlisted")

Try as I might, I adjusted poorly to the business-as-usual attitudes in the stateside military and civilian communities and to the relegating of Vietnam to the nightly news. I doubted the nation was doing nearly enough to support the sons and daughters it sent into combat in an increasingly unpopular war. My disdain grew rapidly for those antiwar demonstrators, reporters, and politicians who blamed the soldiers in the field for the war and for the failings of civilian leadership. These feelings influenced what I did next, as did the fear that I might receive orders to Korea. If I must be away from my family for another year, it had to be Vietnam. I couldn't bear the thought of another year away otherwise. Thus reasoning, I volunteered for a second combat tour.

On December 12, 1968, while in Washington, D.C. on another matter, I visited the chaplain in charge of personnel actions in the Chief of Chaplains Office and said, "I'm here to volunteer to return to Vietnam."

The chaplain eagerly accepted my offer. Then to my chagrin he informed me that I would be assigned to a battalion of Reserve or National Guard engineers that had recently been activated in Idaho, the members of which were 95 percent LDS. This would mean a rear-area assignment. It was too late to say no, but I "belonged" in the 1st Air Cavalry Division, or at least in another infantry unit. Sure, the idea of serving with a modern-day "Mormon Battalion" had its appeal. But I believed with all my heart that I was needed in the field.

Helga was in the hospital recovering from pneumonia

when I returned to Fort Bragg from Washington. No doubt I slowed her healing by informing her that I was returning to Vietnam. She had a surprise for me, too.

"I'm pregnant," she said. Words can't begin to describe the guilt that swept over me.

Orders to Vietnam arrived before Christmas. We would depart from Fort Bragg for Utah in January and take thirty days of leave there. Jim Skelton, the XVIII Airborne Corps Chaplain, upon learning I had volunteered to return to Vietnam, offered, "If you will let me get your orders canceled, I will give you an airborne assignment next spring." I declined his offer.

Christmas 1968 was hectic, a period of checking children out of school, shipping household goods, clearing post, and attending to personal affairs—wills, insurance and so forth—and saying goodbye to very good friends, colleagues, and leaders.

Before departing from Fort Bragg, I made the rounds and bade farewell to selected soldiers, sergeants and officers, mostly those with whom I'd served in Vietnam. When I called on Dowd, my former brigade chaplain, at Post Headquarters, he took me to see the Post Sergeant Major who had been our Brigade Sergeant Major in Vietnam. The Sergeant Major took me to the Corps and Post Chief of Staff who had been in our brigade in Vietnam. The Chief of Staff took me to the Commanding General, John Tolson, as I recall, who had commanded the 1st Cavalry Division during part of my tour in Vietnam. Without any coaxing or hint on my part, the general asked, "Chaplain Newby, do you want to go back to the 1st Cav?"

"Yes, sir, very much, sir," I responded enthusiastically.

Turning to the Chief of Staff, the general said something like, "Bob, call Jim at USARV and ask him to be sure Chaplain Newby is assigned back to the Cav."

I left Fort Bragg somewhat more hopeful of another infantry assignment, but at the same time doubtful it would come about. After all, the "Mormon Battalion" waited in Vietnam and I happened to be a *Mormon* Chaplain. And promises made didn't necessarily mean promises kept. Still, I hoped; this promise came from a three-star general and former commander of the 1st Cav.

On the last morning of a stopover in Chattanooga, we awakened to about seven inches of snow on the ground. The tires of our car never touched a road surface that was clear of ice and snow until many miles and a few days later, when we drove into the Murdoch family garage in Grace, Idaho.

We visited the Murdoch family, rested for a couple of days and attended church on Sunday. Then, leaving the children there, Helga and I went south for a day and rented a home in Ogden. We returned to Idaho to visit and to squeeze in all the play we could before I left again.

Most memorable about our visit in Grace was the deep snow and hours spent pulling the children on a car-hood sled behind a snowmobile. These antics took place on white fields and over and through massive snowdrifts in the Murdochs' front yard—they had few close neighbors then.

On another day during our stay in Idaho, Dallas, Joan, Helga, and I took a daylong snowmobile trek far back into the wilderness somewhere north of Soda Springs, Idaho. During the snowmobile trip, I discovered the true meaning of "white out" in blizzard country. We were standing beside an isolated dirt road. A snow-filled field that appeared to be on level with the road stretched to the south. I started to step onto the field, but Dallas grabbed my arm. Then he dropped a stick or rock onto the seemingly solid snow. The object fell straight down for at least fifteen feet, destroying the illusion of a flat, level field at my feet. But for Dallas' greater experience, I might have broken my neck on the boulders below.

All too soon the fun and games were over. It was time to put our children in school in Ogden, get our household goods delivered, set up a new home, and for me to be on my way to Vietnam.

A day or two before I left for Vietnam, Daniel Lang of *The New Yorker* magazine called for a final interview about the Mao incident that had occurred during my first tour.

That last night home, I dreamed of dying in combat (more in the next chapter). This was one dream that I withheld from Helga for a year. Holding back the dream from her was something of an infraction of our covenant to share everything. I justified my actions to myself because it was only a dream and would worry her, perhaps unnecessarily—though the dream seemed very real. Helga was quite familiar with some of my night dreams, like one that I had in Cameron.

The dream came to me about November 1967, about a month after we settled into our farm home in Cameron, North Carolina. We were sleeping in our bed with me on my back on the right side of the bed. *I'm lying in a prone shelter. Suddenly, a chicom hand grenade—a potato-masher—hurtles from the darkness and lands against me. Frantically, I grab the grenade and attempt to fling it across my body to the right! A bloodcurdling scream shatters my nightmare.* I awaken to find poor Helga half above me and half out of the bed, her frantic eyes pleading to know why I have a death grip on a large cylindrical hair curler atop her head, and why I seem to be trying to hurl her out the window.

The dream I had the night I left to return to Vietnam seemed even more real and is indelibly imprinted in memory.

The landscape is all in shades of black and gray in the pale moonlight. Bushes stand out from the ground in darker shadow. The damp earth presses against my chest and elbows. A patch of gray distinguishes a clearing from the surrounding bushes.

The clearing is roughly circular and about twenty-five feet across. On the other side of the clearing lies an enemy soldier, Vietcong (VC) or North Vietnamese, who is drawing a bead on me with his AK-47 assault rifle. Frantically, I

*try to push up with my arms and fling myself to the right.
But I'm too late. I'm just beginning to push when the AK-47
muzzle flashes and a sledgehammer-like blow slams into my
forehead. Suddenly, I feel myself being thrown upward and
to the right. Then, in an instant, I'm in the air about three
feet above the ground and to the left of my body, watching it
tumble and fall, face upward, dead eyes staring blankly.* I
awoke then, wondering, *am I only dreaming or is it a vision,
an omen, or something else?*

Since I placed little stock in omens and didn't credit myself with frightful imaginations, I was left with something
else. The dream was from a spiritual source, I concluded,
and was intended to reassure and comfort me, that I might
comfort others during the year ahead. I drew comfort from
the dream because it reassured me that change from death to
spiritual existence—from mortal awareness to spiritual
awareness—is quick and sure. The experience left me with
neither a foreboding of impending death nor any reassurance that I would return safely. Simply, it comforted me.

twenty-nine

"Quick to the Field"

(From the hymn "We Are All Enlisted")

March 1 was a bittersweet day of extreme emotions. I finished packing, which wasn't all that difficult because I would deploy laden much more lightly than in 1966. The family accompanied me to the airport, just like last time. I was grateful to be leaving everyone generally well, except for Helga's expectant condition and for Laura, who faced surgery to correct a "wandering eye." Too bad I wouldn't be there to soothe her fears.

At the airport, after sharing final hugs and kisses, I marched onto the plane with feigned courage, wondering how I could do this to my family and to myself again. I almost turned around and stayed home, but a sense of duty or mission, not fear of the consequences, kept me going.

This moment confirmed stronger than ever that war is harder on family members than on soldiers, mentally, emotionally, and spiritually. A feeling in the form of words seeped into my soul: "Your family is not alone. I will be with them." And it was so. Take Laura's eye surgery for example. She was operated on at Hill Air Force Base soon after I departed. Afterward, Helga stayed with her every moment in the recovery room.

"Where is the nice man who was holding me?" Laura asked upon awakening.

"No one was holding you, dear. I've been here beside you the whole time," said Helga.

"But, Mommy, I was so scared, and a nice man came and held me in his arms, and I wasn't scared anymore," Laura said, adding that she had felt overwhelming love and comfort in her "visitor's" arms. Laura recalls those wonderful feelings vividly. Helga and I believed this was confirmation that I wasn't leaving my family alone; He was with them.

At the top of the Salt Lake Airport boarding ramp, I turned for a last sight of and wave to my dear family. I didn't think I could bear it, and I wondered irrationally if it were possible for Helga and the children to hurt as much as I did.

During the flight to San Francisco I swallowed my woes and recalled why I had volunteered to return to Vietnam and to our much-maligned soldiers who were serving faithfully there. A few hours later, at Travis Air Force Base near Fairfield, California, I was booked on a flight scheduled to depart early the next morning. It was delayed until the following evening. I used the delay to attend church meetings, and accepted a dinner invitation to the home of Lewis and Karen Madsen. Over dinner I discovered that Lewis and Karen were good friends of Dallas and Joan Murdoch from their dental school days. In addition to feeding a homesick and Vietnam-bound soldier and stranger, the Madsens also treated me to a telephone visit with Helga and the children.

My assigned seat on the commercial charter flight to Vietnam was on the aisle about halfway back on the right. In the center seat next to me was Lieutenant Colonel Richnak, the same who had been my platoon leader in the 287th Military Police Company, Horse Platoon, in Berlin in 1954–56. I quickly confirmed recognition of Richnak with a glance at his name tag. Richnak seemed even more surprised than I that we were on the same flight in adjoining, assigned seats. We reminisced during much of the flight. Richnak seemed nothing like the spartan, reserved, aristocratic young lieutenant who had commanded the horse platoon fifteen years earlier.

Our flight, having departed America the evening of March 2, arrived at Bien Hoa Air Base in Vietnam the afternoon of March 4. We had skipped a day as we crossed the international time zone somewhere west of Hawaii.

*   *   *

Surprisingly, Vietnam was not nearly as hot as I remembered and expected it to be, coming as I did almost directly from deep winter in the Rocky Mountains.

We replacements were hustled off to in-process at Camp Bravo, 90th Replacement Battalion, Long Binh. Then, in company with the handful of chaplains who arrived on the same flight, I went to the USARV Chaplain's Office to receive my assignment. This was a very anxious moment. Would I get my first wish, the 1st Air Cav? If not, then my second wish, another infantry division?

At USARV Headquarters, on Long Binh post, the Deputy USARV Chaplain welcomed us, gave us a pep talk and, finally, told us our assignments: "We've had several calls and written requests from the USARV Commander's office and the Chief of Staff of the 1st Cav. The Cav wants you back and that's where you're going. But it is not what we had in mind for you. You shouldn't have tied our hands by politicking for a specific assignment."

"There was no politicking," I assured the deputy. "I simply responded honestly to a three-star general when he asked me if I wanted to return to the Cav." I thought it unnecessary to mention my petitions to God, as I didn't consider praying the same as politicking. Nor did I describe how enthusiastically I responded to General Tolson's query about my wishes.

On March 6, at Camp Radcliff, An Khe, I began in processing to the 1st Cav. Why, I wondered, did replacements for the division still come through Camp Radcliff? Radcliff had been turned over to the 173rd Airborne Brigade (or was it the 101st Airborne Division?) after the 1st Cav moved north to participate in the 1968 Tet Offensive battle at Hue and other locations. Now the 1st Cav was operating in its new AO to the north and northwest of Saigon in III Corps, well south of Camp Radcliff and the Central Highlands.

The commandant of the orientation school gave me the option of attending or skipping a three-day combat orientation the 1st Cav provided for new troopers, because I was a "sandwich." Soldiers like me who returned to Vietnam for a second or a subsequent combat tour with the 1st Cavalry Division were called sandwiches because we were authorized to wear the big yellow and black Cav patch on each shoulder. By Army regulations, a soldier ever after is authorized to wear on his right shoulder the identifying patch of any unit with which he or she served in combat, while wearing the unit patch of his current assignment on the left shoulder. Thus, after a combat tour with the 1st Cav, during subsequent assignments with the 1st Cav one could wear the distinctive, "horse blanket" shoulder patches—like slices of bread—one on each shoulder. I opted for the orientation period because it would give me time to begin acclimating to the heat and humidity and to explore old haunts.

Camp Radcliff had the lonely, ghost town–like feel of a schoolhouse during vacation. The camp had bustled day and night when the 1st Cav was here. Now much of the camp was abandoned and some of it seemed on the verge of being reclaimed by the jungle.

I wandered around the camp between rappelling practices and booby trap demonstrations. First I visited what had been the 15th Medical Battalion area on the east-southeast end of the main flight line. The hooch I'd built in 1966 still stood, but no one occupied it. The old 2nd Battalion, 8th Cavalry area was vacant and overgrown. The PX no longer existed at the site where I once faced down a sergeant who tried to deny access to my troopers and me. Pleasing to the eye was the continued presence of the gigantic 1st Cav patch in yellow and black on the side of Hon Cong Mountain. A fellow replacement, LTC Ivan Boon, was pulled out early from the orientation course to replace LTC Peter Gorvad of Oakland, California. I'd soon become better acquainted with Lieutenant Colonel Boon. Gorvad, whom Boon replaced, had been killed the previous night when an enemy 122mm rocket with a delayed fuse exploded in his tactical operations center (TOC). This death occurred during an NVA assault on the 2nd Battalion, 12th Cavalry (2–12 Cav) firebase at an old abandoned French fortress that we called LZ Grant. More than 250 NVA died in the attack.

Alan Syndergaard of Mount Pleasant, Utah, and a door gunner on an LOH (pronounced loach) for Apache Troop, 1–9th Cav, said that after daylight following the attack, he counted 287 NVA bodies—some still showing signs of life—scattered outside the wire around LZ Grant (from *Headhunters*, edited by Matthew Brennan, Presidio Press).

From other sources, I heard that an American listening post (LP) was caught among the NVA outside LZ Grant that night. Shortly after first light, a "grunt," the only surviving member of the LP, attempted to walk into the perimeter. One source said the soldier was small and badly burned, and had been mistaken for an NVA soldier by one or more grunts on the perimeter. A hail of automatic fire cut him down and snuffed out his life as he drew near, after all he'd just gone through. Alan Syndergaard said that a soldier had waved to his LOH from a hole near where all the dead NVA were. The LOH radioed LZ Grant that an American was coming in. However when the guy reached the wire, "shots rang out and he collapsed to the ground. Two guys ran out and pulled open his shirt. He was wearing a crucifix."

On March 9, I reached 1st Cav Headquarters at its latest and last base camp in Phuoc Vinh, about thirty-five miles north of Saigon. There I got the word. "You are going to an infantry battalion, the First Battalion, Fifth Cavalry (1–5 Cav)."

The Division Chaplain received me well, but the Deputy Chaplain, Lieutenant Colonel Frank (assigned alias) reiterated the USARV Deputy Chaplain's accusation that I politicked to return to the Cav. "You will regret returning to the Cav," Chaplain Frank promised me.

The 1–5 Cav battalion would have two chaplains for about a month because Captain Henry Lamar Hunt, Assemblies of God, was staying on until his imminent promotion to major. Combat action was light in the 1st Cav area of operations (AO), insisted the personnel in the Division Chaplain's Office.

It being Sunday, and not having any pressing duties, I located the LDS Group Leader, Captain John Thomas Kalunki, who was the Assistant Division Information Officer (DIO). I attended a service with him, at which I spoke by invitation. Colonel McPhie, an Air Force combat pilot and the ecclesiastical head of the LDS organizations in the Southern Military District of South Vietnam, was present at the services. Also in attendance was a Sergeant Kapule, recently of the elite Army parachute team, the *Golden Knights*, and currently with the 101st Airborne Division.

I spent the night of March 9 with my nephew Pfc. Earl Dyer, my sister Billie June Ramage's eldest son. The next day I reported to the 1–5 Cav field trains in the big 25th Infantry Division base camp at Tay Ninh. Upon arriving, I drew essential field equipment and spent a night under intermittent rocket attacks. Over the next year rockets or mortars exploded on the Tay Ninh Base every time I was there, some quite close to me.

On March 11, I arrived at the 1–5 Cav combat trains on LZ Dolly. Dolly was situated atop Nui Ong, a north-south razorback ridge that rose above the Michelin Rubber Plantation on the east and southeast and jungle on the north and west. From the ridge one could see the Nui Bau Din or Black Virgin Mountain, about twenty-five kilometers to the west. The Black Virgin and razorback were the only prominent elevation features in the western sector of the 1st Cav AO.

When I arrived at LZ Dolly, Bravo 1–5 was fighting down below in the Michelin Rubber. The company was so near we could have seen the action, but for the foliage. At 1435 hours, the second platoon of Bravo 1–5 attacked a bunker complex where it had pinned down three or four NVA.

Between 1618 and 1627 hours, Bravo 1–5 was mortared while it attempted to medevac its casualties. Three minutes later and for the next twenty-seven minutes, the Bravo 1–5 forward operating base (FOB) took heavy fire from three sides, resulting in two friendly WIAs, George Densely and Gary Jolliff.

While Bravo 1–5 fought on, I met Chaplain Hunt, then reported to the battalion operations officer and requested permission to join Bravo Company.

"Not until you meet Colonel Peterson," he insisted. LTC Robert J. Peterson and his executive officer (XO) were in the air over the battle.

By mid-evening Bravo 1–5 had broken contact with the NVA and settled in for the night—a quiet one, the battalion operations officer expected.

About 2000 hours, Lieutenant Colonel Peterson received me cordially. "You know what to do. Get to work. To receive a max OER [Officer Efficiency Report], all you have to do is walk on water," Peterson said, tapping the 1st Cav combat patch on my right shoulder.

Well, it was too late to get to work, so Chaplain Hunt and I got acquainted. He briefed me on his arrangement for area support that he had with Chaplain Hugh Black of the 2–12 Cav. The Army applies the principle of area support to distribute assets across unit lines. Area support is applied most often because some requirements, legal support for instance, are so specialized that the cost of placing such assets in small units would be prohibitive. The same is true of denominational (Catholic, Jewish, Baptist, etc.) religious support. Chaplains provide essential religious support, but each chaplain is an ordained clergy member of a particular religious denomination. Baptists can't conduct Catholic Mass, nor can Catholics conduct Protestant communion services. Consequently, most chaplains support one another across unit lines.

In accordance with this principle, Hunt provided Protestant support for the 2–12 Cav and Black provided Catholic support for the 1–5 Cav in return. I liked this cross-pollinating arrangement and opted to continue it, though I called my support "General Christian support" rather than Protestant. Black and I would usually pass back and forth at will between our two battalions, which usually worked quite well for both of us. Some chaplains preferred to coordinate more closely and even travel together.

* * *

The next day, March 12, Chaplain Hunt suggested I go to Bravo Company. "I don't think B Company is going to have contact today," he opined. He would go to Charlie Company, which he thought was much more likely to see action. Again, I accepted Hunt's suggestion, but dismissed his estimation of the situation; my senses were humming. I could almost feel the sensations of close combat.

At 1410 hours, I hopped a chopper to return to the infantry on the field of battle, eighteen months after leaving Bravo 2–8 Cav on the Bong Son Plain. My arrival in the field had been delayed much of the day because Bravo 1–5 had returned to the area of some of the fighting that had occurred the day before; intense enemy fire promptly pinned down the first and second platoons. Two soldiers died and four were wounded before the platoons could disengage.

When I reached Bravo 1–5 about 1440 hours, the company was in its FOB [forward operating base] among the rubber trees, and preparing to return to where it had fought that morning. From the open chopper door as we swept down past the treetops, I studied the squad of sky troopers who were securing the temporary LZ. Each of their young faces appeared exhausted, wary and old, and each set of eyes appeared to stare a thousand meters beyond us.

My feet hit the ground the moment the skids of the chopper did. Quickly, I moved off in the direction that one of the grunts pointed. Two rows of rubber trees later, I passed a line of log- and sandbag-covered foxholes, each with a couple of troopers sitting nearby. Drawing nearer, I noted their uniforms were black-streaked and soaked with sweat. Obviously, the troopers had recently fought in a burned-over area. Fifty feet farther, at the command post (CP), I easily picked out the company commander.

Approaching Captain Robert Bailey, I began to introduce myself. We were still shaking hands when an excited message blared over a nearby PRC-25 field radio. The message came from a 1–9 Cav scout ship that was flying nearby, part of a two-ship team that consisted of a Low-level Observation

Helicopter (LOH) and a Cobra gunship (or Snake)—a pink team. "Gooks on the bunkers. They're sunbathing," radioed Apache 28, the light observation helicopter (LOH) pilot. "We're taking fire!"

"Our LOH is down at [map coordinates]!" radioed another voice, the pilot of the Cobra. The LOH and its three-man scout crew were down less than a klick from our position. Time: 1445 hours. I'd been back in the war on the ground for less than five minutes.

Immediately, Captain Bailey ordered two platoons of troopers to move out to rescue the scout crew. I joined the rescue and we moved out to the south without our rucksacks. The grunts moved through the rubber plantation on-line (side-by-side) toward the crash site, with Bailey, the platoon leaders and me in a second line about ten to fifteen feet behind them. Here we were heading almost certainly into a fight, and other than Captain Bailey, I didn't know a name or face. We moved out less than eight minutes after I jumped off the chopper.

Meanwhile, at 1505 hours, Lieutenant Colonel Peterson radioed that he had spotted the wreckage of the LOH from his Charlie-Charlie (Command and Control, or C&C) helicopter, with the crew nearby and apparently unhurt.

We quickly covered about half a kilometer, moving easily and at a steady pace through sparse undergrowth beneath the rubber trees—the trees were evenly spaced in rows that were about twenty feet apart.

About 1519 hours, in company with the leaders, I stepped onto an east-west running dirt road and had made it about halfway across the road when the troopers on-line stepped warily past the first row of trees on the south side. Ahead, two rows of trees deeper in, the ground was obscured by fallen, leaf-covered tree branches, as though the branches had been knocked off the trees during earlier fighting, *or intentionally knocked down to conceal something*. My nerves were tingling. Surely, hell would break loose at any moment.

Hurrying on across the road, I reached the first of the downed branches. That's when the NVA opened fire at us.

The first burst of AK-47 rounds cracked past me on both sides as I, on the way to the ground, glimpsed muzzle flashes directly ahead. By the time I reached the ground, several other AK-47s had opened up, joined a moment later by two enemy 30-caliber machine guns.

Right behind the incoming machine-gun fire, NVA snipers opened up on us from the trees. The sniper fire was quite distinct. It came in single shots and was harder on the nerves. It seemed more personal than the automatic fire because I knew each shot was probably aimed at a specific target. Fortunately for us, the snipers were too far back to have much effect.

Notwithstanding combat experience and already anticipating what to expect, for a moment the ambush almost overwhelmed my sense of purpose, coming so suddenly as it did, about twenty minutes into a year-long combat tour.

Sp4 John Bezdan Jr., whose name I learned later, returned M-16 automatic fire at the most immediate threat to the two of us, the automatic weapon that had fired the first burst of the engagement. From twenty feet in front of me, Bezdan fired straight ahead at a concealed fighting position two rows of trees to his front. As I watched from my prone position, Bezdan fired around the trunk of a small rubber tree. Quickly, he emptied a twenty-round magazine in two or three bursts. Then he shifted to his left side to better extract another magazine from a pouch on his right side. His weapon reloaded, Bezdan raised onto his left knee, apparently in an attempt to get a better shot at the NVA in front of him. Quickly, he swung the barrel of his M-16 around the right side of the tree and tracked toward the enemy bunker. A shade faster, the NVA fired. Bezdan's body was flung backward and to the left, with a fist-size chunk of muscle and other tissues torn from his inner right thigh area.

Indescribable shock accompanied the instant realization that I was nearest to Bezdan and he needed help fast, and that rendering that help would probably cost me my life, for he lay wounded in clear sight of the gunner who cut him down. I hadn't been back in combat long enough to be prepared for this.

"Why me," best describes my first impulses. Still, after a moment of hesitation, I began low-crawling toward Bezdan, and promptly got my pistol belt snagged on a root or twig. Awkwardly, taking care not to rise too high, I unhooked and wiggled out of my load-bearing suspenders and belt. While I got unstuck, Sp4 Henglier, the platoon medic, slithered past on my right (he moved on his stomach fast enough to shame a Tennessee blue racer snake). "I've got him, Chaplain!" Henglier called as he scooted past. Word of the new chaplain's presence was spreading.

Henglier, still on his stomach, was examining Bezdan's wounds when I reached their position. Off to the left front I saw Sp4 Robert Lewis, a Kentuckian, low-crawling toward the NVA position. From about halfway between us and the NVA position and a little to the left, he threw a grenade at the machine gun and followed it with a long burst of M-16 bullets. While Lewis suppressed the NVA, Henglier and I each grabbed one of Bezdan's shoulders and began dragging him back toward the road. At the edge of the road, we bandaged his wound as best we could before pulling him across it.

All this activity with Bezdan was accompanied by the continuous din of heavy volumes of American and NVA small-arms and machine-gun fire, punctuated by the distinct chatter of at least one body-shredding NVA 51-caliber. Distinct over all this noise was the dreaded thump of enemy mortar shells leaving the tubes. Luckily for us, the first barrage of mortar shells exploded harmlessly near the company CP rather than in our exposed position. The second barrage, though aimed at us, fell short and caused us no grief.

North of the road, we set about solving the problem of how to quickly retreat with a trooper too badly wounded for a shoulder-carry. Scrounging around on his stomach, a trooper found a single stout pole about ten feet long. The medic and troopers were stumped for a moment; in their experience, a makeshift stretcher required two poles and a poncho or two jungle-fatigue blouses.

The Army belt buckle by chance or design was useful for more than holding up a soldier's pants. So turning on my right side, amid warnings to "Keep down, Chaplain," I removed my standard brass-buckled Army issue belt. Then, after borrowing another belt from a nearby trooper, I laid the pole long ways over Bezdan's body. Then, with the two belts hooked together, I bound Bezdan's chest to the pole. Catching on fast, the troopers used all the belts necessary to secure Bezdan to the pole, from head to foot.

With Bezdan secured to the pole, we were ready to withdraw, but we'd never survive running upright unless the intense enemy fire was suppressed. To keep the enemy off of us, Air Force jet fighters attacked. One after the other, the jets screamed across our front at treetop level from west to east and strafed the NVA with what sounded like mini-gun and cannon fire. Concurrently, artillery pounded the NVA positions farther back. The fighter planes at one hundred feet away roared so loudly that it was hard to distinguish bursting artillery and the ripping blasts of mini-guns and aerial cannon fire.

At 1650 hours, we reached the company FOB without taking more casualties. A lot of thanks for this goes to the danger-close fire support provided by the Air Force fighters, the gunships of Apache 1–9 Cav and ARA (aerial rocket artillery), and tube artillery. This time I arrived soaked in sweat and covered in black soot, just like the soldiers I'd studied two hours earlier. At 1720 hours, we loaded Bezdan and Sp4 James T. Freeman onto a waiting, idling medevac chopper. Bezdan was going home, alive if not quite whole.

Introductions within Bravo 1–5 seemed anti-climatic after what we'd just been through, but Bailey and I completed them anyhow. Then he introduced me to his CP members and lieutenants.

Lieutenant Colonel Peterson, who had landed for a face-to-face conference with Captain Bailey, looked me over and nodded his head approvingly. "All right, my new chaplain walks on water," his eyes seemed to say.

But I was feeling anything but elated. Yes, I was glad to be with the infantry and I felt accepted already, and thankful I had been of some assistance with Bezdan's rescue and care. But I wondered: *How can the grunts keep up with this? How can I? I've had it after two hours, but they've been in action and taking casualties continually for three or four days*. Bravo 1–5 had already sustained two killed and eight wounded this day. Sp4 Robert E. Spires of Tewksbury, Massachusetts had died of gunshot wounds to the head and stomach, and Pfc. James A. Gazze of Chicago, Illinois had died of gunshot wounds to the head.

For their actions in the fight, I recommended Henglier for the Silver Star and Lewis for the Bronze Star with "V" for Valor. They each got their awards. Henglier was Catholic and a conscientious objector, willing to serve, but not to bear arms. He really deserved the Silver Star. He and I would visit often over the next months.

About a month later Lewis became one of only two troopers who were, to my personal knowledge, bitten by a poisonous snake in the reptile-infested jungles of Vietnam. We had found a bamboo viper hanging over the entrance to an NVA bunker. A trooper cut off the snake's head. Lewis picked up the head and it bit him. He lived.

One of the heroes that first day (name withheld) was part of Secretary of Defense Robert McNamara's "Project 100,000." This project was a plan—or special ploy—that made it possible to meet draft quotas by allowing many mentally "below par" Americans to fight and die for their country while others enjoyed student deferments from the draft because of their good grades in college.

Instantly, I respected, admired and loved these troopers in the 1–5 Cav. I'd known these men in the 2–8 Cav, only the names and faces were new.

In most other ways, though, things were different. The society we served had changed; the support we received was different. The enemy was different. Even 1st Cav tactics and equipment had changed. Not all equipment changes were for the better. Notable improvements included the LOH chopper as replacement for those fire-prone death traps called H-13 helicopters, and the modified M-16 rifle, which was less prone to jam and had a muzzle flash suppressor that was less prone to get tangled in vegetation.

For a while this first day, I wondered if I could endure another year, especially if the first hour was any indication of what the year held. That first night I found peace of mind and spirit by reminding myself anew that I was here precisely because everything was different, and because it was worse. I was in the right place to serve these troopers, God's beloved sons, sons so much condemned, neglected and maligned by much of America. But they were obedient sons, all the same, and each one of them laid his life on the altar of sacrifice for a nation that had turned its back on him, from most appearances.

Renewed determination welled up in me as I remembered why I was here, and that the safest place for me was where I was most needed. *To keep going, I must remember why I am here.*

Anyhow, the events of the first two hours certainly cut short the period of "feeling one another out" between my new men and me. Already, the officers, sergeants and troopers appeared to accept me as completely as I'd ever before been accepted.

By the way, we rescued the helicopter crew. The three-man crew of the scout bird simply followed the sound of shooting and linked up with our right flank, without being shot by us in the process.

A minor casualty of the day was my new hunting knife. I'd returned to Vietnam with an expensive Buck knife, only to lose it in the first hour. It was on the load-bearing equipment (LBE) I wiggled out of during Bezdan's rescue. Perhaps my Buck knife brought joy to some NVA soldier.

At 1945 hours, the second platoon, which had just set an ambush 150 meters from the FOB, detected heavy movement and spotted several NVA on every side except the one nearest the FOB. The platoon pulled back and artillery pounded the area. Nearby at the same time Delta 1–5 Cav reported rockets being fired from near its position toward the town and base camp at Dau Tieng. Charlie 1–5 received five 82mm mortar rounds at 2110 hours, and five minutes later about fifteen NVA approached one of its Second Platoon ambushes. Two of the approaching NVA soldiers spotted a claymore mine that the troopers had put out. One of the NVA picked up the mine and the two were examining it when a Charlie 1–5 trooper squeezed the detonator, or klacker as the men called it. There was little left above the chest of either of the two NVA.

The next day, March 13, about 0825 hours, two Bravo 1–5 platoons and the CP moved south. The plan was to go south a short distance, turn east and then north to reenter the area of one of the firefights that had occurred the day before, the area where the two troopers were killed. I moved with the company CP group.

Fifteen minutes later we came onto a freshly buried NVA soldier. After ascertaining what the grave contained, we moved a little farther south-southwest and turned due east.

As we moved, two NVA soldiers paced us from the front, keeping about two hundred meters between them and us. The troopers fired sporadically at the NVA, who simply jumped behind a rubber tree each time until the shooting stopped. These were definitely not the sly, elusive VC and NVA of the 1966–67 days. *We'll not be sneaking up on the enemy today*, I thought.

We turned north after moving eastward a few hundred meters. That's when American artillery began bursting ahead of us. Bravo 1–5's artillery FO walked the exploding shells ahead of us as we advanced northward on a wide front. He kept the rounds bursting near enough to us that shrapnel rained on and around us, but far enough away to avoid cutting us down with shrapnel flying directly out from the bursting shells. In this way we hoped to catch the NVA while they were still in shock from being on the receiving end of heavy artillery. The strategy might have worked, as we reached our objective without receiving enemy fire.

We came to an east-west road, probably the same one I'd become so intimate with the day before. In the middle of the road lay the rucksacks where troopers had dropped them during one of the earlier fights the previous day. Though it didn't seem logical to assume that the NVA had withdrawn, many troopers sighed with relief at the sight of the apparently undisturbed rucksacks.

Captain Bailey established his CP beside a bomb crater, one that had taken out the north side of the road. The Second Platoon spread out east of the bomb crater and settled down along the north side of the road to await orders.

Things were not as they appeared. I suspected the NVA had left the GI rucksacks alone to lull us into a false sense of security, to get us to drop our guard; a successful ploy as it turned out, intentional or otherwise.

Something else bothered me. It seemed the ground north of the road was almost obscured by downed tree branches, presumably freshly blown off the rubber trees during the earlier artillery barrage. But the ground south of the road was almost bare of freshly fallen branches. I suspected that branches might have been moved from the south to camouflage something to the north. If Bailey took my concerns seriously, he didn't show it.

The guys in the CP were too bunched up, so to put some distance between the CP and all those antennas, I walked east along the road, greeting resting troopers as I went. Sp4 Eiker was among the troopers I met and greeted. About twenty-five yards from the Company CP, I stopped and visited with Platoon Sergeant and acting Platoon Leader Gene Nuqui.

Orders cut short my visit with Nuqui at 1118 hours. Bailey ordered Nuqui to sweep his platoon on-line straight north from the road. Without hesitation, the men moved out as ordered. Nuqui and I moved about five feet from the road and stopped when Sp4 Eiker, fifteen feet in from the road and twenty feet to our left, signaled us to hold up. He had almost stepped on a well-camouflaged bunker. Eiker pulled the pin from a CS tear-gas grenade, cocked his right hand low and backward and leaned forward out of sight. *He's throwing the grenade into a firing slit of a bunker*, I correctly deduced. Eiker never finished the toss.

A burst of 30-caliber machine-gun fire nearly cut off one of Eiker's legs at mid-thigh. He fell, terribly wounded and pinned down just inches beneath the flaming muzzle of the machine gun. The NVA machine gunner must have fired a sweeping burst because his first volley also shattered a medic's shoulder and wounded another trooper. The medic ran wildly back past the bomb crater in which the CP was already taking cover, and thus avoided being pinned down. The second wounded trooper fell beside Eiker, as did two unwounded troopers. A split second later enemy fire opened up all along the road.

Sergeant Nuqui and I reacted instantly and reflexively, but slightly differently to that first burst of machine-gun fire. Nuqui dropped flat where he stood, while I dived forward amid cracking AK-47 rounds to take advantage of the meager protection and concealment offered by a small rubber tree.

It was instantly obvious that my reaction served me poorly, for while it gained me meager concealment and protection, it also halved the distance between an enemy soldier and me. The dive also put a small clearing between the road and me, and machine-gun fire was raking that clearing.

From the other side of the clearing, Sergeant Nuqui took stock of my predicament. "Here, Chaplain," he said, tossing a CS grenade next to my left hand. Then, unknown to me, he belly-crawled with most of his platoon to the south side of the road, leaving me behind.

Very carefully and as quickly as I could, I brought the smoke grenade near my face, pulled the pin with my right hand, and lowered the grenade to my leg to prepare to toss it. As I tossed the grenade, an AK-47 fired a burst from about ten feet in front of me and three rounds cracked past my left ear. I saw the muzzle flashes of the AK-47, but not the NVA soldier behind them.

Seconds later, partially concealed by a CS gas cloud, I scurried backward to the road on my stomach, feet-first. I made it unhurt, despite the NVA fire that continually swept the clear area I had to cross.

Once into the roadbed, I spun around and, crawling head-first, quickly caught up with Nuqui and his platoon on the south side of the road. He and his troopers were hugging the ground behind the fence post–size rubber trees and an occasional termite dome. Except for those pinned down with Eiker, and the CP, which was pinned down in the crater, I was the last one on the right flank to withdraw across the road. Enemy machine-gun fire continually raked the rim of the bomb crater into which the whole CP group had disappeared when the shooting began.

At 1206 hours, 82mm mortar rounds started thumping from tubes several hundred meters to our southeast. Simultaneously, Nuqui and his men leaped up and ran westward parallel to and about two rows of trees south of the road. I thought we were running to flee the mortars, which made no sense becuase the shells could just as easily be targeted on where we were headed as where we had been.

Though I ran as fast as I could, bringing up the rear, something much faster pursued me. Over my right shoulder I saw a line of dirt geysers overtaking me; I had an NVA machine gunner's undivided attention!

I knew that hitting the ground probably wouldn't save me, for the machine-gun rounds were striking low. Looking frantically ahead, I spotted a small hump of earth, a termite hill, between two trees. Increasing my speed, I dived, twisting my body in the air as I did so to offer the machine gunner a smaller target. Almost as if in slow motion, I watched the approaching geysers, doubting I would reach cover before hot bullets tore into me. But I made it, barely.

As I sailed and dropped behind the eighteen-inch-high

mound, I saw plugs of wood burst first from the tree on my right and then from the tree on my left, as bullets tore through them and stitched across the face of the mound which protected me.

Meanwhile, that first barrage of enemy mortar rounds, the one which panicked the troopers I was with, landed near the company FOB. Four shells also burst near us, but caused no casualties.

Pinned down but unhurt, I at first thought the mound I was behind offered the only protection from the machine gun for at least twenty yards in any direction. Soon, though, I discovered I could move in the depression between the rows of trees, provided I stayed on my stomach.

Across the road, beneath the hot barrel of the machine gun that had fired at me as I ran, Eiker's unwounded buddies struggled to administer first aid and to keep him and the other wounded trooper alive. A few meters from them in the bomb crater, Captain Bailey and the CP group tried to follow and get control of events via PRC-25 radios. Enemy machine-gun fire had quickly dissuaded most of the CP group of any ideas about eyeballing the scene or evacuating the bomb crater. Fortunately for the CP, Army of the Republic of Vietnam (ARVN) Sergeant Van Nie was not dissuaded.

The following details I learned later. Sergeant Van Nie, in the bomb crater with the CP, repeatedly risked instant death by popping his head up to check the area around the bomb crater. Following one such "peek," Van Nie gestured wildly to the northwest and yelled, "Beaucoup GI! Beaucoup GI!"

Captain Bailey and the artillery forward observer (FO) at first thought Van Nie was trying to give their position away— after all, we were the GIs. "But the Gooks already know where we are," Bailey told himself, and ventured a quick look, just in time.

Seemingly from nowhere, twenty-five NVA infantrymen were advancing on the CP in the crater. Van Nie opened fire first and an NVA fell. The FO dropped another, and the NVA retreated, the element of surprise having been lost.

Help arrived quickly. ARA choppers and gunships came on-station and began taking some of the pressure off us by pounding the NVA with 40mm grenades, rockets, and mini-gun fire. Artillery commenced pounding the area farther to the north. Air Force fighters arrived ready to help. However, we couldn't bring all these supporting fires near enough to be immediately effective because Eiker and his buddies provided an unwilling shield for the closest NVA.

Meanwhile, the First Platoon remained north of the road and west of the CP group during the fight, sustaining friendly WIAs in its efforts to rescue Eiker and his buddies and protect the CP.

My hands were quite full helping with the wounded, so I missed some of the details of Eiker's eventual rescue. It went like this: At great calculated risk to itself and the grunts with Eiker, an ARA chopper hovered in "danger close" and placed a rocket just behind and almost on top of the NVA machine-gun position/bunker. Then, while the troopers of the First Platoon concentrated fire on that bunker and on others that were more exposed because much of the concealing foliage was blown away, one of Eiker's buddies pulled the pin from a fragmentation grenade. Carefully he released the handle to activate the time-delay detonator, counted off the seconds, and then slipped the grenade through the firing slit. The grenade exploded before the NVA could throw it back out. The machine gun was silent after that.

With the enemy machine gun out of commission, the First Platoon pulled back, dragging Eiker and his buddies with them, protected somewhat by an umbrella of aerial rocket and mini-gun fire. Right behind the last of the First Platoon, the CP group escaped from the crater. A rocket exploded on the north rim of the crater just as the last CP member went over the south rim. That's how close we were bringing in the suppressive fire.

Eiker and the other wounded troopers were brought to my location. We stabilized Eiker's flapping leg and attended to the other troopers' wounds. A medevac chopper arrived above the trees to hoist Eiker out, but withering NVA gunfire thwarted the attempt. So Peterson braved the bullets to hover over us in his command and control chopper (Charlie-Charlie) long enough for the door gunner and crew chief to kick out stretchers, some of which hung out of reach in the trees. Thus, with our wounded, we withdrew and left the NVA to the pounding of artillery and air attacks.

It is hard to estimate how long the fight lasted. It seemed like hours. According to official records, the shooting started within seconds of 1118 hours. The CP was still pinned in the crater an hour and thirty-seven minutes later, at 1255 hours. Probably the engagement ended after about two hours. Amazingly, we sustained no friendly KIAs, but easily could have, as events proved.

According to a report I read a few days later, a company of 25th Infantry Division Armor killed some 120 NVA in a tunnel, the exit of which was at the spot where Van Nie first saw the 25 NVA soldiers who attacked the Bravo 1–5 CP in the crater.

Subsequent intelligence revealed that Bravo 1–5 had for two or three days repeatedly bumped into the weaker points of an NVA regimental position. The NVA position was horseshoe-shaped, with the open end of the horseshoe to the west, and defenses around both the inside and outside of the horseshoe. The stronger defenses were presumably on the outside.

Bravo 1–5 maneuvers the day before had taken the company north-to-south past the tip of the north prong of the horseshoe, and into the soft inside of the southern tip. The next day, we'd again maneuvered south past the northern prong of the horseshoe-shaped position, turned east between the prongs and then north into the jaws of a trap.

One can easily imagine our fate had we hit the harder outside of the NVA position, or if Eiker hadn't prompted the NVA machine gun to open fire before the Second Platoon passed the first line of enemy bunkers and fighting positions. Had we gotten farther in among the NVA, the tunnel exit would have been between the rest of the company and us, which would have allowed overwhelming numbers of NVA forces to engage us at such close quarters that outside help would have been impossible.

My instincts had been reliable. Surely, the NVA had left the GI rucksacks in place to lure us in, and had gathered the downed tree branches south of the road to conceal their positions, clearing fields of fire south of the road in the process.

About mid-afternoon, back at the company FOB, it occurred to me I'd been back in combat less than twenty-four hours. A lifetime.

Following a quiet night, Bravo 1–5 moved out to the northwest the next morning, March 14. In the order of march, I was just ahead of the CP group in the lead platoon. We were leaving the Michelin Rubber Plantation, and good riddance. Along the way, we passed a dead NVA soldier. He was about twenty feet off to the left of the path. One of the troopers said Bravo 1–5 had killed the NVA three days earlier. It was amazing how much the NVA soldier's remains had decomposed in so short a time. His torso appeared to be melting and blending into the ground.

A few hours later and a few kilometers farther, the rubber trees abruptly gave way to jungle. Ahead, the trail continued in a northwesterly direction, intersecting a path that went south and disappeared into a draw. The lead platoon turned south along the new path. Suddenly, just as I reached the intersecting path and started to turn south, three bicycle-mounted NVA soldiers came zipping along from the northwest.

The NVA reacted almost too quickly to follow. With practiced moves, they leaped from the bikes while drawing AK-47 rifles from scabbards on the bikes, and sprayed us with bullets. Just as quickly the three abandoned their bikes and disappeared into the brush.

I hastily backtracked toward the CP as troopers moved

forward and blasted the vicinity where the NVA had disappeared. Moments later after the CP moved to the south and against a line of trees on its west, a trooper next to me fired an M-79 high explosive (HE) round. He intended to fire over the tree line and at least harass the evading NVA. His aim was slightly off. The grenade exploded against a tree limb almost directly above the CP Group. A radioman (RTO) caught a piece of shrapnel through the muscle between the thumb and forefinger of his right hand.

After confiscating the NVA bicycles, we moved a hundred feet to the south and set up an FOB. There, beneath heavy foliage, I conducted my first worship service since returning to Vietnam and my first service with an element of the 1–5 Cav.

Late that afternoon I caught a chopper back to LZ Dolly, where a very apologetic Chaplain Hunt waited. Actually, he'd seen action, too. Earlier in the day the NVA had attacked while he conducted a worship service. The enemy quickly broke off the attack because it had mistakenly assaulted the Charlie and Delta Companies of the 1–5 Cav in their two-company position, thinking they were attacking a CIDG (Vietnamese home guard) unit—this according to the confessions of an enemy prisoner of war (EPW or POW).

Hunt continued with the worship service following the aborted attack. Unlike Hunt's experience that day, I never in two years of combat had a worship service interrupted by an enemy attack.

The next day, March 15, I began making rounds to become acquainted with the other units of my new battalion. About noon Chaplain Hunt and I flew from LZ Dolly down into the rubber trees where Charlie and Delta Companies were co-located on an FOB. The companies were preparing to begin air assaults, each onto a different company objective in the jungle. Chaplain Hunt introduced me first to the Delta 1–5 commander, then to Captain Jim Cain of Charlie 1–5, after which I stayed with Charlie 1–5 for the air assault while Hunt returned to LZ Dolly.

Charlie 1–5 air assaulted into a small clearing in the

jungle about two kilometers northeast of LZ Dolly. We came in behind an impressive barrage of tube and aerial artillery. The LZ was green, meaning we received no unfriendly fire. Within minutes of being inserted, the men of Charlie 1–5, all unfamiliar faces to me, had formed up and pushed north and deeper into the jungle. Almost immediately, we found ourselves in a massive, recently-vacated bunker complex.

Captain Cain called in a report on the bunkers and the company pressed on, leaving the complex for others to investigate and destroy. We had contact about 1630 hours when our point man met the point man of an NVA element and they blasted away at each other. We sustained no casualties and saw no sign of NVA casualties.

We stopped an hour later to dig in for the night and I began my foxhole at a spot about five meters or so from where the radiomen were digging in—digging my own hole reinforced my credentials with these men. The FO, Lieutenant Bill Haines, approached me as I dug in. He introduced himself and offered to share a two-man hole with me.

I noted that these troops, like the ones in Bravo 1–5, dug in differently now than had those in 1966 and 1967. First, Cain selected the site of the FOB, a different and more difficult process in the trackless jungle than it usually had been in the more populated areas around Bong Son—areas where land features, rice paddies and villages offered points of reference.

With the FOB site chosen, the platoon leaders promptly sent out cloverleaf patrols to sweep a hundred meters or so in front of their respective sectors of the perimeter. Each cloverleaf patrol went forward a specified distance. Then each patrol turned in the same direction, right or left, and looped back to the perimeter; by this means the patrols usually, but not always, avoided running into one another.

With patrols under way and OPs going into position, it was time to dig foxholes. Every trooper switched back and forth between guarding the perimeter and digging. Each NCO and officer who was not otherwise occupied with vital duties took his turns at pick and shovel. Enough holes had

B Company 2-8 troopers departing on a combat assault from which five grunts would not return, near LZ Santa, Dec. 22, 1966.

Chaplain Newby in front of his bunker, LZ Dolly, spring 1969.

Sp4 Walter Robiston Jr. (Preacher) and Chaplain Newby back in the security of base camp after being ambushed and pinned down along Highway 19 between An Khe and the infamous Mang Yang Pass, Central Highlands, June 23, 1967.

Sixteen-year-old Bau, a Vietcong soldier, surrendered early in the morning to the troopers of B Company, 2nd Battalion, 8th Cavalry, 1st Cavalry Division. April 15, 1967, on the Bong Son Plain.

Chaplain Newby in the jungle.

A wounded B Company 1-5 trooper covered with and surrounded by rucksacks for protection against an impending air strike, War Zone C, May 17,1969.

Terrence Brain of Pasco, Washington, points to a bullet hole in his helmet, LZ Dolly, winter 1969. (Photo courtesy of Terrence Brain)

Pfc. Michael Doughterty, D Company 2-1 (retired NYPD), nurses the ankle he sprained the previous evening while retrieving the body of a fallen comrade.

Chaplain Newby before his one-poncho rain shelter in the jungle, Christmas 1966.

Sgt. Tony Cruz, A Company, 1-5 Cav (center), died in Chaplain Newby's arms, September 1969.

ARVN interpreter, with back to camera, has just shot a conical hat off the head of the child to make her talk. A few minutes earlier, we captured the child's mother, a confirmed VC, but her father escaped.

Montagnard family pauses for pictures as it moves along Highway 19, Central Highlands, February 1967.

Sp4 Walter Robiston Jr. at the spot from which a few minutes before another trooper shot himself in the face and missed hitting Chaplain Newby by about a foot. Central Highlands, July 4, 1967.

A group of nine soldiers. Chaplain Newby is sixth from left.

Troopers of D Company, 2-8 Cav, one of whom is the legendary Sgt. Roy Baumgarner, just after presenting Chaplain Newby with the "Aussie" hat he is wearing. Greenline, An Khe base camp, Central Highlands.

Chaplain Newby's wife, Helga, on R&R with the author six weeks after the death of their infant daughter, Suzanne Marie. Off Honolulu, August 1969.

Deadly waters. Light spots on the side of the well bear witness to the booby-trapped bucket that killed Pfc. Daniel Nelson an hour earlier. The unidentified grunt is a member of D/2-8, Bong Son Plain, May 30, 1967.

An NVA captive, wounded the previous midnight while within "whispering" range of Chaplain Newby, left behind by his comrades in a hammock, with chieu hoi pass and AK-47 in hand. War Zone C, June 1969.

Infantryman of C/1-12 Cavalry at careful rest. This grunt's company was decimated within two hours of Chaplain Newby's snapping this picture, Bong Son Plain, May 31, 1967.

to be quickly dug to permit every man a place under cover from which to stand and fight, if necessary. After the fox-holes were dug in relative silence, the men filled sand-bags—each trooper carried a few empty bags in his rucksack for this daily protective routine. At each foxhole, once the sandbags were filled with dirt from the excava-tions, the men stacked a few bags at each corner of the fox-hole and put the remainder aside for later use. Then with holes dug and sandbags filled, noise discipline was relaxed enough to permit the troopers to chop down small trees (my favorite digging-in task) for overhead cover. Next, short wooden crossbeams were laid across the stacked bags at each end of the hole and four to six long poles were laid across these. Finally, the remaining sandbags were laid across the logs. Thus, in an hour or so almost every day, we dug five-foot-deep fighting positions and constructed overhead cover for protection from mortar, artillery and rocket bursts, including overhead bursts in the trees. After dark, ambushes were set and listening posts (LPs) replaced observation posts (OPs). The dissimilarities between how we now dug in 1969 and how we had dug in 1966–67 re-flected the differences in the war itself. We were definitely in a different kind of war on this, the fifteenth day of March, nineteen hundred and sixty-nine.

Notes

2 March 1969, 1–5 Battalion Journal: A Co WIAs 1LT Cecil Harrison, Sp4s David Witte, Richard D. McCoy, Ralph L. Froehner, Thomas N. Schenvert and D. Knox.

8 March 1969, 1–5 Battalion Journal: 1000, B Co WIA Sp4 Jack S. Keyes, c/a. 1315 B Co WIAs Pfc Wilbert Ford and Pfc. Roy Hudson, claymore.

9 March 1969, 15 Battalion Journal: A Co WIA Aniline, eye. C Co, Appendicitis—Allen Niedwell.

11 March 1969, 1–5 Battalion Journal: B Co WIAs George Desley or Dealey RA52338083 and Gary Tolliss.

12 March 1969, 1–5 Battalion Journal, item 36 cont'd: "[B Co] proceeded into yesterday's contact area . . . 26 element was into

area 50 meters before being pinned down . . . 16 element came in
from north and pinned down after 100 meters . . . 02 US KIA and
04 US WIA." 1505: "B Co at 1445 hrs, reports Apache 28 finding
bunkers with enemy in area . . . Apache 28 reports low bird has
been shot down . . . GM-6 spotted downed bird . . . crew seems all
right because GM-6 sees strobe light 30 meters from downed bird.
B Co is moving into area of downed bird." 1520: "B Co taken
under fire from flank and front." 1525: "B Co at 1520 hrs are now
pinned down . . . enemy on both flanks, firing from bunkers and
fighting positions." 1535: "B Co still receiving fire . . . flanks and
front . . . B Co maneuvering to link up with crew of downed bird."
1650: "B Co has linked with down bird crew at 1540 . . . [crew]
neg injuries." 1650: "B Co has broken contact at this time and is
headed for their FOB." 1650: "B Co request medevac for 02 EM
at 1650 hrs." 1730: "B Co reports knocked out machine-gun
bunker . . . their 35 did it, he [Lewis] crawled within fifteen feet of
bunker and threw frags . . . confirmed 02 NVA KIA." 1945: "B
Co 26 element was moving from FOB to ambush loc, when
spotted 4 to 5 indiv and heavy movement on both flanks, 150
meters from FOB." Casualties today: B Co KIAs—Pfc. James
Gazze and Sp4 Robert Spires; WIAs Pfcs. Jan Bingel, gsw back;
John Bezdan Jr., gsw leg and testicles. Sp4s WIAs were James
Woodall, gsw side and arm; and James Goggins, gsw foot. Charlie
1–5's WIAs were Sp4 Harold Curtis, frag arm, and Pfc Jool P.
O'Kula frag to leg. Delta 1–5's WIAs, were James Sargent, frag
head; and Samuel Hunter, frag head, and James Freeman, frag eye
[shown also in B Co with Sp4 David Bowers, frag. wd. leg].

13 March 1969, 1–5 Battalion Journal, 0840: "B Co has dug up
grave . . . will move into yesterday's contact area."

0846: "spotted 04 NVA 75 meters to the south . . . two carrying 50 cal. B Co has one squad maneuver and rest laying low."

0930: "B Co . . . spotted 2 more individuals, 150 meters to
S.E. . . . area is full of bunkers . . . two contact areas are all one
bunker complex."

1005: "B Co is in contact area . . . thinks this is large complex."

1120: "B Co is in contact . . . 02 US WIAs. B Co will pull back
for arty . . . then proceed to objective." 1145: "B Co 26 element is
pinned down by 30 cal, fire from bunkers 20 meters [actually 20
feet] to their front . . . others flanking 26 element on left. 26 is
trying to pull wounded out. B Co is completely surrounded &
awaiting arrival of ARA." 1206: "B Co FOB is receiving

mortars." 1210: "B Co is receiving mortars in contact area." 1215: "B Co is being flanked to the N. E. Believe they killed 2 or 3."

14 March 1969, 1–5 Cav Battalion Journal, 1013: "B Co is in contact with 03 individuals 45 meters away, running, 3rds returned fire, riding 03 bicycles . . . fork, bamboo on bicycles to carry weapons . . . One WIA, hand, no name."

March 1969, 2–12 Cav Operational Report: On the morning of 8 March Company D's PO/LPs around LZ Grant picked up heavy movement. Shortly after that LZ Grant received a heavy rocket, mortar and recoilless rocket attack, followed by a heavy ground attack. During the mortar attack a 120mm mortar hit the TOC, killing the Bn. Co., LTC Gorvad, the Assistant Operations NCO, the LNO, and one RTO. The round also wounded the Intelligence Sergeant, the Operations NCO, and one other RTO . . . Operations Officer, Major Brown assumed command . . . [105 and 155 batteries on Grant] fired 1400 rounds . . . both direct and indirect fire . . . mortar sections of C and D Companies fired over 1000 rounds of 81mm mortar. Spooky and Blue Max provided additional support. Contact broke at 0530 hrs. . . . 150 NVA KIA, 2 NVA/WIA/PW . . . Friendly losses were 15 US/KIA and 31 US/WIA.

March 1969 1–5 Cav Operational Report: 15 Mar C Company captured POW w/AK-47. When the company's 2nd Platoon blew its ambush, killing one or two of his companions, the POW ran toward company's F.O.B, and was tackled. He was a medic with the 7th NVA Battalion, 29th Regiment.

12 April, 0900, 1–5 Battalion Journal: "B Co requests medevac for Sp4 Robert Lewis, snake bite."

thirty

Best Combat Soldier I Ever Saw

Robert W. (Bill) Snyder

On March 15, Captain Cain and I got better acquainted while we dug in. He, upon learning I was LDS, pointed to a large, sweating trooper who was digging a machine-gun position on the eastern side of the perimeter. "See that man? He's a Mormon, Bill Snyder, and the best combat soldier I ever saw," Cain said.

Casually, I approached Pfc. Robert William Snyder and his machine-gun team, all of whom were shirtless, except Snyder. His fatigue shirt was off, but he wore what appeared to be two green tee shirts. Knowing Snyder was LDS, I applied my keen intellect and I deduced the "tee shirt" next to his skin was actually a religious garment, covered reverently by a regular tee shirt, despite the added heat and discomfort that prompted others to shed every item of clothing they could.

"Hello. I'm your new battalion chaplain," I greeted Snyder and his buddies, concealing my specific interest in Snyder. We went through the usual pleasantries—names, hometowns, days left on short-timer calendars. When Snyder, in turn, said he was from Springville, Utah, I responded, "Mormon country. Are you a Mormon?"

"Yes, I am," responded Snyder, with that combination of confidence and absence of sanctimoniousness of voice and demeanor that I'd hoped for.

"Are you a good Mormon?"

"I try to be," Snyder answered.

"Fine! I'm LDS too," I declared as I again reached out my hand.

"Great!" he said, his countenance beaming like a lighted

Christmas tree. "Now I can write my folks and tell them something good. Now I can receive the sacrament."

Bill Snyder had been in combat for several months and was the only man of his faith in Charlie Company so far as he knew. After promising Snyder that we'd share a two-man sacrament service the next day, I returned to finish my foxhole. It was too near nightfall to have the service then. Little did I anticipate how hard it would be to keep my promise to Bill Snyder, nor the impact his life would have on mine.

A 1–9 Cav scout LOH reconnoitered around our position while we dug in. Soon the LOH pilot alerted us to large stacks of ammunition boxes and probably a bunker complex about 150 meters to our southwest. Exploitation of the information would have to wait for another day, as Cain did not want our patrols to go out that far so late in the day.

It was 2300 hours and the night was pitch-black beneath the triple-canopy jungle. I slept on my partially inflated air mattress beside my foxhole with my head toward the hole. In an instant, I awakened standing upright in my foxhole. My reflexes had carried me faster than my mind could register what had awakened me. The blast of a claymore mine had shattered the night. The chatter of Snyder's M-60 machine gun and of several M-16 and AK-47 rifles shattered whatever was left of sleep. Green tracers snapped across the FOB and exploding hand grenades punctuated the din the automatic weapons were raising.

Men on an ambush out beyond Snyder's position had pressed the detonator, blowing a claymore mine on about ten NVA soldiers. The NVA had stumbled onto the ambush about a hundred feet from me, and some fifty feet beyond Snyder's position. The NVA soldiers' reflexive return of fire showed combat experience and discipline, especially considering that they were walking wounded, as we learned later.

The shooting stopped as quickly as it had begun and someone yelled from Snyder's three-man foxhole, "Gook in the perimeter!" Two NVA soldiers, probably in considerable confusion, had charged straight at Snyder's machine gun. One fell dead in front of the machine gun, and the other one ran past Snyder into the perimeter and threw himself to the ground near Platoon Sergeant Raymond Clark. I heard Clark whisper, "Who's there?"

Silence. . . .

Clark, sensing a presence in the pitch-black darkness, lunged with both hands at where he thought the presence was. One hand clamped onto a head and the other to an AK-47 rifle. "I've got him! Help! I've got him!" Clark yelled. The bewildered NVA soldier surrendered without a fight. Clark and a trooper soon had him searched and tied up, ready for interrogation and evacuation, come the dawn.

The POW said he was part of a group of walking wounded, all dazed survivors of an American bomb strike, and that they had been en route to an NVA field hospital when they stumbled onto our position. We had unintentionally dug in for the night on the eastern edge of an NVA bunker complex that combined a hospital with an ammunition cache.

On March 16, dawn arrived with more shooting, and another NVA dead and two enemy prisoners of war in hand. Sergeant Thomas Eugene Hoover of Dayton, Ohio was either on an LP, not likely considering his rank, or on dawn patrol when he and two other troopers engaged two NVA soldiers about twenty meters outside the northwest perimeter. I arrived on the scene moments later and found one dead NVA soldier and the troopers standing over a seriously wounded one on which a medic worked to staunch arterial bleeding from a mangled thigh. I stopped the bleeding with a combination pressure bandage–tourniquet, using the NVA soldier's own belt.

From their expressions, the troopers disliked my choice of wound bindings—NVA belt buckles made prized war trophies. Later, before the wounded NVA was evacuated, I noticed someone had replaced the belt with a bandanna. No Americans had been hurt in the brief engagement.

Soon, a chopper arrived and took the two POWs off our

hands. We quickly broke camp and moved a few meters to investigate the ammo boxes and bunker complex that the crew of the 1–9 LOH had reported the evening before.

Immediately, the troopers discovered hundreds of mortar and rocket rounds, all in boxes above ground, and all bearing Chinese markings. For the rest of the day the troopers hauled in munitions from all over the area. Army engineers and the press arrived, the engineers to blow the enemy munitions in place and the press to follow the story of the day.

By late afternoon the troopers had finished collecting and stacking scores of boxes of munitions. The finished stack was roughly squared, thirty feet on each side and as high as a one-story building. After the grunts stacked the munitions, the engineers laced C-4 explosives all through the stack and connected the charges to each other with detonating cord. Finally, the engineers ran the det-cord a thousand meters westward into another section of the NVA bunker complex.

While the stacking and lacing were going on, we searched the bunkers closer at hand, which included a forty-bunker hospital complex, side-by-side with munitions bunkers. From one bunker I collected my only trophy of the war, a Bic pen, which prize I justified taking because it was made in America. Later during the tour I would reluctantly comply with a personal request by a friend to bring him an NVA pith helmet.

In one of the hospital bunkers I saw rare examples of NVA personal taste—fresh-cut flowers on a table and a calendar on the wall that had the current date scratched off.

With the munitions pile ready to blow, I followed the detonating cord along a freshly beaten path toward the bunkers where we would take shelter from the anticipated explosion. An engineer was in the lead and an infantry lieutenant was behind me. We passed a trooper, as skinny and bedraggled as any soldier I ever saw. He stood in deep grass at a point where the detonating cord made a slight turn to the left. As the engineer approached, the skinny, slouching trooper said, "Don't step on the det-cord."

The engineer responded, "That's all right, troop. You won't hurt the det-cord."

"Makes no difference, Sad Sack. You keep doing what I told you. Keep people off the det-cord," ordered the lieutenant from behind me.

Dutifully, the trooper advised me to not step on the det-cord. I stopped before him and extended my hand with, "Hi, I'm Chaplain Newby, your new chaplain. What's your name?"

"Sad Sack," he said in a voice every bit as beaten as its owner appeared to be.

While suppressing the mental image of the trooper's sagging body being held upright only by the grime in his uniform, I said, "I'll not call you Sad Sack. What is your true name?"

"Private Rodriguez." Was it my imagination, or did Rodriguez's shoulders straighten just a bit at the use of his own name?

"What's your first name?"

"Ronaldo," the trooper said, though the record reads Ronald.

"I'll call you Ron, for short. Is that all right with you?"

"Yes, sir," Ron answered with a slight smile.

I continued along the route marked by the det-cord toward the NVA bunkers. Once out of earshot of Ron, I asked the lieutenant why he had the trooper performing an unnecessary task. "Because," he answered in effect, "we can't rely on Sad Sack to do anything important. So we look for stuff for him to do, things that won't get others hurt."

Later in the day, after what I considered adequate time for reflection and tactfulness, I challenged a couple of leaders to see what would happen if they started addressing Rodriguez either as Ron, by his last name, or by his rank and last name. "Besides, Ron sees through busy work. I wish you would stop giving it to him," I said.

One of the leaders reacted defensively at first, then agreed to call "Sad Sack" by his name or rank. Perhaps it was my imagination, but Ron looked better, more soldierly, whenever a leader called him by his true name, during the few months he had left.

A few minutes later in an NVA bunker, I placed my helmet on the head of a newswoman, moments before an engineer hit the detonator. The resulting explosion was nothing like the fantastic bang we anticipated. Rather, the placed charges detonated with just enough force to scatter the stacked munitions and render them more dangerous for the grunts to re-collect, which they of course had to do. The Charlie 1–5 troops used the remaining daylight to re-stack enemy munitions. Meanwhile, another day had passed without Snyder and me getting together as I promised.

It rained hard in the late afternoon, which was rare for the season and made for a wet, uncomfortable night in the same FOB we'd used the previous night. I again shared a foxhole with 1st Lt. Bill Haines, the son of four-star General Ralph Haines, Commander-in-Chief of all the American Forces in the Pacific, including us in Vietnam. Bill Haines and I got along quite well during the short few months we were together off and on. His parents invited Helga and me to use their guesthouse in Hawaii for R&R, but the timing didn't work out.

On March 17 I moved on, leaving the troopers of Charlie 1–5 to finish re-collecting and stacking the enemy munitions. Though I was elsewhere when it happened, the engineers did the munitions demolition job right this time, so I was told.

Though I wanted to remain with Charlie 1–5 and have that service with Snyder, I felt I had to move on because there remained first visits and worship services for three other companies in my battalion plus all the companies in the 2–12 Cav. Fortunately, Chaplain Hunt had held services for Charlie 1–5 five days earlier. The troopers were so busy and scattered that I couldn't even locate Snyder to explain the delay in having a sacrament service.

During the period of March 16–26 I visited the rest of the companies in both battalions and got reacquainted with

Lieutenant Colonel Boon of the 2–12 Cav. I was almost constantly on the move and was with units during a couple of fights. My closest call during this ten-day period was probably an incident that occurred in the battalion field trains (rear) area at Tay Ninh. Shouting awakened me there late one night. An intoxicated trooper, one I'd met several days earlier in the field, was waving a loaded M-16 and threatening to kill anyone who messed with him. As I was the only officer on the scene, I approached the trooper very slowly and calmly said, in essence, "Look, I'm your chaplain and I don't want to hurt you, but I can't let you hurt anyone else either."

He blustered for a moment, then handed his weapon to me. I passed the weapon to the sergeants, who put the trooper to bed under watch. I don't think anything else ever came of the incident.

On March 20, we got an impressive demonstration of armor against infantry. The engagement began as an operation to rescue a long-range patrol (LRRP) team. The LRRPs (H Company, 75th Rangers) were pinned down and hard-pressed by a very large NVA force in the jungle near the northeast edge of the Michelin Rubber Plantation.

In preparation for the rescue operation, half of Alpha 1–5 air assaulted in and linked up with a mechanized company of the 11th Armored Cavalry Regiment. While Captain Hurt (alias) placed Alpha 1–5 in a skirmish line between the armored personnel carriers (APCs) and tanks, facing west, one of the five M-60 tanks in the force quickly cleared a field of fire by knocking down a swath of trees around the contact area. Then with the men on-line between them, the five M-60 tanks and eight armored personnel carriers charged ahead to rescue the rangers.

Unfortunately, the tankers demonstrated little appreciation of the difficulties that the downed trees presented for infantry on foot. Soon, the tanks were well out in front of the struggling foot soldiers—a big mistake.

The NVA made their presence known just moments later, at 1300 hours, after the tanks had charged beyond the

LRRP team. Concealed in bunkers and spider holes, the individual NVA soldiers had let the tanks pass over them. Then, before our guys could catch up, the NVA popped up and fired rocket-propelled grenades (RPG) into the soft rear grills of the tanks. Farther back, other NVA took the grunts under fire from behind.

Sergeant Mario Grisanti of Tyler, Texas describes part of what happened next. "We were assaulting a bunker complex on-line. This was the only time I ever worked with an ARVN unit. The ARVN soldiers were interspersed between Americans as we attacked on-line. Ahead of us the tanks were also attacking on-line. An ARVN soldier on my right pointed ahead at an NVA soldier behind a tree and said something in Vietnamese. At that point it became one of those slow-motions deals. I remember slowly bringing up my weapon, firing on full automatic. Even the recoil was in slow motion. I hit the NVA in the chest and watched him throw a chicom grenade as he fell. Then I watched the grenade as, slowly trailing smoke, it arced up and down, bounced, and rolled right between my feet, where it exploded," said Grisanti.

"I wasn't unconscious very long, but when I woke up I was completely paralyzed. And I was aware that my legs were all wet—I thought they were shattered. Someone pulled me behind a tree and a medic came and I could feel his hands when he cut my pants' legs off using a sapper knife that I'd taken off a dead sapper. I kept asking the medic how my legs were and he kept shaking his head and saying something that I could not hear. I interpreted his shaking head to mean my legs were gone. Finally, he . . . lifted my head and made me look at my legs," said Grisanti.

"I never had a scratch. My legs were wet because the shrapnel had hit the American on my right and blown apart his canteen, splashing water all over my legs. I thought my ears were bleeding. They weren't. After about fifteen or twenty minutes, feeling started coming back. The next day, hearing started to return."

Meanwhile, the tanks and their crews were generally less fortunate than Grisanti. Within minutes of beginning the attack, four of the five tanks were burning, total losses, and the fifth tank had a track blown off. A burning tank swung about and attempted to withdraw, running headlong into a bomb crater in the process. The tank came to rest with the barrel of its cannon resting across the rear rim of the crater, the way a soldier on guard might rest his weapon on the berm of his foxhole.

The LRRPs were rescued alive. Alpha 1–5 sustained one killed and nine wounded. An NVA soldier shot Sergeant Victor D. Kahla Jr. of Texas while he, John Gayman, and some others were checking bunkers and fighting positions that had been bypassed by the armor. Kahla was shot from inside the bunker when he leaned down to toss in a hand grenade. The NVA who shot him died quickly at the hands of Kahla's angry buddies. Kahla was alive when he was evacuated from the field, but died later in the day. The mechanized unit sustained eight men killed and thirty wounded, in addition to losing four of their five M-60 tanks. The withdrawing enemy left the bodies of seventy-two NVA. Several NVA soldiers were captured.

While half of Alpha 1–5 was engaged in the action described above, the other half was in action with tanks elsewhere. Of the other action, Tom Holcombe said, "Kimbrough and I dug some NVA soldiers out of caved-in bunkers and took them prisoner. This we did after Rex Storey had seen them behind us after we had passed them. . . . Rex Storey pulled several NVA soldiers out of a bunker and took them prisoner."

"This was the easiest clearing of bunkers we ever did. The tanks would drive on top of a bunker and pivot back and forth until the bunker was collapsed. Then we would literally dig the enemy out with our shovels," wrote Platoon Leader Lieutenant Steven A. Holtzman of Agoura Hills, California.

Trooper David J. De Leon of Alpha 1–5 became a "delayed" casualty during the night after the fighting ended. His platoon was in position on-line about fifty feet from the barrel of the tank cannon, the one that fell into the bomb crater. Sometime after midnight, a flechette round cooked off in the breech of the cannon on the burning tank. De Leon, who was lying barely exposed on his side or stomach, caught one of the steel flechettes (arrows) in one of his lower cheeks.

From the air the next morning, I saw a freshly-beaten trail along the edge of a bomb crater to the north. It looked like hundreds of pairs of feet, many wearing BF Goodrich sandals, had beaten a retreat from the area during the previous night.

About an hour after I joined with Alpha 1–5, we climbed atop the APCs and one remaining tank for a very unpleasant ride out of the rubber trees to the southeast. This ride took us into an area where Rome Plows (giant Army road graders) had cleared away several acres of jungle. These jungle-clearing operations were executed to deny enemy forces the concealment they had to have in order to stockpile war supplies and to assemble in preparation for attacks against us and other lucrative targets like Saigon.

On the way to the clearing we passed through an area that had been seeded with persistent CS (tear) gas powder. The tank and APC treads stirred the CS powder into billowing clouds of tearful misery for us. Crying silently, we survived the best we could.

Once out of the gassed area, I got a bright idea. By rolling down my sleeves one turn at a time, I uncovered consecutive strips of gas-free cloth with which to wipe some of the gas-impregnated dust from my face and eyes. Pretty soon the other troopers were following my example.

Pleasant relief waited ahead. A cool, swift, deep stream ran northeast to southwest through jungle near the north edge of the clearing. The men of Alpha 1–5 went swimming, led into the water by their company commander. They were taking advantage of the security provided by the 11th Armored Cavalry Regiment (ACR). After his swim, an officer went about his duties for an hour or so wearing only his jungle boots, steel helmet, and holstered pistol on a web belt—not an impressive picture.

Sergeant Elvin Jackson of Fremont, Utah, whom I'd just met, wanted a bath as much as anyone else, but he and I held back until most of the troopers finished with theirs. Then we went upstream a hundred feet or so and found for ourselves a pool that promised at least the illusion of privacy. After looking around to be sure we had no unwelcome company, I stood guard with Jackson's M-16 while he bathed and washed out his religious clothing. Then we switched roles.

Following the baths, we gathered the company and held a memorial service for Kahla. I'd already decided to hold memorial services in the field, at company level, as soon as practicable after a soldier fell, rather than to wait for larger services in the rear, as had been the common practice in 1966–67. This policy turned out to be wise because during this tour there were no opportunities for larger-unit services in the rear.

The company commander spoke at his own request during the service and by a poor choice of words he seriously damaged his credibility with the troops. He said something like, "We're sorry Kahla was killed, but we made the SOBs pay for it with seventy-two of their own."

When the captain said this, I sensed an almost tangible wave of anger sweeping through the assembled troopers. Eyes turned cold and faces hard. Sp4 Rodney J. Linn, machine gunner, interrupted his captain. "No way does seventy-two Gooks 'pay' for one grunt, for Kahla," he declared. Later he said, "After the memorial service you came to us, Chaplain, and calmed us down. 'Don't do what you guys are thinking,' you advised us."

The general feelings were that *the old man doesn't care about our lives.* That was too bad. The captain probably meant well, intending only to console the men and perhaps boost their spirits. After all, a ratio of 72 to 9 was impressive as body-count comparisons go. And this time the enemy never got away unhurt, as so often seemed the case; usually we fought at times and at places of the enemy's choosing, and seldom knew how badly the enemy was hurt. But what the troopers heard the captain say was, "Your lives mean nothing to me."

Perhaps with time the captain might have gained the hearts and loyalties of the men in Alpha Troop, but judging from officer and enlisted comments thirty years later, it never happened. Phil Gioia replaced Hurt as Company Commander of Alpha 1–5 soon after I arrived. Captain Joseph A. Davidson (Hurt's predecessor) had established the unoffical position in his company of "pace man." Without reference points, it was very difficult to know one's exact location in the featureless jungle. This made it very difficult to call immediate and accurate artillery and air support early during a contact with the enemy. The lack of exact map coordinates always multiplied the risk of friendly-fire casualties. Consequently, Captain Davidson designated Terrence M. Brain of Pasco, Washington, as his pace man. Brain, standing well over six feet tall and always smiling and friendly, literally counted steps as the CP moved through the trackless jungle from a known to an unknown point. He also served as an ex-officio bodyguard to his commander.

Brain came to his duties as pace man via a very hazardous route. He explained it this way: "I was a fairly new guy and walking point for the first or second time with Smoky [Herb West, according to Rod Linn] behind me teaching me what to do. We were taking a break when I spotted three NVA coming along the trail. They hadn't seen me. I alerted Smoky and he said, 'On my signal, you rise up and fire twenty and dive left. I'll stay low, fire twenty and dive right.'

"Smoky gave the signal, a tap on the shoulder, and we executed the plan perfectly. A fraction of a second later, the NVA answered us with a hail of bullets straight down the trail between Smoky and me.

"Calls from the rear, 'What's going on?' Some guys hurried forward to help without being asked. CO sent patrols forward, about twenty meters to the left and right of the trail.

[The patrols] went forward, crisscrossed the trail and back down the opposite side . . . reported lots of blood ahead.

"CO asked if we wanted to continue in the lead to check out the contact area. 'We spotted them, so we'll lead,' Smoky and I agreed.

"As we moved forward beside the trail, he whispered from ten feet behind me, 'Don't look at the ground. Look straight ahead and left and right. Use peripheral to check the ground. If you see something on the ground that way, then feel for it with your hand and bring it up to your eyes, but keep your eyes up and moving.'

"That way, I spotted . . . tracer and regular rounds and while looking ahead brought them up and whispered to Smoky what I had [found]. . . . Handed them behind me to Smoky without taking my eyes off the front and flanks. . . .

"Again, from about ten feet behind me, Smoky cautioned, 'Keep your eyes up. Be careful, Terry. We're getting close.'

"A moment later, something, like a voice, said to *dive for that tree*! I pulled the trigger and dove just as a hail of fire swept the spot I'd just vacated. Slow motion. Hit the ground hard. Awful pain in my stomach area. . . . Thought I was hit four times in stomach. Became aware of massive fire from my left . . . caught in cross fire. One moment the sixty-pound pack on my back was knocked to the left by a bullet and the next it was knocked to the right. That was one of two times that I had my pack shot to pieces on my back.

"I kept firing magazine after magazine, figuring if I was firing the NVA would not shoot at me. Two machine guns came forward [Rod Linn and Darrell Thompson] and laid down fire on both sides of me, leaving me a lane about three feet wide to pull back. Pretty sure Rod Linn was one of the machine gunners.

"Someone called, 'Brain, are you hit?'

"'Yes!'

"'Check yourself out and see how bad it is.' I felt my chest and stomach. Nothing. Sure thought I'd been hit bad, though.

"By rising to a squat, I made a 180 [degree turn] and

pulled back under cover of the machine guns. Smoky wasn't hit either. Don't know how he survived.

"After all that had happened, I was told I could stay in the FOB while my squad went on ambush. I borrowed a poncho liner (mine had been destroyed along with everything else in my pack) and went on ambush about where I'd been ambushed earlier—the company had moved forward of the ambush site before it stopped for the night."

Brain would be wounded at least twice, once before becoming pace man and again months later. He described the first action this way: "By order of the CO, I took a squad and linked up with a mechanized unit of the 11th ACR. I'm riding the lead APC with my RTO and the rest of the squad is spread out on other tracks. We'd been told how far to go along this road, and when we passed that point, I told the armor master sergeant—track commander—that we'd gone far enough. He said, 'There is lots of daylight. We'll go a little farther.'

"Right after that, I pointed out to the sergeant that smoke rounds were popping on the road behind us. That's when they hit us with mortars, machine guns, AK-47s, and B-40 rockets. The APC driver swung the track off the left side of the road, spun it around and brought the front end back onto the road, at which point in place and time it took a B-40 rocket to the front. The blast took off the track commander's fingers.

"About the same time, a mortar round exploded nearby and knocked me and my RTO off the track. On the ground, and me unarmed, we huddled next to the long horizontal piece of rubber that runs outside the top of the APC track. Again I got one of those premonitions, warning to get lower. I'd just gotten flat and pulled the RTO down beside me when a machine gun stitched that rubber mudguard from end to end. Obviously, the NVA were all around us.

"A crewmember dropped the rear gate on the APC long enough for the RTO and I to scramble inside—didn't like being inside, but had little choice.

"A tremendous volume of NVA fire was coming in. Could hear rounds hitting all over the APC and expected a B-40 to explode inside any moment. Decided to get my M-16 off the top of the vehicle. I reached up through the open hatch and felt around, then raised up until my helmet and eyes were barely out of the track [hatch]. I got hold of the M-16 and, with the barrel pointed straight up, started to withdraw into the vehicle. That's when I felt and heard a loud explosion or bang and felt a tremendous shock to my head and face. A bullet had hit my helmet right on the rim, next to my right eye. The bullet deflected upward and tore a gash in my helmet and helmet liner. I remember being in the APC after that, but I don't remember getting out of it or anything else until later in the day at the 15th Med. They kept me on the firebase for about five days because I blacked out every time I moved or stood up quickly.

"Soon after that, when we were on LZ Dolly, Clemens— just remembered that name—said the CO wanted to see me. Captain Davidson wanted me to be his pace man—to keep track of his position in the trackless jungle, so we could get close artillery and air support quickly when we needed it, without getting it on our own heads. Davidson was a wonderful commander. I loved him. He wanted me to attend the University of Missouri and play football . . . promised to pull strings to get me on the team. . . . I got wounded and that ended that," concluded Terry Brain.

Rod Linn, by the way, didn't seem to be a troublemaker, despite his angry remarks during the memorial service for Kahla. Rather, he seems to have been one who felt very close to his buddies. Thirty years after Vietnam, Linn retains an exceptional memory for names and details. At least two of his leaders describe Linn as the best machine gunner they ever saw. Linn has the same high praise for a fellow machine gunner, Darrell Thompson, who does not appear in the journals or company roster in my possession. Linn said, "Darrell was wounded up north about July 1968 by mortar fragments in the shoulder."

Darrell Thompson shared a close encounter of the odd kind with Lieutenant Steve Holtzman during the latter's first fight with the enemy, sometime before the action on March

20 with the tanks. Holtzman describes what he thought happened. "I was 3–6 [platoon leader] and we had the point. Three Gooks ambushed us. . . . I dropped my ruck[sack] and hid behind it for a while until I realized it would not protect me at all. I then moved . . . behind a tree for cover. Inside my ruck I carried a framed 5×7 picture of my wife, an air mattress . . . etc. . . . the picture had a line of holes across it and the mattress was destroyed." Thirty years later he learned what really happened while attending a 5th Cavalry reunion. At a motel in Peoria, Illinois, "Rod Linn asked me if I recognized some guy he was talking to—neither of us recognized each other. It was Daryl [Darrell?] Thompson, the other M-60 gunner from Third Platoon. He doesn't remember much—sort of like I was ten months ago. Thompson asked me, 'Remember when I shot your pack up?' "

"Why didn't you tell me?" Holtzman asked.

"You don't tell your lieutenant that you almost shot him unless you're very stupid," Thompson replied.

"It seems the ruck was lying next to a log that Daryl tripped over and as he stumbled, he squeezed the trigger," said Holtzman.

Meanwhile, back in Vietnam at 1140 hours on March 24, Alpha 1–5 got into a fight and sustained three KIAs and nine WIAs. Though Rod Linn names Johnny Ray Parker of Idabel, Oklahoma as one of the KIAs, he also says, "The KIAs were machine gunner Monty Gilbert Lackas of Columbus, Nebraska; his assistant machine gunner Corporal Joseph Schimpf of Philadelphia, Pennsylvania; and Ken Richie of Sandusky, Ohio, as I recall."

Earlier in the day, Charlie 1–5 sustained nine WIAs and Delta 1–5 sustained one. Later in the day, Delta 1–5 had three more troopers wounded when the NVA mortared its FOB.

The next day I found Bill Snyder on LZ Dolly. His company was pulling firebase security for a week. Firebase security duty was usually safer than being in the field, especially up on the razorback ridge where LZ Dolly was. While the duty was usually safer, it wasn't always easier, for the grunts spent most of their days patrolling, filling sandbags and hardening defenses; and their nights on perimeter guard, LP duty and ambush. Well, Snyder and I decided to have the sacrament meeting we'd been trying to hold, only to postpone it until the next morning because we could not find an LDS trooper named West who also wanted to share the sacrament. The delay seemed reasonable and practical. After all, we expected Snyder to be relatively safe and available for the next few days—LZ Dolly had never been attacked by ground forces and seldom received rocket or mortar shells, probably because of the difficulty involved in targeting the LZ there on the razorback ridge. I flew out to conduct services and spend the night with Bravo 1–5, intent on returning the next morning for the service on LZ Dolly.

Sounds of explosions and heavy volumes of small-arms fire shocked me awake at 0410 hours on March 26. Bill Snyder wasn't so "relatively safe" after all.

The NVA launched a B-40 rocket attack on LZ Dolly in preparation for a sapper attack. The sappers (demolition engineers) prepared for quick penetration of the perimeter by sneaking in close, taking advantage of soldiers' natural tendency to be lethargic at that hour of the morning—especially in "secure" areas—and by securing defensive trip flares with rubber bands to keep them from igniting. With the flares secured, the sappers snipped concertina wire, then crawled through and waited for the rocket barrage. Simultaneous with the rocket barrage, the sappers tossed satchel charges over the perimeter bunkers, probably intending to cause the men on guard to take cover inside the bunkers by making them think that mortars had zeroed in on them.

The next five satchel charges went into perimeter bunkers, including the one where Snyder slept. Meanwhile, two sappers charged toward the battalion TOC through their own hail of B-40 rockets. About the same time, other NVA soldiers captured a live, dazed trooper on the perimeter and tried to pull him out through the wire.

Snyder had been sleeping in the back of a perimeter

bunker when the attack began, with some of his buddies lying between him and the entrance to the bunker. His buddies, including his assistant gunner Donald Forest—who had been wounded a few days earlier—died in the blast and collapse of the bunker.

Elsewhere on the perimeter, battle-hardened troopers quickly recovered from their initial shock and killed the sappers, including those assaulting the TOC. They also rescued the trooper who was being dragged through the wire, and killed his would-be captors in the process.

With all the NVA inside the perimeter dead, Captain Cain hurried to the perimeter to assess the damage. There he found Bill Snyder surrounded by dead buddies in the midst of a collapsed bunker. Snyder, face toward the jungle with a weapon in hand, was straining to hear any sound from outside the perimeter. He appeared to be blind.

Heroics had been in abundance during the attack. Chaplain Hugh Black from the 2–12 Cav received the Silver Star for his actions there during the attack. He was there to provide Catholic support to my troopers.

A chopper plucked me out of the Bravo 1–5 position shortly after first light. Captain Cain was waiting for me. "Claude, Bill Snyder *got it* last night. He's blind. They medevaced him to Tay Ninh."

Most of the wounded had been evacuated to the hospital in Tay Ninh by the time I reached Dolly, so I went to where the dead were laid out. There I prayed, meditated and said goodbye to our dead, including one we thought dead who wasn't. Then I went looking for Lieutenant Colonel Peterson.

"Sir," I recommended, "it would help the wounded and the men here, too, if you visited the hospital ASAP." Peterson was hard pressed, I knew, but I had to reach the wounded, especially Snyder, for I was feeling very guilty that we'd postponed that sacrament service until today. And Charlie 1–5 really needed a strong, visible demonstration of command concern. So we flew immediately to Tay Ninh on a very tight time schedule.

Snyder wasn't blind after all. He had only appeared to be blind because of all the dust and debris that had been blown into his eyes by the satchel charge that killed his buddies. He expected to return to duty in a day or two. Snyder and I were unable to have a sacrament service during this visit because he was being treated and Peterson couldn't tarry longer at the hospital.

What to do? I was torn by conflicting calls of duty, whether to stay with Snyder or to return to the shell-shocked "non-casualties" of Charlie 1–5. Perhaps my decision was too much affected by my professional determination to not allow service to LDS members to cause me to neglect others. So once again, Snyder and I put off our sacrament service.

Eight troopers gave their lives in the attack on LZ Dolly and twenty-three were wounded. One of those pronounced KIA at the scene by the battalion surgeon was found to be alive later at the morgue. Naturally, the doctor suffered a severe case of self-doubt over his mistake. One of the wounded troopers died later in the day.

Stranger things than live soldiers in the morgue happen in war. During war, in my experience, anything one can imagine happening probably will happen. Often even the unimaginable happens. For example, a trooper in one of the companies was killed sometime before I joined the 1–5 Cav. The unit carried the dead trooper "present for duty" for a month or two, until his dog-tagged skeleton was found by another unit operating in the area where he had been killed. That the body might be "lost" in the night and aftermath of intense battle was understandable, as the trooper's body had been placed behind a bush, he being but one of several KIAs and WIAs being evacuated. How, though, could he be counted present for duty for a month or so, considering all the personnel accounting checks and balances we had?

In addition to several failed attempts to share the sacrament with Snyder, while covering two battalions, and despite frequent battles and firefights, I tried to minister to

LDS beyond the 1–5 and 2–12 battalions and to be liaison between Army and Church.

Sometime in March I attended at least one LDS meeting in Saigon, during which I was called to a leadership position, on the usual condition that it would not be allowed to cause me to neglect my battalions. Besides the general services, I conducted several LDS services in the field and attended meetings at Tay Ninh and Phuoc Vinh, taking my nephew Earl Dyer with me to one in Phuoc Vinh.

A month had passed from the time I left my family. Amid all this carnage, Helga and the children seemed a vivid but distant memory. Well, at least I'd gotten past the period of almost unbearable homesickness. Except for passing the one month in-country point, my journals and memory provide scant details about the first five days of April 1969, except that they were busy days and full of fright.

At 1100 hours on April 2, Alpha 1–5 got in a firefight and sustained six WIAs. Sp4 Tom Holcombe explained, "Alpha 1–5 was walking [in columns] in company strength. Dennis Knoch was walking . . . point for the left column. We walked into a linear ambush. . . . a guy in our squad, Caldwell, took a round through the knee, and . . . J. J. Johnson was hit in the eye by a round that bounced off his M-16. Lieutenant Dave Neff was wounded in the upper torso by a round that hit a frag on his pistol belt, breaking off the blasting cap inside the grenade, but it did not detonate."

Lieutenant Steve Holtzman said of this action, "My Second Platoon was the trail platoon on the right column, parallel to Captain Hurt's CP that was in the left column. When the NVA sprung their ambush, they focused most of their fire on the command post. To a man, my entire Second Platoon flanked left and attacked on-line, passing through the CP and other platoon, without any commands from Platoon Sergeant Nelson or myself.

"We pressed the attack through a bunker complex, one hole at a time. Nelson and I took out one bunker and got quite a surprise for our efforts. Keeping away from the firing slits, we got close to the bunker, then we each tossed a smoke grenade into the entrance, followed by frags. Then we moved away from the opening and lay up against the side of the bunker for protection from the frags, not expecting that the bunker contained a stash of explosives. The resulting blast lifted our bodies about three feet off the ground. Nelson and I lost our hearing for several days."

After the bunker-clearing operation, J.J. Johnson, Caldwell, and three or four others were medevaced out, and the rest of the company went on its way again.

"Later," said Holcombe, "we crossed a field and the CO decided we'd FOB there, to use the field for the LOG bird. Dennis, Bob Fussell, and I were assigned to the same foxhole. We had Dennis pull security while we dug our foxhole because he was beat from walking company point all day. Dennis put on his gear and went out about 10–15 meters in front of our position and we started digging. However, I was pulled away to pull security around the open field so LOG birds could bring in supplies.

"A guy with a PRC-25—who was placing the security detail—pointed me to a section of the wood line that was across a clearing that kind of paralleled the FOB. Right away, I found an unoccupied bunker and a well about twenty meters inside the tree line, and a trail that led deeper into the jungle. On the trail were little beads of water and footprints. I reported what I had seen to the guy with the radio and asked him to send me an M-60 machine gun, then I took a position by the well to watch the trail. A few minutes later two guys show up, one with an M-79 and the other with an M-16. No M-60. . . . One may have been Bill 'Big Daddy' Morris. A couple of minutes later an enemy probe came down the trail and veered off to our right when we opened up on them. Quickly, I shifted position to cover our flank, and discovered a trench. Beyond the trench the NVA were breaking brush as they tried to flank us. At that point the noise of breaking brush stopped and heavy shooting broke out back across the clearing around the FOB. I didn't know until I got off the security detail—only one chopper made it in, only to take off again with most of our supplies when the NVA opened up on it—but that was when Dennis Knoch was killed with a round through the heart.

"No way," Holcombe continued, "was Dennis caught napping. He was one of the most alert, if not the most alert, soldiers I ever knew. Dennis had kept the enemy from sneaking in close enough to open up on our guys digging in. And he had fired two or three magazines before he was hit. Dennis' death shook us. Bob Fussell was severely hurt by it, and later he visited the Knoch family in Ohio after he recovered from the wounds he would sustain on June 5, 1969."

Machine gunner Rod Linn of Marquette, Michigan, added, "When the shooting started, C. Brooks and I were about three or four inches into digging a foxhole for our M-60 position. We both tried to fit into that little depression when the firing started that killed Knoch. Word quickly passed from hole to hole that he had been killed and shortly someone, a sergeant or lieutenant, asked for volunteers to take an ambush out. Brooks and I declined. We'd stay in our M-60 machine gun position. I thought it was bad judgment to try and set an ambush when we were already in contact with the NVA (who were in bunkers nearby). As it turned out Aggie [Sp4 James W. Agnew] volunteered to go. Brooks and I couldn't believe that he would go, being so short."

First Lt. Steve Holtzman said, "Captain Hurt wanted to send out an ambush patrol even as the guys on the LZ were in contact. Both Dave Neff and I argued against the idea. 'When I want your opinion I'll ask for it,' Hurt said. Hurt threatened to shoot or court-martial us when we refused to get up the patrol. I'm not sure who went around asking for volunteers. It wasn't Neff nor me." Brave young men on their own initiative recovered Knoch's body while the lieutenants faced Captain Hurt's wrath.

Captain Hurt got his volunteers. With the coming of the night seven troopers crept stealthily away from the relative security of the foxholes and perimeter and into the position that had been selected for the ambush. At 0145 hours,

April 3, the NVA attacked viciously, not on the company but on the ambush site.

Holcombe described what happened. "Volunteers were sought for ambushes and James Agnew and Keith Welsh went on the one out in front of our foxhole. Way late that night we heard tubes (mortars), and jumped in the hole. But the rounds landed short of the FOB, tragically on the Welsh-Agnew ambush. . . . Agnew was KIA. The rest were wounded. . . . One lost a leg. The NVA followed the mortars with a ground attack. What was left of the ambush, mainly Keith, fought them off. Then the trip flares in front of our hole went off. The hole next to us blew a claymore thinking it was an attack. We yelled, 'Hold off, he's one of ours!' The guy who was trying to come in yelled, 'I can't see!' Another guy from my hole and I went out and brought him in. Soon after that Keith Welsh brought the rest of the wounded in— making more than one trip. One brave son of a gun.

"Rex Storey was beside himself. Someone out there kept calling, like *'oui, oui.'* Rex imagined Agnew was alive and calling 'Storey, Storey.' Welsh had assured us that Agnew was KIA, but Rex couldn't stand it. [Story] rounded up guys from the foxholes near ours to go out for Agnew, but the CO wouldn't allow it. The *'oui, oui'* noises turned out to be a wounded enemy soldier," said Holcombe.

Though the enemy fire let up once the surviving members of the ambush got inside the perimeter, the grunts still had good reason for concern. Reports of heavy movement and Vietnamese voices were coming in rapidly. The NVA were pressing toward the perimeter on three sides. Lieutenant Holtzman said, "I remember that we got hit some time after dark. . . . We could hear moaning all night. Both Neff and I asked Hurt to let us go bring the LP back in but he turned us down. He didn't want to risk any more people. We explained to Hurt that Foggy Day [Alpha Company] had never left wounded or dead in the field and we didn't want to leave anybody to become a POW either. Hurt flatly refused to let either of us go . . . [and] threatened courts-martial against us if we couldn't get all of the troops to stop mumbling about how dangerous he was. . . . It was at this time that I first started to hear troops talk about fragging him. . . . prior to this . . . the term fragging was totally foreign to us."

Holcombe said, "I spent the night in my foxhole with Dennis' poncho-wrapped body beside me, a very sad and lonely night."

Early on April 3 a patrol sustained more WIAs at the same time that others were recovering Agnew's remains and the destroyed radio. Cautiously, the patrol moved past Holcombe's and Fussell's foxhole toward where the repeated mournful wails of chieu hoi were coming. "They hadn't gone far when a claymore mine went off and wounded several of them. The enemy had set up a claymore and used one of their own wounded as bait. Pretty ruthless I think. Soon after that we got into our holes for a napalm strike—real close. After that there was no more resistance. We carried the wounded enemy soldier all day, until we could send him out on a chopper." Holcombe added that, "Chaplain Newby, you are the first other than myself to recall the chieu hoi aspect of that action."

Also in early April, I hitched a ride in an LOH from Bien Hoa to LZ Dolly. En route, I snapped a picture of the pilot. He was shot down the next day along the Saigon River, in the area we had flown over. Wild pigs partly consumed him before rescuers found and reached the crash site the day after he went down. I hope he was already dead.

For Easter services, April 6, the Second Brigade Commander dedicated an LOH for Chaplain Hugh Black and me to share so we could conduct both General Christian and Catholic Easter services for all the companies in the 1–5 and 2–12 battalions, an all-day operation. We began the operation by having the chopper drop Black at one 2–12 company and me at another. Next the chopper picked up Black, brought him to where I was, and took me to yet another 2–12 company. Thus, we leapfrogged through most of the 2–12 Cav. Later in the day, Black conducted masses for my 1–5 companies, where Henry Lamar Hunt was providing Protestant Easter services.

To deliver me so I could conduct a service for Alpha 2–12, the pilot of the LOH hovered over a small, cluttered clearing amid smoldering jungle while I jumped to the ground. The troopers were already gathering in an area on the west side of the clearing where the vegetation had already burned away. The line of still-smoldering vegetation was about thirty feet north of where we were and was burning away from us.

My part of setting up for the service consisted simply of removing song materials and scriptures from my pack and placing my helmet atop the pack with the insignia of a chaplain facing the congregation. The Easter service for Ace High (Alpha 2–12's call sign) was underway within minutes of when I jumped from the LOH.

Almost every trooper who could get free from pressing duties was there to worship. We'd sung and prayed, and I was well into a sermon that focused on the significant linkage of Easter and Christmas, when I of necessity paused to wait out the noise of an H-model helicopter. The chopper slipped carefully between the trees to hover about five feet above a bomb crater. Simultaneously, the crew chief and door gunner kicked out supplies while grunts hustled on both sides of the chopper to get the supplies away from it and the crater.

Suddenly, the chopper engine stalled. Without a sputter it dropped like a rock toward the bomb crater and came to rest with the front end and tail rotor on opposite sides of the rim, and with the main rotor skimming at full speed toward the rear and on both sides.

We worshipers abandoned the service and dashed to the crash site, fearing troopers were being cut to pieces by the spinning main rotor. Amazingly no one was hurt. Even more amazing, about the time we made that happy discovery, a 105mm artillery round exploded in the burning vegetation, about a hundred feet behind where I'd stood to conduct the service. The falling chopper had drawn Easter worshipers from the "kill zone" just in time! Apparently, the burning vegetation set off the 105mm round, a dud left over from the earlier fighting.

The crashing chopper and exploding dud were the closest I came during two tours to having one of my worship services interrupted by combat.

That afternoon we had a service for another 2–12 company, commanded by Captain Shine. (I believe that was his name because I remember this captain's last name as Star, and Shine comes closest to that of any of the officers listed as commanders in the 2–12 Cav at that time.) This CO asked for permission to address his troops during the Easter service. Of course he was welcome to do so; it was his company. He began his remarks by identifying himself as a devout, born-again Christian, and said in essence, "I claim all your lives in the name of God. None of you will die while you are in my company."

I liked this captain. I admired him for his spirituality, and understood his desire. In my heart, though, I *knew* he couldn't keep his promise to the men, and I feared some would be spiritually worse off when his promise failed. I regretted letting him speak, and hoped the best—a futile hope as it turned out.

By late afternoon I had conducted three Easter services in the field and one on LZ Grant. I was aboard the LOH on the way to conduct a service for Bravo 2–12 when the pilot said, "Alpha [1–5] is in a fight and has sustained twenty casualties."

We changed course toward Alpha 1–5 in the jungle northeast of LZ Dolly. The company had disengaged from the enemy and pulled back about three hundred meters to set up an FOB and cut a PZ (pick-up zone) so the wounded could be evacuated. The last of the wounded were being placed aboard a medevac chopper when I arrived. Among the wounded was Private Ernest K. Baller—Baller had taken a bullet through his helmet some months earlier, up near the DMZ.

320 Claude D. Newby

Upon reaching Alpha 1–5 late Easter afternoon or early evening, I arranged for and conducted two small, low-key services. After the services, I visited one-on-one with small groups of men and tried to help restore individual and collective spiritual resources, part of the Army reconstitution process. The company definitely needed reconstituting, because it had been at about half strength going into the Easter fight.

Notes

15 March 1969, 1–5 Cav Battalion Journal, 1906: "A Co, 2–6 WIA, serious leg wound."

16 March 1969, 1–5 Cav Battalion Journal, 1010: "? Co received AK-47, B-40, MG from bunker . . . 6 WIA."

18, 19 March 1969, 1–5 Battalion Journal: A Co WIAs Seikert, US 544452112 and N. RA55380871.

1308, D Co KIA Sp4 Barry Jackson; WIAs Robert Vastu [?], US51983981, AK rd. hit claymore and M16 mag, frag stomach and side; Rosado RA67194464, heat stroke.

19 March 1969, 1–5 Battalion Journal: B Co casualties, KIA, Sp4 Roy Womack and Pfc. Peter McCallum

20 March 1969, 1–5 Battalion Journal: A Co KIA Victor D. Kulla; WIAs Holmes, Schraud [Schrauer]. [Douglas A.], Lightfoot, Wess and Hecke or Heikle, and Jones (1/77) [FO?]. "A Co, opcon 11th Cav, reports . . . 04 tanks destroyed. 09 WIA from A Co, also about 30 US WIAs, 08 KIA from Armor . . . Name of A Co WIAs: Holmes, Savard, Lightfoot, Wess, Kulla, *serious* D. O. W., Chenvert, Heckle, De Leon, Jones of B 1–77."

21 March 1969, 1–5 Cav Journal, 1850: "D Co taking incoming 82 mortars . . . resulting in two [?] WIA . . . Joseph A. Gatto, Arnold W. Wright and James A. Lukas."

22 March 1969, 1–5 Cav Battalion Journal, 1630: "A Co inserted 30 feet from tree line . . . received AK-47 fire. Sp4 Moises Tapia [Los Angeles, California] is KIA and Clement is WIA."

23 March 1969, 1–5 Cav Battalion Journal, 1600: "D Co, WIA, Pfc. Barry Overlee." 1927: "[company?] WIA, Rudy M. Blehm."

24 March 1969, 1–5 Cav Battalion Journal, 0945: "C Co 3 US

WIA, Pfc. Eddie Ellis, Sp4 Curtis Harold and Sp4 Rudy M. Reyes." "B Co, Joe L. Fergerson, appendicitis."

1125: "C Co, 3 WIA . . . Pfc. Donald Forest, Pfc. Benny Gerrell and PSG Raymond Clark."

1150: "D Co Robert Karasturdy, WIA."

1330: "A Co 1 US KIA."

1345: "A Co 2 US KIA, 5 US WIA, KIA . . . additional KIA . . . [KIA were Sp4 Johnny Parker, Sp4 Monty Lackas and Pfc. Joseph Schimpf. WIAs medevaced, Sp4s Eppy, Ruty and Harper, and SSG Dayton. WIAs stayed in field, Rash, Schmidt, Pierc and Anderson. Norman Brimm, no company given, medevaced with head cut." [Note: Terry Harper's arm was broken when the canister from an artillery marking round fell on him. He was previously wounded up near the DMZ in July 1968, at the same time as Baller, when a bullet penetrated Baller's helmet and cut a groove on his head, according to Rodney Linn.]

26 March 1969, 1–5 Battalion Journal: "0410, LZ Dolly. Started receiving . . . B-40 rockets also 6-7 sappers on NE side of perimeter . . . total number of WIA 21, 19 medevac & 08 KIAs." KIAs from Charlie 1–5 were Sp4 Patrick Benze [of O'Neill, Nebraska], Pfc. Donald Forrest, Pfc. Robert E. Green, Pfc. Edward Lamoureux [of Plainfield, Connecticut] and Sp4 Carlton Monroe [of Portsmouth, VA]. Other KIAs were Sp4 Theodore Heinselman of HHC 1–5 [Jacksonville, Florida], Sp4 Terry Moore of Bravo 1–5 [Washington, Illinois], and Greg Mills of 1–8 Cav [of Mendota, Illinois]. WIAs from Charlie 1–5 were 1LT Stephen Grubb; Sp4s Jimmy Brown, Frank Marshall, Gary J. Walz and Eddie Melendez; Pfcs. Steve Gonzales, Louis O. Kroh, Allan Jewell, Joseph LePoint Jr., Robert W. Snyder, Thomas Bieme and Thomas W. Kreuger. Bravo 1–5's WIAs were Sgt. Darrel R. Rutz and Sp4s Louis A. Bachus, Ireland G. Hassler, Richard G. Bergeron and Dickie L. Nelson. Also wounded were Sp4 James Adams of Echo 1–5, Maynes and Blanchero of 1–8 Cav, and 1LT Smith and Sp4 Young of 13th Signal-Division Relay.

25 March 1969, 1–5 Cav Operational Report: Early on 26 March, LZ Dolly came under attack by B-40 rockets and 6 or 7 sappers . . . received 9 KIA and 21 WIA before enemy fled.

27 March 1969, 1–5 Battalion Journal: "1150, D Co an individual stepped on a mine, butterfly type, 8 WIAs, Jeffry Gelden, Thomas Robben, Everett Roberts, Angel Hosea Bonilla, Douglas Miller, Bartel Caklo, Thomas James and David Beeker."

28 March 1969, 1–5 Journal: "1505, B Co 3–6 element
engaged . . . two WIA, Richard Barker and Samuel Usted."

30 March 1969, 1–5 Journal: "Beginning at 0006 to 1300, B Co . . .
two KIA, Sp4 Roy Womack and Pfc. Peter McCallum; WIAs,
Sp4 Sergeant James, 1LT Chester Hargrewski, Sp4 LeRoy
Hopes, Sgt. Robert Dykstra and Pfc. Charles Kritt."

2 April 1969, 1–5 Journal: "1100, A Co. (firefight) . . . 6 WIAs,
Sgt. Pedro Trevino, Donald Davis, Pfc. Dale Carr, Pfc. Dale
Caldwell, Jackie, 1LT David Neff." "1815, A Co. hit by smf and
1 B40, 1 KIA, Sp4 Dennis Knoch [Ohio]."

3 April 1969, Battalion Journal, 0753–0815: "As A Co was policing
area of last night's contact, heard someone yelling Chieu hoi . . .
walked into an NVA ambush . . . 02 US WIA." 1130, A Co KIAs
Sp4 James W. Agnew; WIAs, Sp4s Tomie Parker, Keith Welsh,
Thomas Harris, Michael Maphis, Jazquez Cruz, Joseph Couie;
Pfc. Robert Davidson; Injured, non-hostile were Pfc. John
Hoffman, Sp4 Joseph Casonhr [?] and Sgt. Gerald Phiehl.

6 April 1969, Battalion Journal, 1215 hours: "A Co contact . . .
received 13 WIA: Eugene Davis, Michael Schroch, Donald
Savlier, Stacy Holmes, Robert Hunder, Ernest Baller, Charles
Truitt, Michael O'Connel, Jeus Jimenez, Thomas Rudy, Kenneth
Deal, John Hoffman [again] and Ronald Tipton B/177 Arty."

1 April 1969, 2–12 Battalion, Operational Report/Lessons
Learned. Friendly casualty in March: KIAs, 23; WIAs 100;
Non-hostile wounded, 1 Enemy casualties: KIAs 261, WIA/PW,
2, Chieu Hoi, 2."

thirty-one

No Greater Love

Before dawn on April 7, orders came for Charlie 1–5 to attack the objective that Alpha 1–5 had assaulted the previous day. At first light a log bird (lift ship) transported me from Alpha Company to Charlie 1–5. There I found Captain Jim Cain and his men breaking camp, emptying sandbags, collapsing fighting positions, destroying unwanted, less desirable C-ration items like peanut butter and ham-and-eggs chopped, redistributing ammunition for the heavy weapons, and making a final check of weapons.

"Move out," Cain ordered a few minutes after I arrived. I joined Cain's CP group, which was with the Second Platoon, and fell in about five positions behind the point. A moment later we crossed the east perimeter of the FOB and came on Bill Snyder and his M-60 team. He would stay behind us during the fifteen hundred-meter hump (jargon for moving, patrolling by ground troops) to the objective, unless we hit the enemy on the way.

"Bill, we'll have a sacrament service today, no matter what," I promised. Snyder agreed. We would share the sacrament, even if we had no time for any other elements of the service. Snyder's sincere desire and eagerness to renew his covenants exceeded anything I witnessed in any other soldier. *With God's help, I'll not let Snyder down again.*

We moved out in three columns with a platoon and part of the weapons platoon in each column. The company CP group and I were in the middle column. To lighten some trooper's load and, consequently, be a less-inviting target myself, I carried a half-filled plastic water bottle in one hand and a pick or shovel in the other.

We'd moved more than half the distance to the objective when the point man for the left column ran into red ants. Everyone held in place while he, throwing caution to the wind, did a quick striptease, which anyone familiar with Vietnamese red ants will understand.

While we waited, Captain Cain crawled to me and, in violation of his own strict rule against nonessential talking in the jungle, said, "Claude, I want you to teach me about the Mormon religion."

"I'll be glad to, Jim," I answered, surprised, "but why now?"

"Because of Bill Snyder," he answered, and added, "Snyder is the most honest, trustworthy, cheerful and best infantryman I've ever known." It sounded like he was describing the perfect boy scout.

In fact, Snyder was an Eagle Scout, who had ridden horses at a gallop by age four, hunted and tamed wild horses as a youth, played the saxophone at school and church functions, and taken second place at State one year in high school wrestling.

"I want to know about a religion that makes a man like him," said Cain.

"I'll be glad to teach you about the Mormon religion," I assured Jim Cain. Of course the teaching had to wait. It was time to move on.

A little before noon we swept through a new, fancy bunker complex and held up in a north-south running ditch just beyond it. There we waited out an Air Force bombing attack that we hoped would soften up our objective.

New NVA fighting positions were spaced about every ten feet down the center of the ditch. The condition of the newly-dug soil suggested the NVA diggers had abandoned these positions barely ahead of our arrival. The fighting positions confirmed what we already knew. The NVA were ready for us, and they knew exactly where we were. I confess to hoping that our foes were waiting where we expected them to be, right where the bombs were raining down. The NVA were even nearer to us, as it turned out.

Snyder and his machine-gun team had moved forward of the ditch when we stopped to wait out the bombing strikes, as had Cpl. James Derda of Albuquerque, New Mexico, with his 90mm recoilless rifle. Following the bomb runs, I went ahead of the CP and paused to speak with Bill Snyder and his buddies while I waited for the CP element to catch up. With Snyder were Cpl. Derda, Sergeant Thomas Hoover and others.

"Chaplain, don't look so serious. It hasn't rained, and maybe it won't rain bullets today," Snyder chided me.

We all chuckled, heartened by Snyder's attitude. A moment later I fell in with the CP element as it passed. I was about six men back from Pfc. William Allen Jr. of Cantonment, Florida, who had the point. Hoover, Derda, Benny Gerrell (nicknamed Gator) and Snyder's machine-gun team fell in behind the CP. Gator was among those between Allen and the CP. Gator's nickname reflected his roots in the swamps of north Florida and South Georgia. The time was 1433 hours.

We moved forward with Second Platoon and the Company CP element in a column on a well-used path with the First and Third Platoons in columns on our left and right flanks. The platoon on the left faced tough but safer going through thick jungle with no trail to follow. The other platoon entered an open field after moving five meters from the ditch where we had waited out the air strikes.

An NVA machine gunner opened fire at 1435 hours from a well-concealed position about a hundred feet ahead, where the trail turned sharply to the left and where the open field on our right ended. Less than a minute had elapsed since I left Snyder and his buddies to move forward.

With his first burst, the machine gunner killed Allen instantly and drove everyone ahead of me to the ground. While I hit the ground slightly to the left with my feet still on the trail, Captain Cain and two radiomen dived behind a large termite mound to the right of the trail. Simultaneously, 1st Lt. William (Bill) Haines, his RTO, and the company medic dove to cover behind a mound on the left side of the trail. The mound on the right, behind which Cain took cover, was closer to the enemy machine-gun position by about five feet.

Up ahead, Gator hit the ground behind the meager protection of a tree, unhurt. All the other troopers between the NVA machine gun and Cain's CP were wounded.

Several AK-47s joined the enemy machine gun almost immediately, firing on our front and left flank. Simultaneously, our platoon on the right flank moved into the tree line from the open field, unhurt—presumably the NVA hadn't covered the field because they couldn't imagine Americans approaching in the open.

While others scurried to cover, I lay where I fell, confused because a hearing handicap prevented me from pinpointing exactly where the fire was coming from. I knew I had to move, but *which way*? Carefully, I raised my helmet-covered head in an attempt to pinpoint the source of enemy machine-gun fire.

In an instant the NVA gunner answered my unasked question with bursts of machine-gun bullets. The first burst clipped off a half-inch-thick stem of a bush where it pressed against the left side of my neck. Reflexively, I dug my left cheek into the ground, a split second before the second burst filled my face with stinging gravel as the bullets dug into the ground and ricocheted past my face. I decided to play dead for the moment.

"Get the 90 [recoilless rifle] and machine gun up here!" yelled Captain Cain.

A moment later Snyder came into view with Hoover right behind him. In response to Cain's call for the machine gun, Snyder hurried forward at a crouch, keeping to the right of the trail for the little protection that Cain's termite hill offered. Hoover was right behind Snyder. Dropping to one knee as he drew even with me, Snyder looked directly into my eyes, a look that haunts me still. "Goodbye, Brother," his eyes seemed to say.

Then he leaped forward and threw himself onto the path slightly ahead of where Cain crouched behind the termite hill. Instantly, the machine gunner shifted his fire from me to Snyder. Almost simultaneously with Snyder's move, I rolled to the left behind the relative security of the termite hill on the north side of the trail, timing my move to coincide with the first burst of fire that at least now didn't crack right in my ears. That burst of fire was aimed at Snyder, who was trying to take the enemy machine gun under fire. From ten feet away Captain Cain watched helplessly as Snyder's head jerked backward from the impact of a bullet between and just above the eyes. Snyder died instantly.

Derda had arrived perhaps a moment behind Snyder, keeping left of the trail. Dashing to the left, Derda dropped to one knee and fired a flechette round, which he had already loaded, against the NVA forces that were assaulting our left front. The Third Platoon yet struggled through thick undergrowth, trying to get into position to protect our flank.

From behind Cain's termite hill, Hoover yelled, "Gator! Snyder's hit! Here!" With that he threw his heavier-hitting M-14 rifle to Gator and dived for Snyder's machine gun. Hoover died before he could pull the trigger.

"Hold this for me, Chaplain," Derda said, tossing me the strap he used to carry the heavy 90mm recoilless rifle. Then he too was gone around the termite hill into the line of fire. Perhaps the blast of the recoilless rifle had temporarily dampened enemy enthusiasm, for Derda made it to slight cover. But upon seeing that Snyder and Hoover were hit, Derda abandoned the recoilless rifle and dove behind Snyder's machine gun. He took a round in the head before he could fire, and joined Snyder and Hoover in instant death.

"Snyder is dead," Cain called to me, after watching helplessly as the sequence of death played out ten feet before his eyes. I had no doubt Cain knew what he was talking about.

Snyder's death shocked me more than all that had occurred before. Sorrow, remorse, even guilt almost immobilized me, but people were still being hurt. The enemy machine gun yet fired, and NVA soldiers were attacking our left front. For the moment the defense of the left flank was left to a medic, the FO, his RTO, and me. Our only cover was the termite hill behind which we had gathered a few wounded grunts.

Very quickly, the urgency of the situation snapped me into action. Leaving the wounded to the medic's care, I picked up an M-16 rifle that a wounded trooper had dropped and helped defend the left front flank long enough for the Third Platoon to get into position to take some of the pressure off us.

Meanwhile, Lieutenant Haines already had high-explosive shells pouring in as near to our front positions as he dared. But the artillery coming from several directions could do little more than suppress enemy maneuvering to the rear of the NVA fighting positions. We were too close to the enemy for anything better.

After the Third Platoon relieved the pressure on our left front, and with the wounded troopers within our reach attended to, I looked around. Suddenly, I felt very exposed, vulnerable. In a flash of insight, intuition or inspiration, I *knew* what was wrong. While our attention was focused forward, the NVA were about to hit us from another direction: *from across the field! The NVA are about to mortar us from there!*

I pulled on Bill Haines' leg to get his attention. "Better get some fire across the clearing to the south. They're going to mortar us from there," I advised. Haines, his hands already quite full, put me off for a moment—understandable, as he had only my word on a threat from any direction but the front and left flank. Finally, perhaps to humor me, Haines targeted a single barrage of artillery where I asked him to. "First rounds HE [high explosive]. Fire for effect," Haines radioed to a battery fire controller.

"On the way, wait," replied the fire control officer a moment later.

In the few seconds that the shells took to arrive, five enemy

82mm mortar rounds thumped from tubes located behind the tree line across the clearing. The NVA shells exploded harmlessly fifty feet or more out in the clearing, just outside our position. Our artillery shells exploded right on target before the NVA mortar men could adjust their fire. Enemy mortars stayed silent for the rest of the engagement. *How many NVA soldiers died there because of my insistence? How many Americans lived?*

Another "truth" flashed into my mind sometime after the mortars threat had been taken care of. *The NVA are moving into the fortified ditch behind us to cut off any withdrawal!* Calling across to Cain, I recommended, "NVA are going to occupy the ditch to our rear. You'd best secure it." Reacting immediately, Cain ordered the First Platoon to secure the ditch, and just in time too. NVA soldiers were coming along the ditch from the north when our trooper arrived. The enemy pulled back without much of a fight.

After almost two terribly frustrating hours, Cain became fed up with the NVA machine gun which yet pinned down some of our troopers and kept us from recovering our dead. I had joined him behind the mound on the right, having crossed the machine gunner's sights unhurt.

A hard, grim look of resolve came over Jim Cain. Without a word, he laid his weapon down, withdrew two grenades from his webgear (pistol belt and suspenders—LBE) and pulled both pins. It dawned on me that Cain intended to take out the machine gun single-handedly, or die trying. "Wait," I said, as I picked up another M-16, checked the magazine and simultaneously chambered a round, and moved the selector switch to semiautomatic. "Now!" I yelled.

Cain charged the machine-gun position, straight down the path past his dead troopers. Simultaneously, I laid a steady stream of well-aimed single-shot covering fire directly on the machine gun position. With only AK-47 rounds cracking about both of us, Cain charged to about twenty feet from his objective and dropped—rather than threw—the hand grenades into or very near to the enemy machine gun. He was halfway back to me when the grenades exploded. He returned unhurt to the protection of the termite hill.

The enemy machine gun stayed quiet during and following Cain's charge. Though I can't know for sure, I believe my support made the difference. And though several troopers had sprayed the area with automatic fire as Cain charged, no one else placed steady, aimed rounds straight into the machine-gun position.

With the enemy machine gun finally silent, we soon succeeded in pulling our four dead and the wounded troopers back behind the termite hill on the left side of the trail.

After almost four hours in close contact, and with the enemy pressing as hard as ever, less the machine gun, we withdrew behind the fortified ditch with all our dead and wounded. To keep the NVA at a distance as we withdrew, we set a line of claymore mines across our front, then backed off a few meters and set another line. We blew the first line of claymores while backing away from the second line to set up yet a third line. Thus, we kept the NVA at bay while we withdrew behind the ditch, which, fortunately, we didn't have to fight our way across. At 1711 hours we arrived in an old FOB about 200 meters west of where we had fought all afternoon.

Sergeant Clark had been outstanding during the whole battle. He was everywhere, constantly risking his life to fill defensive gaps and maneuver his men. Without his valiant efforts the company CP group probably would have been flanked and possibly put out of action early in the fight. Clark had maneuvered his platoon to take the pressure off us as I fought beside a medic to hold the left front. Clark frequently exposed himself to enemy fire to help retrieve wounded troopers. I nicknamed him "Audie Murphy" after the most decorated American soldier during World War II.

After our withdrawal to the old FOB, Cain put a few men to work turning a small clearing into a PZ so medevac and re-supply choppers could come in. He ordered the platoon leaders to get the men to work filling sandbags and digging out old, partially collapsed foxholes. I intended to stay with the wounded until they were picked up, but changed my mind when all around the perimeter as far as I could see, grunts sat immobile in a daze and stared blankly, silently into the partially collapsed foxholes or into space. None dug or filled sandbags.

Approaching a foxhole, I suggested we'd better dig in for the night. One or two troopers glanced in my direction. The others just stared glassy-eyed at nothing. None started digging.

I picked up a shovel, dropped into a hole and started throwing out dirt. After a minute or so, a trooper nudged me from the hole and took over the shovel.

Going from hole to hole, I dug until someone nudged me aside. Gradually the effect began spreading ahead of me as troopers in adjacent holes began digging before I reached them. Soon, everyone who had nothing else to do was either digging, filling sandbags or collecting logs for overhead cover.

In the telling of this, I don't wish to give the false impression that I was tougher than those troopers were. Sure, I'd had some rough moments today, but nothing like what these young men had endured. And I'd had advantages that most of those guys lacked. I had a termite hill to hide behind and had been close enough to the commander to have some concept of the whole picture. It is amazing how it helps one to have some idea of what is going on in the chaos and confusion of a battle.

By the way, while I'd been close enough to the CP to have some idea of what was happening, a lot more occurred than what I perceived. For example, several times during the fight, I had urged Haines to get us more artillery support, only to discover later that more than fifteen hundred rounds of friendly artillery had been expended during the fight. And the artillery barrages continued after the fight, off and on all through the night, as it seemed likely we would be attacked in the FOB before dawn.

For me, personally, the night was tumultuous, not because the NVA attacked, but in consequence of my internal struggle with remorse, guilt, self-recrimination and even shame, tempered with amazement that I was alive. Over and over, I relived the events of the day.

Repeatedly, I considered everything from every angle. I replayed in my mind each contact I'd had with Bill Snyder. These thoughts gave me little solace, for I felt I had let Snyder down. Rationally, in the light of circumstances and conflicting demands, each delay in sharing the sacrament with Snyder seemed logical and reasonable, given the limitations of human foreknowledge.

All night long, following the deaths of Snyder, Hoover, Derda and Allen I wrestled with very strong emotions and feelings. And I reflected anew about how amid all the chaotic sounds and furies of close combat, for me the worst combat noise of all is the profane use of God's name and of motherhood by young men in the face of imminent death. Cursing under fire hadn't changed since 1967, except perhaps for the worse. Men continued to employ the most sacred of names and titles during the vilest, most frightful moments of war.

Profanity and obscenity during battle were reflexive, I thought, and reflected habits formed during individual struggles for peer acceptance during youth. Some of the cursing was probably intended as "tokens of bravery" or "manliness." This most disturbing of battle noises bothered me because, as I had cautioned Sergeant Wade back in '67, "God will not hold him guiltless who taketh His name in vain."

But Snyder was gone, forever beyond the limits of mortal ministrations and sacraments. *How does Bill feel now*, I wondered? *Did his last, deep gaze into my eyes include understanding as well as goodbye?* Yes, Robert William Snyder was gone, but he was not forgotten. I did not forget him, nor, it seemed, did the surviving troopers of Charlie 1–5. Gator revealed something of his esteem for Snyder about a month later. "Chaplain, I've quit smoking," he announced.

"Great, Gator," said I, "but why are you telling me? I never told you to quit smoking."

"No, Chaplain, but Bill Snyder told me to."

Later, a lieutenant asked me to help him deal with a moral problem and to straighten his life out in preparation for reunion with his dear wife. He, like Gator, credited Snyder's counsel and example for bringing him to see me. A private first class counseling a lieutenant. Now that's unusual.

I found a semblance of peace days later while I prepared to conduct a memorial service for Snyder and his fellow grunts. Bill Snyder had lived in accordance with God's will as he understood it, which truth I discovered in a spiritual, powerful, sure manner. Thus was I convinced that Bill Snyder had been chosen for higher purposes in God's plans, purposes in which he was already engaged, among the spirits of recently killed soldiers, American, Vietnamese, and many others, spirits with whom he held special standing. Snyder had served as a missionary in Canada for two years, then dutifully submitted himself for military service, which service he could have avoided simply by remaining in Canada to greet the hoards of draft dodgers who were flocking there.

Notes

7 April 1966, 1435: "C Co is in contact with an unknown size force." 1450: "C Co engaged . . . trying to pull back." 1600: "C Co received 04 US KIA and 02 WIA . . . still in contact . . . received 05 60mm incoming rounds." 1637: "C Co is moving back to FOB about 200 meters to their west, enemy is following, still in contact." 1820: "C Co requests medevac at 11 . . . completed at 1804 hrs . . . Contact was broken at 1720 hrs." KIAs: Hoover, Derda, Snyder and Allen. WIAs: Alfman, Franklin, Cole, Heriot, McDonald, Castaneda, Mahler, O'Neill and Wacker.

HQ, 1st Cav Div (AM) Journal, 1530 hrs: "At 1425H C/1–5 made contact w/est en plt . . . Contact broke 1444h. Neg. assess. Neg frly cas. 1500H. C Co began sweep of area . . . 1800 hrs. Contact w/en was reestablished w/est 4 to 5 indiv. Rec SA & AW fire . . . 4 to 5 rds 60mm mort . . . Res 4x US KIA, 2x US WIA. Contact continues." 1830 hrs, Item 46 [foxhole strength]: A Co., 2–65; B Co., 3–80; C Co., 2–62; D Co., 3–92; E Co., 2–39.

thirty-two

Renew the Attack!

In the wee hours of April 8, Captain Cain placed Charlie 1–5 on full alert, just in case the NVA tried to take advantage of our depleted stamina and resources. No attack came, though. What came instead was an order from battalion for Charlie 1–5 to renew the attack after dawn. We few who knew of the new orders waited in silence for the dawn and wondered what the new day held for us. We took some comfort from the promise that Air Force bombs would attempt to soften up the target prior to our assault.

Sergeant Clark came to me just after dawn. He looked very somber. "Chaplain, when I looked at my men this morning, some of them had no features where their faces should have been. It was like no soul existed behind each blank face." Clark interpreted the illusion, if illusion it was, as an omen that those particular soldiers would soon die.

I'd heard reports of this sort of "vision" during the World Wars and Korea. Though I was inclined to not give much credence to Clark's premonitions, I remembered an Indian trooper, Prentice LeClair, who had come to me about premonitions of his own death just days before he died on 9 August 1967. Because of this and other experiences, I found myself unable to shrug off Clark's impressions as meaningless.

In fact, several of Clark's men would give their lives in days to come, but he wouldn't be around to confirm whether those who died were the same faceless ones in his "vision." Clark had about six hours to go in the field at the moment he shared his premonitions with me.

* * *

Combat doctrine, I was told on high authority, called for at least 500 meters distance between friendly troops and Air Force bombing targets. But we were only 200 meters from our objective. So to ensure that the air strikes would be more effective than those on the previous day, Captain Cain gave our position as about 250 meters farther away to the west. Consequently, seven air strikes came in at half the "required" distance between friendly troops and the bombing target. I had thought that eight-inch shells at fifty meters were horrendous, but they paled in comparison to 500 pound and heavier bombs at 200 meters.

The circling Air Force forward air controller (FAC) warned us that the first bombing run was coming in. Casually we took cover in holes or behind trees just before the jet screamed across our front from the south, and almost instantly the jungle floor slammed like a sledge hammer into our chests or whatever body part we rested on. Concussion and the sound of the exploding bombs came so close together that I couldn't tell which arrived first. Waves of concussion swept over us with such power that even the largest trees seemed to lean away. The blasts were so loud that I doubted our tender eardrums could survive. Waves of shrapnel and debris flashed straight outward from the blasts, over and around us, sounding like thousands of giant, angry wasps. Secondary shrapnel and debris rained straight down from the sky moments after each concussion wave swept past us.

Faces paled in awe before the terribly destructive powers unleashed so near to us. Many eyes focused on Captain Cain, and behind those eyes lurked traces of hope and suspicion— hope that the terror of the bombs would spare us more intimate terror when we assaulted, suspicion that our leaders up above might kill us with the bombs in order to save us.

Spaced moments to minutes apart, six more air strikes followed, each just as impressive as the one before. *Surely any NVA left alive are too stunned to resist us*. Not so, as we soon discovered.

Following the concussion and initial sweep of shrapnel from one of the latter air strikes, Captain Cain dropped his helmet between his folded legs to relieve a terrible headache. He got them frequently, the result of an earlier wound, which I'll explain later. "Jim," I chided, "you're setting a bad example for the troops, taking off your helmet at a time like this."

"Right," Cain said, with just the trace of a sheepish grin, as he replaced his helmet on his head. His hand was still on the brim of his helmet when a chunk of hot shrapnel fell from the sky and caved in his steel helmet a good half of an inch.

"Thanks, Claude," Jim said simply. Enough said.

We assaulted eastward right after the last air strike, moving steadily and unopposed for a hundred meters, which brought us to the north-south running ditch with the new NVA fighting positions that we had found the day before. After a brief pause at the ditch we moved forward with the men on-line across a thirty-meter front with Cain, the lieutenants and me about ten feet behind the line. Perhaps we were feeling more confident than was justified following the bombing.

Sure enough, the NVA opened fire across our front with AK-47s before we'd moved more than 50 feet. Three troopers fell wounded in as many seconds.

For the next hour we lay where we were and exchanged sporadic fire with the NVA—they seemed content to stay where they were too. Two more troopers were wounded during that hour. Finally on Cain's command, Haines called in ARA to attempt to end the stalemate. It was doubtful that ARA could make much difference, considering the fight still left in the NVA after those bomb strikes.

During the ARA attack, we were lying on our stomachs facing the enemy when shrapnel wounded the man to my left and a bullet laid open the left cheek—nose to ear—of the man to my immediate right. It took a very brave or an extremely foolhardy NVA soldier to rise up and fire so effectively with those ARA rockets raining down on him.

A trooper lying about ten feet to my left escaped bodily injury when a bullet cut a path in the ground beneath his prone body. The bullet, perhaps fired by the same NVA who hit the man on my right, drilled a cigarette case—top to bottom—in one of the trooper's upper blouse pockets and passed on without touching his flesh.

Charlie 1–5 moved forward again a little past noon and advanced unopposed for a hundred meters. We skirted the northern edge of the area where we had fought the day before, and stopped atop a steep bank that dropped to a debris-choked stream. Bombs and artillery had literally destroyed the jungle to the east of the streambed. A single dead NVA soldier lay in plain sight by the stream.

After a momentary pause the Second Platoon crossed the stream and reconnoitered among the fallen and twisted trees. When they drew no enemy reaction, Cain swung the line of troops south for a sweep through where we'd fought and been pinned down the day before. He halted the company in and around a small clearing east of and separated by a thin line of trees from the large clearing that had been on our right flank during the fighting the previous day.

Taking advantage of the stop, I sat down and leaned back against the termite hill that Cain had taken cover behind. For several minutes I stared, deep in thought and with churning emotions, at the spots where Snyder, Derda, Hoover and Allen had given their all. Suddenly, heavy small-arms fire shattered my contemplation, just as I was about to take pictures of the scene.

With all thoughts of a pictorial history temporarily forgotten, I rushed past the hole from which the NVA machine gun had given us so much grief the day before, turned south and dashed across a clearing to where a medic was tending Sergeant Clark. The two were behind a large tree near the south edge of the small clearing and about ten feet from where Clark's men lay on their stomachs and poured automatic fire into the jungle to the south.

A moment before the shooting had begun, Sergeant Clark had raised up, much as he'd often done during the fighting the day before, to get his reluctant troopers moving to the south. Standing there and facing south, Clark looked over his right shoulder at his unmoving men, and with a follow-me-forward swing of his left arm he said, "Come on.

If Gooks were out there, they would already have shot me."
Bam! His arm signal was cut short by a shot from about
twenty feet to his left front. Keeping his feet, Clark swung
around, yelled to someone to take charge, then ran back and
dropped behind the tree where I joined him and the medic.

An AK-47 round had torn through Clark's left wrist and
buried itself and parts of his wristwatch in his left shoulder,
which was bleeding profusely. Sergeant Clark was very calm.

The medic had a bandage on Clark's wrist when I
reached them. A moment later sniper fire interrupted our
joint efforts to tend to his shoulder. The single-fire rounds
came from some trees about fifty feet to our left—from the
east. The troops on the line couldn't help us; their hands
were full. Across the clearing behind us were several troopers that didn't seem so occupied in the fight. I caught their
attention, pointed eastward and yelled "Snipers in the trees!"
They never reacted. So, assuming they could not understand
me above the din of battle, I ran toward them with the intent
of directing their fire against the snipers. What I did instead
was draw the snipers' fire away from Clark and the medic.
More than one sniper was shooting at us, no doubt about it.

I had covered about ten or fifteen feet when suddenly I
realized that I was at the center of the focus of several
snipers. In the same moment, I spotted an empty NVA fighting position off to my left front. I dived into the position
with bullets cracking all about me. That's when I became
aware of Clark's M-16 in my left hand. So I popped up just
enough to blast away at where I thought the latest sniper fire
was coming from. I didn't do the snipers any harm, though.

After the fight, several grunts expressed amazement that
I wasn't hit. "Dozens of rounds followed you into the hole,
Chaplain Newby, and they continued to pepper all around
you until we finally realized where the shots were coming
from and hosed down those trees," said a trooper to agree-
ing nods of his buddies. I'd been shooting in the wrong direction, betrayed by my ears, again.

After the men put a stop to the sniper fire, I helped the

medic with Clark and the other wounded men until the company, down to 48 men as I recall, pulled back to the position we had occupied the night before. From there we evacuated the wounded.

In the quiet of the following night, I recommended to Captain Cain that Clark be put in for the Distinguished Service Cross, the second-highest award our nation gives for valor in combat. Cain declined to support my recommendation, so I recommended Clark, Snyder, Hoover and Derda for the Silver Star—Cain wrote up Allen—and later was assured the awards were approved posthumously for all but Clark.

The NVA mortared us during the night, but the incoming ordnance made very little impression on my memory.

Probably, some will criticize me for taking up arms in three instances during the engagements of April 7 and 8, but I offer no apologies or excuses. What I did was done reflexively, for what seemed very appropriate causes under the accumulated heat of those particular battle conditions. It was, perhaps, another case of former infantry training and reflexes kicking in and overcoming chaplain education. The Geneva Conventions were definitely not on my mind.

It occurs to me that I've said almost nothing of my family since I began to describe the first month of this tour. Suffice it to say, I wrote almost every day, often in the dark out in the jungle. Helga and the children wrote, though incoming mail was as sporadic and unpredictable as incoming mortars.

Helga's letters came in bunches, with painful gaps in between. Still, they were filled with love and spiritual support, which is what counted. The mail also raised some concern about things on the home front. For one thing, Helga kept threatening to miscarry. I lived with the premonition, the certainty almost, that I would never see this baby alive in this world. Concerns for Helga and our children helped me to appreciate the cares and worries that so many troopers went through, and perhaps helped me to minister to them more effectively.

True to my call, though, I resisted the urge to quit and find a way to go home to Helga and the children. Actually, I'd never entertained the idea of going AWOL. Even as an enlisted man, I had always been paranoid about sometime being AWOL because of events beyond my control.

Notes

8 April 1969, 1–5 Battalion Journal, 1113: "C Co is now receiving s/a fire from their front . . . one burst of AK-47 fire 15–20 meters away, from the southeast . . . 01 US WIA."

1137: "C Co received another burst of automatic fire . . . believes fire is coming from a bunker instead of a tree. The bunker is center of mass of C Co line . . . will swing right and left and try to frag bunker."

1204: "C Co had made repeated attempts to maneuver on bunker, with negative results. There appears to be more than one individual firing . . . Enemy has two well-placed auto weapons and has been throwing chicom grenades."

1850: "C Co in contact today, had 05 US WIAs, 02 were wounded this morning, 03 were wounded this afternoon . . . medevac completed at 1825 hrs. C Co pulled back . . . tomorrow, C Co will sweep area." WIAs: Mario Trevino, Eddie Ellis, Raymond Clark, Richard Higgins, Donald Phillips and Douglas Barron.

April 1969 2–12 Operational Report: On 8 April contact was heavy. [In] A Co . . . claymore mine was detonated, causing 1 US/WIA . . . [later] point element engaged 2 NVA . . . found 2 additional claymores . . . minutes later ran into 5 individuals . . . while they were moving from LOG site, point element tripped a booby trapped claymore mine resulting in 1 US/KIA and 7 WIA. B Company made contact . . . resulting in 1 US/KIA, 8 WIA and 1 MIA. Next day B Company was in contact area and again received heavy fire, Results 10 US/WIA. On 11 April A Company made contact with enemy in bunker. Results, 5 US/KIA, 9 WIA and 1 NVA/KIA.

thirty-three

Circuit Riding

Area Support

On April 9, after conducting several small group worship services (small, to avoid bunching the troops) I returned to LZ Dolly. Over the next five days, I divided my time between efforts to get LDS troopers to a conference in Bien Hoa and quick visits to conduct worship services for companies in the field and on LZ Dolly and LZ Grant. Charlie 1–5 must have returned to LZ Dolly soon after I did, following the fighting on April 7 and 8, for there I conducted a memorial service for twelve troopers, including Allen, Derda, Hoover and Snyder. Meanwhile, Bravo 2–12 still hadn't received its General Christian Easter Service.

Three days later, at 0820 hours, Alpha 2–12 moved by foot away from LZ Grant. An hour later they reported finding new graves and said the company was moving on. At 1150 hours, the RTO reported that the company was in a firefight and had sustained two wounded from small-arms fire. A few minutes later he radioed that the company was receiving heavy automatic fire and had one grunt dead and two more wounded. By 1301 hours, the American casualty count was two killed and four wounded. The company was still engaged in heavy fighting. Two hours later the count was three killed, nine wounded, and three missing in action. At 1710 hours, Lieutenant Colonel Boon reported from his command chopper that he had found two of the three MIAs.

While all this was happening to Alpha 2–12, I completed my first month in the field—with Bravo 1–5 elsewhere in the jungle. Sometime that day I left the field for a religious retreat at Bien Hoa. I stopped on the way and picked up a contingent of 1st Cav troopers, including Sergeant Elvin Jackson and my nephew Earl Dyer. We flew to and from Bien Hoa on an Air Force Caribou that I had laid on for the retreat. By invitation, I spoke during the retreat and turned one session into an informal memorial service for Bill Snyder and others.

Following the retreat, the Caribou dropped some of the troopers at Phuoc Vinh and dropped the remainder at Tay Ninh—we arrived there after dark. On the way from the airstrip to the 1–5 Cav rear area, Jackson and I stopped by to see Chaplain Black in his combination office and sleeping quarters.

When we walked in, Black tore into me angrily, without any courtesies or preliminaries. He was very put out that Bravo 2–12 was still waiting to receive a non-Catholic Easter service. "I didn't let your men go without an Easter mass, and Black Gold still hasn't had a service."

I explained about the heavy casualties and subsequent events in Alpha 1–5. Clearly from his religious perspective Black considered Easter services to have precedence over casualties. I didn't agree, but we parted on good terms and remained so for the duration.

The next day, April 13, I conducted several worship services for the 2–12 Cav at and around LZ Grant. One of the services was a belated "Easter Service" for Bravo 2–12, for which Chaplain Black thanked me profusely. "The men say you are just great, that you speak just like me," he said. This compliment I took as Black's peace offering.

Following the field services, I hitched flights to Ton San Nhut via LZ Dolly. Elder Ezra Taft Benson, former Secretary of Agriculture in President Eisenhower's cabinet and a very high ecclesiastical official in the LDS Church, was conducting the conference. The conference was more than half over when I landed at Ton San Nhut.

Out on the street, dozens of military vehicles ignored my outstretched thumb. Finally, I ran what seemed like a mile to get to the service, laden with full rucksack and field gear. Come to think of it, perhaps the traffic passed me by precisely because of my laden, scruffy, filthy, sweaty appearance. Fear of being mugged?

Elder Benson was delivering the concluding talk of the conference when I sneaked in and took a seat on the back pew. Among the things he spoke of were the importance and divine origin of the Constitution of the United States.

After the session, I held back from the crowd that gathered around Elder Benson because I knew that I smelled rather strong compared to everyone else. This self-awareness did not equate with any sense of being inferior or subordinate to the others, except Elder Benson. Like most of the front line troops that I served, I felt a bit superior to rear-area soldiers, because of my combat experiences and existence. I appreciated the sacrifices that many rear-area soldiers made, and understood how impossible our situation at the front would have been without their support, but it was hard to avoid this attitude.

Well, Elder Benson shook my hand in passing, but never commented on my aroma and appearance.

Between April 17 and 23, I concentrated on the companies of the 2–12 Cav, but not exclusively. My journal got behind, so consequently I must fill in the blanks with vividly remembered incidents, without positively linking them to dates in every case.

It was during this time with the 2–12 Cav that several well-remembered actions and events occurred. One involved a young lieutenant in command of a company, reinforcing the concept that preparation makes a difference. Another action exposed the hope- and promise-shattering vagaries of war. Yet another incident shattered any illusion that chaplains lead charmed lives.

About mid-April, I joined Alpha 2–12 for an afternoon and a night. The company was receiving supplies when I arrived. It had a temporary perimeter near the eastern end of an east-west running swath of open terrain. A recent B-52 bomb strike (Arclight) had recently created that swath in the jungle. The NVA demonstrated that they knew precisely where the company was by firing an occasional 60mm mortar at it.

Fortunately for the grunts that were not dug in, the NVA mortar man was a poor shot.

The new company commander, a lieutenant about to be promoted to captain, appeared oblivious to the risks he was exposing his men to. He kept his company in the open for three hours following my arrival, to receive and break down supplies.

To make matters worse, this new commander—I believe he was John F. Kopacz, but can't confirm that—used up the last hour and a half of daylight to move his company toward the westward end of the bombed-out area. There he stopped the company for the night in plain sight of watching eyes around us in the jungle. While the perimeter was being laid out, I picked a spot near the center of a mass and started digging a one-man foxhole. A few minutes later I gave myself a break and looked around. To my dismay I was the only one within my sight who was digging. Everyone else, it seemed, had things to do that they considered more important.

The troopers, following the lead of their commander, were wasting the remaining daylight on personal comforts, reading mail, erecting rain shelters and sorting out C-rations. Calling the CO aside, I offered some unsolicited advice. "Lieutenant, you are setting a bad example for the men." With that "tactful" opening, I told him why.

"You tend to your business and I'll tend to my company," he retorted as he turned and stomped away in a huff back to his CP group.

Shortly after dark, a subdued commander came to my foxhole, the only decent hole inside the perimeter. "I apologize for reacting the way I did, Chaplain. I'd appreciate it if you would explain what you meant," he said.

I gladly complied with his request, beginning with a critique of how the unit had stayed too long in the open while receiving supplies, and how he selected the FOB out in the open when he knew the NVA were watching. Then I pointed out how he and the troops had squandered the remaining daylight hours on creature comforts and then settled in for the night with poorly planned defenses and no overhead protection.

"Overhead cover isn't a big concern out here in the open tonight, but it is very important in the jungle and prevents mass casualties from mortar and rocket bursts in the trees," I explained.

The lieutenant acknowledged the wisdom of my observations and then impressed me by asking, "What do you recommend I do?"

"First, pray we are not hit tonight. Second, include in your resupply list for tomorrow picks and shovels to distribute between the platoons, and several empty sandbags for each man in the company. Third, starting tomorrow and from then on, put security before creature comforts," I advised.

"Why the picks and shovels? How do we use the sandbags?"

I explained how the 1–5 Cav and other 2–12 Cav companies developed an FOB. Perhaps the lieutenant said his prayers. We had a quiet night and Alpha 2–12 got itself out of the open first thing the next morning.

After we had moved a good ways into the jungle, we learned another 2–12 company was having a very loud morning following a quiet night. Boon radioed me to meet him at LZ Grant, and sent his C&C chopper to pluck me out of the field. While we waited for the chopper, the troopers blew down some trees to create a PZ. In the process, a trooper stuck his head up to watch the explosions. For his curiosity he caught a piece of shrapnel that might have cost him the sight in one eye. He left the field with me on Boon's C&C chopper.

Lieutenant Colonel Boon met me at his helipad, just outside the south side of the LZ Grant perimeter. Boon wanted me by his side when his dead troopers arrived. Soon a chopper came into sight from the southeast, made a 180-degree turn to the right and settled on the pad before us, facing east, with rotors turning. A detail of men ran forward and started unloading the chopper. A moment later, five poncho-wrapped bodies lay out on the ground in a neat row, their feet toward the chopper. At the last moment before taking off, the crew chief of the chopper tossed a wadded-up poncho out the door. The wadded poncho came open when it hit the ground. Its contents rolled out and came to rest at the feet of one of the troopers on the unloading detail. Dead eyes "stared" up at the trooper from the severed head lying at his feet—the eyes of one of his closest buddies. Understandably, the young man almost lost control of his emotions. And undoubtedly the memory is never far below the surface of his mind, assuming he survived Vietnam.

After we'd done what we could there on the helicopter pad, Boon had his chopper drop me off at the company of my born-again friend, where I got the rest of the story.

The night had been quiet, but for the usual defensive artillery fire. Next morning, the company broke camp and prepared to reconnoiter in-force to the west, in a column, with flanking security.

Unknown to my friend, the NVA had left him alone during the night in favor of a more elaborate plan, an ambush designed to catch the company outside the FOB between two forces of NVA. The captain said that his company might have been annihilated except for the nervous trigger finger of an NVA soldier in one of the NVA elements.

As the lead element of the company moved west, the remainder of the company gravitated toward the west side of the FOB. About half of the company was still inside the FOB when an NVA soldier opened fire on the point element, prematurely triggering an L-shaped ambush.

Simultaneously, the second NVA force attacked the company from the rear with heavy small-arms fire, hand grenades, and RPGs. This attack came from the foxholes on the east side of the FOB, holes the NVA had slipped into as our men abandoned them.

Thus, while the guys in the lead platoon fought off the ambush and dragged their dead and wounded away from the kill zone, the remainder of the company counterattacked to expel or destroy the NVA on the other side of the FOB. It was during this battle inside the perimeter that an enemy RPG decapitated the trooper.

The company commander was understandably dejected that his faith and prayers had not protected his men as he had promised them. Though I tried, there was little I could do to console him. I never saw him again after that visit to his company. A few days later at LZ Grant a hand grenade went off on a trooper's pistol belt or load bearing suspenders while my friend was checking some of his men in formation prior to them going out on ambush. He and several of his men fell, wounded severely.

Word came that my captain friend died of his wounds, but I can't confirm it. Boon insists only one of his company commanders was killed, in different circumstances than those described here. Another problem I have with this account is that, though I saw the bodies and got the story first-hand, I can find no official record of an engagement quite like the one described to me. The lack of records doesn't mean the fight didn't happen the way the captain said. I just wish I could verify the details.

It was mid-April and I was in a chopper at about 2000 feet elevation with a squad of infantry. We were southeast of LZ Grant headed toward LZ Dolly. Eight or nine infantrymen plus their chaplain with all their gear was more than a full load for a Huey helicopter. I sat cross-legged on the floor with my knees sticking out of the open left doorway directly behind the copilot's seat. While I was watching jungle and bomb craters sweep beneath us, the helicopter suddenly, without warning, banked sharply to the right and went into a steep dive. Only the quick reflexes of those sitting back from the doors kept others and me from being flung from the chopper to certain death. Our saviors had kept us in the chopper by grabbing our packs and suspenders.

At LZ Dolly the pilot apologized and explained. He'd been forced to perform the violent maneuvers because

37mm anti-aircraft guns had targeted us. The 37mm anti-aircraft gun, he explained, was aimed and fired electronically, during which process it emitted three electronic beeps. The first and second beeps occurred when the gun's targeting device gathered some aspects of the target's height, speed, and direction. The third and last beep signaled completion of the aiming process and firing of the gun.

"When we hear the distinctive signature beep of a 37 mike-mike, we react instantly and violently to thwart its electronic brain. We don't wait around to see if what we heard was the first or the second beep, for if we miss one and hear the third beep before we react, it is too late," the pilot explained.

Another night, Chaplain Black and I were both in the jungle with Charlie 1–5. The next day the company patrolled from the jungle eastward through the northern edge of the Michelin Rubber Plantation. Captain Cain was suffering one of his frequent and severe headaches. His eyes were glazed over and his demeanor and countenance broadcast a man on the verge of screaming. During a stop, Cain sent a squad along our back trail for rear security, then forgot to call it in before we moved on. The error was soon noted, and a platoon returned and brought in the lost squad.

Cain had been wounded twice before I joined the battalion. Once a bullet entered his lower abdomen and exited through his left hip. The other time, Cain took a piece of shrapnel in the face. The hot steel entered the side of his nose and lodged under the skin above the nape (back) of his neck. This injury accounted for his blinding, agonizing headaches.

After retrieving the lost squad, we moved farther east and into the edge of the jungle. There under the trees just outside the rubber plantation, we established an FOB. As we dug in, I saw VC punji stakes for the first and only time in War Zone C—this was quite different from the highlands in 1966–67, when punji stakes had been a common threat.

Cain and I discussed the dilemma of headaches from the perspective of command and career. He very much wanted to finish his six months in command, but in light of his error earlier in the day, he worried that another mistake might get people killed. Still, he believed it could end his military career if he requested his own relief from a combat command. He believed his career concerns were justified because Peterson had reprimanded him for leaving his artillery FO in command when he was medevaced out from his company after being wounded.

The next day, with Cain's reluctant permission, I talked with Lieutenant Colonel Peterson about Cain's demonstrated courage, efforts, and performance, and the debilitating effects of his headaches. I recommended that Jim be reassigned short of the completion of six months in command for medical reasons. Cain was reassigned to the battalion staff ahead of schedule and replaced by Bill Kehoe, a newly promoted—or about to be promoted—captain who worked in the TOC.

The division sustained a chaplain casualty about this time in April. Chaplains James Carter and Nicholas Waytowich, like Black and me, shared coverage of two battalions, but with a different modus operandi. Waytowich and Carter focused almost exclusively on providing worship services. Normally, the pair traveled together, hopping from company to company to provide concurrent or consecutive Catholic and Protestant services. Often they spent a night in one or the other's rear-area accommodations.

Waytowich and his assistant's sleeping quarters in Tay Ninh were in a rectangular room at the back, south end of a building. The middle and north end of the building served as a unit chapel. This was but one of several identical buildings aligned with military precision in rows running east to west near the north perimeter.

The sleeping area contained two cots, one on each end, with enough space between them for cots to be set to accommodate guests. Steel and sandbags enclosed the cots at the east and west ends of the room, leaving small openings for getting in and out of bed. During a visit with Waytowich and Carter, I concluded that I did not like the bunkered-in cots. But events were about to prove them quite effective and worthwhile.

Waytowich and his assistant went to bed one evening a few days after my visit, each in his own cocoon. Chaplain Carter bedded down in the guest cot. During the night their building took a direct hit. An NVA 122mm on a delayed fuse crashed through the roof and floor and exploded in the ground beneath Carter. The rocket's entrance or explosion took off both of Carter's legs at the hips. Waytowich and his assistant were shaken but unhurt. Carter lived and received a medical discharge.

thirty-four

Mind Your Own Business

On Wednesday, April 23, I accompanied Delta 1–5 on an air assault into the western part of the 2–12 Cav AO. Delta Company was temporarily under the operational control (OPCON) of Lieutenant Colonel Boon and the 2–12 Cav. The next morning, following a hot and uneventful night, the company split into platoons. I went with First Lieutenant Larry Dee Brock's platoon. About midmorning, Brock received orders to find a PZ. We did so, and shortly were picked up and flown to the southwest, where we became OPCON to a mechanized company of either the 11th Armored Cavalry Regiment or the 25th Infantry Division.

When we arrived, the tankers were in the process of destroying a Sheridan tank, one the NVA had disabled with an RPG. The Sheridan had been declared unsalvageable under current combat conditions. The tankers finished stuffing the Sheridan with explosives. Then they (with Brock's platoon atop tanks and APCs) moved off a kilometer to the northwest. From that distance, an M-60 tank fired a single HE (high explosive) shell at the disabled Sheridan, with very impressive results. The turret flew upward about one thousand meters, as I recall, and returned to the earth through a rising, mushroom-shaped cloud.

We spent the rest of the day riding atop tanks and APCs, with occasional stops. Snipers usually took advantage of these stops to take potshots at us from distant tree lines. On the move, standing behind the turret of the lead tank with Brock and his RTO, we watched a long ugly gash being torn through the virgin jungle as small trees and forest giants yielded to the irresistible power of the M-60 tank. It seemed that nothing nature-made could resist "our" tank as it rumbled forward with its cannon pointed slightly off to the right or left. As I recall, the mechanized unit moved in two or three columns, each with an M-60 tank in the lead to cut its own swath through the jungle parallel to ours.

At one point a five-inch-diameter limb shook loose from a falling tree. It broke across my helmet, knocking me to my knees. Three factors combined to spare me injury: my helmet, a hard head, and the fact that the limb was rotten.

A little later, our column turned south along a swath in the jungle that had been made previously by these or other tanks. The going became much more difficult for both tanks and APCs because we were moving against the lay of the fallen trees, opposite from the direction they had been pushed down.

Lieutenant Brock of Oklahoma City, Oklahoma was sitting on a tanker's waterproof bag atop the right side of the turret as we rumbled over and through this mess. Suddenly, the forward movement of the tank drove the sharp end of a small, broken tree into the bag on which Brock sat. The scene was reminiscent of a medieval knight driving his jousting lance into an opponent's saddle. The bag catapulted into the air with Brock on it. Reflexively, I caught Brock as he flew over my head, and dropped him with a thump onto the tank. This rescue may or may not have kept Brock from being crushed beneath the treads of the second tank in the column, from breaking bones on fallen trees, or impaling body parts on broken limbs and splintered tree tops. Brock believed it did, and thanked me profusely. I felt great satisfaction that I had reacted quickly enough.

Well past twilight the tanks and APCs stopped for the night. I recalled anew one reason I hated working with tanks. Armor types had a habit of continuing until dark, stopping too late for accompanying infantry to dig in properly. Digging in was no big deal for the armored people. They had the equipment for the job.

To establish an impressive FOB, the mechanized folks simply used the tanks to knock down the local flora to clear both the areas inside of the perimeter and fields of fire. This done, they drew into a circle like a herd of musk-oxen, front armor and cannons outward, with the tanks interspersed among the APCs. As final preparation, the tank gunners loaded their cannons with flechette rounds and lowered them for direct fire. Defensive matters attended to, the tankers and APC crews attended to personal matters, preventive maintenance, and equipment repair routines, with very little concern for light and noise discipline. The tank and APC crews were content to spend the night inside their armor.

Cringing at all the noise, with images of NVA swarming toward them, the grunts dug in as best they could in the darkness or made do on the open ground. One thing experienced infantrymen weren't about to do in an attack on the perimeter was take cover beneath a tank or APC. Proximity to tracked combat vehicles greatly increased the odds of ending up crushed, punctured, or burned—tanks were like magnets to enemy rockets and they burned hot when their ammo load and fuel cooked off. We had a quiet night, fortunately.

The next day, April 24, Brock's platoon rejoined Delta 1–5. I remained on the chopper that picked us up and had it deliver me to Bravo 1–5, in the jungle northeast of LZ Dolly. Newly promoted Captain King (an assigned alias) had recently taken command. All day, King's men kept turning up fresh signs that the NVA were active in the area, but the enemy themselves remained elusive.

King stopped his company at 1630 hours, in one of those rare areas of old-growth forest that reminded me more of hardwood forests back home than jungle in Vietnam. The trees were huge and the undergrowth was sparse, which meant good fields of fire for us but also an easy approach for any NVA who might want to attack us in the night.

A chopper resupplied us soon after we stopped for the night. My assistant and I, with no other pressing duties, commenced digging a foxhole. Something was bothering me as we dug. A quick glance around the perimeter during a rest from digging told me what it was. Every man in sight was busily sorting C-ration and care-package goodies, reading

354   Claude D. Newby

mail, or constructing a rain shelter. None was digging or filling sandbags. My first thought was that the forest-like surroundings had pacified the troops into a false sense of peace
and security, but the real problem was something else.
Captain King, having stretched a hammock between two
trees, was testing it for comfort as he surveyed his new command—leading by example, deadly example.

I called King away from the CP and said, "You are setting a bad example for the troops, and it's going to get them
hurt or killed."

"What do you mean?" he demanded testily.

"When the troops see you relaxing, they relax, assuming
you know more about the situation than they do. When you
spend the remaining daylight attending to creature comforts,
the troops do too," I explained. King's facial muscles tensed
up. He just stared at me silently. I added in essence, "By using a hammock out here you do more than set a bad example.
You also place yourself right in the line of grazing fire and in
the most lethal path of shrapnel from bursting mortars."

"Mind your own business, Chaplain," King snapped,
"and I'll take care of my command. Besides, when the mortars start popping I can be out of my hammock and into my
foxhole as fast as anyone on the ground can."

So my assistant and I attended to "chaplain stuff," which
stuff never pleased my assistant. "It doesn't seem necessary
for us to be the only ones digging in," he opined. We dug,
and only then did we set up a rain shelter.

Perhaps it wasn't so, but for the first and only time among
a CP element in a combat unit, I felt unwelcome. I avoided
the CP and spent the remaining daylight with grunts on the
perimeter and talked with three visitors, actually four counting a beautiful German Shepherd scout dog. Division had attached a scout-dog team and a chemical specialist to the
company for this operation. A civilian reporter had attached
himself for his own reasons. The trooper from Division
Chemical packed a fancy, non-regulation chrome-plated
Army .45-caliber pistol in an army-issue leather holster.

The night was quiet. Sometime the next day I returned to

LZ Dolly without another word exchanged between King and me—we'd never have another chance. I've often wished we had parted on cordial terms.

On Friday, 25 April, Bravo 1–5 continued to follow fresh signs of enemy activity, right into a recently-vacated NVA bunker complex. None opposed their entry into the complex, so they commandeered it for an FOB. Perhaps King was pleased with all the overhead cover just waiting for new occupants. For a second night, there would be very little digging of foxholes.

An embankment about two to three feet high meandered through the center of the complex from southeast to northwest. In its center the embankment turned sharply north and then swung westward, creating a crescent around a cluster of bunkers and a well. King chose these bunkers with their overhead cover for the CP element and visitors. Resupplies arrived and were distributed. Among the resupplies was a lot of CS gas. The trooper from Division Chemical used the gas to contaminate the well and deprive the NVA of water. Some of the troopers on the perimeter had to dig fighting positions, while others like the CP pressed NVA positions into service for the night.

True to current leadership style, many of the troopers settled in casually. King again erected his hammock, this time between two trees. This arrangement put him about four feet from a bunker, on the opposite side from the entrance. The rest of the CP got comfortable among the cluster of bunkers about the well. The dog handler tied his German Shepherd on an unnecessarily short leash to a tree root that protruded from the bank, then settled down for the night.

The NVA mortared the FOB fourteen minutes past midnight on April 26. First came the frighteningly familiar *thump, thump, thump* of mortar rounds leaving tubes out in the nearby jungle. "Incoming!" yelled several troopers on the perimeter. Experienced grunts slipped under cover even as they snapped awake. Some of the less-experienced troopers frantically scurried about the middle of the perimeter in the darkness in search of the cover that they'd thought was well-fixed in their minds when they went to sleep.

No one knows how Captain King reacted. One of the first incoming 82mm mortar shells exploded beneath his hammock and decapitated him.

The dog handler and reporter made it to cover. The dog died at the end of its leash with its body stretching toward the entrance of the bunker where its handler had taken cover. The trooper from Division Chemical was killed. His .45 pistol was missing.

The ARVN scout/interpreter (not Sergeant Van Nie, I think) came close to dying when he jumped up instead of going for cover at the yells of "incoming!" He was understandably perturbed that no one had explained the meaning of the term to him.

On the south side of the perimeter, a mortar shell exploded on the overhead cover of a foxhole, wounding Pfc. William Brown and destroying an M-60 machine gun.

Back on LZ Dolly in the early morning light, Captain Jay Copley asked me to accompany him on the flight that would take him out to replace Captain King.

Copley had entered the Army from Kentucky in 1949 as a private. He went into combat as an infantryman on July 31, 1950 with the 5th Regimental Combat Team. He left Korea as a WIA in May 1951 and returned to combat in 1952. In May 1967 he joined the 1st Cavalry in Vietnam as the Sergeant Major of the 2–5 Cav, operating out of LZ Uplift, just a few kilometers south of my unit on the Bong Son Plain. He received a battlefield commission with the rank of captain in February 1968 and moved across the LZ to take command of C Company, 1st Battalion, 50th Mechanized Infantry, 173rd Airborne Brigade. On May 1, 1968 he sustained gunshot wounds to the neck, right lung, and shoulder blade. After several months in military hospitals, Jay Copley arrived back in Vietnam just when Bravo 1–5 suddenly needed a commander.

Copley and I offloaded from the chopper in a small clearing. We moved quickly out of the way of a detail that waited to load poncho-wrapped bodies onto the chopper. Moments later a cursory look around the FOB told the story. King had ignored common-sense advice and gotten himself killed. By accepting NVA hospitality, he'd placed his command in a position with which the NVA were intimately familiar. They responded by lobbing in twenty 82mm mortars, almost without having to pause to adjust fire. Every shell exploded inside or on the perimeter.

One of Copley's first actions was to order a search for the late Division Chemical trooper's chrome-plated .45. It was found off in the bushes. Copley ordered that the pistol be sent to the rear and placed with the trooper's personal effects.

As soon as the casualties were evacuated, Copley had his men check the immediate area and then move out on a company-size recon toward the east. We continued to see lots of evidence that the NVA were very active in the area, but got through the day and following night without a fight.

Beginning at 0832 hours the next morning, choppers flew a series of round-robin sorties to concurrently move Bravo 1–5 to LZ Dolly and to combat assault Delta 1–5 from Dolly to a point a little east of where Bravo 1–5 was picked up. This rotation was timely, though it had been planned at least a day earlier. A week on and around LZ Dolly would allow Copley and his new command to get used to one another and get over some of the shocking events of the previous night.

I returned to Dolly with the first group, to prepare for the worship service Copley wanted his men to have as soon as possible. With the change of command, I was again welcome in the Bravo 1–5 Command Group.

At 0856 hours I hopped off the chopper, ducked low beneath the whirling rotor blades and headed up a gentle grade toward the TOC and my bunker. Captain Patrick Greiner, Delta 1–5 Company Commander, and Lieutenant Larry Brock met me halfway up the hill. "Sir, Chaplain Newby saved my neck the other day on the tanks," Brock declared to Greiner, and described how I'd grabbed him in mid-air to keep him from falling off the tank.

Pat Greiner thanked me for keeping his lieutenant out of

trouble and asked, "How about making the air assault with us this morning? We'd really appreciate it."

"I promised Bravo Company a service as soon as we're all on the LZ. I'll conduct the service and come back out," I promised. I headed for the TOC to get word out about the service. Pat and Larry Brock boarded a chopper with the first lift and went to war.

It was hard to put Greiner off, but the men of Bravo 1–5 desperately needed immediate spiritual support, interlaced with specific counsel about vigilance in the jungle.

Most of the Bravo 1–5 troopers attended the worship service as did Lieutenant Colonel Peterson and many others, sitting on the ground on a slope near the aid station and my bunker, facing south. The service was simple. My assistant passed out some laminated song sheets. We sang a song and I prayed, and was well into the sermon when a call from the TOC interrupted us.

"Sir, you'd better come quick. Delta is in deep sh—. Four friendly KIAs and lots of WIAs, still in contact," yelled a sergeant.

"Sorry, Chaplain," said Peterson as he took off for his TOC. For the remainder of the service, I gazed into the eyes of Bravo troopers that were filled with relief, remorse, regret, even guilt: relief because Delta 1–5 guys were in the fight and not themselves; regret, perhaps even guilt, because others were dying in their place.

The service over, I flew to Delta Company and helped load several dead and wounded men onto the chopper that delivered me there. Then I went looking for Captain Greiner and found him on the opposite side of a termite hill from where the ambush had occurred. He was wounded, but refused to be evacuated until his CP and Delta Company were reorganized. In Greiner's words, here is what happened:

"We were completing our week of base defense . . . when word came that Captain King had been killed . . . [in a] mortar attack. . . . [He had been] sleeping in a hammock when the attack occurred. The timing was good for our relief. Jay Copley had taken command of B Company, replacing King, and would be bringing them in to replace us on base defense on LZ Dolly.

"On the morning of 27 April, as we were preparing for the combat assault, Mateus, one of my best men, mentioned a continuing problem with one eye. And though the medics had cleared him for the field and I would have liked to leave him behind for treatment, I briefly emphasized how shorthanded we were, and how much we needed everyone on this assault, especially someone with his experience. Mateus was an excellent soldier who never asked for special treatment, and he didn't this time. Instead, saying no more, he got his gear and headed for the pickup zone.

"As we lifted off from LZ Dolly, I continually rubbed the silver spoon I carried to eat my C-rations with—a kind of joke that had become my good luck charm. The combat assault was uneventful. The first element, which included my CP, landed without opposition or incident, even though we landed forward of the planned set-down point because of heavy smoke and dust that had been kicked up by a massive preparation fire from artillery and Blue Max ARA gunships.

"Once all the company was on the ground, we moved out to the east toward our objective, to check thick jungle, trails, and small streambeds for hiding places that could not be spotted from the air. Almost immediately, our lead element encountered bunkers. We stopped and formed a perimeter and sent out cloverleaf patrols. We weren't about to walk carelessly into something big. . . . At this point Sergeant James Meyer led his Third Platoon out, and just minutes later he radioed that they had come onto a T-intersection trail (a trail where another trail joins it) and running into heavy signs of recent activity—a 'Gook' latrine that had recently been used. We continued to check the area.

"A few moments later all hell broke loose—heavy fire and explosions accompanied by the dreadful realization that the majority of it was coming from the enemy.

"At first there was no response to our radioed request to

3–6 for a sitrep. Then after what seemed like minutes but was probably about 30 seconds, the call came back. 'Six! Six! We are hit! We are hit! We are all down, need help!'

"Translated, this meant thirteen wounded or dead grunts were pinned to the ground in the kill zone of an enemy ambush by a continuous heavy volume of enemy fire.

"I immediately ordered Lieutenant Brock and his Second Platoon and my CP forward, and directed the First Platoon to attack more or less straight ahead toward the enemy's left front. I intended that these two platoons would force the enemy back so they could recover the dead and wounded 3–6 troopers.

"As I was positioning my CP behind a termite hill, Brock's men moved on past and immediately began to lay down a heavy volume of fire on the enemy's right front. By this time many wounded and pinned-down members of 3–6 element were also returning fire.

"The enemy small-arms and B-40 rocket fire continued without letup, but now we were firing back with everything we had. And Lieutenant George T. Prosser, my artillery forward observer—call sign, Birth Control Four-Niner—was adjusting artillery and ARA fire. It looked like we were quickly getting the situation under control. But just as our artillery began firing for effect, a B-40 rocket landed in my CP. It detonated as best we could determine on the point of my rifle, which at the time I was holding lightly in my right hand as it lay beside me on the ground.

"The instant the round hit I saw a ball of fire by my right foot at the same time that I was thrown back. My first thought as I pulled myself up was that our own artillery—a short round—had hit us. 'No,' Prosser assured me later. The rounds he called in had exploded on target a few seconds earlier.

"As I looked around, I noted Brock's horribly mangled body lying a few feet in front of my position, as was the still body of his RTO, Sp4 Gary Roy Smith of Laconia, New Hampshire. I didn't recognize Brock or Smith at the moment. It was later that the pieces all came back together.

Brock had been out in front of his men gallantly directing their efforts during the extremely heavy contact. Smith, his RTO, was right where he needed to be—beside his platoon leader. Among the other wounded were three other RTOs and Lieutenant Wendling.

"My rifle peppered me when it exploded, but the wounds were minor, kind of like getting stuck a hundred times with a lead pencil.

"The next few minutes were a blur. But during those minutes we directed the troopers and they continued to lay down a strong base of fire, while we popped smoke and marked our position for Blue Max and continued to direct artillery support. Soon, Prosser had the gunships spray the trees around the contact area, which allowed us to break contact—total elapsed time was probably thirty minutes that seemed like hours.

"As we pulled back to the LZ that we'd assaulted into an hour or so before, I lugged one RTO's radio and Prosser another one. On the way we added a machine gun and other assorted gear that our dead and wounded had dropped. Back in the enemy bunkers, we huddled for protection as fighters swished overhead and each dropped their six 750-pound bombs on the contact area. Prosser directed those too. His coolness and professionalism under intense enemy fire saved a lot of lives that day.

"When the first medevac arrived, I was both pleased and surprised to see Claude Newby walking my way. I always thought Newby was really a frustrated infantryman. He knew infantry tactics and was quick to provide his opinion when he thought it appropriate. I had no problem with this—I needed all the help I could get, both tactically and spiritually, and Claude gave good advice on both accounts.

"Among the wounded I saw Mateus lying on his back on top of a bunker. He was alive but had a sucking chest wound. 'How are you doing?' I asked him.

" 'Well, my eye doesn't hurt anymore, Six.'

"As we completed the evacuation and regrouping, my XO Lieutenant Ash arrived and took command."

Pat Greiner's account as given here agrees mostly with what he told me that day on the scene, except that I distinctly remember him updating me at the very spot where the B-40 rocket killed Brock and wounded Greiner. I recall concluding from the nature of Brock's wounds that the rocket hit him in the back from the rear even as he faced toward Greiner and the enemy out beyond the termite hill. I remember as Greiner described these events, I looked around for a likely place for the rocket to have come from. I concluded that it had to have come from high in the largest tree in the area, about twenty meters behind the mound. With that conclusion came the eerie feeling or impression that another B-40 rocket waited in the tube on an NVA soldier's shoulder, just waiting for him to get his fill of satisfaction from the results he'd already achieved before he let fly another blast of destruction. My impression was taken seriously. I'd finished relaying it when several grunts hosed the tree with M-16 and M-60 machine-gun bullets.

Lieutenant George T. Prosser, Greiner's FO, provides this graphic description of the engagement. "Chaplain Newby . . . I am sure Pat's account is accurate in every way, with the exception that in his modesty he does little justice to his own role. We all know the commander is vital. . . . We expect him to be a major factor . . . [under] duress. I'm convinced we dodged a much worse outcome (I'm talking overrun) without the leadership we had to have and got from Captain Greiner. He very casually dismissed his own wounds. Let me tell you, he was a mess, [and] in pain. He did not have the use of his weapon or his hand. . . . [For a time] the bad guys had fire superiority and it was possible Pat was going to have to fight with [one useless] hands. . . . While Greiner was shredded and bleeding, [and] covered with matter from Lieutenant Brock . . . we didn't know that the partial body in our CP was Lieutenant Brock. . . . Captain responded like the seasoned veteran he was. How . . . he remained calm and capable of giving coherent directions is beyond me—if he had not, the results would have been appalling. [Nothing] can take away from . . . the amazing bravery of our troops in that war. . . .

that they displayed if they had direction. That's what got us through—Pat Greiner's cool direction under intense fire [despite his own] intense pain.

"First Lieutenant Brock died doing his job . . . an incredibly brave man. I remember in several conversations with Larry that he knew he would not survive the war. I don't know why he felt that way; he didn't resent it; he just knew it. How we wish he had been wrong!

"I remember the terrifying realization that the enemy was in the trees. [My] recon sergeant [Rodriguez] and an RTO [Francis, a Navajo] with me . . . [we] fell to the ground . . . with Rodriguez between Francis and me. . . . I first realized we had a tree problem [when] Rodriguez was shot, while Francis and I were spared. That is extremely bad news in triple-canopy jungle. . . . I have to give immense credit to the Blue MAX [gunships] for saving us from that most diabolical and dire situation.

"As a forward observer I recall many times when we had high explosives . . . explode in close proximity. Only once, that day, do I recall [that] air support [jets] so close that I tasted the cordite before I experienced the flash/bang/concussion. I don't know if that is even possible, but I know it happened—I can still taste it after thirty-one years.

"Finally, I remember the bodies lined up, covered with ponchos, awaiting removal after the wounded had been evacuated. Then, and how do you make sense of this, I remember it rained that night—a slow, drizzly, soaking, mournful rain; the first rain we had seen in months. The rainy season had begun."

In retrospect, someone on the NVA side that morning and the night before possessed excellent tactical skills and lots of combat savvy and insight. These traits he demonstrated by how he (one leader might have orchestrated both actions) anticipated Captain King's decisions the day before and Greiner's reactions this morning. The NVA ambush was superbly placed and executed. And it was eerie that the

NVA leader had possessed enough insight to cover the likely place for our CP to take cover.

Consequently the NVA ambush and subsequent attack killed five great soldiers, including Lieutenant Larry Brock, and wounded about thirty-three others and a civilian reporter. Except for a few blood trails and an occasional piece of NVA equipment, there was little evidence that the enemy had paid a price for their success. The Delta 1–5 First Sergeant would become a casualty of this action in a very unusual, unexpected way.

Meanwhile, Lieutenant Brock's death left me pondering, coming as it did within an hour of his heaping praise upon me for saving him from serious injuries, injuries that might have saved him from a violent death four days later. *Did I get Brock killed by rescuing him? Would things have turned out different had I accompanied Delta Company instead of delaying on LZ Dolly to provide a worship service for Bravo Company?*

Reason quickly dispelled these doubts, and unreasonable guilt yielded to spiritual solace and relief. Right there where Brock sacrificed his life, a powerful sense of peace and confirmation poured into me, bringing with it reassurance and insight. In an instant, I saw clearly that I'd done the best I could with Brock on the tank and later with him and Greiner on LZ Dolly, limited as I was by mortal foresight and reasoning powers. And I "knew" that my presence during the ambush and fight would have changed nothing, except perhaps for my family and me. I knew deep inside where it counts that I'd done right to keep Brock from being thrown from the tank, as he would have done for me, had our roles been reversed. No, my actions on Thursday did not make me responsible for what happened on Sunday. Ever since that moment there by the termite hill, I've been free of any conscious guilt for Lieutenant Brock's death—not grief, but guilt. Consequently, I've been better able to hear and counsel other long-suffering veterans during times of grief and unreasonable guilt.

*   *   *

After a quiet night to lick their wounds, except for the frequent "swoosh" and "karrump" of friendly artillery, Delta 1–5 swept through the area where it had been ambushed the day before. Where giant trees and thick foliage stood twenty-four hours earlier, now stood splintered tree trunks, some with a few bare branches still attached and dangling. The ground was littered with fallen, mangled foliage.

In the midst of all this destruction and bad memories there appeared something quite beautiful and seemingly out of place. An amazingly colorful, crow-size tropical bird perched on the branch of a small, shattered tree. Apparently the bird was shell-shocked, for it did not react when a trooper took it in hand and checked it for injuries. It appeared to be unhurt. Those battle-hardened troopers evacuated the beautiful bird to LZ Dolly and made it Delta Company's mascot.

At LZ Dolly, Delta Company's first sergeant built the bird a cage in his bunker—he usually stayed on the LZ to coordinate and ensure adequate support for Delta Company out in the field. I saw the bird in the cage a few days later. It appeared to have recovered from its ordeal in battle with Delta Company.

A few days or a week or so after that found me waiting in the early morning darkness on the "Dust-Off" pad at the hospital in Cu Chi. I had come to visit some of my troopers and then spent most of the night trying to hitch a ride back to the 1st Cav AO.

About 0300 hours, a medic alerted me that a 1st Cav chopper was coming in with a fever-of-unknown-origin patient. The odds were small that the chopper was from my battalion AO, but I prepared to board it to get back to the Cav AO where I'd have a better chance of getting to one of my battalions.

The medevac chopper landed and medics quickly offloaded the first sergeant of Delta 1–5. He was comatose—encephalitis, inflammation of the brain. The first sergeant was evacuated to the states, and word came back that he was a "vegetable" for life, however long that might be. The medics believed the first sergeant caught the deadly disease from vermin living on the beautiful tropical bird that he'd made a home for in his bunker.

Notes

26 April 1969, 1–5 Battalion Journal, 0020: "B Co received 20 rds of 82mm mortar in FOB, resulting in 02 US KIA and 02 WIA . . . evacuation of wounded will be at first light. Note: One of the KIAs was their C.O. B 16 has shrapnel wounds and is assuming command of company. Also B Co lost M-60 as a result of direct hit . . . Scout dog wounded, seriousness unknown at this time." KIAs: Captain [name withheld] and J. Balou [James D. Valov from "the Wall"]. WIAs: 1LT James Joyner, Sp4s Roger Mendell and David Boudeau; Pfcs. William Brown and Irvin Barnett. Also WIA were S. Theil, Division Chemical and John Bordas, a civilian reporter.

  0945: Questions and answers between Bde S-3 and Div 6-B:
   1. What time did unit move into RON position? A. 151600 April.
   2. Distance to LOG pad? A. No Log pad, between 1720 and 1810, they took a kickout of 2 sorties, 100 meters away. Also had penetrator medevac at 1850 hrs.
   3. Was unit dug in? A. The 2 KIAs were sleeping above ground—the rest were dug in with OHC [overhead cover].
   4. Was FOB used previously? A. Negative.
   5. Status of noise and light discipline? A. Status good—no unusual violations.
   6. Readout: Area had been used by 1–3 individuals in last 2–3 weeks.

27 Apr 1969, 1–5 Cav Journal: "At 1125 hours they [D Co] came into heavy contact . . . enemy probably in bunkers. The 36 element was in the lead and what they hit appears to have been an ambush. The 26 element moved forward quickly and also came under heavy fire . . . mostly B-40 rockets and small arms . . . B-40s causing the most casualties. Contact broke at 1158 hours . . . 3 NVA killed by air strikes."

  1300: "D Co became in contact with unk. number of NVAs

while searching bunker complex. Contact began at 1137 ... stopped getting returned fire at 1150 ... friendly casualties, 21 WIAs and 4 KIAs." Delta 1–5 KIAs: 1LT Brock, Chambers [of Maysville, Oklahoma], Pfc. William W. Henderson [Lyndhurst, Virginia], Smith [Laconia, New Hampshire] and Bray [Paris, Texas] died later of wound. Delta 1–5 WIAs: Erford, Crismore, White, Rodriguez [of Fallon, NV], Davis, Erickson, Mougthty, Hunter, Meyers, Mateus, Gary, Anthont, Ford, Guss, Jardell, Actquilar, Gatto, Grandchamp, Sargent, Hughes, Karastory, Blehm, Bonimi, and Greiner (Company Commander). Other WIAs: Casey and Wendling of HHC (medics) and Groves of B/1–77 (artillery FO); and Wigham for shell shock.

thirty-five

Double Jeopardy

A season of less-intense combat settled over the 1–5 Cav AO for a few days. Consequently I focused a little more time and energy toward the 2–12 Cav AO, where more was happening. I ended my second month in the field—lifetimes compressed into sixty days.

On May 6, Alpha 2–12 was engaged in close, furious combat with a strong NVA force. American casualties mounted rapidly, and the Company Commander called in medevac to extract the three most serious of its nine wounded infantrymen. The battle raged beneath triple-canopy jungle, so the most seriously wounded guys would have to be extracted by jungle penetrator—a buckle-in stretcher at the end of a cable.

Several minutes before 1700 hours, a medevac chopper came to a hover above where the appropriate color of smoke trickled up through the trees. Over the next several minutes, the penetrator hoisted out two wounded grunts. Naturally, the NVA were busy too, trying to move into position to shoot down the chopper.

The third WIA had cleared the trees and was dangling below the hovering choppers when, at 1704 hours, the NVA opened fire. What happened next chilled the hearts of the troopers on the ground.

Concurrent with the NVA fire on the chopper, the troopers on the ground saw the chopper speed away, as their wounded buddy, wire litter and all, hurtled into the trees. "D—them . . . Gooks. They shot the cable in two!" a trooper shouted.

Later I learned different. And I kept what I learned to myself because I didn't want the grunts shooting down a medevac chopper the next time they saw a casualty fall from the sky. By mid-1969, medevac choppers were rigged with explosive charges so the penetrator cables could be *cut* in the event the chopper was about to crash onto a wounded patient or onto troopers on the ground.

Well, in this instance the chopper wasn't about to crash. Someone on board had apparently panicked and cut the cable at the first sound of AK-47 rounds cracking nearby. The wounded soldier fell into the trees and the medevac chopper returned to Tay Ninh without any bullet holes in its skin. An hour and a half later, the grunts found their buddy in the wire litter, barely alive, hanging head-down from a tree. He may have survived.

On May 7, Platoon Sergeant Elvin Jackson and his men came upon a bomb crater in the jungle. The bomb that made the crater had also cleared the bamboo back about five feet from it. The platoon continued through the clearing one man at a time, skirting the edge of the crater on the left. Three squads had crossed safely when Jackson entered the clearing. As he started around the crater, three NVA soldiers appeared and knelt down in the edge of the bamboo just ahead of him and to his left. They were looking right toward him. "I quickly dropped into the crater and motioned for my RTO to get down too—he was following fairly closely to keep the radio handy to me," said Jackson.

Even in the crater, Jackson and the RTO remained clearly exposed to hostile view, and were certain they'd be cut down by bursts of AK-47 fire if they attempted to swing their weapons up. After a moment, the NVA turned around and disappeared back into the jungle. "It was as if blinders were placed on their eyes so that they could not see me, though I was in plain sight. It's hard to explain, but I believe God shielded me from the NVA, so they could not see me," Jackson said.

Jackson reported the incident to Captain Hurt, who asked, "Why didn't you open fire?" Despite Jackson's explanation that it would have been impossible to take out the

NVA under the circumstances, and suicidal to try, Hurt said, "Sergeant Jackson, tonight I'm writing up charges against you for dereliction of duty." Hurt came down with malaria before the day was over. First Lieutenant Phil Gioia took command of the company, and Jackson heard nothing more of the threatened charges.

The beginning of my third month in country found me in Saigon. I had arrived there at 2200 hours on May 9 to attend a conference scheduled for May 11. I spent that night and May 10 with Major Rulon Paul Madsen, whom I first met in April 1967 at a conference in Japan. His billet in a hotel in the middle of Saigon was air conditioned and had hot and cold running water, maid service, and a hotel-style GI mess. I enjoyed a rare and long hot shower. The next morning a sedan, compliments of Madsen, delivered me to Ton San Nhut Air Base, where I spent the morning shopping for gifts for the family, a very neglected family the past two months.

At 1300 hours I attended an ecclesiastical leadership meeting. During the meeting Navy Captain Payne in his farewell remarks—his tour in Vietnam was at an end—said, "Chaplain Newby, you will never know what a wonderful effect you had on my family at the Mt. Fuji Conference in 1967. I will be ever grateful to you." A very kind tribute.

Paul Madsen inadvertently complicated my return to the 1st Cav AO by turning over to me an M-16 rifle, the old style with the open-pronged flash suppressor so handy for opening C-ration boxes. Madsen said he had no idea who the weapon belonged to, and asked me to get it into the proper channels when I was finished with it. So, with an olive drab towel around my neck to hide my chaplain insignia, I hitched a ride to Bien Hoa with an Army chaplain and his assistant. My benefactor assumed I was an infantryman, an understandable and welcome mistake considering my grubby clothing and hidden insignia of branch and rank.

Early on May 12 the NVA simultaneously attacked the 1st Cav base camp at Phuoc Vinh and every battalion firebase in the AO except LZ Dolly. I was asleep on the concrete floor of the Division Chaplain's office when the attack on Camp Gorvad (Phuoc Vinh) began. For the next hour I lay there and listened to the explosions of incoming rockets and the occasional rattle of shrapnel on the tin roof. From off in the distance came the sound of close combat, the unsynchronized fire of small arms, machine guns, and exploding hand grenades and claymore mines. An ineffectual ground attack was being beaten back at one point on the perimeter. Camp Gorvad was named in honor of LTC Peter Gorvad, the same who was killed back in March while I was still processing in to the division up at An Khe.

On the morning of May 15, following a quiet night on LZ Dolly, I entered the TOC for a sitrep. Based on skimpy intelligence reports, it looked like there would be no combat that day. Lieutenant Colonel Peterson was about to fly toward the area he thought any combat would be most likely. I boarded a slick ship (resupply helicopter) and flew to Bravo 1–5, in the other direction. Bravo Company was on its third futile day of searching an area suspected to harbor a large cache of NVA supplies. Peterson would move the company unless it found something in the next few hours.

On the ground, the company commander and I decided to hold a worship service as soon as a squad-size patrol closed with the perimeter. After two or three nights in the same place, the FOB was taking on the appearance of a permanent camp, and the troopers appeared much too relaxed. In an instant, though, everyone was awake and looking sharp.

The returning patrol had just radioed in. "We're about two hundred meters to the west and coming in," when a burst of AK-47 fire added a stuttering exclamation point to the radio transmission.

The patrol leader, perhaps having lapsed into a false sense of security as the patrol neared the company, had led his patrol across an open field, the easiest, most direct route back to the FOB. The AK-47 opened up on the patrol even as the squad leader was delivering the radio message, just as the point man passed on the east side of a small clump of trees. The men hit the ground among the clump of trees and one shocked, happy squad leader gawked at his helmet. It had three bullet holes in it, but he was unhurt. A minute later, I arrived on the scene in company with Captain Copley and reinforcements.

Copley sent two platoons, well dispersed in a wedge formation, across the clearing and into the jungle to the west of the clearing. We easily found where the NVA were hidden when one of them "couldn't" resist such an inviting target.

The platoon I was with scouted about fifty meters into the jungle and then turned right to skirt a small clearing, keeping it on our left. Chest-high grass rimmed the clearing, except for an eight-foot wide section that we had to cross. The NVA let a few troopers cross the gap in the grass unmolested, then fired short bursts at the rest of us as we dashed across the gap one by one. We all made it. Obviously this NVA was not the same soldier who'd hit the squad leader's helmet three times at ten times the range here.

We continued on along the north side of the clearing and soon discovered the outskirts of the NVA stronghold for which the company had been searching. Several times, we attempted to maneuver against the nearest NVA bunkers, but were driven back each time by chicom grenades and bursts of AK-47 fire. The company commander ordered us back and called in artillery to pound the complex for the rest of the day. Meanwhile, Lieutenant Colonel Peterson flew over and radioed:

"Is One-Niner [Chaplain call sign] with you?"

"That's a 'rog'," the RTO replied.

"I knew it," answered Peterson.

Sometimes it seemed Peterson trusted my instincts more than he did Division Intelligence. Another time, following one of my rare orientations for replacements, Peterson said, "Chaplain Newby, having you is like having a second executive officer." I hadn't known he was listening in on the orientation.

In the morning on May 17, we swept back across the clearing and into the NVA bunker complex without meeting resistance at first. Apparently, the NVA had faded away during the night. Appearances were deceiving.

The CP of one of the platoons settled around and in a bunker while the platoons spread out and searched the area. Two troopers, for unexplained reasons, brought armloads of B-40 rockets and chicom grenades into the bunker where we waited in the cooler shade. I thought that was a good time to relate an incident that occurred two days earlier.

It happened on LZ Phyllis, south of the Fishhook and north of LZ Dolly nearer the Cambodian border. The NVA attacked LZ Phyllis viciously, then withdrew leaving lots of NVA bodies, rockets and shells scattered about. The next day a detail of troopers went about collecting the shells and rockets into a jeep-pulled trailer. Then for some reason the detail moved the vehicle and its deadly cargo inside the perimeter, where by accident or by NVA design the rockets and shells exploded. In an instant the lives of eight American infantrymen were snuffed out in a blinding flash of light and concussion. Ten other soldiers were wounded by the blast. A few days later I would visit abandoned LZ Phyllis and see the burned and demolished skeletons of the jeep and trailer that marked the exact spot where the eight troopers were blown away.

After listening to my story, the platoon leader called a halt to the collection of enemy rockets. We got ourselves out of that bunker, just in case, and were putting some space between the bunker and us when B-40 rockets started exploding.

Apparently the grunts got too close to something the NVA wanted to keep hidden. So from a well-concealed position they fired three or four B-40 rockets, one after the other along the same trajectory. Each rocket penetrated farther through the foliage until the last one exploded in the midst of the Americans and wounded some of them, one badly. Other NVA opened up with automatic weapons in support of the B-40 grenadiers.

Under covering fire being laid down by the rest of its platoon, the squad pulled back from the kill zone with their wounded. Quickly, we improvised a stretcher by chopping down and stripping two small trees and slipping them into a

folded, snapped-together poncho. With me carrying the
right rear corner of the stretcher, at the wounded man's right
shoulder, we withdrew under fire to the edge of the jungle.
Then, while 105mm and 155mm artillery rained down on
the NVA positions, we moved across the open field, past
where the patrol was fired on the day before, toward the
company FOB. We were about halfway across the clearing
when the trooper on the stretcher yelped in surprise and new
pain. A large chunk of sizzling-hot shrapnel had hurled
from the sky and buried itself in his right leg. Amazingly, he
was the only trooper seriously wounded in the engagement—"twice"—first by the B-40 rocket, and then by
friendly artillery at what was considered a fairly safe distance from the exploding shells. Little wonder the wounded
trooper was anxious later, when we were ordered to get under ground for overhead protection because air strikes were
coming in. He couldn't be placed in a foxhole because of his
wounds. And I couldn't leave him like that.

Quickly, I stacked rucksacks all around and over the
wounded trooper, leaving only his face partially exposed,
then laid down beside him to wait out the air strikes. I have
a picture of the trooper's grateful, smiling face, one someone snapped while I was barricading him. He survived the
air strikes without sustaining any more wounds. The following sky troopers were wounded in that engagement (he was
one of them): John Coates, Willie Chavez, Benny Wallace,
Thompson, Gordon Holtrey, and Edward Schulnerrich.

Unknown to me, my old Delta 2–8 Cav became OPCON
to the 2–12 Cav at 1840 on May 25. Soon after that, the
Angry Skipper troopers were hit by fifteen B-40 rockets and
perhaps some mortars. At 1930 hours, the point element
walked into a claymore mine and sustained three killed and
one wounded. Those killed were First Lieutenant John
Preston Karr of Kenner, Louisiana; Corporal Richard Neal
White of Golden Valley, New Mexico; and Pfc. Wayne Eric
Garven of Mt. Vernon, Ohio.

Sergeant Stephen R. Atchley of Odon, Indiana, whose

squad had the point for Delta 2–8 as it moved out that evening, tells what happened. "We left the firebase late in the evening of May 25, 1969. Choppers had dropped us off just as it was starting to get dark. We moved out with my squad on point. I was the squad leader of 2nd Squad [White Skull platoon].

"We soon came up on a bunker complex. It seemed to be empty [of NVA]. Captain Livingston, the CO, ordered us to keep moving, so we did and started finding stacks of mortars, grenades, and other ammunition, quite a bit of it.

"I thought we were getting into something bad, and reported what we were finding and my suspicions, and suggested that because it was getting dark we should pull back and set up, or set up where we were for the night. The CO said, 'No. We have to get to a certain place first.' He was green and had no idea what it was like to be on point, the time it takes to check things out, to cut a path . . . and then how all that becomes harder in the dark!"

Atchley continued. "We kept going and came upon a booby trap, a claymore mine—one of ours. We continued and soon came upon another booby trap and were trying to figure out what it was and how to get around it. All the time we were moving real slow, chopping through bamboo, and the CO kept calling to know what was taking so long, and pushing us to move on. Sp4 Fred Metz butted in on the radio and started needling Lieutenant Karr by telling him it was the platoon leader's job to move up and see what was going on. . . . Metz's squad leader shouldn't have let him touch the radio. . . . Metz was too *gung ho*, most of the guys in White Skull thought. Karr trusted me to know what I was doing. I'd been there longer than he had.

"But anyway because of Metz's needling, Karr and Wayne came to the point . . . when they got up there to us there was a blinding flash and I felt great heat and pressure. Don't remember any sound. Don't know if it was another booby trap, a command-detonated mine, or what.

"I tried to get up immediately . . . couldn't hardly hear and was dazed. Wayne was on the radio to the CO. Kept repeating, 'The lieutenant's been hit! I think he's . . . I think he's. . . . ' Wayne just couldn't say that he thought Karr was dead—couldn't get it out. I'd crawled to Wayne when he passed out . . . had to use his radio because Dick's was destroyed. Called for a medic, then started trying to get the other guys posted around for security . . . it was kind of chaos.

"The medic arrived by the time I got the guys in position, but there was nothing he could do for John [Karr] or Dick [White] or Wayne [Garven]. He thought all three were dead, but . . . this young black kid noticed that Wayne was still trying to breathe [and] started giving him mouth to mouth. . . . I took over and administered CPR . . . he [medic] . . . never checked Wayne out or anything, saying it was a lost cause. But I maintained a pulse for about twenty minutes.

"I had some metal in my leg, and my right knee was hurting badly. . . . The next morning . . . I helped carry Dick, and returned us to the LZ where we stayed about three days."

Atchley was evacuated a few days later. A four-star general, perhaps Creighton Abrams, visited him in the Army Hospital at Tan San Nhut to pin a purple heart on him. "I asked him what Karr, Dick and Wayne were getting.

" 'Their families will get purple hearts.'

"I told him [the general] to take my purple heart and 'stick it.'

" 'Son, you'll be sorry one of these days,' said the general.

"I am sorry. I didn't get any of my medals. Nothing," said Atchley.

Chuck Hustedt, another participant in the Delta 2–8 action wrote, "Lieutenant Karr got a letter . . . his wife was pregnant. [Atchley was] hit by a B-40 . . . command detonated. It appeared the Gook had suspended the B-40 above [Atchley]—there were wires hanging from the trees . . . looked like the wires suspended . . . the B-40 in the middle [over the path]."

Elsewhere, the last half of May was the quietest period of this tour to that point, but still plenty hot down at the grunt level. I was with Delta 1–5 one day during this "quiet" period when Alpha and Charlie 1–5 discovered a huge cache of food, weapons and munitions. Delta Company was sent into the area to help them search the site. This was the sort of pre-positioned cache that the NVA needed for serious attacks on American or ARVN forces and population centers. Somewhat reluctantly, the NVA moved out of the cache site as we entered it. As I recall, Alpha 1–5 first discovered the cache and Charlie 1–5 approached later from a different direction to help search the area.

Terry Brain said, "Alpha Company entered a bunker complex that seemed to have been abandoned." Savaard and I jumped into a bunker to check it out and I heard a hollow sound when we landed. After jumping up and down to be sure, we alerted the CO. Then we pulled up a false floor and discovered a cache of weapons. About then, someone from another platoon called and reported that the men were finding all kinds of stuff."

A trooper in Charlie 1–5 fell dead to machine-gun fire as we entered the cache site a little later. About the same time, I came upon a fighting position that had been evacuated so hurriedly the ground still seemed to retain body warmth, and chicom grenades lay where they'd been abandoned by reluctant defenders of the cache.

A cache like this one drew generals and reporters like honey draws flies. Both types descended on the scene as soon as the area was pronounced secure. Those who came for pictures got them, and those who found the cache, the grunts, got to perform unaccustomed stevedore-like chores for the next couple of days, without benefit of heavy-lifting equipment. I'll not discuss the firefight Delta 1–5 got into— can't remember it.

Friday, May 30, nine Latter-day Saints, infantrymen and artillerymen, and I met on my side of a cramped bunker and shared the sacrament and our testimonies. We'd finished the sacrament and begun to share testimonies when a young Jewish officer, the medical platoon leader as I recall, stuck his head in the door. "Chaplain Newby?" Upon realizing a service was in progress, he froze. I invited the lieutenant to

finish his message. "I'll wait," he said. Instead of withdrawing to return later, he remained for thirty minutes, standing
bent over, just inside the bunker doorway.

The service and testimonies completed, I thanked the
lieutenant for waiting and asked what I could do for him, to
which he responded, "Chaplain Newby, that was the most
meaningful religious service I ever saw."

I arrived on LZ Dolly one day about noon and while going from the chopper pad to the mess tent I passed two new
troopers who were quietly praying over their food. Something was familiar about the way they did it.

The pair's blessing finished, I introduced myself and
asked their names and from where they came. "I'm Pfc.
Ramone Banks and this is Pfc. Theodore (Ted) Pierce [of
Layton, Utah]," said the larger, fair-haired trooper.

So, in my usual style, my LDS affiliation hidden behind
the anonymity of the universal Christian chaplain's insignia,
I asked if the men were Mormons. They were, and they
were replacements bound for Delta 1–5.

While I humped the jungles with Bravo 1–5 on 1 June,
the men in Charlie 1–5 were following a strand of NVA
communications wire. The NVA ambushed the point element and killed Sergeant Ray Edward Knoll of Michigan.
The NVA, like any effective military force, were very protective of their communication assets.

The next day, June 2, Delta 1–5 engaged the enemy in the
jungle not far from LZ Dolly and quickly sustained eighteen
casualties—two KIAs and sixteen WIAs, including three
medics. One of the medics died later. Private First Class
Bowen and I accompanied a chopper load of ammo out to
Delta 1–5. Bowen, who had recently arrived in country, went
to replace the three experienced medics.

The fighting was beginning to slack off when we reached
Delta 1–5. After helping offload the supplies from the chopper
and with a cumbersome ammo box in hand, I slipped and slid
off the muddy LZ, through the equally slippery and muddy

jungle to the company CP. Later, after we settled down, I visited Bowen to help him adjust to being an instant replacement for three seasoned medics in a very violent environment.

Bowen was concerned about his standing in the LDS church because he was also a conscientious objector. No problem, I assured him, for while the Church supported its members serving in the armed forces of their countries, it held very high the individual's agency and right to act in accordance with conscience. This counsel I had previously confirmed with the proper authorities.

Meanwhile, back on LZ Dolly, Platoon Sergeant Mario Grisanti waited at the helipad with some of his platoon for a chopper that was carrying someone who rated a welcoming committee. While they waited, one of his men, Arnold R. (Swamp Fox) Boggs casually drew his .45 pistol, pointed it at his own right leg just above the knee and fired. Grisanti said, "Swamp Fox had been growing increasingly agitated during the preceding days on LZ Dolly, getting more and more flaky. One day he started shooting hand illumination flares at the observation tower in the center of Dolly. I was having a real hard time keeping him out of trouble. Swamp Fox and his squad were at the LZ Dolly helipad to provide security for somebody important who was landing, when he calmly pulled out his .45 pistol and shot himself. I came running when I heard the shot and saw what had happened. After Boggs was taken care of, I dug the bullet out of the dirt. I've kept it for 30 years, hoping to run into Swamp Fox someday and return it to him."

Sergeant Grisanti was unusual in his own way in that he secretly humped a super-8 movie camera in his rucksack. With it he filmed quite a few of the things happening in and to Alpha Company. All this came as quite a surprise thirty years later to Phil Gioia and Steve Holtzman, who had been his CO and platoon leaders at the time.

Now back to Delta 1–5. The night of June 3 was quiet, surprisingly so, considering the NVA knew exactly where we were. Expecting an attack that never came, I stood two radio watches so the exhausted RTOs in the CP could rest, and to improve the likelihood the radio watch would be awake if someone yelled "incoming."

Early on June 4, we assaulted some NVA bunkers located less than thirty meters from the FOB. Here was where Delta 1–5 had fought a very costly battle the previous day. We took advantage of the NVA bunkers to call air strikes in closer than usual, almost as close as Captain Cain had called them the morning of 8 April.

The air strikes came in really close, and terror filled the eyes of the five or six troopers with whom I took cover in an NVA bunker, most of whom were new replacements. This seemed like an ideal time for an impromptu worship service. So with the eager consent of all present, we prayed and worshiped to a background of diving jets and exploding five hundred- to one thousand-pound bombs. I like to believe a few violently trembling body limbs were calmed somewhat by the experience.

The enemy had pulled out, or they were killed during the air strikes. At least none made his presence felt as Delta 1–5 searched through the bunker complex and southward for the rest of the day.

The company dug in for the night about a klick from the site of the fight the day before. We held a worship service after everyone was dug in. Then at twilight I attached myself to the Third Platoon so Banks, Bowen, Pierce and I could share the sacrament, which we did beneath a poncho for privacy. Moments later the platoon, just sixteen strong, moved out about a hundred meters to set up an ambush at a point where a well-used path approached from the northwest, curved about 40 degrees and continued to the northeast toward the Saigon River. We met the trail at a point where the vegetation was relatively low and beaten down. A stretch of high grass and shrubs separated the path from a thirty-foot-wide, oval-shaped clearing on the south. Lines of shrubbery separated that clearing from similar clearings to the east and west. The near rim of a bomb crater came within a foot or two of the west side of the middle clearing. These details were just barely discernable in the thickening darkness.

The main body of the platoon set out claymore mines between the middle clearing and path, then settled down near the north edge of the clearing with about ten feet of higher grass and a fallen tree between them and the path. The main body included the lieutenant and five troopers, all of whom lay left of me with their faces toward the claymore mines and path beyond. The lieutenant had, I learned the next morning, divided the remaining troopers between two five-man flank security positions, each near the path and about fifty feet to either side of us.

Not bothering to roll down my sleeves, I wrapped in my poncho liner and lay with my head toward the path, behind the trunk of the small, downed tree that lay parallel to the trail. The rain, which had begun at 2200 hours, stopped at midnight, which I confirmed by the luminous dial on my watch. I was feeling the usual appreciation for the poncho liner, which kept me quite warm though I was soaked. The stage was set for an up close and personal experience with the NVA.

Notes

1 May 1969, 2–12 Battalion Operational Report/Lessons Learned (1 thru 30 April): Friendly Casualties: KIAs, 10; WIAs, 54; non-hostile wounded, 7.

6 May 1969, 2–12 Battalion Journal, 1704: A/2–12; medevac of 2 litter patients complete "while third litter patient was being lifted out, bird took fire and patient was dropped . . . 7 more [WIAs] to be taken out." 1825: "A/2–12; They found the missing man about 100m south from their location. He is line 2 [wounded]." 1925: "A/2–12 total of 13 line 2s [WIAs]; C/2–12 had 1 line 2, accident; D/2–12 had 5 line 2s and 2 heat casualties."

13 May 1969, Fm. Bde 3B, 2020 hrs: At LZ Phyllis, a great number of mortar rds and rockets were found around the LZ at the battle. These were policed up, placed in a trailer and brought into the LZ. One of the rounds went off somehow, exploding the pile of ammo and killing 9 while wounding 10 nearby. All . . . reminded of longstanding policy of blowing all but small arms ammo in

the field . . . preferably by EOD Team . . . ammo should not be gathered . . . nor should it be tampered with unnecessarily.

14 May 1969, 1–5 Battalion Journal, 1559 hrs: Fm B. Co: 26 ele . . . was engaged by 4–5 indiv fm tree line w/AK-47 . . . Entire [company] moving to check out area . . . found small bunker complex . . . 26 ele received AK-47 fire and 4–5 chicom grenades were thrown from a bunker 15 m to left of kitchen bunker.

15 May 1969, 1350, 1–5 Battalion Journal: Names of indiv . . . Rec #18 & 26: John Coates, Willie Chavez, Benny Wallace, Thompson, Gordon Holtrey and Edward Schulnerrich . . . treated at Dolly, Gordon Holtrey, Edward Schulnerrich. Four indiv wounded by shrapnel and remained in the field, 1LT James Joyner, SSG Thomas Newburn, Sp4 Jackie Burns and Pfc Aleya Hodroowich.

25 May 1969, 2–12 Cav Journal, Item 92: Fm D/2–8, incoming . . . 15 B-40 rockets (possibly a couple of mortars) . . . became opcon to 2–12 at 1840 hrs . . . at 1930 hrs . . . point element walked into a claymore. Casualties 3 line 1 [KIA] and 1 line 2 [WIA].

31 May 1969, Military Index: KIA Cpl. Landrus S. Taylor Jr. of Madison, Georgia.

1 June 1969, Military Index: KIA, Sergeant Ray Edward Knoll, Michigan.

2 June 1969, 1630, 1–5 Battalion Journal: "D Co 16 engaged 15–20 enemy in bunkers and trees . . . has 05 WIAs, still receiving sporadic fire." 1735: "D Co requests medevac, blood, doctor and penetrator . . . medevac 7 completed at 1719 hrs. Medevac 2 completed at 1731 hrs . . . 02 KIAs were extracted on medevac bird. KIAs: Sp4s Duane Baumgardner [Cloverdale, California] and Jeffrey Geldin [Lindsey, Ohio] [both of whom are officially listed as having died on 2 June '69]. Delta 1–5 WIAs: Whatley, Alicea, Booker, Smith, Spruill, Wright, Hansen, Overlee, Ashburn, and Hernandez; 1SGT Prosser of B/1–77; and medics/ Pfcs. Larsen, McFarland and Alonander [one of whom reportedly died of his wounds, but neither name is found on the Wall]. 1842 hours: medevac requested at 1820 . . . D Co contact today . . . GSW in leg. Also A Co had 01 indiv shot himself in leg at LZ Dolly, D Co, Thoma[s?]; A Co, Boggs w/45 pistol.

4 June 1969, 1–5 Battalion Journal, 2310: "C&E 1–5, LZ Dolly, 2240H. Reports lightning struck several times in the perimeter, igniting several trip flares, fougasse, detonated several claymores. . . ."

thirty-six

Déjà Vu

It was June 4 and my watch read 0015 hours. I had just checked it and was about to turn over on the wet ground to relieve aching muscles. Suddenly, the RTO who was sitting radio watch next to me blasted off a full magazine from his M-16. He was shooting toward the rear.

"Gooks!" he shouted, and kept firing until his weapon clicked on empty. That's when he abandoned it and the radios and fled from sight around the rim of the bomb crater. Later we learned he'd run to the security element on the west flank, almost getting himself shot by friendly troops there in the process.

Simultaneously, the lieutenant and three troopers leaped over the small downed tree that lay crosswise between our position and the claymore mines we had set along the trail. The other trooper, Edward P. Woll, and I had the same idea—to stay put until we got a clearer idea of what was going on. Meanwhile, my left hand reflexively wrapped itself around the grips of a pistol.

There followed a moment of suspenseful silence, except the pounding of our own hearts. Then from the bushes near the bomb crater, we heard voices whispering in Vietnamese. A distinct, commanding voice said something. Another less-authoritative voice responded. One voice was obviously female. Into my mind flashed the image of a sergeant telling privates to do something dangerous and unpleasant, and of privates complaining about their orders.

Upon hearing alien voices so near, I retrieved four grenades that a trooper had laid out for the ambush, and passed them to Woll. Woll knew what to do. He lobbed the

hand grenades into the row of bushes and beyond, in quick
succession.

The grenades exploded about two seconds apart. A moment later, a shadowy figure moved from the bushes and
dropped into the bomb crater. I could easily have dropped
him, but I held my fire—the shadow might have been our
RTO, and the muzzle flash from the pistol would have pin-
pointed my position. Besides, no one was threatening
wounded troopers, so I felt constrained somewhat in my
role as chaplain.

The moment passed and a shadowy head popped above
the rim of the crater. A NCO-like voice barked something,
probably a demand for us to identify ourselves as "friend"
or perhaps to get us to fire at him and reveal our location.

Woll and I simultaneously took the NVA soldier's challenge as our cue to move, though no signal passed between
us. Automatic fire tracked me as I leaped into the air and
dove across the fallen tree into the midst of our comrades and
the claymore mines. The burst probably would have caught
me had I not twisted in the air to create a smaller target. Even
so, the last AK-47 bullet cracked near enough to cause a stab
of pain and momentary vacuum-like sensation in my left ear.
As I landed in the grass, a chicom grenade exploded within
three to five feet of the spot Woll and I had just vacated.

There on the ground, striving to maintain perfect silence,
with my wet body rapidly chilling in the absence of a body
heat-retaining poncho liner, I mentally replayed what had
happened. I concluded that the NVA unit had stumbled onto
us as it came through the jungle to get on the trail. We had
come close to being wasted because we had no rear security.
This shortcoming surprised me, what with an OCS-trained
platoon leader, new to combat though he was.

With six more hours of darkness to kill, I spent the first
one carefully rolling down my sleeves for the meager warmth
they offered, and for protection from the mosquitoes. The insect repellent was back in the clearing with the radios.

Meanwhile, the company commander was very concerned. He'd heard in quick succession an M-16 in panic

mode, four American grenades, AK-47 fire, and a chicom grenade. Then for six hours there was nothing. The RTOs had left their radios in the clearing and were understandably reluctant to return for them.

Later in the night, while Third Platoon lay silently at the ambush site, an NVA element hit the company perimeter on our side. This was probably the same unit that stumbled onto us, engaged in yet another unintended encounter with Delta 1–5.

Meanwhile, up on LZ Dolly Lieutenant Colonel Peterson probably wondered if he had lost an under-strength platoon. I doubt that the Delta 1–5 commander informed Peterson that he might have lost a chaplain.

Back on the ambush site, we lay quiet as death for six hours. At 0615 hours in the dawn's earliest light, the lieutenant stood up to see if he would draw fire. Instead of fire a mournful call of "chieu hoi" came from the jungle.

Carefully, we followed a trail of NVA packs and gear into the jungle, where we found a wounded NVA soldier in a hammock. His body was riddled with fresh shrapnel wounds. On the NVA's chest lay a Chieu Hoi pass—one of the open-arms certificates our psychological operations people spread around to entice the NVA and VC to come over to the South Vietnamese government side—and by his side an AK-47. America paid cash for surrendered weapons.

A few minutes later, I paced off twenty-three feet between where I had lain and the spot on the crater rim from which the NVA shot at Woll and me. This pacing I did while we waited back in the clearing for a chopper to evacuate the wounded enemy POW (later called EPW, for enemy prisoner of war). This experience was similar to the dream of death I had the night before I left home for this tour, except in real life the NVA missed me! We sustained no casualties during this engagement. Three months later, Woll would suffer a dreadful tragedy—the accidental killing of one of his buddies.

*   *   *

The chopper that came for the POW brought the new Second Brigade Chaplain, who stayed only long enough to pay his respects to the company commander. I accompanied the chaplain and POW to LZ Dolly, where lightning had struck the evening before with results similar to those during another strike when I was present.

LZ Dolly, in keeping with its defensive needs, was surrounded by a perimeter of bunkers, and with rolls and layers of concertina wire. These were supported by cleared fields of fire, trip flares, claymore mines, machine guns, CS gas grenades, and barrels of fougasse—a homemade napalm-like mixture of fuel and some thickening compound—set to be detonated on command by an explosive charge. The fougasse and other defenses frequently showed their value against attacking enemies. They were formidable weapons in the hands of determined troopers. Defensive plans included using these measures selectively, depending on the nature and ferocity of any given threat against the LZ. I doubt anyone ever envisioned the level of shock and noise should all these perimeter devices explode simultaneously.

The lightning strike that hit when I was present came about 1600 hours, a moment after Colonel Peterson passed my bunker headed toward the north. The lowering clouds threatened a monsoon downpour at any moment. I'd just greeted Peterson, stooped and gone inside and sat on the edge of my litter when a blinding flash illuminated the dark recesses of my bunker. Simultaneously, there came an earthshaking, ear-shattering blast from everywhere at once. A ripple of smaller explosions followed the big one.

Daisy cutter, I thought, one of those ten-thousand-pound bombs the Air Force used to create instant landing zones in the jungle.

Outside, thick black horizon-blotting smoke billowed up all around the perimeter. A stroke of lightning had spontaneously ignited scores of claymore mines, drums of fougasse and most of the CS gas and flares on the perimeter. And nature continued to add its own voice to the tumult with each new bolt of lightning and simultaneous thunderclap; we were at ground zero.

Peterson hurried tearfully past me toward the TOC, his journey helped along from that point by the loan of my gas mask.

At 1033 hours on June 5, Alpha 1–5 engaged in a vicious, costly firefight that raged for more than an hour. The shooting began within a few minutes of my arrival on LZ Dolly with the chieu hoi–turned POW.

Larry (Shorty) McVay described events leading up to the fight this way. "Just that morning I was moved over from Sergeant Jack Hatfield's Second Squad, Third Platoon to walk point for another squad." This would be his first time at point.

"We had been humping long enough that it was time to take a break, when I spotted the bunker complex. The complex had recently been destroyed by a B-52 strike. The NVA had moved right back in and built new bunkers and fighting positions under the brush and rubble caused by the bombing. They were waiting for us. I spotted something suspicious and reported it. Captain Phil Gioia called the company to a halt and sent out cloverleaf patrols. Sergeant Jack Hatfield of Ohio led his squad—my squad until a few hours earlier—into the bunker complex with Corporal David Mann of Iowa at the point. Mann moved forward as cautiously and carefully as he could, with Hatfield backing him up, but it was not enough. The NVA held their fire until Mann and Jack were well within the kill zone. The patrol hadn't been out but minutes when gunfire and explosions began."

McVay continued, "Jack and David were gut shot. David died instantly, cut in two by a 30-cal. water-cooled machine gun. Jack died slower. The last thing he said in this life was, 'Mother,' and he closed his eyes.

"Benny Swan, a husky black man and Hatfield's assistant machine gunner, rushed forward. . . . The rest of the 2nd Platoon and a few men from other platoons rushed forward to support Hatfield's squad. Benny was like a man possessed—like John Wayne to me. Although being severely wounded, Benny poured accurate fire into the enemy positions and kept them at bay until our KIAs and WIAs were pulled back. There was much bravery that day. The KIAs could have easily been left behind but these brave young men fought until all their buddies were brought back."

Sergeants Elvin Jackson, whom our previous company commander had intended to court-martial, and Robert Fussell of South Carolina were among those heroes from other platoons that rushed forward into the jaws of death to help rescue the wounded and recover the dead. For their actions that day, Jackson and Fussell were recommended for the Silver Star.

Sp4 Tom Holcombe said, "He [Fussell] was next to me when the fight broke out with Jack Hatfield's squad on the fifth of June. He got up and took off to help, even though it was another platoon and they were handling the situation—he didn't have to go but he did. But that was Fuzz."

Only after Hatfield, Mann and all the wounded were recovered did Gioia pull away from the contact area so they could be medevaced and the area pounded by artillery and Cobra gunships, and napalmed by Air Force F-4s. Then about dark Gioia moved his company to another nearby site and set up a new FOB. He wisely avoided returning to the positions Alpha 1–5 had used the previous night.

"As I recall, the NVA mortared the position we had stayed in the night before," said McVay, and continued, "Claude, I remember it well. As corny as it may sound, I felt for years that I should have been on the patrol with my squad, from which I'd been gone only half a day. The fourth of June 1969 plays over and over in my mind while sleeping and awake. I've been treated for post-traumatic stress disease at the VA. . . . I am doing okay now. . . . I also accepted Jesus Christ as my Lord and Savior."

McVay's guilt is typical, unjustified, and definitely not corny. Though he never said it, added to his feelings of guilt is the haunting fact that his alert led the squad into the ambush without him and to the horrible deaths of Hatfield and Mann, close buddies; he'd joined the company about the same time as Mann.

Those who fell wounded during the attempt to recover Hatfield's and Mann's bodies included Platoon Sergeant Fussell (1st Platoon), William S. Haj, Swan, Theil, John Stumpt, and Charles Spliker.

Fussell was awarded the Silver Star and went on to become a platoon sergeant before being severely wounded in the leg and medevaced to the states. Back home, following a long and painful convalescence and rehabilitation, he married and became the father of three sons. These days, he walks about performing his duties as the pastor of a Friendship Baptist Church in North Carolina, aided in his efforts by a special built-up shoe.

The Army downgraded Sergeant Jackson's award to the Bronze Star Medal for Valor. He would become a platoon sergeant and be wounded, though his wounds would not be serious enough to cut short his Vietnam tour.

Blissfully unaware of the action Alpha 1–5 was engaged in or of the casualties they sustained, I arrived at Ton San Nhut Air Base in Saigon about 1800 hours. A few minutes later, I dined with Paul Madsen.

After dinner I returned to Madsen's hotel room to write letters and prepare a monthly report. The next day was a rare goof-off one for me. The day after that, between 1300 and 1505 hours, I attended the ecclesiastical meeting that brought me to Saigon. By evening I was in Lai Khe in 1st Infantry Division (Big Red One) AO, and quite ill. On June 8, I went to the hospital in Cu Chi, where a doctor diagnosed strep throat. I visited twelve of my wounded troopers while I was there and spoke in an LDS service, with thirty-three members of the 25th Infantry Division (Tropical Lightning) in attendance.

Feeling ill wasn't unusual. The weekly big (as opposed to the daily little) malaria pills usually made me sick, which explains why I sometimes "forgot" to take them. Frequently I got fever blisters and sore throats, and numbness in my left big toe would continue to interfere with humping during most of this tour. And there were the rashes, constant sores and irritations to sensitive body areas in consequence of sleeping most nights in dirty clothes and going weeks, day and night, with my boots on. On the other hand, my metabolism worked well in combat. These were the only years since about age thirteen that I could eat without concern for weight gain. Still, I had it easy compared to the men in the companies. At least I could change clothes during stops at LZ Dolly.

On June 9 I returned to LZ Dolly, intent on joining Charlie 1–5. When that proved impossible, I flew on to Tay Ninh, and was there when my third month in the field ended. The beginning of my fourth month found me recuperating from strep throat to the tune of exploding rockets and mortar shells and the rattle of shrapnel against the roof and walls. I endured the rattling because I felt too ill to take cover in a bunker. While I slowed down to nurse my health, the action was hot for the 2–12 Cav the next day, June 10.

On June 10, Bravo 2–12 moved into a bunker complex and in exchange for one American life and seven wounded, captured one rifle, ten bicycles, and other assorted items of NVA equipment. While that was going on, Alpha 2–12 made contact with a battalion-size force of NVA and sustained three killed and twenty-eight wounded. The Alpha Company troopers killed fifteen NVA that they could confirm. On June 11, another unit entered the area and found twelve more NVA bodies.

At 0545 on June 11, I snapped awake on LZ Dolly to the distant sound of mortar shells leaving tubes from too far away to be ours. Several seconds later, the barrage rained down on LZ Dolly and wounded two troopers on the LZ. One had arrived in the battalion as a replacement the previous day and was slightly injured while he pulled perimeter guard. A senior NCO "jokingly" expressed envy of the trooper's "easy" Purple Heart on his record.

The enemy mortars, though they did little damage, validated my avowed belief that the NVA could precisely target LZ Dolly up there along the crest of the ridge.

Bravo 1–5 got through a mortar attack on its FOB unhurt on June 12, but wasn't so fortunate a day later while crossing a deep tree-choked draw. One man was killed and another seriously wounded during the crossing. At 1300 hours on June 13, I joined Bravo 1–5 for a sweep along both banks above the draw. The NVA were gone or lying low.

From the draw, the Bravo 1–5 troopers pressed on and did a battle damage assessment on a bunker complex located just beyond the draw. The BDA turned up scattered pieces of equipment, clothing, and body parts amid a wild tangle of downed trees, craters and angry red ants. None of the body parts was large enough to join together as a body, had the troopers been so inclined. It would have been hard to tell that the body parts were human but for the occasional pieces of clothing attached to them. An NVA helmet with a hole in it lay among ruins. I passed it on to Madsen to fulfill a promise I had made him.

That evening Bravo 1–5 dug in near the bunker complex, after which we held a worship service at twilight. Afterward word came that Charlie 1–5 had sustained one dead and one wounded when two of its patrols bumped into one another.

With Charlie 1–5 the next day, June 14, I got the details of the fatal mishap the day before. The company had moved early into a night position and each platoon had sent out the usual cloverleaf patrols. Somehow in the featureless jungle, one of the patrols stopped in the path of another. Moments later, the point man heard the other patrol stealthily approaching his position. His patrol leader got on the radio and requested that all friendly troops freeze in place. The sounds of movement continued to draw nearer, even after confirmation was received that all friendlies were stopped.

Thus reassured, the point man on the patrol-in-waiting blasted away with his M-16 when the first shadowy figure broke through the underbrush. He killed instantly the point man on the other patrol and seriously wounded another man, who soon died of his wounds. Killed by friendly fire were Pfc. Theodore Heriot Jr. and Sp4 James Burton. One of them had been a best friend with the shooter.

As best I could, I consoled the trooper who killed Heriot and Burton, but don't know whether I had much effect. "I didn't kill and wound my buddies. My leaders killed them by losing control and by assuring me no friendlies were moving in front of me," he said with calm and cold logic; he had a point.

About this time in June, I became upset because the CP group and some other elements of Alpha 2–12 bunched up badly in an open area. Later in the day, I got some negative feedback for raising my concern during a worship service. A trooper, and former LDS missionary to Hong Kong or Japan, said that some troopers in attendance griped that it wasn't my place to chasten them for bunching up.

My informant had his own sad story to tell. Back about February or early March, he'd been in night position beside a bomb crater. He and his buddies were licking their psychic wounds following a nasty fight. Out of the night he heard movement on the other side of the crater. His whispered challenge drew no response. He opened fire when a human shape rose up before him, silhouetted by the starlit sky. A fellow trooper fell dead, one that presumably had played dead since the earlier fighting and was making his way back to the company. Perhaps he'd been too shell-shocked to respond to his fellow trooper's whispered challenge.

While many accidents ended in tragedy, some had humorous properties, like what happened to a visiting chaplain. I ran into this chaplain on a firebase and commented on a large bandage across his nose: "What happened to your nose?"

"I was sleeping in the field and a grunt stepped on my nose and broke it. He was on the way to relieve himself," the chaplain explained.

Tactlessly, I said, "Man, you were lucky."

"What do you mean, lucky? Look at my face!"
"He could have stopped a step or two sooner."

Notes

5 June 1969, 1–5 Battalion Journal, 1410: "A Co WIAs . . . Fussel, Haj, Swan, Theil, Stumpt, and Spliker. Two KIAs: Hatfield and Mann. 1411 hrs: A Co received AK-40 and MG fire at 1033 hrs from approx 10–12 indiv in bunkers . . . contact broken at 1144 hrs, most . . . resulting in 02 US KIA and 05 US WIA. Enemy losses, 05 NVA KIA."

13 June 1969, 1–5 Battalion Journal, 1124: "C Co made contact w/unk size enemy ele, friendly cas—1 line 1 & 1 line 2, contact broke at 1126 hrs."

1230: "C Co request medevac at 1135 for 1 ind . . . request doctor, ind has wounds in the chest. Names, Pfc. Theodore Heriot Jr. and Sp4 James Burton."

1253, Readout: "C Co, 36 element was . . . securing a trail . . . the 26 element was given the coordinated mission of swinging down the same trail . . . The 36 lead element setting in place, heard movement and opened up. CPT Cain is appointed as investigating officer."

thirty-seven

Fraggings

Though I saw more combat action with the companies of the 1–5 Cav than with the 2–12 Cav, I provided about the same number of worship services for each battalion. Early in June during a visit to Alpha 2–12, I learned of threats to frag a company commander. Several troopers confided to me that most of the men in the company believed Captain James Robert Daniel of Atlanta, Georgia, cared very little for what he put them through. "Plans are afoot to 'frag' Captain Daniel next time the company's in a fight," I was told.

The phrase "fragging" came into use early in the war and described the rare practice of troops killing unpopular leaders, by tossing a hand grenade in their hooch or whatever. I knew personally of no fragging incidents during my first tour in Vietnam, but I heard of two or three alleged incidents—all involving rear-area personnel. The closest I came to a fragging, or anything like it, during my first tour was when troopers allegedly attempted to kill a fellow grunt for reporting an atrocity, the Mao incident.

But this was a different war in a different time, and we heard of fraggings almost weekly, some quite close. By 1969 fragging meant killing friendlies by any means, including shooting leaders and others in the back. This evolution of definition made sick sense considering the different conditions between the rear and the field.

In the rear, the grenade was often the weapon of choice because small arms were more carefully controlled than in the field. Usually, with patience, an unpopular individual could be found alone and blown away without anyone else being hurt. And hand grenades left no tell-tale fingerprints and rifling marks to lead the Criminal Investigation Detachment (CID) back to the guilty party(s).

In the field, on the other hand, small arms, which were in abundance, were weapons of choice for fragging. This made morbid sense. First, in the field it was difficult to isolate an individual from his RTO and others for a grenade attack. Second, it was extremely easy to shoot backward or sideways at the targeted individual during the heat of a firefight. Finally, even if a fragging were suspected, an adequate investigation under field conditions was very difficult, and successful prosecution was unlikely. Rifling marks on full-metal jacket M-16 bullets and markings on shell casings didn't carry the same evidential weight in the field as these would in rear areas.

Knowing all this, I alerted Captain Daniel and Lieutenant Colonel Boon about the fragging threats, and assured them the threats were serious, based on my confidence in my sources. Captain Daniel reacted with, "Chaplain, there is nothing I can do about that, and worrying won't change it. If the troops frag me, they frag me. I'm doing my job the best I can." Another tragedy intervened before we could find out how these fragging threats might have turned out.

On June 17, the Deputy Division Chaplain accused me of neglecting my battalion and troopers. This chaplain took almost every opportunity to show hostility toward me, whether for personal, professional or religious reasons, I knew not. But this accusation was too much.

The chaplains in the division had just completed a conference and I yet basked in good feelings over a moment of praise that the USARV Chaplain had just given me in the presence of the 1st Cav Chief of Staff. The compliment was for my work while at Fort Bragg. A few minutes later in the officer's mess, the Deputy Division Chaplain joined two other chaplains and me at our table. I hoped this chaplain, by joining us uninvited, meant to signal more openness and cordiality toward me. Not so, I soon discovered.

"Chaplain Frank, Chaplain Martin wants to send me an LDS chaplain assistant. Does Division have any problem with that? Do you?" I asked.

His response shocked me. "Chaplain Scott is considering moving you out of the division because you are neglecting your assigned battalion."

What? I couldn't believe what I was hearing. "Why?" I asked.

"Because three times in your weekly report, you showed more LDS services than Protestant ones," Frank said.

"Those instances don't mean I've neglected my battalion. To the contrary, they reflect the once-per-month occasions when another chaplain came into my battalion and provided communion services, while I went about the division AO conducting sacrament services for as many LDS troopers as I could reach."

This practice, I insisted, showed concern for the religious needs of my men, without bias. "Besides, I could legitimately have lumped LDS and general services together to impress you. Instead, I reported them separately to give you a clearer picture."

Chaplain Frank said he understood and accepted my explanation, then added, quite out of context, "Your being selected for promotion to major from the 5 percent zone means nothing. You don't fit here."

The next day I discussed my weekly reports and the threat of a transfer out of the 1st Cav with Chaplain Scott, the Division Chaplain. Chaplain Scott said he thought unfair to isolate me in a battalion rather than assign me at a headquarters above division so I could minister to LDS personnel over wide areas.

We discussed this concept from my perspective. First, I reasoned that LDS members were well organized and empowered to care for one another. Second, in my present assignment I was chaplain to men of all faiths and those with no faith, which was what my church expected of me. Third, the chaplains would have a difficult time convincing my chain of command that I neglected the unit or could be better used elsewhere. Chaplain Scott promised to not try to move me from the division.

Thus, the matter was settled, at least on the surface. But the hurt simmered long. It tore at my heart to be accused of neglecting those whom I loved and tried so hard to serve. Considering the source of the accusation helped a little to ease the hurt. Chaplain Frank's irrational hostility toward me continued.

On June 18, while Chaplain Hugh Black went to the only 1–5 company that was receiving log (being resupplied), I conducted a memorial service for Bravo 1–5 on LZ Dolly—don't recall who the service was for. Next, I conducted three field services for companies in the 2–12 Cav, in their positions on the rocket belt (the area around a target from which rockets can effectively be fired) around Phuoc Vinh. In the evening I taught a lesson to some LDS troopers about the virtues of possessing a forgiving heart. My treatment at the hands of Chaplain Frank was on my mind.

The next day, June 19, a spur-of-the-moment decision saved my life. The fateful decision occurred at Phuoc Vinh. Boon's 2–12 Cav had moved from LZ Grant to assume palace guard around Camp Gorvad, the Division Base Camp. Battalions on palace guard kept one infantry company on the perimeter near the battalion headquarters and TOC, while three companies lived and patrolled beyond the perimeter to suppress rocket and mortar attacks and to deny the NVA opportunity to mass undetected for ground assaults. The line companies took turns spending a few days on the perimeter, where they enjoyed rare hot showers, three hot meals per day, cots, and other trimmings of rear-area life.

About 0900 hours, June 19, having conducted three field services, I flew back to the Phuoc Vinh and entered the 2–12 TOC to seek a ride to Captain Daniel's company. There I found Daniel and Major Robert William O'Keefe of Davis,

California. They were preparing to depart on Boon's Charlie-Charlie. I accepted a seat on the chopper, only to change my mind for some long-forgotten reason. The pilot of the Charlie-Charlie promised to return for me in a few minutes.

Ten minutes later, at 0940, Alpha 2–12 reported seeing a chopper explode in the air. LTC Boon's Charlie-Charlie had collided with a 105mm artillery shell. Captain Daniel and Major O'Keefe were dead, along with the four-man crew of Boon's chopper. This I learned a few minutes later when I reentered the TOC.

So mangled were those bodies that had been blown out of the aircraft that we could not tell by sight to which body some parts belonged. The bodies of those who rode the chopper into the ground were mangled and severely burned, skulls exploded from the heat.

Understandably Boon and many of his staff were deeply distraught. After ministering to Boon as best I could, I went seeking solace of my own, solace which wasn't easy to find. One might expect my heart to be filled with gratitude for having been spared. Instead, my heart, mind and senses reeled, my emotions all mixed up, and terrible smells lingered inside and outside of me. I was in no mood for what happened twenty minutes later at LZ Dolly.

At Dolly, I stepped into the medical aid station for a cold soda. The only other person there, a medic and sergeant, reacted badly when I took a soda from the blood box. "Chaplain, no disrespect, sir, but you're just a big, F— S—," he said.

All my pent-up emotions burst inside of me. Instantly, I wanted to demolish that sergeant, who at the moment epitomized every rear-area snob I'd ever met. Just barely, I suppressed these destructive impulses and said: "Sergeant, you are taking advantage of me. I want very much to stomp a mud hole in you, but I can't do so because I'm your chaplain."

"I'll gladly ignore your rank and position if you will," the sergeant snapped back.

His offer was sorely tempting, but of course we had no barn or other private place to go behind. Anyhow, while considering the sergeant's invitation, I collected myself. *How did I offend him so*, I wondered? So I asked him.

"You come in here like you own the place and help yourself to other people's sodas," he said.

"You don't understand. I contribute to the soda fund so I can have an occasional cold drink when I come in from the field," I explained.

The sergeant's apology didn't help much. I had arrived at LZ Dolly with my feelings and reflexes on supercharge because of my near miss and what had happened to those on Boon's chopper. These factors combined with the confrontation with the sergeant and a lack of mail from home— it had been days since I got a letter—affected my mood for the worse. So I joined Alpha 1–5 in the field for a day and two nights of humping, during which time I managed to get my feelings into a precarious balance.

Sometime in May or early June there occurred an incident that lives vividly in my memory, but for which I cannot find records that the final outcome is as I remember it.

Three troopers in one of my eight line companies refused to go on an ambush. Their company had remained for a second night in an FOB near where one of its ambushes had been very successful the previous night, having killed several NVA without taking any casualties.

The ambush had been set up along a well-concealed trail about fifty meters from the FOB. As part of its preparations, the ambush team aimed a 90mm recoilless rifle straight down the trail, chambered a flechette round, and waited.

About midnight the point element of an NVA unit came along the trail. The troopers fired the recoilless rifle. At first light they found several dead NVA on the trail. One was literally pinned to a tree by flechette darts. The surviving members of the NVA unit had retreated leaving their dead behind. An NVA unit, probably the same one, dogged the company the next day. I joined the company as it was digging in for the night.

The company commander directed one of the platoons to put an ambush on the trail, the same as the night before. The platoon leader designated a squad for the ambush, and three squad members refused to go out. "It's stupid to put an ambush in the same place as last night. We'll be killed if we go," a spokesman for the three had insisted.

The company commander said, in essence, "I hate it, Chaplain, but I've no choice. If they don't go on ambush, I must bring charges against them. Would you talk to them?"

I found the three sullen men in a small, clear spot beneath the bamboo. "Don't try to change our minds, Chaplain. We'll be killed if we go out tonight," one of the three said.

"I don't intend to change your minds. All I intend to do is help you consider the alternatives and consequences. Yes, you might be killed if you go out tonight. It's very possible. On the other hand, if you don't go on ambush tonight, you *will* go to LBJ [Long Binh Jail] tomorrow and you *will* face a general court-martial. That is a certainty. You three are the only ones left with any choice. You can go out or stay. The company commander has no choice. He can't back down, no matter how much he understands and sympathizes with you. You made sure of that when you openly refused his orders."

In conclusion, I asked the three troopers how they'd deal with it if others died in their stead, and added, "I wish I could promise you'll be okay out there tonight, but I can't. But if you decide to go on ambush, I'll go with you."

The three troopers looked back and forth at one another in silence for a minute or so. Some signal must have passed between them, undetected by me, for their spokesman said, "We'll go out on ambush, Chaplain Newby, but you can't come. No use you being killed too."

The three troopers went on ambush with their squad.

During the night the NVA attacked viciously, its assault focused directly on the ambush site, which led me to suspect this was the same NVA unit our ambush had hurt the previous night. The three troopers were killed.

Without self-recrimination, I grieved hard for the men who died acting on my counsel. I sorrowed long for them, wishing there had been another way.

On June 22, Alpha 1–5 moved through the jungle to a clearing. We were to be picked up by choppers to relieve Bravo 1–5 on LZ Dolly. While most jungle is indistinguishable from other jungle, this was different. I sensed I'd been here before as we neared a clearing that was designated for our pickup zone.

A powerful sense of awe came over me as we entered the PZ. Looking to the north side of the clearing, I suddenly knew why. Here, Snyder, Derda, Hoover and Allen gave their lives; here I came mighty close to dying. That day after Easter, two and a half months before, seemed to be in the far distant past.

Reverently, I walked twenty feet into the jungle and stood in contemplation and prayer at the spot where those great men gave their all. No longer did the events seem ancient. Memories and sensations flooded through me as if the experiences there had happened the day before, though much had changed and so many troopers had died and been wounded since then.

Even this sacred spot was rapidly changing, being reclaimed by the jungle. The termite mounds, trail and the caved-in NVA machine-gun position were still there. Otherwise, there was little evidence of the terrors shared and blood spilled on that frightful day.

On a whim, I looked at the scene from the NVA machine-gun position. The line of fire was perfect. The machine gunner couldn't have missed me. *Impossible*. He'd had a clear shot with nothing to deflect his fire, but he had missed me! Snyder, Derda, Hoover and Allen hadn't had a chance, either. *Why did the NVA machine gunner miss me and not the others*?

This would have been a good time to experience survivor's guilt, a malady so common to survivors of traumatic incidents. But instead I was having an indescribable, deeply spiritual experience. I understood, like Moses on Mount Sinai, that I stood on hallowed ground. I intend to return to Vietnam someday as a reverent pilgrim.

As I paused there and turned inward, deep into my soul, I appreciated more deeply than ever how unfathomable are the vagaries of war, and how the soldier can't always be responsible for them.

Sometime after the middle of June, I tallied the friendly KIAs and WIAs in the 1–5 and 2–12 Cav battalions, beginning with when I arrived in the unit and going through about the middle of June 1969, or three and a half months. One hundred and twenty-eight troopers had died and eight hundred had been wounded—though I can no longer find all their names in the records. Amazed at the number of casualties, almost all of them infantry and medics, I checked morning reports for foxhole strength to compare casualty numbers with the number of fighting men and medics actually in the field. The results were sobering.

Between March 11 and mid-June 1969, the combined strengths in my ten infantry companies hovered just below eight hundred, far below what the strength should have been. The flow of replacements couldn't keep up with the casualty rates. Thus, 800 wounded and 128 killed represented a casualty rate of more than 100 percent, albeit a skewed casualty rate because some soldiers were wounded, treated and returned to duty only to be wounded again or die. This brings me to one other major difference between 1967 and 1969.

In 1966–67 a wounded trooper could usually expect to be in a chopper en route to expert medical care in sixteen minutes, on average. In 1969 in War Zone C, the wounded waited as much as ten hours for evacuation by a medevac chopper or slick ship. This change I attributed to the loss of so many great medevac crews; exhaustion of the ones remaining; the difference between fighting VC and NVA regulars; and the affect of war protests on everyone, especially on the pilots, who generally were better educated than infantrymen.

At 0800 hours, June 22, I conducted a memorial service for Alpha 1–5, followed by a worship service. Though I was with the company when these troopers died, I can't remember the details of how the deaths occurred. Perhaps my emotions and mind had all the horrors they could deal with at the time. Still, I feel disloyalty to the dead whose names I can't remember.

Following the services, I flew to Tay Ninh and almost got hit by one of three 122mm rockets—it exploded next to the latrine while I was inside "reading." Next day I was back in the jungle with Second Platoon, Bravo 1–5, searching the banks of the Saigon River on foot and via Army boats. Choppers had lifted boats in. This was one of the worst nights ever for mosquitoes. Those NVA mosquitoes along the Saigon River appeared to relish insect repellent; they came out in the daylight too.

On June 24, a Delta 1–5 patrol discovered NVA "commo" wire within six hundred meters of LZ Dolly. We followed the wire and were pleasantly surprised that none of us got shot in the process. This time, the NVA had moved on, leaving the strung wire behind.

Delta 1–5 stopped for the night about halfway up the south slope, in the northernmost saddle of the razorback ridge, between LZ Dolly to the north and Dau Tieng to the south. In the afternoon I held a service for the company followed by a sacrament service with Banks, Bowen and Pierce. Later we entertained ourselves creating pizza from C-ration items. The night sky was brilliant, unusual for the rainy season.

All seemed so peaceful. I really needed this moment to contemplate situations here and at home. I was growing more and more concerned about Helga and the baby; her letters described increasing threats of a miscarriage.

Notes

16 June 1969, 1–5 Battalion Journal: "0920, A Co had two claymores blown at it . . . 2 WIAs, Sp4s Ronald Anderson and Thomas Spratt."

　1400: "A Co, while checking bag of rice, booby trap went off . . . 1 WIA, Gerald Peihl, eye."

18 June 1969, 1–5 Battalion Journal: B Co, Nickolas Rutvicror [?], appendicitis.

19 June 1969, 0940, 2–12 Battalion Journal: "A Co 16 reports seeing a bird go down . . . probably the CC. Also probably hit by friendly arty."

　1035: "medevac 6 extracted 1 line 1 and part of another body." KIAs: Major Robert O'Keefe [of Davis, CA]; Captain James R. Daniel, Warrant Officers Ralph Clime and Jerrold Pearlstein, and Sp4s Raymond Voss and Henry Matthews.

　1300: D Co Heatstroke, Pfc. Barry Overlee.

30 June 1969, 1–5 Battalion Journal: "1650, A Co WIA, Pfc. James Beroney, frag leg."

thirty-eight

Grief on the Home Front

Delta 1–5 moved out early on June 26, and by 0930 hours we'd moved west through the saddle in the razorback, crawled through bamboo thickets contaminated with persistent CS gas, and were in position to assault a recently-discovered NVA bunker complex. The complex was near the base of the razorback ridge and almost within spitting distance of the southwest perimeter of LZ Dolly. Battalion thought we'd need more ammunition and medical supplies, so we delayed the assault to await resupply.

Battalion Operations called about 1000 hours. "Is One-Niner at your location?"

"That's a rog [roger]."

"Instruct him to report to Phuoc Vinh ASAP. Emergency message from home."

A slick ship landed half an hour later. While his men off-loaded ammunition boxes, the company commander, with the radio handset still to his ear, relayed a message from Battalion. "Get on the chopper, Claude. Battalion is delaying the assault to fly you to Tay Ninh, where you are to prepare for travel to CONUS [Continental United States]." Under the circumstances, I appreciated this gesture.

A few minutes and kilometers later at about two thousand feet in the air, the crew chief suddenly hustled out of his rigging and started erecting a jump seat; I was sitting on the floor, as usual. The seat ready, the crew chief hollered in my ear, "Buckle up, Chaplain! We're having transmission trouble and might crash." This was very bad timing. Helga needed me too much for me to crash now. We made it to

Tay Ninh, "coming in on a wing (rotors in this case) and a prayer." On several prayers, no doubt.

At Brigade Headquarters the Red Cross director handed me two messages. The first message said a daughter was born and not expected to live. The second message said she had died. Somehow, I knew as I read the messages that our baby's name should be Suzanne Marie and that Helga would agree. Helga, on her own, had the same impression. We had never before discussed this name.

Many hours later I landed at Travis Air Force Base, California, on the same day and close to the same hour that I'd received the first emergency message in the field, in consequence of crossing the international time zone in the middle of the Pacific Ocean. It took almost as long to go the 850 miles from Travis AFB to Utah, via San Francisco, as from Vietnam to California.

Bishop David Taylor met me at the airport and took me straight to Helga's bedside in the old Dee-McKay Hospital in Ogden. Helga and I clung to each other for several minutes. It was a bittersweet moment. We were so glad to be together, even under the circumstances.

With her faith, Helga was handling Suzanne Marie's death very well, and so was I. We knew, nothing doubting, that our baby was beyond such conditions as I'd left in Vietnam and she was ours eternally, provided we lived for the blessing.

The children appeared to be doing very well too. They were accepting what was and what could be, or so it seemed. But James was hiding his true feelings, which I'd learn more than a year later in Germany. Meanwhile, the children had grown during my almost four-month absence.

Helga, the children and I had three days together before Suzanne's funeral, time to comfort one another and become reacquainted.

On the day of the funeral, I saw Suzanne Marie's remains in her casket. Her infant face is burned indelibly in my memory.

At 10:00 a.m., June 30, 1969, we held a graveside funeral

and buried Suzanne Marie in the All-To-Rest Memorial Park Cemetery in Ogden, Utah, a temporary grave because we intended to move her someday to wherever we settled after retirement. Dallas Murdoch opened the service with prayer. Bishop Taylor gave a eulogy and Lynn and Sharon Cruiser sang "I Stand All Amazed." Like angels they sang. Elder Marion D. Hanks spoke about faith, hope and God's love.

Suzanne Marie's funeral marked the completion of four months on my second tour in Vietnam.

Following the funeral, Helga and I spent a few days trying to help each other regain our physical and emotional strength. I had come home with the fabled "thousand-meter stare" common to soldiers too long in combat. Later I wondered how this leave with Helga and the children contributed to my being able to complete this tour, painful though the occasion was. We had several impromptu family home evenings, times to talk and share and watch and play, and to reinforce the truths of Christ's redeeming love. We visited Joan and Dallas Murdoch and played and fished and water-skied and worshiped. Helga and I clung to each other, spirit and soul, trying to give and receive enough strength and memories to carry us through yet another parting.

Elder Marion D. and Maxine Hanks, sensing our emotional needs, invited us for an afternoon in the Hanks' co-op swimming pool, followed by dinner at their home. The children loved the pool and the new Ping-Pong table they discovered on our hosts' back porch. The Hanks showered us with hospitable kindness and showed sincere interest in Helga, the children, and my experiences in Vietnam. About 10 p.m., as we prepared to leave, Elder Hanks folded the new Ping-Pong table and tied it atop our car.

We think the *Hanks' Table*, which is how we thought of it, followed us four times across the Atlantic Ocean and at least as many times across the American continent. Finally in 1981 we donated its shaky remains to a poor, struggling seminary teacher in Orem, Utah.

The parents of one of my troopers called the day before I left to return to Vietnam. He had written home about my leave. It meant so much, I knew, to the parents to talk to someone who had recently "touched" their son, to receive reassurance firsthand that his assignment was as "easy and safe" as he claimed it was.

Fortunately, before I had to answer their inquiry about the dangers, the mother diverted me with a more delicate question.

"Sonny [assigned alias] said his company just got in a lot of—" Embarrassed, I got around the question with some vague comment and a promise to *visit* Sonny the moment I returned to Vietnam. Her question gave me an idea for a sermon for all the troops, about avoiding the use of certain acronyms and phrases, especially in letters home.

As I recall, Bill Snyder's brother visited us during my short leave, seeking a personal account of how Bill served and died. Sergeant Elvin Jackson's brother also visited.

Sometime during the emergency leave a reporter from the Deseret News, a Salt Lake City afternoon paper, interviewed Helga and me in our home. *Almost a Legend in His Own Time* was the heading for the somewhat accurate article that resulted from the interview. I about had to get a larger helmet.

My mind refuses to release the details of our final parting on July 15, except the pain. Though I had to go and was being pulled back to Vietnam, leaving was so hard. It was probably harder for Helga than for me, weakened as she was by giving birth and losing her precious daughter.

I departed Travis Air Force Base, California, at 2300 hours, July 15, and was back with my unit at 1600 hours on July 17. During the return flight I decided I would take a rest and relaxation (R&R) with Helga in Hawaii at the first opportunity, to take her away from the pressures of home and help her through her grief.

At 1600 hours on July 17, I arrived back in country. The 1–5 Cav had replaced the 2–12 Cav on Palace Guard. LTC

Ronald R. Rasmussen had replaced Lieutenant Colonel Peterson as Battalion Commander. It was almost too good to believe that the 1–5 and 2–12 Cav battalions had sustained just one KIA while I was gone! Very sad for the fallen trooper's buddies and family, but what a relief that there had not been more.

Chaplain Hugh Black had been sent to Korea and replaced in the 2–12 Cav with a non-Catholic, which ended our reciprocal support arrangement. As the leaders said that chaplain support had been inadequate in my absence, I felt especially grateful for unusually low casualty rates during this time. The new commander, Rasmussen, and other leaders welcomed me back with enthusiasm and surprise. I wasn't due to return for another two weeks, but Helga and I both knew we couldn't leave the unit without its chaplain for so long.

Private First Class Robert F. Bacon of Alpha 1–5, from Phillipsburg, New Jersey, was killed by a sniper's bullet within minutes of my return to the battalion. Two men were wounded with him. We almost made a combat assault my first evening back, in response to Bacon's shooting, but it was called off after we were aboard the choppers.

When I met Lieutenant Colonel Rasmussen, he said he'd heard only nice reports about me. He asked me to go over a sympathy letter he'd just roughed out to Bacon's wife or parents, and to rewrite it if necessary. I recommended he change the word *lost* to *gave* in the phrase, "your husband lost his life while . . ." to better express the sacrifice every trooper stands ready to give when he answers the call of his country. This characterization fits Bacon, who according to other sources was a schoolteacher and thus could have been exempted from the draft. Rasmussen liked the change, and we became instant close friends who shared comparable ideas about and respect for the troopers we led and served.

Casualties remained low and the action light for the 1–5 and 2–12 Cav battalions between July 18 and August 12, thanks at least partly to palace guard duties and rain hard enough to discourage even the NVA. I took advantage of this to increase the number of worship services for small units, to counsel soldiers, send sage counsel to my children, tighten up denominational leadership, get troopers to a conference, and arrange R&R in Hawaii. I recall but one personal close call during these days, when a sergeant almost shot me in the back.

On my first full day back from leave, July 18, I conducted two platoon-size worship services in the field. Over the next two days I visited the new 2–12 Cav Fire Support Base (FSB) O'Keefe. About this time, a high-ranking general ordered that henceforth battalion-size firebases would be called fire support bases and the designation Landing Zone (LZ) would be applied only to temporary landing sites out in the field. Unofficially, we continued to designate places like Dolly and O'Keefe as LZs.

LZ O'Keefe was named in honor of Major O'Keefe, the same who was killed when artillery blew Lieutenant Colonel Boon's chopper out of the sky back in June. Colonel Barker (from Fort Bragg) arrived at LZ O'Keefe as I was tromping about through mud and heavy rain. We met, and he seemed pleased to see me. He said he would get me as his brigade chaplain, provided he could arrange a transfer. Though it would probably have been a great career move, I hoped he would not succeed. I didn't know it then, but position would count for more than combat experience in the future peacetime Army. Even had I known this, I think I still would have wished to be left with my battalions, which wish I confided to Chaplain Scott.

On July 21, a shot-up helicopter limped in for an emergency landing at LZ Ike while I was stranded there. At the control was the same pilot who had interrupted my Easter service by crashing into a nearby bomb crater. We were pleased to see each other alive.

Eventually I got off Ike, only to be stranded again on LZ Dolly, where Delta 1–5 was engaged in the destruction of what remained of the firebase. The work of demolition stopped while we held a memorial service for Bacon, followed by a worship service, and then a sacrament service with four in attendance.

Later in the day, stranded again by weather, I spent the night at Lai Khe. That evening on Chaplain Allen's television we saw Neil Armstrong make footprints on the moon, a "giant step for mankind . . . the greatest event in the history of mankind since the creation," exaggerated President Richard M. Nixon. I made a mental note to remind the troopers of Christ's atonement—*the* greatest event since the creation.

On July 24, frustrated in my efforts to reach a 2–12 Cav company (none were receiving log), I gave up trying and tackled an administrative backlog. After writing several official letters and counseling several troopers, I went to Saigon to celebrate Pioneer Day.

At Ton San Nhut Air Base, I attended meetings with Colonel McPhie and USAF Chaplain Robert Christiansen. Afterward, the three of us celebrated the day over steak and a special cake at the officer's club, quite a different celebration from the one near An Khe in 1967.

A counseling moment of note occurred on July 25. It involved a young officer who sought spiritual counsel because he, a married man and a Christian, had gone with a prostitute at the coaxing of another officer. This reminded me of the destructive, wasteful nature of short rounds—artillery, mortars and bombs that land off-target and harm friendly troops and non-combatants. Short rounds would be my sermon topic the next day.

On July 26 I made a rare trip via jeep, to visit a 1–5 Cav unit which was protecting a major bridge on the Song Be River. The unit was down in the dumps because the muddy, swollen river had swallowed up a rucksack-laden grunt, never to be seen again, as I recall. I say "as I recall" because though I've been unable to find any record of a trooper being drowned at that time, I find records of troopers drowned a month earlier, and suspect a trick of memory here. We held another memorial service in the driving rain for Bacon and (presumably for) the drowned trooper. The service I'd held several days earlier had been with a smaller element of the company. A worship service followed the memorial service.

Elsewhere in the rocket belt—area from which rocket can reach target—the Third Platoon of Bravo 1–5 combat assaulted into a hot LZ. Another platoon was boarding choppers to reinforce it when I arrived. Captain Copley asked me to go along. We loaded into Chinooks in terrible flying weather.

A Chaplain Allen and I had an interesting conversation at Lai Khe the evening of July 27. The exchange began with his challenge of my operational methods. He insisted that staying in the field and accompanying units on combat operations had negligible benefit to the troops, though it earns lots of points with commanders. Allen offered two arguments to back up his premise. First, it is too hard on unit morale and effectiveness to have the chaplain become a casualty. Second, he argued, the chaplain is too valuable an asset to risk losing in close combat.

My response was that the chaplain, in order to influence the soldier and unit, must accompany the soldier wherever duty takes him, as far as that is possible. He must share the soldier's experiences and fears. "Only in this way can the chaplain's influence remain with the soldier when he is not there, as a constant reminder of higher values and hopes," I insisted.

I countered the arguments about effect on morale and effectiveness and the chaplain's value as an asset. First, the chaplain is negligent who waits for the soldier to come to him in the rear, for the field soldier seldom has the opportunity to do so. Second, the soldier heeds the sermon he sees, and what he sees influences what he hears. Third, the chaplain's voluntary presence with the soldier during hardship and danger preaches a mighty sermon about the soldier's worth and lends credence to what the chaplain says and stands for. Finally, those things the chaplain represents are reinforced for the soldier during times of terror.

In conclusion, I insisted the chaplain is a valuable asset precisely because, and only if, he accompanies the soldier wherever the soldier is sent. Thus, the chaplain's life is worth risking for the sake of the soldiers' souls and well-being.

"Besides," I added somewhere in the conversation, "I know the safest place for me to be is where I should be, for then if I die, I live in the Lord."

We cordially discussed these topics without either of us noticeably changing his opinion or without Allen attempting to change my modus operandi by force of his position. This exchange gave *me* more clarity and helped me focus myself in ways that prepared me for future duties as a combat developer (yes, chaplains do combat developments too).

Notes

17 July 1969, 1–5 Battalion Journal: A Co KIA, Pfc. James Bacon, sniper; WIAs, Robert Davidson and Occheuzzie. Sgt. Timothy Dagin was evacuated from the field with FUO.

27 July 1969, 1–5 Battalion Journal: 1013 D Co, head [wound], Gerald Lawton.

thirty-nine

Beginning of the End

President Richard M. Nixon visited Vietnam and got a sanitized tour. USARV pulled 1st Infantry Division company onto a firebase and issued each man a new, clean uniform and jungle boots—even new helmet camouflage covers, free of short-timer calendars, salutations, crosses, peace symbols and the like.

Meanwhile, other companies were shifted around in country so the president could visit the squeaky-clean companies on secure firebases. I spent the day with a 1–5 Cav company patrolling out beyond a firebase near Bien Hoa.

Having moved by Chinooks to an area south of Bien Hoa, we transferred to liftships and combat assaulted into a swampy area interspersed with clumps of jungle. Our mission was to suppress any rocket and mortar attacks that might threaten the president.

This was a bad day, not because of enemy action, but because the troopers behaved as if the enemy were all elsewhere. Perhaps the guys acted this way because we were south of Bien Hoa Air Base and a great distance from War Zone C.

Never had I seen such slothfulness among 1st Cav troopers. Troopers talked loudly, laughing and joking as we patrolled the area. Some even hung items on their packs to rattle and clang about. Under these conditions I had another close call with death by non-hostile means.

We'd been patrolling to the south but a few minutes, and had just entered a patch of jungle, when a shot rang out almost in my ears. Ignoring the principle of dispersion, plenty of space between soldiers on patrol, the platoon sergeant had closed within a yard of me and accidentally fired his M-16. Fortunately for his conscience and my health, the bullet passed harmlessly over my head or shoulder. The accidental shot was the only one we heard all day, except for artillery and ARA.

The whole Nixon visit agitated me, all the scrubbing and polishing to create a false image for him. It would be much better, I thought, for him and all the visiting commanders and politicians to see conditions as they really were.

But as matters turned out, I deduced what the President saw was irrelevant, for he came not to see but to tell. His visit provided a dramatic backdrop for announcing the beginning of the American withdrawal from Vietnam and "peace with honor."

Thus, I considered President Nixon's 1969 visit as the official beginning of the end. I would soon conclude that his visit marked the beginning of a rapid decline in unit cohesion, combat discipline, dedication, aggressiveness, and the general racial blindness that was common among the front line troops. These negative changes, marked by a rapid increase in disciplinary problems, reflected a loss of *sense of mission* by the Army. In hindsight I believe this event marked the beginning of a collective unwillingness to waste life in a lost cause. This attitude grew rapidly and affected soldiers all the way down to the foxhole. But the war still continued hot and furious for my units and men.

Back at Phuoc Vinh that evening, after a day of patrolling to support the President's visit, my nephew Earl Dyer met with two troopers who also served as LDS missionaries. Earl returned to his unit with lots of new questions spinning in his head.

Now, I always exercised extreme care to avoid the very appearance of unethically misusing my position and influence to convert soldiers from other faiths, as all chaplains were supposed to do. Earl is close blood kin, so I made an exception when he asked me specific religious questions about my own religious preferences.

* * *

Combat was light August 2–5, and so were casualties in my two battalions. Private First Class Johnson became my chaplain assistant in July, and promptly announced that he wanted to accompany me to the field and "see what it is like." He soon got his wish, a combat assault with Bravo 1–5.

Unchallenged, we made the assault and jumped off into waist-deep water, in a spooky area of dead trees—victims of Agent Orange spraying. Johnson and I linked with Second Platoon and moved out to the east on a company-size search for an NVA bunker and village complex that was supposed to be in the area. We waded in the chest-deep water for several hundred meters to reach wet ground, there being no dry ground nearby.

We continued eastward the next day, until late in the afternoon, when the point man began reporting signs of NVA—tracks, fighting positions, finally bunkers. As we moved among the fighting positions, I, in a whisper, pointed out and explained tell-tale signs of the enemy's presence to Johnson. Johnson appeared increasingly uncomfortable the deeper we moved into the NVA complex. Finally, Johnson crept to me, holding his stomach. "Chaplain Newby, I don't feel well. My stomach really hurts."

"Know what you've got?" I asked.

"No. What?"

"A severe case of fear," I diagnosed.

"Really? That's what fear feels like?" Johnson seemed relieved and satisfied, even pleased to know how it felt to be afraid.

Well, his fears were for nothing. The NVA chose not to fight. While the grunts pushed on to the east side of the NVA complex, where the flooded area began anew, the CP set up for the night among the bunkers. They soon wished they hadn't. The complex swarmed with little red leeches; they rose from the ground wherever one looked.

We'd been in the complex an hour or so when from the east side of the perimeter came the dreaded cry, "Medic! Medic!"

The company medic and I rushed toward the sound of the alarm, wondering what could be the matter. We'd heard neither shooting nor explosions. Just beyond the complex and undergrowth, knee-deep in water, stood a very upset trooper.

A leech had crawled inside him. The unwelcome guest was discovered when a buddy asked the trooper why his trouser-front was covered with blood. The leech had sucked blood until it burst and kept right on dining.

We could do nothing for the poor trooper. A lighted cigarette to the head of the leech was out of the question, as was a squirt of insect spray and other tried and proven methods of making a leech turn loose.

The trooper's medical evacuation, which began when he climbed into a chopper hovering over the flood waters, ended at Walter Reed Army Medical Center, in Washington, D.C. There, surgeons removed the unwelcome guest from the trooper's anatomy. What a way to get out of Vietnam early.

Meanwhile, back among the leeches, none envied the trooper his unusual method of escape.

After the medevac was completed, Johnson and I made a rain shelter and settled in to wait for the dawn, which I thought would never come. All night long, I imagined leeches crawling on and into my body, especially into the more sensitive parts. Vainly I tried to sleep while limiting contact between my body and the ground. Great was my relief next morning after Johnson and I checked each other and found we were free of leeches, except in the mind.

Sergeant Elvin Jackson came in from the field the evening of August 7. He showered and donned dry underclothing for the first time in 57 days. The next day he and I hitched a ride to Bien Hoa on an *Air America* (Central Intelligence Agency "Airline") fixed-wing aircraft. At Bien Hoa we treated ourselves to some commercial food and a movie and then visited until midnight. This day, August 8, held special religious significance for Helga and me—the anniversary of our baptism. I began and ended that day reflecting on our blessings, and feeling especially close to her despite the distance between us.

As the concluding speaker at an LDS conference, I paid tribute by name to Sergeant Jackson and many others the next day. My remarks led many rear-area people to a clearer understanding of the nature of the war and to a greater appreciation for the sufferings and sacrifices of the faceless men they supported. At least that is what several of them told me afterwards.

Following the conference, I placed a call to Helga via the MARS system, and waited until 0300 hours the next morning for it to go through. The call went something like this: "I love you. Over. . . ."

Six hours after the call I was in the field conducting worship services for the platoons of Delta 1–5, followed by two more general worship services for other units and two LDS services, all at different sites.

The pace of war increased the night of August 12. NVA forces attacked American firebases throughout the 1st Cav AO. In response to the attacks, the 1–5 Cav was pulled off palace guard and air assaulted into the jungles northwest of Quan Loi, near Cambodia. I moved forward with Alpha 1–5 to LZ Shirley at An Loc. There we offloaded from Chinooks and stood by on the airstrip to await the Huey choppers that would carry us on the air assault.

The terrain was fairly clear for about 2000 meters west of the north-south running airstrip, which airstrip was just inside the firebase perimeter. The Alpha Companies of the 1–5 and 2–5 Cav battalions were spread out along a descending embankment on the west side of the airstrip. Lieutenant Colonel Rasmussen, the Sergeant Major, the operations officer and their RTOs huddled in a sandbagged gun pit several meters east of the runway.

Without warning a 90mm recoilless shell exploded about eight feet behind the huddled CP group, followed by the sound of a round being fired from the west. More shells followed. I became edgy because the two companies of infantrymen were bunched up and very exposed. So I dashed across the runway, followed by two companies of infantrymen, who knew a good example when they saw one. Of course, we were bunched up again, but not as exposed.

The incoming shells exploded among positions fifty feet behind us at the rate of two per minute. We counted our blessings; the NVA weren't targeting the unprotected infantry along the airstrip. Then to the north I saw something that would surely bring the shells nearer.

A C-130 cargo plane, laden with infantry I later learned, was on final approach. It would stop beside us. Those around me did not appear interested in the approaching plane, nor in the likelihood that its arrival would draw enemy shells onto the infantry.

Hoping I knew what I was doing, I ran onto the runway and, with incoming recoilless shells whizzing overhead, I waved the cargo plane off. Apparently, upon seeing me, the pilot refused to land until the enemy fire ceased. Soon friendly artillery rained onto the area to the west and the 90mm shelling ceased. Captain Gioia's memory of this morning differs from mine in two ways. First, he is certain that Rasmussen and his CP did not arrive at An Loc while we were there. Second, he recalls personally waving off some choppers because of incoming 90 recoilless fire. He doesn't recall the C-130 being waved off, and I don't recall the choppers being waved off.

Soon after that the choppers arrived, and I accompanied Alpha 1–5 on a combat assault into heavy jungle within four kilometers of Cambodia. Though the jungle we moved through was somehow different, eerier than any other jungle I'd seen in Vietnam, we made no contact with the enemy as we humped the rest of the day, dug in for the night, humped another day and dug in again. We saw little sign of enemy forces in the area or of recent American ground troops having been in the area.

Termites attacked during the second night and ate holes in some heavy rubber air mattresses. While the termites feasted, NVA mortars rained destruction on the 1–5 Cav's LZ Eagle One, which had opened on 12 August. The bombardment of LZ Eagle One began a few minutes past midnight and continued for an hour. The enemy tubes fired from about five hundred meters east of our position, almost on-line between the firebase and us.

Repeatedly, we called in coordinates and requested counter-fire on the enemy mortars, but never got it. Meanwhile, I quit counting the mortar shells at one hundred. On the firebase, the battalion sustained several casualties, mainly because of unfinished defenses on the new LZ.

The next day, August 14, I conducted worship services for Alpha 1–5 and shared the Sacrament with Elvin Jackson before returning at noon to Phuoc Vinh to prepare for R&R.

I spent August 15–17 at Bien Hoa and getting to Ton San Nhut for my R&R flight, which flight got off to a bad start on August 18.

We boarded an air-conditioned commercial airplane about mid-afternoon, eagerly anticipating a quick takeoff and smooth flight to Honolulu and into the arms of loved ones. I sat next to a window on the left several rows forward of the rear door of the aircraft. The engines, and with them the air conditioning, stopped several long minutes later: "Sorry gentlemen, but we have a little light here that we shouldn't have. We'll take off after it is checked out. Meanwhile, Customs says everyone must stay on board. Relax, gentlemen. The smoking light is on," said the pilot in his best *don't worry, everything's all right* voice.

Once the air conditioning was turned off, the passenger compartment quickly became a torture chamber in the intense heat and humidity. It was no place for a nonsmoker to be trapped in starched khakis. I spent the next 180 minutes sweltering with my head beneath a wool blanket, as I tried to filter the effects and disgusting stench of tobacco. I dreaded the assault this stench would have on Helga when we next embraced at the Honolulu airport.

Many hours later in Hawaii, the torture chamber forgotten, I passed through customs and hurried into Helga's waiting embrace. She seemed hardly to notice my smoke-cured aroma. In my journal I described the moment: *18 Aug 1969 . . . Hawaii . . . To see Helga was joy beyond description . . . very romantic, lovely, and memorable . . . only regret . . . temple is closed.*

On this R&R, like the one in 1967, we spent a wonderful, romantic, memorable six days and five nights. Helga grew stronger physically and emotionally day by day. Alas, all too soon the adventure was over and the sorrow of parting was upon us. But we appreciated what we had between us and knew it was worth the pain of another parting.

On August 25 I returned to the 1–5 Cav. The fighting was similar but less frequent and intense than it had been in the spring and early summer, but morale and esprit de corps, spirit of the unit, were falling at an almost discernable rate. Racial tensions were mounting even in the foxholes, though nothing like they were doing in the rear areas. Back there blacks and whites glared at one another with hate-filled eyes. White troops averted their eyes as black *brothers* exchanged the closed-fist black-power salute, or "dapped" one another with their imaginative handshakes. Things were changing for the worst, the first signs, I think, of the impact of President Nixon's announced American withdrawal from Vietnam.

An attack on Quan Loi two days before I returned from R&R inflicted casualties in every unit in the 1–5 Cav, except Echo Company.

My first night back from R&R I spent under the stars at LZ Eagle One. My assistant hadn't constructed a shelter or cover for us in my absence. The LZ enjoyed a quiet, wet night, nothing like what was in store for it the next night, when I would be in the jungle with Delta 1–5.

The NVA launched a heavy mortar and rocket attack on

LZ Eagle One, beginning at 0030 hours, August 27. Two troopers died and several others were wounded. I monitored the standoff attack by PRC-25, from out in the jungle.

Phil Gioia described the attack: "Terry Brain (my pace-man, also known as Biggy) and I were sitting on the sand-bag ring around an 8-inch howitzer on LZ Eagle One; Foggy Day [Alpha 1–5] had that afternoon been airlifted into the LZ. The very first round of an incoming sheaf of mortars or rockets hit right inside that gun pit, killed several members of the gun crew, flipped the gun on its side, and blew Terry, myself and a couple of other people into the side of a bunker. Dazed, shaken and temporarily deafened, we quickly scrambled to cover in one of those hasty-bunkers that consisted of a half-culvert laid on the ground and covered with sandbags.

"Terry, I believe, lost a kidney (or so we heard later), and was sent back to Ft. Lewis, WA, where he sorted mail until the Army let him out. I wasn't scratched, but to this day I have serious hearing loss in my left ear, which was toward that 120mm mortar or 122mm rocket. We were so close to the explosion that I didn't hear a thing when it went off . . . just remember a blue flicker, like when you switch on a flu-orescent light tube. Couldn't hear anything out of that ear for days afterwards. Still have a constant ringing in it."

Said SSG Elvin Jackson: "I was in a bunker with another soldier when a mortar round hit outside of it. RTO Carl Bahnlein was in a bunker some 20 to 30 feet from ours. Shrapnel hit me in the shoulder and arm when I ran from my bunker to check on my men. That's when I found Bahnlein lying half outside and half in his bunker. He was seriously wounded in the chest, the result of shrapnel. A trooper, the company mail clerk, who had been stranded on Eagle One for the night, responded to my repeated calls for assistance, and he and I carried Bahnlein to the medics under a continu-ing barrage of heavy mortars or rockets."

After we left the medics, the mail clerk began crying. "I've lost my weapon! I can't find it," he told Jackson.

"I gave him my weapon, and told him to watch the

perimeter. He stayed on watch there behind the sandbags all night, and was still guarding the perimeter when I checked on him at dawn. In the daylight, we found his weapon and he returned to his job in the rear. I was very impressed with his courage and willingness to help me under those dangerous conditions. I hope he got a medal," said Jackson.

Three troopers were with Bahnlein in the bunker just before he was hit—Platoon Sergeant Mario Gristani, Larry Smith, and a blond medic. "Bahnlein had just come back to the field after recuperating from previous injuries, and had just started humping an M-79 that he was dying to shoot. We were having movement around LZ Eagle, and he kept pestering me to let him shoot it, but I said no. Then when the NVA started mortaring us, I said 'Go ahead. Knock yourself out.'

"Bahnlein was just running out of the bunker when a mortar round landed right in the doorway and blew him right back into the bunker. Smitty looked down at him and said, 'Oh my God! A sucking chest wound!' and I thought Bahnlein would go into shock."

Jackson received word the next day that Bahnlein had made it out of the unit alive, but he didn't know how long he lived. "It wasn't until 1999 that he and I made contact again. He is alive and well, but badly scarred, and living near Washington, D.C.," Jackson said.

Bahnlein told Jackson that, "Working in a VA hospital, I know that I had but minutes to live with the kind of wound I had, and I would have died if you had waited until the mortar barrage stopped before you came out to help me."

This is how Terrance Brain (pace man) remembers that morning. "As we came into the LZ earlier, the NVA kept popping up, shooting a few rounds at us and disappearing. That night I was sitting between two of those bunkers made out of half-culvert corrugated steel—first time I saw bunkers made that way—and reading my mail in between mortar and rocket attacks. When the barrage started, I headed for a bunker, then turned aside to grab a radio that was separated from the CP— Captain Gioia needed two radios, one to communicate with the perimeter and one to coordinate fire support.

"I grabbed the radio and headed at a crouching run for the bunker about 12 feet away. There was a big explosion and something slammed into my back just as I reached the entrance, threw me right on top of Captain Gioia. He and the medic, a large black man and really nice guy, kept telling me to quit putting my hand in my wound . . . they had to turn me around inside the long narrow culvert/bunker so they could get my head up . . . burned and pained awfully. The blast didn't just ruin my kidney. It completely destroyed, disintegrated it—nothing left.

"Because one of the troops was too badly wounded to wait, a medevac chopper crew braved rockets, mortars, and small-arms fire to come in and hover while the worst wounded were loaded. I also got aboard, wrapped in a blanket and sitting upright.

"A few minutes later at one of those blow-up medical places, probably the 2nd Surg, I sat next to a wall and observed the medics chasing around and trying to find a really seriously wounded guy. No luck. A doctor said, 'He's got to be here. He was on that chopper. Start checking the medic tags.'

"Soon, a medic reached inside my blanket and pulled out my tag. 'Here he is!' he shouted. That's when I knew I was in trouble . . . Later, at a hospital in Saigon, a doctor told me I was going home. 'No,' I said, 'I'm going back to my unit.'

" 'You're badly wounded, son, and you are going home.' I came home."

Between August 27 and 29, the battalion sustained at least seven more KIAs, including three more on LZ Eagle One and one at Quan Loi. At Quan Loi a 107mm rocket burst in the battalion rear area. The field trains had recently moved there from Tay Ninh. Also, on the night of August 27 the NVA viciously attacked Bravo 1–5 in its FOB. I can't recall the outcome.

On August 30, I left Delta 1–5 and headed for Quan Loi via LZ Eagle One. My objective was to visit the troopers of

Bravo 1–5, who had come in to "enjoy" a 48-hour stand-down in the Division "VIP" Center there. The VIP Center was nothing more than a place to provide the grunts, a company at a time, two days and a night away from the constant patrols, ambushes, bunker building, and firefights, where they could get a real shower, eat a little better and drink if they wanted to. I came to the VIP Center to provide the men a rare opportunity to worship as a company and to help restore their spiritual strength and stamina.

One look at the VIP Center and I wished these men were somewhere else. Sure, they had showers and cots, but very inadequate overhead cover. *They will have little rest and recuperation here*, I thought, correctly as the next hour proved.

I'd barely left the VIP Center to visit Chaplain Lamar Hunt at his nearby hooch when several mortar rounds and rockets came in. I hurried back to the VIP center, but a 107-mm rocket beat me there by mere seconds and exploded in the branches of a tree. Hot shrapnel and debris wounded three troopers. This "break" from the field was the first for Bravo 1–5 since late in April.

The next night was another bad one for Delta 1–5. The company had stopped early, dug in well, built overhead cover and set out plenty of claymore mines, trip flares, LPs and ambushes. None of these things kept a very capable NVA unit from sneaking right up to the FOB without being detected until an NVA point man finally tripped a flare. The instant the flare popped, the NVA point element opened fire, killing a trooper as he scrambled for his foxhole. Reacting almost as quickly, the men in Delta 1–5 killed several NVA soldiers, including the point man, who fell between two perimeter foxholes.

On September 1, I passed the halfway mark on this tour, grateful to have apparently escaped the threat of being reassigned to a rear area unit, I thought, as was customarily the fate of captains and above. The troopers in Alpha 1–5 marked the new month in a much more dramatic way.

Captain Gioia grew tired after waiting several hours on
LZ Eagle One for choppers to arrive to carry Alpha 1–5
back into the field. "We are infantry. We will walk," Gioia
said, according to Larry McVay.

Tom Holcombe said, "We simply walked off Eagle One
in the usual two-column company formation with my squad
about in the middle of the left column. Around midday we
came upon a field that was too large to go around. We were
about halfway across the field when one of the men farther
back in my squad passed up word that he'd spotted NVA
out to our left front. I got on the horn and reported this to
Six [Gioia], who stopped the company and sent a large patrol ahead to check the sighting out. The patrol moved forward in two columns, with half of my squad at the head of
each, and me in second position on the left."

Holcombe continued, "We took off at a fast walk trying
to overtake the enemy and had gone about 400 meters when
Ed Atkinson, point man for the right column, spotted something and signaled the patrol to stop by raising his hand,
palm forward. Ed signaled Bob Ahern to come forward with
his M-79. Meanwhile, Lieutenant Williams moved everyone on-line and I positioned my men to provide fire support
for Ed and Bob. 'Open fire at the first shot from either side,'
I whispered. Then I stayed kneeling on one knee in the
waist-high grass so I could watch Ed and Bob. After a moment, Bob Ahern saw the NVA Ed was pointing at and
fired. Instantly, both sides opened up, and the B-40 and
small-arms fire seemed to last forever."

McVay added, "As Ahern's squad leader in the First
Squad of the Second Platoon, I was standing right beside
Ahern when he fired the first round, and Holcombe was to
my left. Despite the intense small arms and rocket fire we
were taking, we swept forward. During the charge, Williams,
our platoon leader, fell seriously wounded . . . I was hit too;
however, I didn't realize I was hit until it was all over."

"My squad's M-60 machine gunner and point man and
Lieutenant Williams were among those evacuated. McClelland
went home. The point man eventually returned to the squad.

Several others were wounded, including some who rushed forward from other elements in the company to reinforce us," said Holcombe.

"I believe we killed a couple more with small arms before the NVA made a hasty exit," McVay said.

It is amazing that Americans did not die in this action. Things were definitely in the enemy's favor. They were in hiding and the Americans were moving toward them in the open, which gave the NVA the element of surprise and a better fix on the Americans. That Atkinson saw the enemy soldier lying in the elephant grass at all is extraordinary. That Ahern got off the first shot, and by so doing thwarted the ambush and wrought the most damage in the fight is almost beyond comprehension, given the other factors. "The enemy had fared much worse before they pulled back from the ambush they had attempted to draw us into. Bob Ahern's first M-79 grenade hit one of the ambushers right in the face, killing him and the poor soul next to him," said Holcombe.

According to Shorty McVay, "Williams . . . was wounded and returned to the states . . . I received shrapnel from a B-40 rocket . . . stayed in the field. Also wounded were Robert Braud . . . remained in the field . . . [and] Charles Robbins. May have been others. Some of the A1–5 troopers dubbed this action the 'Ahern Ambush'."

On September 3, in the field with Alpha 1–5, everyone dug in with zeal, spurred on by fresh NVA signs and the occasional clank of metal-on-metal in the nearby jungle, that distinct, nerve-stressing clank of a gun barrel against mortar tube or base plate. Obviously the NVA knew our location, and lately they'd shown little reluctance to engage us up close.

Shortly after full darkness, Sergeant Tony Cruz of Phoenix, Arizona took his squad and set an ambush about 100 meters north of the FOB. We settled in, fully expecting to be mortared, and perhaps hit by a ground attack. I dozed off once sometime after midnight, only to be snapped full awake by the clank of metal against metal out in the jungle. The clanking came from the east of our perimeter, and close.

Captain Gioia put us on 100 percent alert at 0355 hours in response to a whispered radio message from Sergeant Cruz. "Gooks all around us! Heavy movement and Gook voices!"

Gioia considered ordering Cruz to withdraw his men into the FOB, but rejected the idea when Cruz reported hearing Vietnamese voices between his position and ours.

At first light, according to the plan, Cruz and his men would blow their claymore mines, which they'd rearranged facing in all directions. Then simultaneously, each squad member would throw two hand grenades and fire off a magazine in every direction except toward the FOB, then the squad would dash for the FOB along a narrow, specified lane between heavy covering fire by Second Platoon. "The tension in the minutes before I withdrew the OP/LP was so thick you could cut it with a knife . . . there was a big unit out there, moving across our front, and Tony and his people heard them very clearly. We shot artillery to cover their withdrawal into the main body of the company," said Gioia.

Preparations for the withdrawal went according to plan. Cruz and his men threw the grenades and each blasted off a magazine. But Cruz was hit in the back almost as soon as he and his men jumped up and began their dash for the perimeter. A green tracer round (red, according to an entry in the Battalion Journal) entered his lower back and traveled upward slightly to leave a fist-size exit wound in his chest, just right of center.

Seconds later Tom Holcombe swept forward with the rest of his squad in response to a radioed plea for a medic, and reached the ambush site in a few seconds—Holcombe had been Cruz's squad leader until Cruz got his own squad just before this action. "When I got there, one of the guys from the ambush was with him [Cruz] calling for a medic. He left and I stayed with Tony and tried to calm him. When I saw the wound, I knew he wasn't going to make it. All I could do was tell him help was on the way. I'm sure Tony knew he was going to die," said Holcombe.

The NVA withdrew without putting up a fight, for reasons known only to them.

The company medic and I reached Cruz within a minute, followed shortly by the company commander and first sergeant. For the next fifteen minutes, while some troopers provided security and others cleared an LZ for medevac, I held Cruz's head and upper torso in my arms and literally watched his heart beat through the hole in his chest.

During those minutes, while I comforted Cruz and the medic attended him, his buddies pleaded for him to hang on. "You've got it made, Tony! On the way home, man." Standing by helplessly, the first sergeant vented his frustrations on medevac for taking so long to reach us, which frustrations he expressed with obscenities sprinkled with a divine title.

"I don't want to die," Cruz gasped, as he looked into my eyes and grasped my right hand with his right hand. His grip became vise-like, superhuman as his life ebbed away. "I feel my life slipping away," he whispered.

Then turning his eyes on his men, he spoke a few words in Spanish, and died. "So long. I'll see you guys later," he said, according to a member of his squad. "Sal later translated to us that Cruz said 'see you in heaven,'" said Holcombe. "He must have died shortly after that while you were holding him, Claude. I remember that I was low on ammo that day and wound up taking Tony's . . . had to . . . wipe the blood off of each magazine."

McVay said of this incident: "Your [my] account of the day and night of Sept. 3, 1969 is just the way I remember it. I had Second Squad and Tony had the First Squad in the Second Platoon. . . . I remember tying claymores up in trees . . . we were expecting to get hit . . . I also recall Sergeant Cruz calling in Arty most of the night. His Arty missions are most probably what kept the enemy off the FOB that night. Anyway, that's how I felt at the time and still feel today."

Contrary to the battalion journal entries about this incident, Tony Cruz was killed by a green tracer round and not by a fragment from friendly artillery that he himself had directed, nor from a grenade that he or his men threw. And he died on the scene, not on the way to Quan Loi. I know an exit wound made by a high-powered weapon when I see one.

Captain Gioia wrote, "I've always been convinced that Tony Cruz was killed by small arms . . . [I] shot artillery to cover their withdrawal into the main body of the company, and the staff types later inferred that he'd been hit by secondary frag (as though seasoned field soldiers didn't have the sense to stay down). But as you say—and I remember quite clearly—the other people in his group reported incoming green tracers as well."

About September 5, following a night on ambush with Echo 1–5, I held a worship service on LZ Eagle One. At the meeting were the Commander and the Command Sergeant Major of the 11th Armored Cavalry Regiment. The NVA shot down the Commander's C&C helicopter thirty minutes later, and the sergeant major was wounded.

Later that day I provided worship services for Alpha 1–5, then joined Delta 1–5 for two nights, during which time we conducted a memorial service, followed by some worship services. That evening Banks, Bowen, Pierce and I shared the Sacrament. It was the last time with all of us present.

It was during this visit with Delta 1–5 that Lieutenant Colonel Rasmussen performed an act of leadership worthy of special mention because it contrasted so much with some other leader's examples. The Battalion Command Sergeant Major said that back in July and early August when the 1–5 Cav was on palace guard, the engineers demanded tribute of the infantry in exchange for water for the grunts' showers. He said that each afternoon the engineers expected a case of beer in exchange for a daily delivery of water to the battalion area on the perimeter. If the engineers found no case of beer waiting for them, the infantrymen received no water for showers the next day.

My upset over this system of tribute affected my reaction to what was happening on LZ Eagle One early in September—people were eating lots of ice cream, but ice cream was not getting to the field. An S-4 officer justified this. "We can't get ice cream to the field before it melts."

So I took my observations to Rasmussen and on September 6 he personally radioed Delta 1–5. Sp4 Ted Pierce took the following message and relayed it to Captain Nishioka: "If you can find an LZ within the next thirty minutes, ice cream is on the way!"

We immediately stopped in place, set up a perimeter, and while patrols cloverleafed the area, other troopers went to work. Well within thirty minutes, an oval-shaped patch of sky appeared where triple-canopy jungle had reigned. Those highly motivated grunts created that hole by blowing down trees with plastique explosives. Compound-4 (C-4) was in abundance because most troopers, and I, carried a pound or two in our packs for "emergencies" like this and for heating C-rations, though using C-4 to heat C-rations was forbidden because C-4 fumes were—according to medical sources—hazardous to one's health.

Exactly thirty minutes after we received Rasmussen's ice cream message, a chopper settled carefully down through the hole we'd provided and kicked off a half gallon of ice cream for every man who wanted it, including me, very little of which was wasted. Ron Rasmussen made lots of troopers happy with this gesture.

Two NVA stumbled onto an Alpha 1–5 observation post early the next evening. One NVA fell with wounds to the body and the other one fled to the north. Moments later I passed the fallen NVA soldier, by which time he was quite dead from a shot to the head. A few minutes later back in the FOB, someone snapped a picture of me with two troopers, one of whom, I was told in privileged communication, had delivered the *coup de grâce* to the NVA soldier.

Notes

18 August 1969, 1–5 Battalion Journal: Attack on LZ Eagle 1. [no names].

19 August 1969, 1–5 Battalion Journal, 1322: "C Co at 1145, w/2 WIA by friendly claymore, Schinowski, hand and Kellerhaus."

24 August 1969, 1–5 Battalion Journal: Casualties from Attack on Quan Loi, WIAs, "HHC, Pfcs. Cook, Rook and Hernandez; A Co. L. F. [SSG Larry C.] Fields and (check with clerk for name; B Co, Hafley or Haeley, M. M. Morris, S. K. Kreiger, Trainer; C Co, Phillips (Donald?); D Co, Wenick."

27 August 1969, 1–5 Battalion Journal, 0030: "Fr GM 1/8: Reports Eagle 1 was mortared w/unk no. of 120-mm mortars . . . Pfc. Gardner Brown [Union, ME], Sgt. Guy Inkle [Beecher Falls, VT], both B 1–77 were working their 105mm howitzer when 01 120mm mortar impacted within the pit, killing both ind. instantly. WIA: Pfc. Martin Butler, B 1–77; Sp4 Joseph A. Gatto, D 1–5; Sp4 Carl Bahnlien, A 1–5; Sp4 Jesus Jimenez, A 1–5; Sp4 Terrance Brain, A 1–5." Attachment to Journal: B Co. WIAs [lists thirteen by initials and nature of wounds, only].

29 August 1969, 1st Air Cavalry Division General Order 10571, Purple Hearts for Wounds received: 24 Aug. Sp4 Ronald C. Biaisdell; 25 Aug D 1–5 Sgts John P. Roland and Tyson W. Caitano, Sp4s Jerry E. Wilson, Edward F. Reddek Jr. and William D. Gahacyn, Pfcs. James R. Neely and Benito L. Alba Jr.; 26 Aug. Sgts Henry W. Dickinson, Elvin C. Jackson and Jack D. Morrison, Sp4s William C. Scott, Carl B. Bahnlein II, Joseph A. Gatto, Jeses R. Jiminez and Terrance M. Brain, and Pfc. Michael S. Asbury; 27 Aug 1LT Dale D. Koonce, Sgt David T. Widey [sp] and Pfc. Paul R. Wagers.

31 August 1969, 1–5 Battalion Journal: ". . . 0410, D Co . . . several trip flares set off by small arms fire and B-40 rocket . . . enemy evaded N. E. some 600 meters, again engaged by 1–6 element w/claymore and smf. One friendly KIA, Pfc. John A. Polefka, WIAs, Stroh, McCoy and Adams. Five NVA KIA and 1 NVA WIA."

1 September 1969, 1–5 Battalion Journal: A Co, 4 WIA, no names; 5 NVA KIA.

3 September 1969, 1–5 Battalion Journal, 0355: "A Co 21 ele reports having movement." 0720: "A Co: A medevac was requested at 0645 hrs for 01 litter case. Individual was injured when A Co sprung an ambush . . . in response to heavy

movement; a doctor and blood requested. The ind has fragmentation wounds. Medevac completed at 0710 hrs." 0800: "A Co 6 readout on 21 element. 21 ele blew their TT and received return fire. The 21 leader was hit in back by a red tracer and came out the front. A Co 6 thought the size of the enemy was about 30–40 ind." 0830: "65 Relay: Ind who was wounded in action in A Co became a line 1 [died]. Name; Cruz, Tony, E-5. It is not available as to what ind was wounded by, an autopsy will have to . . . determine cause of death . . . Ind died enroute [not so]." 1230: "GM6: Readout on A Co contact . . . At 0706 medevac 14 picked up ind, at 0710 was taken to Quan Loi . . . Dr pronounced DOA. The type of wound was frag wound to chest. Do not know if friendly or hostile."

4 September 1969, 1–5 Battalion Journal, 2201: "C Co, 2 WIA, while on bunker guard, mortar short round, last of fifteen rounds fell short, WIA Millard Layne and Mason Sims."

5 September 1969, 1–5 Battalion Journal: "0305, LZ Eagle 1 taking incoming . . . 8 to 10 mortar and 1 120 rocket, 4 WIA, Stanford and Eigel, all frag wounds."

7 September 1969, Battalion Journal, 1932: "D Co reports one indiv wounded at 1825 hrs in stomach due to an accidental discharge of an old 45 pistol found in the rubble . . . man who found the weapon was trying to unjam it when it accidentally went off . . . Casualty: John L. Erford [Toledo, Ohio] . . . man who shot [him], Edward P. Woll."

forty

Your Numbers Are Up

On September 9 at Phuoc Vinh, Chaplain Scott announced he was transferring me from the infantry before "you are killed. You've used up all your 'numbers'."

"But, sir," I reasoned, pleaded, "I'm just at the point where my reflexes and skills improve my chances of survival."

Chaplain Scott, after putting up with my begging for a few minutes, promised to reconsider the transfer. But alas, during an afternoon meeting the same day, my finely honed survival reflexes betrayed me and brought Scott's reconsideration to a screeching halt. I sat in a circle in company with a dozen or so other chaplains. We were toward the front in the Division Chapel, between the altar rail and the pews. Each pew had hinged kneelers, rails used by Catholics and some other high-church denominations, which usually were turned up when not in use.

I came late to the meeting and reluctantly took the only chair available, which left me with my back to the pews and front door. Doors to my back tense me up.

During the meeting, a kneeler fell to the concrete floor with a bang. Most of the chaplains present seemed not even to notice the sharp crack. But as I left my chair, spinning toward the "threat," I noted a couple of them glanced over their shoulder in mild surprise, not at the noise, but at my reaction. "It's just a kneeler, Claude," laughed one of the chaplains.

"That's it, Claude. You are moving. Pick any available assignment, so long as it isn't infantry," said Chaplain Scott. My fine reasoning and heartfelt pleas fell on deaf ears from that moment on.

The non-infantry positions open or opening included the

8th Engineers, an aviation battalion and the 1–9 Cavalry Squadron. Without hesitation, I chose the 1–9 Cav because it was a combat unit, perhaps the most famous battalion-size unit in Vietnam, even though it operated out of forward-rear area base camps. Most importantly, from my perspective each of the three 1–9 Cav air-cavalry troops—same as companies in infantry battalions—had a platoon of infantry.

Chaplain Scott introduced me to my replacement, Chaplain (Captain) James Thompson, and allowed me a few days to introduce him and say goodbye to the 1–5 Cav. I felt very anxious. Thompson was quiet and nice enough, but I sized him up with the critical subjectivity of a father appraising a suitor to his favorite daughter's hand, not very generously. *Will Thompson feel about my men as I do?* Still, I yielded to the inevitable and took him under my wing, intent on taking at least a week to introduce him around the battalion. Rasmussen tried to block the transfer. His efforts were futile, as I expected they would be.

On September 10, I took Chaplain Thompson to LZ Eagle One and introduced him to Lieutenant Colonel Rasmussen and the TOC personnel. Ten minutes later, we attended a change-of-command ceremony and congratulated Captain Paul H. Reese upon his assumption of command of Echo 1–5, call sign Big Sioux Six.

About thirty minutes later, at 1240 hours, several explosions on the north perimeter interrupted visiting between Chaplain Thompson, the senior medical NCO, the battalion surgeon and me. The medic-sergeant and I dashed to the scene of the explosions.

Smoke billowed from a berm-protected pit as we broke from between the bunkers near the north perimeter, where enemy munitions had been collected and stowed following a recent attack on the firebase. Two bloody, mud-covered men were writhing in pain. They lay where the blast had thrown them, some 20 to 30 feet from the smoldering pit.

Fearful that the whole pit would explode, others were

fleeing or backtracking quickly away from the pit and from the two men lying in the road, even as we came on the scene.

Splitting apart without conscious coordination, the medic and I each ran to one of the wounded troopers. As I hit the ground by the farthest soldier, I saw over my left shoulder that the medic was shielding Captain Reese with his own body. Quickly then, with the help of several men who had turned back when the medic and I arrived, we placed Sergeant Perra of Charlie 1–5 and Captain Reese on litters and hustled them away from the still-smoldering pit. I vaguely recall that the medic and I each carried a folded litter during our dash to the scene.

Paul Reese was wounded a half an hour into his new command. Sergeant Perra, whose company had base security, had been escorting Captain Reese on his first inspection of perimeter security. The two were apparently investigating a trace of smoke coming from the munitions pit when some of the dud shells or rockets exploded.

We hustled Reese and Perra onto Rasmussen's C&C chopper and the medic and I accompanied them to the 15th Medical Clearing Station at Quan Loi. Captain Reese was obviously the more seriously wounded, with a leg blown off and one eye gone. Perra had multiple shrapnel, debris and blast wounds, and internal chest injuries.

The 1–5 Cav's medical NCO and I helped the doctors and medics at the clearing station until Reese and Perra were stabilized. Reese had quickly lost consciousness, but Perra stayed awake and alert through all sorts of painful lifesaving procedures—slashed arms to expose veins for IVs, a hole in the right side to admit a large drainage tube, and so forth.

I'd often seen the tube-in-the-side procedure, but never when it took all the strength of two doctors to push the tube between the ribs, while four men pushed from the other side to keep Perra on the operating table. Perra endured this without benefit of anesthesia. I've no idea what Chaplain Thompson did during this emergency or what he thought about it. He never said.

*   *   *

The next day, September 11, I began Chaplain Thompson's introduction and my goodbyes in earnest. We began with visits to the 93rd and 24th Evacuation Hospitals, where we checked on Reese and Perra. Reese was conscious, barely. Perra was wide-awake and overjoyed seeing us. "I owe my life to Chaplain Newby. He threw himself between me and the ammo pile and got me out alive," Perra said to a doctor standing nearby. Captain Reese died soon after this visit.

Next, we flew to LZ Kelly at Loch Ninh, where we landed on its PSP (perforated steel plating) covered airstrip at about 1600 hours. From Kelly we flew northwest to a field location where Delta 1–5 was co-located and operating with a mechanized company—APC-mounted infantry. The companies were set up in the southeast corner of a large clearing, between sections of old rubber trees, and very close to the massive NVA sanctuaries in Cambodia.

A cold, steady rain had been falling all day, and the red clay had been churned into a morass by the metal treads of the APCs. Chaplain Thompson was miserable from the start, but became downright discouraged when, following introductions to the company commander, we started digging our foxhole. Chaplain Thompson hadn't had time to acclimatize. Soaked and mud-covered as we were, he was in for a very miserable and chilling night.

The next morning, the infantry and mechanized companies split up. The APCs moved off to the east and Captain Nishioka's Delta 1–5 moved to a rubber tree-covered knoll just south of the position where we had spent the night. We intended to stop on the knoll just long enough to conduct a worship service under the cover of the rubber trees, at Nishioka's request.

The company stopped about 200 feet into the trees and established a temporary perimeter. Cloverleaf patrols went out to check the area on the east, south and west sides of the knoll. We'd been there only a few minutes when I got a strong impression that we were being watched. To Captain Nishioka, I said, "I recommend we not bunch up here for a service because the NVA are close and they have us in their sights."

Nishioka agreed and told his RTO to have the platoon leaders recall their patrols and get ready to move out. Thus, I maintained my perfect record of never having a worship service interrupted by an enemy attack. We also avoided taking heavy casualties among troopers gathered to worship.

Moments after Nishioka recalled the patrols, one of them made contact with an NVA unit. The patrol had come in behind the NVA unit as it was moving in to attack us on the knoll. The resulting firefight prompted us to dive for cover in very old weed- and spider-choked trenches that ran among the rubber trees—just in time, too.

We'd barely gotten in the trenches when other NVA elements swept the knoll with a heavy volume of 30-caliber machine gun and AK-47 fire. Moments later, we cringed at the sound of mortar shells leaving NVA tubes about 500 meters to our southwest—the trenches would provide us no protection from mortars burst above us in the rubber trees. Unexplainably, the mortar shells exploded harmlessly among the buttoned-down APCs that by then had reversed course in response to the heavy gunfire and were rushing to our aid.

The mechanized company took but moments getting back to the clearing we had all just left, where the APCs got on-line and charged toward our position on the knoll, with jumpy trigger fingers at the ready.

Again, the drainage trenches were our salvation, because another spattering of small-arms fire drove us back under cover. At that moment, a trooper waved at the approaching APC's crews to mark our perimeter. A 50-caliber machine gun on the nearest APC responded to the wave with a burst of fire. Sixteen M-60 and seven more 50-caliber machine gunners joined in immediately, and for a moment that seemed much longer, the slower chump, chump, chump of eight 50-caliber machine guns and the faster tat-tat-tat of sixteen M-60s resounded over us as thousands of hot bullets swept our knoll. None were hurt by the NVA and friendly fire that swept our position, thanks to those trenches and the sniper fire that drove us into them!

After the commanders got the friendly fire stopped—which didn't take long—the Mech Company Commander opted to stick around and cover us while we withdrew into the jungle across and east of the clearing, rather than pursue the NVA.

We dug in among the trees at the edge of the same clearing we'd tried to sleep in the previous night. Chaplain Thompson and I conducted small-group, small-target worship services and visited troopers for the rest of the day, to the accompaniment of frequent sniper bullets cracking and the pop of an enemy mortar shell fired from behind the knoll we'd just vacated. For some reason, the NVA shells fell on a Vietnamese Popular Force (PF) unit that was two klicks from us, though we offered a more lucrative target.

"Is it always like this?" Chaplain Thompson asked.

"No, not always. Sometimes it is rough," I answered truthfully, rubbing it in a bit. I wanted Chaplain Thompson ready to care for "my" grunts.

Delta 1–5 linked up with the mechanized company again the next morning, September 13, and we rode atop APCs back to the airstrip at Loch Ninh. Chaplain Thompson left me there and returned to LZ Eagle One. But before he departed, I arranged with him for me to return to the battalion for a day or two each month "to give you a break from the stresses," *and give me an excuse to return to my battalion.*

Meanwhile, I joined Bravo 1–5, which was about to leave Loch Ninh, for one final mission with the battalion, as I supposed. We left Loch Ninh atop the same APCs I arrived on. The NVA mortared us half an hour later as we rode north-northwest toward Cambodia. Fortunately the mortar shells fell too short to force us into the APCs. We stayed atop the armored personnel carriers (tracks), suspecting the NVA were trying to drive us inside before they opened fire with rocket-propelled grenades. No experienced foot soldier wanted to be caught inside a thin-skinned APC should an RPG hit it.

After a few kilometers riding atop the tracks, we dismounted and the mechanized company departed. Bravo 1–5 patrolled to the west, with air scouts from the 1–9 Cav screening ahead of us in the face of sporadic 51-caliber anti-aircraft fire.

That afternoon we spotted NVA pacing us from the front. They were still there when we stopped and dug in for the night. While some of us dug, others kept watch on several NVA soldiers as they worked through the rubber trees row-by-row to within about 150 meters of our perimeter. The troopers fired at the NVA several times, but the NVA simply stepped behind trees or pulled back when the grunts pushed toward them, only to move closer when we returned to our perimeter. Apparently, these NVA soldiers were intent on staying close to us, correctly assuming they'd be safer from our artillery and gunships. Not once did these NVA return fire or snipe at us. They just stayed close and watched in silence, like they were taunting us to draw us out beyond our rapidly developing night defensive perimeter.

All night we waited for the attack we were sure would come. However, the closest thing to an attack was NVA mortars being fired from about 500 meters to the east, along our back trail. Those rounds, however, exploded farther away, perhaps on the mechanized company that was still out there somewhere.

Captain Copley's company broke camp at dawn and patrolled to the west until the afternoon. They stopped after we crossed a narrow, chest-deep, north-to-south running stream. Beyond the stream, we passed through a thin line of trees and thick underbrush into a wedge-shaped stretch of rubber trees. The rubber trees were bordered by jungle on three sides and very near to Cambodia. The clearing was about 35 meters wide on the north end spread to about 400 meters wide on the south, and was about one kilometer long, with a slight rise in elevation to the southwest.

This afternoon was like the previous one in that the NVA

crept close as we dug in near the narrow end of the patch of rubber trees. They came out of the jungle to the west. While out alone chopping logs for overhead cover, I spotted an NVA soldier about 30 or 40 feet away. Unbelievably, he just stood there next to a tree and watched me work. Not having many options, I kept a wary eye on him and continued chopping. He was still there when I returned to the perimeter.

The LPs went out at twilight and we settled down for another night of waiting to be attacked. Some of the CP members settled down to rest and sleep without any apparent regard for where they laid down in relation to their foxholes. I suggested to them, "Always lie with your head oriented toward your foxhole. Then when incoming jars you awake, you'll automatically scoot into it without losing precious seconds getting oriented."

"I'm always oriented. I'll beat you into the hole when the shooting starts tonight," said one of the CP members, with a chuckle.

Some members of the CP group rearranged their sleeping positions as I advised. Attack was certain tonight, this near Cambodia, with our exact location known to the NVA.

At 2130 hours, dozens of mortar rounds began thumping from tubes in the jungle about 200 meters to our west. Instantly, I was in our hole, where the medic and an RTO had arrived even sooner. Moments later, my focus on a trembling trooper beneath me was broken by the noise of someone scurrying about in the darkness, bouncing off rubber trees and cursing, "Where in h— is the d— foxhole?"

That individual, who shall remain anonymous, finally made it into a foxhole. He would have been too late had not the shells burst on a different unit farther away. All was quiet after that until just before dawn.

In the predawn gray on September 14, a whispered message came over the radio from troopers on the south side of the perimeter. "Beaucoup gooks coming at us through the rubber!"

"It's too dark to see movement. You're seeing shadows, not gooks," someone responded.

The troopers on the line knew better. A trooper opened fire with his M-14 rifle and the attack was on.

Through the mist and dawn's early light charged about 100 NVA soldiers. Courageously, foolishly, the NVA charged across hundreds of yards of almost open ground beneath the rubber trees. From the south they came. Most were firing AK-47s from the hip without pausing, while others paused only long enough to aim and fire B-40 rockets from the shoulder. The ground inside our perimeter shook and trembled with the explosions of incoming rockets.

From well-placed and protected foxholes, the grunts met and repelled the attack with withering defensive fires laid down by small arms, M-60 machine guns and recoilless rifles. Accurate enemy mortars entered the fight too late for NVA purposes. Their shells began exploding in our midst about the time the attack began to falter. The mortars were no more effective against us than the ground assault had been, though shrapnel wounded three troopers on LP duty who had no overhead cover.

"Medic!" cried one of the wounded troopers, loudly enough to be heard over the din and tumult of exploding mortars and rockets. Captain Copley and I quickly reached the wounded troopers amid bursting mortar shells. Fortunately, the barrage was tapering off. Upon finding that the troopers were only slightly wounded, we waved the medic back and withdrew with the wounded to our foxholes. That's when the second wave of the NVA attack came.

The second wave displayed much less enthusiasm and lots more respect for us. The charge fizzled out well short of where the first attack had stopped.

ARA choppers arrived and pounded the NVA mercilessly as they withdrew from the second attack. Our M-60 machine guns added to the retreating NVA soldiers' woes with devastating, tracer-marked grazing fire.

One by one, the troopers stopped shooting. We watched silently as NVA soldiers carried their dead and wounded across our front into the jungle, like ducks in a shooting gallery. It seemed that these young Americans empathized with their enemy for just a moment. These NVA impressed me for their courage, but not for good sense. *Surely, despite all their courage, they are not of the caliber of fighters we've faced the past days and months. Perhaps they just arrived from the north and have unseasoned leaders. These are certainly some of the most brazen, unpredictable and seemingly uncoordinated NVA I've ever seen.*

It was suggested that these NVA mistook us for a Vietnamese PF or ARVN unit, a fatal miscalculation, if true. It was hard to imagine them attacking us the way they had, otherwise.

Even considering all this, I couldn't understand why the NVA attacked across a kilometer of relatively open terrain when the jungle offered concealment to within thirty feet of the west and east sides of our perimeter. Why did their supporting mortars delay until it was too late to influence the outcome of the attack? Often I'd seen the NVA act very courageously, but never this foolishly.

Though we confirmed only six enemy dead, sometime called "step-ons," NVA losses were heavy and would have been worse, had the troopers not withheld their fire while the NVA carried away at least as many casualties as they left behind.

It was a credit to Copley's integrity that he didn't pad the after-action report with *probable* enemy casualties. One could call our light casualties miraculous—only the three on an LP—especially considering that a foxhole took a direct hit by a rocket, and the rubber trees inside our perimeter bled white on all sides from hundreds of shrapnel cuts.

After beating off the NVA attacks, we linked up with an ARVN unit that had come to reinforce us. Next, we moved eastward, back across the stream. Then, circling to the right, we crossed back over the stream and searched the area from which the NVA had attacked us, then dug in for the night in an overgrown, probably long-forgotten, cemetery. Most likely, we would have moved the FOB, had we arrived while there was enough daylight to make out where we were.

It was a very miserable night for everyone, especially

me, for I had given my air mattress and poncho to a trooper who lost his during the dawn attacks. Like everyone else, I was soaked to the skin and covered head to foot with red clay and mud. No pretty sight, we.

Late the next afternoon I conducted a worship service for Bravo 1–5 and delivered my farewell address. Most of the company attended, as we were well concealed.

Heavy sadness descended over me when it came time to go. The sadness was heavier than what I felt when I left the 2–8 Cav troopers back in September 1967. This was so partly because, I believe, I no longer had any hope that our sacrifices would make a difference in the future of Vietnam or that our service and the faithful sacrifices would be appreciated by the nation which had sent us here.

I arrived on LZ Ann during a driving, frigid rain. LZ Ann was a secondary 1–5 Cav firebase opened that day to bring artillery nearer where the companies were operating.

Notes

10 September 1969, 1–5 Battalion Journal, 1240: "B Co: 36 reports an explosion in the ammo dump near them (B Co rear) . . . some individuals were wounded."

    1325: "Fm GM 6: An explosion occurred at 1240 hrs at Eagle I in an area used to secure unserviceable ammunition prior to its being destroyed. The exact cause . . . unknown. Big Sioux 6 and leader of Fence Post 46 were both injured and evacuated to Q.L." WIA, Captain Paul Reese, E Co and Sgt. Perra, C Co 4–6.

14 September 1969, 1–5 Battalion Journal: "1800, B Co at 0700, 3 WIAs, Pfcs. Stephen Taylor, Darrell G. Harley and Guillemet or Bellimet."

    0845, B Co was in contact with approximately 100 NVA.

forty-one

The "Real" Cavalry

I left LZ Ann after spending only a few hours there and reached Phuoc Vinh by late afternoon or early evening, where I dined in the Division Officers Mess in company with the chaplain I was replacing in the 1–9 Cav. My unkempt, mud-covered presence drew stares and frowns from many patrons, perhaps because I left red smears on everything I touched. My "grunt pride" rendered me immune to the glares and stares of the upper echelon brass.

Following dinner, my predecessor showed me where to bunk, shower and so forth. A few minutes later, my wristwatch disappeared while I was showering with real, steady, hot water. That watch had served me well in the field.

Well, wristwatch or no, I'd entered a different war and joined a unique unit, the First Squadron, Ninth Cavalry Regiment or "First of the Ninth" (1–9 Cav), also known in an esprit sort of way by its members as the *Real Cav*. I'd joined a unit that didn't quite fulfill Chaplain Scott's intentions of removing me from the field and away from combat situations.

Between 17 and 19 September, I turned gear in to the 1–5 Cav, drew gear from the 1–9 Cav, and settled into a four-man room in the 1–9 Cav headquarters area. A major had commandeered my predecessor's private room and a bunkered-in cot. I never objected, though I could have because as a chaplain I required private accommodations for counseling. But after all those months in the open, I didn't relish being enclosed in a crypt-like, sandbagged bunk.

For sleeping, writing letters, and so forth, I had an area

about seven by ten feet, just inside the front door against the east wall of a north-facing building. From my bed, a real cot, I looked out on a small quadrangle and beyond to the revetments which protected the Cobras, LOH, and Huey choppers of Headquarters and Charlie Troops, 1–9 Cav. The pilot on the other side of the door from me had a battery-powered Sony television set. An officers club, the unit's very own, was around the west end of the building. Yes, I'd definitely entered a different war.

Regular infantrymen and enemy alike recognized and respected the 1–9 Cav. One day in the fall of 1969 a pink team was flying in the vicinity of abandoned LZ Becky when the LOH crew spotted something that had not been there the day before. The NVA had pinned a sign to a tree. It read, "Welcome, Scouts, to battle."

On my third day with the 1–9 Cav, September 20, I conducted my first official duty, a memorial service for an infantryman—a Blue Platoon member—who had been killed by friendly fire. Afterward, the troop commander said this was the best memorial service he'd ever attended.

LTC James W. (Pete) Booth commanded the 1–9 Cav. Company-type units were called troops. The squadron consisted of a headquarters troop, three air cavalry troops, and one motorized troop. Additional assets included the divisional long-range patrol (LRRP) or H Company, 75th Rangers, and the 62nd Infantry Platoon (Combat Trackers [tracker-dog teams]). And the 98th, 151st, and 545th Transportation Detachments—helicopter mechanics—were each attached to one of the air cavalry troops to keep the birds in the air. During my time with the 1–9 Cav, its Headquarters Troop, Charlie Troop and Delta Troop were co-located at Phuoc Vinh, as was the H Company, 75th Ranger Company. The 62nd Infantry Platoon (combat trackers and their dogs) were at Tay Ninh with Apache Troop, and Bravo Troop was at Quan Loi.

Each of the identically organized and equipped Air Cav

troops had a complement of scout crews, cobra crews, and a platoon of infantry. The squadron's infantry platoons were known throughout the Division and Vietnam as the "Blues."

Delta Troop usually patrolled roads around the base camp, set ambushes, and provided ground security to motorized convoys.

The Blues were true infantrymen. They regularly carried out very dangerous missions for which they were often inadequately armed. But unlike typical infantrymen, Blues spent most of their nights in camp sleeping on cots, taking warm showers, taking in movies, partying in clubs, or whatever they wished. The Blues were generally credited with the second-highest number of enemy killed of any units in the war, second only to the 1–9 Cav aero-cav teams.

Before the introduction of the Cobra into the unit, machine gunners on Huey gunships were considered to be the most lethal American weapon in the war. The crew chiefs on the LOH quickly took over that distinction. On the LOH the crew chief, also known as the "torque," served as both crew chief and door gunner. Without question, the LOH crews' life expectancy was shortest of any in the division, except for infantry point men and perhaps grunts who happened to be following NVA commo wires.

In my time with the 1–9 Cav, the primary aerial scouting and fighting element of each troop was the pink team. A pink team consisted of an LOH and a Cobra gunship. Fighting platoons were designated by color in Troops A, B, and C: infantry was Blue Platoon, scouts were White Platoon, and guns were Red Platoon. Red (guns) and white (scouts) equal pink. Thus, a team made up of at least one each of gunship and scout bird was designated as a pink team.

During pink-team missions, the LOH flew near the earth to seek out the enemy and draw fire while the Cobra followed at a higher altitude. Sometimes, to cover distance or to arrive on top of the enemy before he could react, a pink-team LOH skimmed the trees at breathtaking speed. More often the LOH maintained an almost leisurely pace, the better to spot enemy sign and draw fire.

On-station over an objective or an area from which they received fire, the scout choppers moved slowly back and forth, sometimes hovering and even flying backward or sideways to blow foliage off trails so they could look for tracks. They even flew beneath the long branches of trees for the same reason. Often, from the ground with the 1–5 or 2–12 Cav, I'd been impressed as these little choppers buzzed about, dashing forward, backward and sideways like oversized bumblebees.

Normally a pilot or crew chief stayed with a pink team for six months, unless they volunteered to stay longer. Their chances during the six months were by my estimation about one in four of being killed, two in four of going home seriously wounded, and only one in four of going home whole or only slightly wounded. Those scout crewmembers that survived for six months tended to seek other duties for the second half of their tours. Because of the high mortality rate, I would conduct memorial services almost weekly in each of the Air Cav troops.

Notwithstanding the high casualty rates and almost daily contact with the enemy, the aircrews were distinctly different from typical infantry. I credit this difference in large part to the types of personalities drawn to flying and to their almost nightly return to the comforts of base camp life. Religious attitudes were distinctly low-key in the 1–9 Cav, compared to regular infantry. In the field, troopers flocked to worship services at almost every opportunity. In the 1–9 Cav, troopers practically shunned worship services, at least until they got to know the chaplain. Well, I knew how to become acquainted with my new troops—share their life and go with them on missions, except LRRP and tracker-dog missions, of course.

Early during my new assignment I watched would-be rangers, all volunteers, running around the airstrip at Phouc Vinh in the intense afternoon heat; they were each laden with a rock-filled rucksack and other equipment. Those young men would soon be going out on very dangerous and difficult long-range patrol missions, provided they survived two weeks of training. Two of those rangers that I visited may have been Kregg P. J. Jorgenson of Seattle and Jerry Clayton of Downey, California. Both men had arrived in country in September—Jorgenson on the same day that I signed into the 1–9 Cav, September 17. Our paths would cross again.

Church attendees or not, the 1–9 Cav certainly supported my efforts. Each Sunday I had a helicopter and crew dedicated for religious support operations. With those assets I routinely conducted Sunday services across the 1st Cav AO, from Phuoc Vinh (Headquarters, Charlie and Delta Troops) to Quan Loi (Bravo Troop) and Tay Ninh (Apache Troop).

Between and after services at these key bases, I flew wherever else I needed to in the line of duty, which included ecclesiastical meetings and hospital visits in Long Binh and Saigon. Sp4 Harold Lewis came with the assignment as my chaplain assistant. He was LDS and a draftee from the Denver, Colorado Police Department. Lewis usually accompanied me on these Sunday rounds. Overall in this new assignment I think I had more freedom to move according to my own priorities than any officer in Vietnam, in part because Lieutenant Colonel Booth trusted me to do my job as best I could.

The basic pattern of the demands of duty became evident during my first week in the 1–9 Cav. As mentioned earlier, I began my new duties on September 20 with a memorial service for a soldier that was accidentally killed by a ranger. The next day, following my first Sunday services for headquarters, my departure from Phuoc Vinh was delayed because the chopper assigned to me was shot down. Eventually, in another chopper, I visited Tay Ninh and Dau Tieng, visited wounded Blues of Bravo Troop at Quan Loi, canceled worship services twice because the troops were in contact, and attended an LDS service and spent the night at Quan Loi.

On September 22, I traveled around the division AO

making acquaintances with 1–9 Cav officers, noncommissioned officers, and troops. Over the next few days I flew to Tay Ninh and Quan Loi for worship services. Services were canceled at both locations because the troops were unexpectedly inserted into the jungle. One platoon went in to secure a downed aircraft and the other to rescue a team of LRRPs that was fighting off the NVA. At Tay Ninh that day, an Air Force FAC pilot invited me to accompany him on a mission and watch him orchestrate close air support (Air Force support) of infantry and bombings of enemy targets; he was shot down and killed before I could accept the invitation.

On September 24, I awoke on someone else's cot at Tay Ninh. At 1000 hours I conducted a worship service with twelve men in attendance. After the service I played chess with a pilot, then flew to Phuoc Vinh and attended evening meetings. I became frustrated because I couldn't get a flight to the hospital to visit the crew of a Bravo Troop scout LOH that had been shot down to the east of Quan Loi. The LOH had crashed into the bamboo, promptly broken off all four main rotor blades, which kept the destruction down, and came to rest on its nose, tilted over so that the rear end of the skids pointed upward and angled forward. A nearby LRRP team hurried to the crash site and found the pilot, WO Russel, with both legs broken and his knees being pushed into the ground by the weight of the chopper and crew. Four rangers simply lifted the chopper up while the fifth one pulled Russel out of the wreck.

At 0745 hours, September 25, I visited wounded troopers at Bien Hoa. Later at Lai Khe I was able to visit Warrant Officer Russel and Sergeant Fasthorse. Sp4 Early, the most seriously wounded crewmember of the LOH, had been evacuated to Saigon.

Back at Phuoc Vinh, I petitioned Booth to fly me to Saigon. We arrived there too late again to see Early. He was already on a medevac flight to the states. Late at night we returned to Phuoc Vinh where I fell asleep on my own cot.

The next day, September 26, I deployed with the Charlie

Troop Blues to LZ Buttons where we remained on standby the whole day. I used the time to conduct services, and to visit and counsel with the Blues. Seldom did they have uninterrupted days like this one. At Phuoc Vinh for the evening, I attended a scripture study class.

On September 27 I accompanied the Bravo Troop Blues on an insertion to recover key components from Russel, Fasthorse, and Early's LOH. We followed preparatory artillery and ARA fire into a small LZ, then made our way through giant bamboo for two hundred meters to where we found the chopper. Anyone flying directly overhead would have seen the skids and underbelly of the aircraft.

That evening I attended an obligatory *hail and farewell*, where Booth jokingly introduced me as one whose sanity might be in question because I willingly accompanied the Blues into the field. Booth would make up for the less serious part of the introduction in August 1995 by introducing me as a former "real Cav" man, "the bravest man I know"—quite a compliment, coming from a former combat commander of the famous 1–9 Cav. Thus ended what was probably the quietest, least eventful week during my time with the 1–9 Cav, a week of unusually low American casualties.

At 0800 hours, September 28, I conducted a worship service for Headquarters, 1–9 Cav. Booth missed the service because of operational demands, a rare omission for him. Later at Quan Loi I conducted another service for three men, Harold Lewis, the Bravo Troop executive officer, and me. Having reached Tay Ninh, via II Corps and Phuoc Vinh, I reorganized the LDS group and offered an evening service for Apache Troop, to which no one came, due to poor communications and a last-minute mission, I supposed.

A couple of times during the first half of this tour, I had tried to visit my old unit, the 2–8 Cav, which at the time operated out of LZs Caroline and Becky in a nasty area northnortheast of Tay Ninh, between the Black Virgin Mountain and Cambodia. I visited LZ Caroline once shortly after its perimeter had been overrun by the NVA, but found no familiar faces. With the 1–9 Cav, I often flew over LZ Becky, which was abandoned and flooded by monsoon rains. On 29 September, upon learning the 2–8 Cav was pulling palace guard, I volunteered to augment its religious support during the palace guard stint.

It was during this period, I believe, that I visited Sergeant Major Wiley L. Watson, formerly First Sergeant of Alpha 2–8 Cav. Watson and I talked of acquaintances in common, rehashed shared experiences from 1967, and reported on what we'd each been doing since. Watson, I realized, felt out of place operating at battalion level, which I understood.

I spent the night of September 29 with Bravo Troop at Quan Loi, where I slept in the TOC. Next morning I held a worship service that was attended by 23 Blues, almost the whole platoon. The increased attendance suggested that the men of the 1–9 Cav were beginning to accept me. On Sunday, October 19, I conducted four services around the 1–9 Cav AO, with between 18 and 37 present in each service.

Other indicators of acceptance included invitations to go along on operations and to learn to fly. Frequently I got to handle the controls of an LOH from the left copilot or observer seat. I became adequate at flying straight and making gradual turns and changes in altitude, but never advanced to landings, which skill the pilots liked observers to have. Just in case.

In the 1–5 Cav, I'd counted off months beginning with March 11, the day I joined the unit. Now, in the 1–9 Cav, I counted off months from March 1, the day I left the states to begin this tour. Though I never counted the days, I was conscious of them, especially with the draw-down of American troops, which President Nixon had begun. Consequently I was ripe for rumors like most everyone else.

Word had spread throughout South Vietnam that each soldier's tour would be reduced so many days for each month he completed in country. According to the formula described, I might be home by late January 1970. The "word" was everywhere, even in semi-official unit newspapers, until the bubble burst.

A reporter, according to the *Stars and Stripes*, asked a senior official at MACV or USARV to confirm significant tour curtailment based on months served. He quoted the official in essence as saying, "I'm sure the curtailment is official, though I haven't seen the order. I'll get back to you." Well, no such orders existed, the embarrassed official discovered. So applying his snooping skills, the journalist tracked the "word" to its source.

In northern South Vietnam, in or near Danang, two rear-echelon types, while seated on commodes, discussed the traditional source of Army rumors—the latrine. The discussion led to a plot to start a rumor and see how far it went. While their success surpassed their wildest expectations, it worked extreme cruelty on thousands, especially those lonely grunts in the field. As the rumor spread throughout Vietnam, it raised and then dashed the hopes of many lonely soldiers, marines, sailors and airmen, and their loved ones. It also messed up wedding and planned conception dates and such. This was a true "latrine rumor" in every way, as such were known in less delicate terms.

Though I've intertwined discussion of family affairs with this combat tour much less than I did for 1966–67, Helga and the children always supported me, inspired me, pulled at me, and occasionally worried me. Often, I considered what price each family member would pay for my long absences during critical years in the children's development. Would these absences during James' and Jeannie's early teen years deprive them of an essential role model and maybe stunt their development—social, emotional and spiritual? *If I survive only to see my children become casualties of this war, is the price too high?*

To perhaps limit the damages and help the older children progress, I frequently sent each of them their own personal letters and reel-to-reel tapes, crammed full of love, encouragement, and counsel. Jeannie yet has some of the tapes I sent her, she says. Helga gathered the family around to listen to the first tape that I sent them. This was five-year-old Brenda Lynette's first experience with reel-to-reel tapes. So, recognizing my voice, she stared closely at the machine and demanded, "Come out of there, Daddy!"

On October 3, I operated with the Charlie Troop Blues, which gave me a good opportunity to compare a Blue platoon to regular infantry. I found among the Blues a sincere respect for the regular infantrymen, tempered with pride in being Blues and a hint of gratitude that they were Blues, rather than regular grunts. The Blues, though, didn't really appreciate and understand the lot of regular troopers, though they came closer than most to doing so. But no one can appreciate the life of a regular grunt unless he has been in the field continuously for days and months on end. Regular grunts and company leaders generally respected the 1–9 Cav, though many in the field never knew the Blues existed.

Operationally, the Blues were well-disciplined in the jungle, all the time, I hoped. Man for man, a Blues platoon member carried much more weaponry and ammunition than a regular infantryman. Blue troopers could afford to do so because they seldom carried rations and survival gear to last them several days, as it was rare for them to stay overnight in the jungle or to hump farther than a kilometer during an operation. In addition to their personal and team weaponry the Blues usually had very good air support of both the logistical and firepower sort, dedicated and on-station.

Blues lived on the edge of the war with frequent dashes into the middle of it. Regular infantrymen lived in the middle of the war with all the perils, stresses, and strains that went with it. However, they usually experienced less-frequent periods of actual fighting. The Blues usually knew where they were going and had some idea what awaited them there—downed aircraft, hot LZ, and such. Regular grunts seldom knew what was ahead and the fighting, when it came, was usually unexpected and a total shock to their souls.

The regular infantryman's combat tour was a year—if he made it all the way—of near total misery. He was always wet and muddy or hot and soaked with sweat, engulfed in the stench of unwashed clothing and bodies. Often he drank water that was "fortified" with dead polliwogs and leeches; and he was accustomed to finding leeches in unpleasant places on his person.

Several factors rendered the regular field troopers' existence incomparable to that of anyone else. These factors included carrying everything they needed on their backs; constant vigilance around the clock; unending danger; spirit-draining, backbreaking, and exhausting labor; and an existence almost devoid of such creature comforts as frequent baths, clean clothes, beds, and uninterrupted nights. They humped and dug every day. They pulled perimeter guard, OP duty, or ambush every night, no matter what else occurred. All this was interspersed with intentional dashes into combat and those totally unexpected times of terror during firefights and ambushes by the enemy. And with all this, the regular infantrymen got few breaks even during occasional stints providing firebase security or palace guard. Exhaustion and sleepiness were the grunts' constant companions.

The infantryman came to the war alone, committed to a one-year tour. If he survived the first battle, he was accepted as a veteran. He lived in unrelenting stress, and endured unimaginable horrors. Often he would carry the bodies of killed or terribly wounded buddies, sometimes for hours until they could be flown from the field; there was no escape from close companionship with death and maiming. Nothing compares to the regular infantryman's existence in combat, not in the Army and not in life.

A *Stars and Stripes* article unintentionally helps explain the disparity between all other troops and regular infantry. The article, in praise of the support provided to American forces, bragged that 93 percent of all meals served to U.S. forces in Vietnam were hot. The piece failed to mention that this statistic applied mostly to troops located well behind the infantry line companies or that C-rations constituted at least two-thirds of the meals eaten by the grunt. It didn't mention that "hots" served to men in the field frequently consisted of the likes of cold or lukewarm, often watery potatoes and stringy beef served from olive-drab, oval mermite (thermos) cans.

Though I have no statistics on awards, I expect a disparity because the regular grunt's valorous actions were seldom witnessed by anyone but his buddies, buddies just as exhausted as he, and as unlikely to find a moment's peace to write up recommendations for awards. His actions, even when noted and written up, frequently became lost between pen and the awards board, or were depreciated by those who suffered from poor memory or who had never known the infantryman's existence.

All too often in the regular infantry, witnesses to a trooper's valor carried that knowledge to an early grave or to a distant hospital where names, faces, and deeds of valor took second place to personal pains and medical concerns. Just as often, acts of heroism, which in other environs merited recommendation for a Silver Star or higher award, passed with little notice.

Another factor working against the interests of regular infantrymen was that recommendations had to pass through several layers of command for final approval, and paperwork could get lost at every step. In the 1–9 Cav, on the other hand, only the troop and squadron commanders stood between the trooper and General Casey, who had approving authority for most impact awards. Even here things sometimes went awry. Once Booth contacted a master sergeant in Awards and Decoration to ask why no awards had come down for about a month. The master sergeant explained that a storm had blown a large stack of recommendations out into a muddy field and he'd had no way to identify which ones were lost or to reconstruct them. There is no way to tell how many well-deserved awards got lost in situations like this—a lot of them for certain.

Other factors influencing the awards system included proximity to the *flagpole*, uninterrupted esprit between members of unique units like the 1–9 Cav, and operational relationships. For example, the Apache Troop Blues worked closely day after day with the same Apache Troop pink teams and liftships, especially the LOH crews. Almost daily the Blues and aviators got one another out of trouble. And each evening, with few exceptions, both Blues and aviators returned to base camp, where deeds of valor could be written up without the distractions of ambush duty, radio watch, and enemy probes against defensive positions just meters away. Also, the exploits of Blues and aviators were more likely to be observed by officers from higher echelons who knew who they were by name, even reputation.

The well-deserved reputation of the 1–9 Cav had a distinct effect on the number of individual awards recommended and approved. The 1–9 Cav was there at the beginning of almost every major battle and most minor skirmishes that the division got into. The troopers and aviators of the 1–9 Cav earned their reputation the hard way. They accounted for the highest number of enemy killed and consistently sustained the most casualties of any American unit in the war.

Having said all this, I intend to take nothing away from the Blues, LRRPs, aircrews, and leaders of the 1st Squadron, 9th Cavalry. I salute them for their outstanding and effective exploits. I salute the regular ground troopers in recognition of their mostly unsung valor and for all they endured, routinely, "above and beyond."

On October 3, upon returning from the insertion with the Charlie Troop Blues, I traveled to Saigon with Captain John Thomas Kalunki, where we visited USAF Chaplain (Captain) Robert Christiansen. Tom Kalunki and I had a private showing of *2001: A Space Odyssey*, courtesy of Kalunki's contacts with the media. He was Assistant Information Officer for the 1st Cav. For dinner we dined on steak in company with Colonel McPhie (Air Force) and Paul

Madsen. Afterward, Tom and I visited until 0140 hours. My path would cross Kalunki's often in years to come. For example, I piggybacked my 1981 master's thesis on one Kalunki did in the 1970s.

In 1994, emotional exhaustion and a vague sense of depression would weigh down on me when I transcribed my war journals and memories into the computer. Later, these same sensations arose as I attempted to turn my journals into an autobiographical account of the war years. These sensations and emotions were replays of those I endured, especially in the last half of my second tour, as it became obvious America was throwing away our sacrifices in Vietnam in exchange for President Nixon's promised *peace with honor*.

From this point on, I will touch on the highlights of those last months in Vietnam. By doing otherwise, I would be repeating much that Kregg Jorgenson, Matthew Brennan, and others have already chronicled in their books about the 1–9 Cav.

On October 7, I rode for the first time in the *middle* seat on Lieutenant Colonel Booth's gunships. As I mentioned before, the Charlie-model Huey gunships bristled with rockets, a mini-gun, a grenade launcher, and M-60 machine guns, and was more potent and versatile than the newer Cobra gunships which replaced most of them, in the view of many aviators.

The Charlie-model gunships were crewed by four men, a pilot, copilot, crew chief in the left door, and door gunner in the right door; the chief and door gunner each manned an M-60 machine gun. Behind the pilots, against the back of the passenger/cargo section, a jump seat reached from door to door. I sat in the middle of this seat during flights on the Charlie-Charlie, so I could see ahead between the pilots' heads with a clear view out the open left and right doors. Of course, in the 1–9 Cav I had my own aviator helmet and no-max (fire resistant) flight suit. I used the helmet so I could listen in on and take part in onboard communications, but never wore the nomax suits because I performed my duties in jungle fatigues. I appreciated these rides because it was cool at higher altitudes, no matter how hot the weather, and in the Charlie-Charlie chopper I knew what was happening to the Blues and flight crews. As an added bonus, Pete Booth and his successor LTC Clark Burnett were good company, as were their crews.

On October 9, I flew with Booth and his crew, which consisted of Warrant Officer Danner in the left copilot seat, door-gunner Godfrey, and Svafen, the crew chief. We intended to visit Tay Ninh. We were barely underway when we diverted to the scene of a downed scout LOH. Tay Ninh would have to wait.

October 10 began like a replay of the previous day. After spending the morning on administrative details, I took off with Booth to visit crewmembers that had been wounded the day before. On the way, we stopped briefly at Quan Loi and LZ Buttons, and again, the NVA interrupted our plans.

"We received a report that a slick ship with about eight men from Charlie 2–5 had been shot down and was burning in a small clearing north of LZ Buttons near the Song Be River on the south side. The call came just after we lifted off from LZ Buttons in my Charlie-Charlie, a C-model Huey gunship. One of Major George O'Grady's Saber pink teams (Bravo Troop) was en route to provide danger-close support," said Booth.

In the situation that was developing, Booth would show his savvy and skill as a commander. It is as natural as breathing for a commander to try to get near the action so he can know what is happening and ensure that adequate support is provided to subordinate commanders and leaders. Consequently during the Vietnam War C&C helicopters tended to stack up in the air over extended engagements. In a matter of minutes, the battalion or squadron C&C would arrive and start circling the battle at, say, two thousand feet altitude. The brigade C&C would follow shortly to circle a thousand feet higher. Then the commanding general or one of his assistant commanding generals would circle higher still. Unfortunately some commanders got in the way instead of helping.

We arrived over the downed chopper just behind the pink team, and Booth immediately began showing that he could support the commander nearer to the ground without usurping his authority and responsibility. The men down there belonged to Major George O'Grady (Saber Six) and it was his AO. As the situation developed, Booth ordered in Charlie (Cavalier) assets and turned them over to O'Grady. Then he moved Alpha (Apache) Troop assets into the area to stand by prepared to become OPCON to O'Grady, if needed.

Below us a mangled chopper burned in a small clearing. Several apparently dead bodies lay on the south side of the downed chopper, opposite from where rockets from the pink team Cobra were already exploding and where a continual stream of tracer rounds from the LOH was impacting. As we watched, the LOH took hits and crashed near the burning Huey. Three crewmembers quickly scrambled out of it and joined the surviving 2–5 Cav grunts and Huey crewmembers who were hugging the ground among their own dead.

A second Saber pink team arrived on-station and added the firepower of another LOH and Cobra to the support of the troopers on the ground. As I recall, Booth's Charlie-Charlie also contributed firepower at this time. However, he doesn't remember firing rockets then or later. Captain Lou Niles, then Platoon Leader of the Bravo Troop (Saber White) aero-scouts insists that Booth held off on firing his rockets until a later, critical point when no other gunships were on-station.

Booth continued: "The Saber Blues, led by Lieutenant Maurice (Mike) Murphy (call-sign Saber Blue) of Peach Tree City, Georgia, were just seconds out, en route to attempt to secure the crash site and rescue the survivors. With two choppers down in the small clearing, the Blues would have to rappel in because there wasn't room for the Hueys carrying them to land. Hovering over or near the clearing so the Blues could rappel in was out of the question due to intense enemy small-arms, rocket and machine-gun fire from very close range. To make matters worse, the nearest clearing that might serve as an acceptable LZ was at least fifteen klicks away. Fortunately a very small clearing with two overlapping bomb craters in it was about one and a half klicks from the clearing that the Huey and LOH had gone down in. Unfortunately, though, the potential LZ was barely large enough for a Huey to land. Limbless trees stood like telephone poles around the craters. The Blues would have to rappel in and then tear their way through trackless jungle to reach the downed infantrymen and chopper crews.

"Saber pilot Kenneth Caudill of Oklahoma hovered his chopper just high enough above the clearing to ensure that the rotor blades cleared the surrounding jungle. The chopper crew lowered four ropes, two from each side, and the first four Blues rappelled to the ground.

"The second set of four Blues, one being Lieutenant Murphy, was standing in the doors and hooking up to go down the ropes when the NVA opened fire. Suddenly the Huey tipped sharply to the left and crashed straight down into the clearing. The momentum of the dip and crash almost threw Lieutenant Murphy up into the main rotor blade. In 1998 Murphy told me [Booth], 'It threw me up almost into the rotor. Still attached by the rope, I landed on my back across the hot transmission and engine. It was *hot*!'

"Hot was nothing compared to what happened to one of the two Blues dangling from the left door of the crashing chopper. The chopper landed on top of him and pinned him against the side of a crater or depression, promptly covering him with a growing pool of inflammable JP-4 aviation fuel.

"Quickly scrambling off the hot engine, Murphy took stock of the situation and scurried into a crater both for cover from heavy enemy small-arms fire and to communicate with his troop commander, Major George O'Grady, who was nearby in the air. Murphy knew the trooper pinned beneath the chopper had to be gotten out very quickly. He knew it wasn't possible to lift the ship off the man with the manpower available on the ground and that the volume of incoming enemy fire would render that impossible, even if they could. Rescue efforts were further complicated, he realized, because the downed chopper took up most of the tree-studded clearing.

"The two remaining Saber liftships returned to Quan Loi to pick up more Blues. Coming in at Quan Loi, one of the pilots flared his ships too steeply and drove the tail rotor into the ground. George O'Grady now had one liftship left.

"About that time, while circling the contact areas," Booth continued, "I made a wide left turn and saw the big red ball of the sun just touching the horizon to the west and starting to sink. Thinking that *this is going to be a very long night*, I ordered Major Tredway to send me every available ship and also his Cavalier Troop Blues. I also ordered Apache Troop to deploy from Tay Ninh to Quan Loi and stand by on five-minute alert. Next, I called for all available Blue Max (ARA gunships) to help the Saber gunships keep the enemy off the men on the ground. The Cobras came and from then on one or more were almost constantly on-station to provide extremely close aerial rocket support to the troops.

"Fortunately, I had my artillery FO on board. He did a beautiful job of calling in and coordinating massive artillery. But as the commander there was nothing else I could do. If those pinned Blues, 5th Cav grunts and aircrews were to be rescued, it would be up to individuals to take the initiative and do what American soldiers do when it becomes necessary. 'White-Six just let down and brought out two wounded,' radioed O'Grady. It was starting to happen."

It was happening on the ground too. While Murphy coordinated and worked the radio, four of the remaining Blues on the ground fought off the NVA and provided cover fire for the men pinned beneath the chopper. The other two Blues each grabbed a fire extinguisher from the downed chopper, threw themselves to the ground by their buddy who was pinned beneath it, and lay in the open ready to protect him if fire broke out. No doubt those two Blues knew that those fire extinguishers would be of little use if the fuel in the depression caught fire. They knew if this happened they would likely die with their trapped buddy in the resulting explosion. But that guy beneath the chopper, immersed in fuel, needed support—and he got it, despite the risks involved to those who gave it.

Captain Lou Niles carefully lowered his LOH over the bomb craters, down among the limbless trees, to hover motionless a few feet above the ground while wounded troopers were loaded on.

Niles explained. "I used my rotor blades to widen the hole for the chopper [by chopping branches and leaves off the trees that surrounded the clearing] and then hovered a few feet above the ground because there was no place to set down."

"Niles balanced one skid on a log and had his front seat gunner hold it steady," said O'Grady.

Niles continues, "The pilot of the slick ship leaped over a log with his arm above his head as he ran toward me. There was nothing I could do as I watched my rotor blades chop off his fingers. After the wounded were loaded on, I called over to Blue Six, 'What do you need?'

"'Chain saw and hydraulic jack,' Lieutenant Murphy called back."

Mike Hanlon, Niles' crew chief, stayed on the ground after helping load the wounded. Then he added his machine gun and a lot of ammunition to the defense of those in the small clearing. O'Grady said Niles left both crewmembers behind to join with the infantry in the clearing.

After lifting out of the clearing, Niles dropped the wounded at the 15th Med at Quan Loi. "Then I picked up the chain saw and hydraulic jack—part of a packet I had prepared for situations like this—and returned. Meanwhile, all the Cobras had expended their rockets, leaving a temporary lull in the danger close air support while they rearmed at LZ Buttons. You guys were the only ones with any rockets left. Pete made several very effective runs to keep the NVA off the downed crews, Blues, and Charlie 2–12 grunts until the Cobras returned. He literally pinned an NVA to a tree with one of his flechette rounds," said Niles.

From my position behind and between pilot and copilot, I watched the action and followed it over my helmet headset. Booth made several diving runs, each time placing flechette rounds where we hoped they would do some good without injuring our own. During one attack dive, I distinctly saw the rapid muzzle flashes of a heavy machine gun and several small arms that were firing at us. Mr. Danner, the copilot, let go with a roaring, ripping burst of mini-gun fire a moment after I saw the flashes. The trajectory of the mini-gun's red tracer bullets showed that he was right on target. Booth, having failed to see the muzzle flashes and rising tracers, sharply rebuked Danner for firing so close to American troops without a clear target. I keyed my microphone and assured him that we'd been receiving heavy fire, which took the heat off Danner. That Booth never saw the muzzle flashes was understandable; he was fixated on the target he'd selected for our rockets while at the same time flying the chopper and avoiding hitting friendlies or becoming part of the target.

Meanwhile, Niles braved heavy NVA fire to reenter the clearing and deliver the chainsaw and hydraulic jack to the Blues. "On the ground some Blues and crewmembers started cutting down trees to expand the LZ while others attempted to free the two troopers by jacking up the chopper. The jack did not work, so they took one of the trees that had just been cut down and, using the jack as a fulcrum, they lifted the chopper high enough to pull out the fuel-soaked trooper," Niles said.

Next, while other ships extracted the 2–5 Cav and crews from the larger clearing, three Charlie Troop liftships took turns entering the slightly enlarged, hot LZ to lift out the Blues and downed liftship crew. It turned pitch dark as Warrant Officer Smith piloted the last bird up and out of the LZ. "This story shows that when the commander has done all he can and can't figure out what else to do, some soldier will stand up and save the day," said Booth. It also shows that a tremendous amount of action can be squeezed into the few short minutes between when the sun touches the western horizon and full darkness. Heroics on and near the ground reversed a situation that had looked hopeless a few minutes before. Booth praised everyone who took part, especially Captain Lou Niles who saw what had to be done and did it, at extreme risk to his own survival.

According to O'Grady another Saber LOH was downed several hundred meters away and Niles also helped rescue that crew, still flying a helicopter that should have remained grounded in Maintenance.

Afterward Booth highly praised Major O'Grady for the way he handled the multi-faceted situation. O'Grady extolled the contributions of his artillery FO and Lou Niles. He considered recommending Niles for the Medal of Honor for his deeds that day. However, my sources said twenty-year-old Niles prevailed on O'Grady not to make the recommendation because that would have meant the end of his time as Saber White—the scout platoon leader. Niles understood that 1st Cav policy required the removal from combat of anyone who was recommended for that award. General Shoemaker presented Niles with an impact award of the Silver Star instead. Everyone extolled the courage and conduct of Lieutenant Murphy and his Blues.

While the efforts of Niles and others saved the day for the 1–9 Cav, seven of the 2–5 Cav men died when that first chopper was shot down and during the subsequent fighting. All the 1–9 Cav aircrews and Blues survived, including the one who had been pinned beneath the liftship, though some were wounded.

Again we aborted our mission to visit the hospitals and returned to Phuoc Vinh, it being too late to continue on. That evening, a group of troopers and I listened to religious tapes that Helga had sent me. Attention shifts very rapidly for those who fight and serve from rear areas.

During a discussion of the events of October 10, 1969, Booth described Captain Niles as a fantastically daring and effective helicopter scout/fighter. Niles describes himself as a smart scout leader who applied good sense and tactics to survive and keep his men alive. "I detested the *kill* mentality that led to tactics that cost the lives of many young scout crewmembers. So, I established a school for scout pilots that candidates had to pass before they flew scouts in Saber Troop. None who completed the course were killed during my time as their leader—quite a change for you, Chaplain. No more weekly memorial services for Bravo Troop."

Though I wouldn't learn of it for another three days, Ted Pierce of Delta 1–5 had been dying nearby in the jungle while I was over our downed aircraft and casualties. Another trooper I knew, Pfc. Robert L. Lazarus of Honolulu, Hawaii, was among the dead troopers on the first Huey that went down in the larger clearing, I believe.

On October 11, I visited and conducted a worship service for Charlie 2–8 Cav, one of my old units. There were no familiar faces from 1966–67. Again, Booth and I were unable to visit the hospital, so I scheduled another tape-listening session. We finally reached the hospitals at Long Binh and Saigon on October 12.

At the Third Field Hospital in Saigon, I found Sergeant Elvin Jackson of Alpha 1–5. He was recovering from a shrapnel wound to the right arm and malaria and soon would return to combat. Later, the wound would cripple him for life. No problem! The Veterans Administration would magnanimously grant Jackson a 10 percent disability, with the promise of an increase "when they cut the damn thing off."

That evening, following a worship service back at Phuoc Vinh, I filled two cassettes with words of wisdom for Helga and the children on a new cassette player/recorder.

October 15 brought reminders of the inherent dangers of helicopters, which some "experts" insist can't fly. "Because of combat losses, there will be no flights to Tay Ninh tomorrow," I was warned the night before. A ride came though, and I flew west about midmorning.

We were moving along nicely at about three or four thousand feet elevation, somewhere between Lai Khe and the Michelin Rubber Plantation. Suddenly the chopper went into an ear-popping, spiraling, almost vertical dive. That was scary enough, but inside my flight helmet and on the crew's faces, I heard and saw concern sufficient to create extra anxiety in me—a critical fire warning light glared on the instrument panel.

At the right moment, the pilot skillfully pulled the chopper out of the dive and into auto-rotation mode, and the skids thumped safely on the ground. We needed security fast. The regular door gunner was not aboard, so while the crew chief dashed off a hundred feet to the east with one M-60 machine gun, I went west with the other one.

Air cover and aircraft technicians soon arrived and diagnosed the problem. A relatively harmless short-circuit had necessitated the emergency landing. The trip to Tay Ninh would have to wait for another day. The hour forced us to return to Phuoc Vinh, where I wrote a message for inclusion in the *Cavalair*, the 1st Cav's newspaper. Then I turned my attention to administrative stuff. That's when I found Ted Pierce and Robert Lazarus listed as KIAs on a five-day-old casualty report.

According to Banks, Bowen, and some other troopers in Delta 1–5, Ted Pierce was humping a radio on one of countless recon missions when the point element called a halt to check out some suspicious sign ahead, the first fresh NVA sign all day. Trouble was, the troopers with Pierce didn't receive word of the fresh enemy sign.

Pierce left his PRC-25 radio and stepped behind some underbrush a few feet away from the column. Moments later, he was attending to personal matters when an NVA soldier initiated a B-40 rocket attack on the flanks of the column. The first incoming rocket blew off both of Pierce's legs as he squatted in the underbrush. He might have lived, had he not lain where he fell, un-missed by his buddies during the precious minutes it took for much of his blood to drain away. In the heat of the surprise attack and ensuing fight it was some time before Pierce's buddies got to him.

Pierce was conscious when they found him and complained of terrible pain in his legs, one of which dangled in view high in a nearby tree. His last words before losing consciousness were an avowal of love for his wife. Banks and Bowen provided religious administrations to Pierce. He died about an hour and fifteen minutes after being wounded, still waiting for the medevac chopper, which might have saved his life.

Ted Pierce missed *making it* by just a few hours. He'd been selected to leave the field later in the day to fill the coveted and relatively safe rear-area position of company mail clerk.

Some days later, Elder Marion D. Hanks contacted Mrs. Pierce and conveyed to her Ted Pierce's dying declaration of love for her. I missed Ted Pierce's unit memorial service on October 1. It occurred while I was on the way to LZ Vivian to attend it. The next day the LDS men at Phuoc Vinh held a service for both Pierce and Lazarus.

That was also the day—October 15—that I was awarded the Combat Infantryman Badge (CIB). Unknown to me, Captain Copley of Bravo 1–5 recommended me for the award. Rasmussen told me the award went through only with the help of influence in high places, and over the division chaplain's dutiful objections because "chaplains are neither infantrymen nor combatants."

Part of the story I got in early 1977. I was en route to Modesto and Fresno to notify a mother and father of the death of their son in Germany. At the beginning of the trip, I stopped at the convience store in Marina, California. The attendant, who looked familiar, pointed at my CIB and said in effect, "I helped you get that. Everybody insisted a chaplain could not receive the CIB, but with Lieutenant Colonel Rasmussen's permission, I took the matter to General Casey. The general overrode all objections and ordered that the CIB be approved for you."

The attendant was Command Sergeant Major (Retired) Raymond Ballentine, formerly of the 1-5 Cav Battalion. I confirmed his name with my uncle Thomas E. Newby (U.S. Army, retired), who lived in Marina at the time.

The *rest of the story* came out during a ceremoney at the

U.S. Army Infantry Training Center, Fort Benning, Georgia, in September 2000. In his remarks, former Bravo 1-5 Company Commander Jay Copley said, "I wanted Chaplain Newby to receive the Combat Infantryman Badge because he deserved it, so I put him in for it, knowing full well there would be problems. Sure enough, the Division GI and Division Chaplain recommended disapproval because 'Chaplains can't qualify for the CIB.' So I went to General George Casey, Assistant Division Commander. He listened to me and said in effect, 'I always see Chaplain Newby in the field with the troops whenever things are bad for them. He deserves the CIB and I think I outrank the regulations.'"

This was a great tribute coming from great men and leaders, each of whom wore the CIB with a Star, meaning they earned the honor to wear the CIB in two different wars, and consequently had great interest in making sure that it was not trivialized by being carelessly bestowed on those who were not deserving of it. Both General Casey and Copley had served in both Korea and Vietnam.

According to reliable sources and my best knowledge, the CIB was awarded only twice to chaplains for periods of combat in which they served as chaplains. The first CIB went to Holland Hope who, upon finding himself the last officer alive, took charge and successfully led an infantry unit through a furious battle during the Korean War. The other CIB was awarded to me, not for any single action, so far as I know—though I had led an ARVN band on a combat operation back in '67.

On October 16 an incident occurred which reminded me of March 13. That was the time that ARVN Sergeant Van Nie with Bravo 1–5 shouted "beaucoup GI!" when lots of NVA were sneaking up on the CP group that had taken cover in a bomb crater. This time, a Blue trooper died when a Kit Carson scout didn't understand that "Friendlies coming in" meant "Don't shoot, the next people you see are on our side."

*　　*　　*

The Blues, like other troopers, seemed at times to be losing their aggressive spirit, to be yielding to the changing *climate*. Still, I was surprised on October 20 when during a search for an NVA communications source, a Blue Platoon leader "missed" an obvious sign of recent enemy presence in a bunker complex and then led the platoon over clean, freshly laid strands of enemy communications wire as if it wasn't there. The lieutenant was embarrassed when I pointed out and explained the sign to him. Looking back, I believe the lieutenant ignored the commo lines in order to avoid getting more troopers killed in exchange for intelligence of dubious value in a no-win war.

Back at Phuoc Vinh for the night, I sulked because I'd not received mail from home for days. My recent mail consisted only of a letter from my good friend Dallas Murdoch, which contained something that impressed me. He suggested I write a book. That suggestion might have been the seed which bloomed (or festered) into *It Took Heroes*. The next day at Ton San Nhut, Chaplain Robert Christiansen nourished the seed by making an identical suggestion.

A letter from home focused my thoughts and energy on October 22 and 23. Helga wrote of Jeannie being lured into an oath of secrecy regarding criminal activities by a classmate. My concerns became a taped message discussing an error in logic that is common among law-abiding people, an error that fits in well with criminal designs upon them. My message was that, contrary to the flawed logic, we have a civic duty to act on knowledge of criminal intent and action, and it is wise for us to be very careful in the promises we give.

The next day, October 24, Lieutenant Colonel Booth flew and worked the western part of War Zone C, between the Fishhook and the area between the Black Virgin Mountain and Katum, near Cambodia. We were flying northward near flooded LZ Becky when we heard the muscle-tightening, relatively slow *chunk-chunk-chunking* of incoming—upward-coming—51-caliber machine-gun bullets. We could easily hear the burst, despite the muffling effects of flight helmets. "What is that?" a crewmember asked.

"Fifty-one caliber," I answered. In retaliation, we shot a few rockets and some mini-gun bursts at spots from which the enemy fire may have come.

Having spent the previous night at Tay Ninh, I spent much of October 27 trying to accompany the Apache Blues on a mission, only to remain behind because the choppers were overloaded. So I returned to Phuoc Vinh, only to turn around and go back to Tay Ninh for no other reason than that I felt impressed that I should do so.

Back with Apache Troop at Tay Ninh, I found two pilots who wanted to discuss theology, which we did until quite late in the evening. Then I turned in for the night on the cot of a pilot who'd invited me to use it any time it was unoccupied. I lay awake for a long time, wondering about the impression that brought me back and if the theological discussion with the two aviators was the reason for it. *No, I don't think so*, I concluded before finally falling to sleep.

The next day the Apache Blues assaulted into an NVA-infested area near LZ Jess. A new man, the platoon medic, struck up a whispered conversation during a pause in the sweep through the area. He looked at me curiously and inquired, "Where are you from, sir?"

"Ogden, Utah, and you?"

He said his name was Steve Blake. "I'm from Salt Lake City and I served as a missionary before getting drafted. You're LDS, aren't you?" I nodded.

"I knew it! I really need to talk with you, Chaplain Newby."

Back at Tay Ninh, Blake and I visited until late into the night. He had recently transferred from the only 82nd Airborne brigade that was serving in Vietnam, which had been designated to be one of the first combat units to withdraw from Vietnam. Blake wasn't *short* enough to return to the States with it.

"Yesterday, I prayed hard for someone to talk to about spiritual matters, about this environment and the concerns it causes me," Blake said.

After Blake explained his concerns, I thought I knew why I'd been prompted to return to Tay Ninh. He needed to talk with me now, not at some convenient date in the future.

On October 29 I came across Daniel Lang's *New Yorker* magazine article, "Casualties of War," an extensive recounting of the Mao incident in 1966 and the subsequent actions related to the case. This magazine piece and subsequent book formed the basis of an underground movie titled, *Mao*, circa 1970. The producers of *Mao* were sued in world court for violation of movie rights. The incident was portrayed in a late-1980s Hollywood movie titled *Casualties of War*, starring Michael J. Fox. The magazine piece was accurate on every point where I have personal knowledge, except that I have brown hair, not blond, and I was a police officer in Ogden, not Salt Lake City, Utah. The story is told from my perspective beginning on page 51 of this book.

forty-two

QRFs and Crocodiles

October 30 began quietly enough, but ended on the loud side. At 0730 hours Lieutenant Dave Jenkins' Charlie Troop Blues flew to LZ Jamie to stand by as a quick-reaction force in support of Charlie Troop pink teams that were operating in the area. On the way we made what became my last visit to LZ Grant, a ghost base compared to when the 2–12 Cav had been there.

At LZ Jamie a bunker was placed at our disposal to provide us minimum shelter from sun and rain. We took advantage of the temporary quiet there to hold a worship service, after which I became better acquainted with members of the platoon, including Sp4 Eugene Carroll, a squad leader. Then I visited with Captain Norman Childs, commander of Delta 2–7. We knew each other from Fort Bragg. Childs' company was also on standby as a quick-reaction force (QRF) in case the Blues got into something that was too big for us to handle. We would need the whole Delta 2–7 QRF before the day was over.

We scrambled onto choppers at 1030 hours and headed for the Cambodian border near the Fishhook. Our mission was to circle the area while a pink team conducted a BDA (battle-damage assessment) of an arclight (B-52 bomber strike). The strike, according to the plan, was to have been right on the border with Cambodia, and supposedly had occurred a few minutes before we arrived.

We'd been on-station a few minutes, circling lazily about five hundred feet above the jungle and wondering where the pink team was, when suddenly the chopper lurched right into a steep dive to gain speed. I was sitting cross-legged directly behind the left pilot's seat. The violent maneuver caught me off guard. I remained in the aircraft only by catching hold of the doorframe and with the help of the troopers deeper inside who reflexively grabbed onto my LBE (pistol belt and suspenders).

Meanwhile, whole trees leaped into the air as a quarter-mile-wide line of explosions marched straight across the area we'd just vacated; it looked as though some trees were coming right at us.

With my balance reestablished and my seat secured, I took out my camera to record the scene, but, alas, the camera was broken. The previous day, I'd forgotten my LBE in the Apache Troop latrine and had to go back for it. Someone had stolen the film and returned the camera to the ammo pouch, broken beyond repair. It was my misfortune to discover the theft and damage at the very moment when some fantastic, never to be repeated camera shots could have been taken.

We survived the arclight, thanks to the timely arrival and keen eyesight of an Air Force FAC pilot. The FAC had arrived on-station after we did and began circling several thousand feet above us. From that height he spotted our slow-moving, camouflaged chopper against the jungle background. The higher-flying B-52 bombers had already released their bombs when the FAC warned us to get out of the way. That was the warning that prompted our chopper pilot's violent and evasive maneuvering. Thanks to the chopper pilot's skills, we got clear of the target area, barely in time to avoid being knocked from the sky by the falling bombs or the subsequent concussion and air turbulence. As it was, the last of the bombs seemed to pass almost beneath us in their angled descent. Now, all this might make little sense to experts on bomb trajectories, but it's what we saw.

We returned to the area after the bombs stopped falling and stayed at about two thousand feet altitude until the pink team arrived and completed the bomb damage assessment. We arrived back on LZ Jamie at noon, ready for a hot meal.

The Blues scrambled again at 1215 hours, this time to rescue an LRRP team, call sign Talon 4–3. Hot lunch would have to wait. Sergeant Henry Morris' team of five rangers was pinned down and surrounded by NVA a few klicks from LZ Jamie. Other members of the LRRP team were Charlie Steel, assistant team leader; Howard Shute; Julius Zaporozec of New Jersey; and Kregg P. J. Jorgenson.

Our combat assault ended unopposed in a clearing southeast of LZ Jamie, where we arrived five minutes after we took off. From the clearing, we humped southward for fifty-five minutes, moving with relative ease through sparse undergrowth. The NVA were giving every indication of breaking contact and withdrawing by the time we reached the ranger/LRRP team. Linkup was established with the rangers without anyone getting shot at, by friendlies or NVA.

The LRRPs were in a tight defensive position about a hundred meters to the west of the swamps along the Saigon River. An almost circular clearing a little smaller than the top of a five hundred pound bomb crater, maybe twenty to thirty feet across, lay ten yards north of them. Jungle hugged the clearing on the south and east and brush encircled the rest of it, except for a four- or five-foot opening in the brush on the northwest side. A smaller clearing just beyond the opening in the brush joined a much larger clearing about thirty feet beyond us. A water-filled foxhole just inside the first clearing bore evidence of American presence before today.

After the successful linkup, Lieutenant Jenkins and Sergeant Morris conferred and then radioed their respective higher commands to report. It appeared that the NVA had withdrawn in the face of reinforcements, but Morris didn't think so, according to Ranger Kregg Jorgenson. We received prompt orders to sweep southwestward and see what it was that the NVA were hiding in the area that made them so touchy. Having not heard the new orders, I took a seat in the southeast clearing and leaned back against a bank on the north side. The clearing was in a depression, bordered on three sides by the embankment.

I'd barely sat down when thirty feet away Sergeant Morris disappeared from the clearing followed by Carroll and part of his squad. About twenty feet into the jungle, Morris rejoined the other four LRRP rangers at the place they had earlier fought off the NVA.

Sp4 Carroll, who had fallen in behind the rangers, was the only Blue trooper not wearing a steel helmet, an issue I'd talked to his lieutenant about earlier. Carroll turned his head or body to the left, apparently, soon after he disappeared from view, which may have caused an NVA machine gunner to conclude that Carroll had spotted him. A burst of 30-caliber machine-gun fire cut Carroll down from a distance of seven to ten meters. Carroll fell mortally wounded, his head laid open by an upward-angled gash from just below the left eye to above and back of the left ear.

Instantly, the rangers and Blues hit the ground and scrambled for meager cover behind the rangers' massive packs. In response to the yell, "Medic!" I dashed across the clearing and dropped to my knees against the embankment, beside the Blue platoon leader and his RTO. Carroll lay in plain view some fifteen feet into the jungle, his face to the sky and his brain clearly visible through the gash in his skull.

Already, the Blues and rangers were blasting away in response to the distinct cracks of NVA machine-gun bullets, mingled with a heavy volume of AK-47 bullets that were distinguishable for their sharper cracks and faster firing rate. Heavy fire followed immediately on the machine-gun burst. Everyone to the front had his hands full. I went over the embankment, slithered to Carroll, grasped him by his shirt collar, and started dragging him toward the clearing. The platoon medic joined me and helped get Carroll into the clearing. From there, two Blues helped the medic and me carry Carroll back the way we had come to where a small opening in the brush led to the smaller middle clearing. There the medic and I fought death for forty-five minutes while the RTO pleaded for medevac to hurry.

Meanwhile, the LRRPs and Blues pulled back across

the depression and established a defensive line in the bushes about ten feet from us. My assistant Harold Lewis voluntarily joined a Blue in the water-filled foxhole and spent the rest of the afternoon firing at the enemy. He got shrapnel in his back and neck for his troubles, but was not seriously wounded. Earlier Lewis had begged to come along today to "see what it's like on the ground." Now he knew, sort of.

We continued working on Carroll, holding onto the illogical hope that the wound would not be fatal if he reached a doctor soon enough. Carroll's heart stopped beating even as I gave him mouth-to-mouth resuscitation. Medevac was canceled before it ever arrived. A call went out for a resupply of ammunition.

Soon Major Robert Tredway, Charlie Troop Commander, call sign Cavalier 6, slipped his Charlie-Charlie chopper in from the northwest and hovered in the air about thirty feet above the ground while the crew chief and door gunner kicked out boxes of ammunition. Delivery of the ammo had hardly begun when NVA fire raked the chopper, driving metal fragments from the aircraft into Tredway's arm. The chopper beat a hasty retreat with a lot of the much-needed ammo still aboard.

Meanwhile the ammo boxes had fallen some fifty feet away from us in the exposed larger clearing to our northnortheast. None showed any inclination to risk death to retrieve it. After quickly considering the risks—death or capture—involved in running completely out of ammo, I stooped low, ran into the field and returned lugging a box of ammo. On the way back to cover I passed several Blues who were headed out to retrieve the other boxes. Soon our return fire increased in volume, only now firing discipline was more obvious.

Once more, I intervened in tactical matters by urging Lieutenant Jenkins to call aerial rocket fire into the trees beyond a big clearing to our east and rear. We had received no NVA fire from that direction, but I figured if I were the NVA, I'd be setting up mortars there. After repeated urging on my part, a cobra fired a few rockets where I wanted them, but the pilot didn't do it without questioning Blue Six's sense and reasoning. I don't know whether those rockets were necessary. We were not mortared, which was exactly the result that I hoped for.

About 1700 hours, a platoon-size QRF from Captain Childs' Delta 2–7 Cav linked up with us, having combat assaulted in somewhere near and humped to our position. Blue Six conferred a moment with the QRF platoon leader and immediately instructed the Blues to pull out and leave the situation to the Gerry Owen troopers—Gerry Owen was a nickname for the 7th Cav dating back to America's western frontier days. The Gerry Owen QRF platoon leader objected angrily, so Jenkins agreed to stay until the rest of Delta 2–7 arrived.

While we waited, the men fashioned a makeshift stretcher for Carroll by running two green poles through the buttoned-up jungle fatigue shirts of the lieutenant and another man. Captain Childs and the rest of the QRF company arrived a half hour before twilight, and the Blues pulled back and headed for a designated PZ several hundred meters off through the swampy river bottom.

This hasty withdrawal so bothered me that I was tempted to stay behind with Delta 2–7. It seemed we were abandoning the very troopers that had come to our rescue. Rationally, though, I knew the Blues were not equipped to stay long in the field. As it turned out, our hasty departure made no difference. We were in for a miserable overnighter.

Heavy, damp darkness descended on us before we'd gone a hundred meters through the swamp. We kept slipping, splashing and slurping over and under logs and other slimy, barely seen things. By 1930 hours we still hadn't reached the PZ. The rain was coming down hard. Because of the worsening weather, the liftships could wait for us no longer. "We'll see you at first light," the flight leader radioed.

We stopped in place about fifteen minutes later, strung out in a column. To prepare for the night, I backed up to a thick bush beside the trail we had broken, stood still until I stopped sinking into the muck, which came above my knees, and leaned back into the bush until its resistance created a very uncomfortable cradle.

The cold, miserable rain stopped about 2300 hours, but by then there was no drying out or warming to be had. Reluctantly, I proffered my shirt to the platoon leader at 0110 hours. It was much colder after that. The lieutenant's shirt was still under Carroll's body.

At 0200 hours, an artillery battery began walking artillery toward us. Individual shells were exploding successively in a line. The first shell exploded several hundred meters to our east-northeast, the next a little closer, the third one closer still, and so forth. First calmly, then with growing urgency, Lieutenant Jenkins worked the radio to stop the barrage. With nothing else to do, I estimated how many shells would fall before one exploded in our midst. Soon a 105mm shell burst about seventy-five meters from us, in water from the sound of it. We held our collective breath waiting for the next shell to hit us. It didn't come.

After the barrage, to escape the cold and to ignore the slow creep of the second hand on my watch, I focused heart, mind, and soul on considerations of life's stages and Christ's atonement for this miserable world. I considered the close calls and escapes, and whiled away some of the night in grateful appreciation for life, hope, and the strength to carry on.

Though the dawn arrived on schedule, it seemed like it came many hours after it should have. The lieutenant returned my shirt. We pried our feet and bodies from the mire, picked up Carroll's litter, and moved toward where we thought a PZ might be. Shortly the friendly clap-clap of Huey rotor blades were overhead. The Blues popped smoke. The pilot confirmed that the smoke was ours by its color and said, "Be advised. You are surrounded by crocodiles!" Then he stayed close overhead to better see the big, dangerous amphibians as he guided us around and through them to a PZ.

Carroll's blood and the occasional shrapnel wound on our bodies had probably attracted the crocodiles to us. Perhaps the crocodiles left us alone during the night, postponing their meal so to speak, until the warmer dawn because they were even colder than we were.

According to the *Stars and Stripes*, more than thirty NVA soldiers died in the engagement of October 30. The body count figures must have come from the folks in the air, for the Blues and rangers saw very few dead NVA that day.

Kregg P. J. Jorgenson, one of the rangers we rescued, would become the author of *Acceptable Loss, MIA Rescue*, and other books. Jorgenson, who received his baptism of fire this day, described the engagement a little differently than how I remember it, which is to be expected given our different perspectives and levels of experience at the time. For example, Jorgenson thought Carroll would die almost instantly. "While I knew there was little hope for the wounded machine gunner, I was moved that the chaplain never gave up trying to save him—all the while under enemy fire. This was the heartbreaking reality of war and was true and genuine courage. God bless Chaplain Newby," Jorgenson wrote. Jorgenson had good reason for his conclusions because parts of Carroll's body had sprayed over his body and soaked into his trousers as he lay there fighting off the NVA.

I appreciate Jorgenson's perspective. I owe him for providing the names of the other rangers on his team, and for his account of what transpired before the Blues arrived on the scene.

Quite a few valorous awards were given for this action, including Silver Stars and Distinguished Flying Crosses. The medic and I each received the same type of award for getting Carroll out from under direct fire. I received my third Purple Heart for minor shrapnel wounds and for bleeding from both ears, caused by the concussion of numerous explosions. In my journal for that day I wrote, "One day we might need heroes again. Who will be able to tell them [true heroes] apart from the ones who received awards for minor wounds like mine?"

Two days later I wrote, "One day I'm in the swamps surrounded by crocodiles, and the next day I'm sitting here at the feet of a great spiritual leader and theologian, miles away and worlds apart."

The day after the action with the Blues and rangers, November 1, I stopped at Tan San Nhut long enough to arrange for a bus the next day to transport 1st Cav troopers from the airfield to a religious conference site. Then I flew to Cam Ranh Bay and attended a meeting under the direction of Elder Bruce R. McConkie, noted ecclesiastical leader, author, and father of an Air Force chaplain who had recently served in Vietnam.

The next day, following a conference session at 0630 hours, I hitched a ride on the flight that took Elder McConkie to Saigon. At his urging I sat beside him and told war stories, including the action among the crocodiles two days previously. Apparently Elder McConkie was impressed for that evening he introduced me to someone as "one of the great men of the church." I could have temporarily let my helmet band out an inch.

Notes

30 October 1969, 1–9 Cav Journal, 1035: "Fr 1-9-G2 TN X415885. C/1–9 1000 hrs; BDA of A/L [B-52 strike]."

　　1140: "TM 43 [LRRPs] has singing and talking about 500m to their south. Going to try an ambush if possible."

　　1155: "TM 43 in contact at this time at XT491677."

　　1345: "medevac bird requested for TM 43, either Blue or 1-Talon member wounded in contact with unknown number of indivs . . . 1 member of the Blues is KIA."

　　1430: "Heavy Bones QRF [quick reaction force, a platoon of Delta 2–7] in on the ground with Blues."

　　1605: "Cav 6 A/C down at 'Jamie' has to be slung out. No injuries."

Closing Summary: "H. 43 . . . were engaged by 2 indiv while
setting ambush. No cas, radio antenna shot off, commo went
through 2–7 . . . At 1315 Blues linked up with 43, came into
contact with USEF, resulting in 1 US KIA . . . C Troop at
XT491677 UH-1H recd S/A fire, hovering 60 ft while
resupplying Blues with smoke and ammo, no inj., hit A/C no fly
at LZ Jamie . . . Blues, H43 and D/2–7 neg sitrep, will be
extracted when weather breaks. Total killed for 30 Oct 69—A
Trp 5; B Trp 5; C Trp Pink Team 12; C Trp Blues 10; H-43 3 . . .
We had a good day, looking for a better one tomorrow. Good
Night, signed by Captain James A. Price."

30 October 1969, 1/9 Cav S-3 Log Item 1, 1140 hrs.: TM-43 has
singing and talking about 500m to their south. Going to try to
ambush . . . 1155 hrs, TM-43 in contact. Cav [Charlie Troop,
call sign Cavalier] en route . . . 1220, Cav
Blues inserted. 1345 hrs, medevac requested for TM-43 either
Blues or 1 Talon member wounded in contact with unknown
number . . . 1 member of blues is KIA. 1420 hrs, Heavy bones
QRF is on the ground with Cav. Blues. 1605, Cav [Cavalier] 6
A/C down at "Jamie," has to be slung out. No injuries.

31 October 1969, 1–9 Cav Journal, 0810: "C Trp Blues
extracted . . . TM 43 extracted w/C Trp Blues. PZ green."

forty-three

The Vagaries

It was time to keep a promise. On November 4 I left Phuoc Vinh intent on returning to the 1–5 Cav so Chaplain Thompson could take a few days in the rear to recuperate and attend to personal affairs. En route I visited Kurt Ruth of Alpha 1–5 at Quan Loi and spent the night in the 1–5 Cav field trains area.

It took three hours the next morning to get a flight to LZ Vivian, the 1–5 Cav's new firebase north of Quan Loi. To maintain my excuse for being there, I checked in with Chaplain Thompson and sent him to the rear. Then, after several futile attempts to reach one of the companies in the field, the Division Artillery (Divarty) Chaplain Charles H. Hosutt and I conducted a joint service on LZ Vivian. Then I spent the afternoon with LTC Ronald Rasmussen on his C&C chopper.

First we flew north several kilometers to the Bu Dop Special Forces Camp, adjacent to the Vietnamese district headquarters town of Bo Duc and about five to seven kilometers from Cambodia. We'd flown there so Rasmussen could coordinate with the Special Forces commander. However, our landing was delayed because two separate battles were raging, one around the camp and the other near an ARVN camp at Bo Duc. Just ahead of us, an Air Force CV-2 Caribou sustained more than one hundred hits from automatic weapons while trying to land. Rasmussen kept his C&C on-station above the battles and directed artillery for several hours.

Lieutenant Colonel Rasmussen spent the afternoon in anticipation of orders to combat assault the 1–5 Cav into the

Bu Dop area. The orders never came. Instead General George Casey, the Assistant Division Commander, called him to a high-level strategy meeting at LZ Vivian, where it was decided to let ARVN forces respond to the threat to Bu Dop and Bo Duc. The generals were concerned about putting American infantry into the area again, partly because mortars and rockets out of Cambodia had mauled a company of 7th Cav troopers near Bu Dop. As it turned out, American forces became heavily involved in the Bu Dop buildup and fighting during November, with the 1–5 Cav and my Bravo Troop scouts in the forefront.

At 0800, November 6, I held a worship service for Alpha 1–5 on LZ Vivian. Again unable to reach a company in the field, I flew with Rasmussen. This time we made it into the Bu Dop Special Forces Camp for another strategy meeting.

To avoid ground fire during our approach into Bu Dop, Rasmussen's C&C chopper pilot flew in fast at treetop level, skimmed over the Bu Dop camp, flared, and hovered just long enough for Rasmussen, the 1–5 Cav Operations Officer, and me to jump to the ground. Then the chopper sped off to wait for us out of range of the enemy's guns which were in Cambodia and around the camp.

Moving quickly off the exposed chopper pad, we hurried north up a slight incline to a wooden structure. Waiting inside was the Special Forces Camp Commander and his operations officer. General Casey joined us moments later, having arrived unhurt in the same manner we had. The two Green Beret officers shared a familiar *under siege* appearance—drawn faces beneath heavy tans, and staring and shifting eyes that belied the calm of their professional voices. These men had been through a lot, and they knew it wasn't over yet.

General Casey acknowledged everyone who was present. He expressed only mild surprise at the unexpected presence of the 1–9 Cav Chaplain in his Bu Dop strategy meeting. At 1140 hours, two minutes into the meeting, heavy mortar shells and rockets began exploding on Bu Dop and Bo Duc.

The Green Beret commander calmly recommended to General Casey that we move the meeting to his TOC in the command bunker, which we did—walking, not running.

The command bunker was impressive in its size and construction. It was protected by yards of overhead cover. Inside, the bunker was well laid out and compartmentalized. Obviously this was no temporary TOC such as those on infantry firebases.

After a few minutes, I excused myself from the meeting and went to assist with wounded civilians who were being brought into the bunker, victims of the latest shelling. Among the victims were a baby with a gaping shrapnel wound over its right eye, a little girl, two women, and an elderly man. The little girl died there in the bunker while being treated, despite excellent care by the Special Forces medics. One medic said this was the second child he'd lost in two days, the previous loss being a four-year-old girl the day before. The NVA, he said, systematically and regularly targeted the civilian sectors of Bo Duc.

The wounded attended to and the strategy meeting over, we started to depart. A new barrage of incoming mortars, on us this time, prompted a delay. A row of sand-filled fifty-gallon steel drums sat just outside the inclined ramp that led from the bunker. The drums sat back from the entrance enough to allow people to easily walk around them, but were close enough to shield the entrance ramp from all but direct hits by heavy rockets or artillery.

General Casey, Rasmussen, their entourages, and I waited out the barrage standing halfway up the ramp. General Casey's demeanor was impressive. He remained calm, even when a shell exploded just a few feet beyond the barrels at the entrance. Three civilians dived over the barrels just ahead of the near miss. The civilians were a CBS news crew, one of whom was killed there the next day, I was told. According to J. D. Coleman's book *Incursion*, the special forces commander at Bu Dop refused the media admission to his camp, but November 6 was an apparent exception.

After the incoming rockets and mortars let up, General

Casey's and Rasmussen's groups headed one at a time to the chopper pad. On the pad, we waited in trenches for our respective choppers to swoop in for us. All got off from Bu Dop unhurt. Unknown to me, my nephew Earl Dyer was also on the receiving end of the frequent barrages being thrown at Bu Dop. He ran the refueling (POL) point there.

Our casualties during the barrage at Bu Dop included one American soldier killed and one wounded, eight CSF wounded, two CSF dependents wounded, and one CSF dependent killed—the little girl. Two CBS reporters were also wounded.

Back at LZ Vivian, a strategy meeting continued past midnight. American infantry was going in after all. The ARVN units could handle Bu Dop and Bo Duc alone, General Casey believed, provided we reopened an old firebase to provide a conduit through which ARVN forces could be channeled.

Early the next morning on November 7, Captain William Vowell and his Charlie 1–5 Cav prepared to combat assault into LZ Jerri—the abandoned firebase situated two klicks south of Bu Dop. He and a lieutenant colonel arrived on Vivian to coordinate the assault. The lieutenant colonel would lead and command the liftships in support of the assault.

The flight leader attended a worship service I held at 0800 hours, as did Sp4 Charles N. Harris, a former Alpha 1–5 trooper who was serving as a photographer/reporter for the battalion. Both the aviation commander and Harris were rapidly approaching the end of their time in combat, though neither of them knew it.

The combat assault began as soon as the worship service ended, with the flight commander in the lead of the first gaggle of choppers and Charlie 1–5 troopers. They got on the ground without taking casualties. As soon as the troopers jumped from the chopper, the flight leader took off from LZ Jerri in a rapid climb to the west and quickly banked left toward LZ Eagle Two. An enemy 51-caliber machine gun opened up about halfway through the turn, and the chopper went down in flames. The flight leader or copilot skillfully skimmed the flaming helicopter across the treetops to a controlled crash in an open field. During the descent, the forward speed of the chopper blew the flames away from the pilots onto the crew chief and door gunner behind them. To escape the flames, both enlisted men jumped into the trees from about three hundred feet in the air. The flight leader and copilot survived.

Even as the combat assault into Jerri continued, my Bravo Troop Blues arrived to search for the crew chief and door gunner. Other units joined the search later, but the search turned up no immediate trace of the two men or of their remains. They may still be listed as missing in action.

We flew past the downed and burning chopper moments after it crashed, en route to LZ Jerri to reinforce the Charlie 1–5 sky troopers. Sporadic AK-47 fire contested our arrival on the LZ. It was 0910 hours.

Jerri had a long way to go before being reborn. A large, topless pit near the center of the perimeter marked the spot for a once and future TOC. Overhead cover was not to be found, except under the trunks of some giant trees which lay along parts of the perimeter, especially on the west side.

Soon the intensity of incoming bullets increased, and Captain Vowell led part of Charlie 1–5 into the jungle to suppress it. The NVA withdrew just enough to keep thirty to fifty feet from us as we pressed forward. It was during this suppressive effort that four American snipers, who were attached to Charlie 1–5 from Division, discovered a Chinese detonator switch or klacker in the tree line. Wires from the klacker led across the cleared fire zone to the west perimeter berm and attached to a concealed mine that looked like it was intended to take out an M-60 tank. The claymore was well concealed and had been set facing toward the center of LZ Jerri. It was at least two feet in diameter and very nasty looking.

Safely back inside the perimeter, with less NVA lead cracking around us, we labored all day and into the night to dig holes, harden positions, and prepare for a bad night. These preparations took shape under the direction of the battalion executive officer, Robin Mangum, whom I recall as a major, though records a month later give his rank as lieutenant colonel.

Reinforcements arrived while we worked, including an artillery battery with its guns slung beneath Chinook helicopters. Most welcome among the new arrivals was Special Forces Captain Robert C. Beckman and his *Mike Force*, the 2nd Battalion, 3rd Mobile Strike Force of about five hundred Cambodian mercenaries. Also welcome was the 36th ARVN Ranger Battalion that arrived in the evening, though I don't think the latter came onto LZ Jerri.

Beckman was very impressive. Standing about six feet, six inches or more as I recall, he towered trunk, shoulders, and head above his command—an obvious, enticing target for snipers. I wondered how he could survive, standing out as he did.

After consulting with Mangum and Captain Vowell, Beckman settled his Mike Force down inside the perimeter to rest until dark. After dark, the mercenaries sneaked from the perimeter and dug in under the trees to the west of the LZ.

Earlier, while we pushed the NVA deeper into the jungle on the west, General Casey had arrived on LZ Jerri and remained there with his aide and some hangers-on while his chopper returned to Quan Loi to refuel. Someone said General Casey was very impressive and inspiring as he walked about the LZ, not even flinching when bullets cracked about him. This is believable, based on his calm behavior the previous day at Bu Dop.

Long after dark, I joined Mangum and a couple of his CP group under a partially-sandbagged half culvert. Mangum insisted I keep his .45-caliber pistol for him "just in case." The first action of the night came at 2355 hours, when probing NVA soldiers bumped into some mercenaries and quickly retreated.

*   *   *

The anticipated attack began at 0220 on November 8 with a standoff barrage of about eighty rockets and mortars, followed by a ground assault from the west. I waited out the barrage under our half culvert, and for the first and only time in combat my legs trembled uncontrollably. On occasions I'd felt greater fear than this, but this time the incoming artillery got to my knees.

Most of the grunts endured the barrage without benefit of overhead protection. Ronaldo Rodriguez was one of those. Someone on LZ Jerri that night said that at the first *bloop* of NVA mortar shells leaving tubes, Rodriguez dashed with his team from meager shelter into a hastily-prepared mortar pit, a three-quarter circle of sandbags. The same person said Rodriguez's team got two rounds into the air before NVA shells began exploding on LZ Jerri, the first or second of which exploded in their mortar pit, wounding all the team.

It happened differently according to Staff Sergeant Ray Easton. "I was Sad Sack's platoon leader," said Easton. "The day before when we landed . . . I told everyone . . . to get the sandbags filled and put on the half culverts because we would probably get hit that night. Sad Sack and his partner for whatever reason did not get their bunker protected, and decided to sleep in the mortar pit because it at least had a sandbag wall.

"I was laying in my bunker half asleep when the incoming started. It woke me up and as I raised to put on my flak jacket, the round that Claude said exploded in Sad Sack's mortar pit actually exploded in my bunker. My radio operator who was sitting closest to the blast sustained the most damage, mainly in the head area. I was hit in my left side and back. Another person in my bunker received slight damage.

"After collecting myself, I crawled out to get help for my radio operator and to check on my men and try to get a gun firing. That's when I found Sad Sack and his buddy. I went to Sad Sack first and talked to him and turned on a small flashlight so that I could look him over . . . the enemy outside the perimeter fired a rocket at the light. Thankfully it was about five feet too high. 'Where are you hurt?' I asked Sad Sack.

" 'Sarge, I'm okay. I just have a little metal in my leg, but get help for [his buddy]. His guts are on the ground.'

"I looked over and sure enough they were. I yelled for a medic and soon one came . . . we decided to get Sad Sack's buddy out first, because he appeared worse off. As it turns out his buddy survived. I was told afterwards that Sad Sack died on the helicopter, with a sucking chest wound that no one was aware he had," ended Sergeant Easton.

Rodriguez and his buddy would have been no better off by staying under cover in their culvert, because an 82mm mortar shell exploded just inside the open west end of it.

Meanwhile, in the jungle on the west side of the LZ, a massive NVA assault came up short against the Mike Force. The Mike Force sustained one killed and nine or ten wounded during the fierce hand-to-hand fight that followed. We could offer little help to Beckman and his Cambodian strikers because our mortar was knocked out and the artillery battery had failed to move its munitions from the helipad to the gun positions.

Within minutes of the last exploding shells inside our perimeter, we had gathered the wounded Americans and mercenaries inside the topless TOC. Of the six American casualties, Rodriguez was now obviously the one most seriously wounded.

"Hang in there, Sad Sack. You've got it made, Sad Sack! You're going home, Sad Sack," his buddies encouraged.

Rodriguez appeared unconscious as the medics fought to save his life. Yes, it was Ronaldo Rodriguez, whom I'd refused to call Sad Sack, the private whose leader hadn't trusted him with important tasks six months earlier.

Kneeling with Rodriguez's head cradled in the crook of my right arm, I asked softly, "Ron, can you hear me?" A faint smile or grimace flickered across his lips and his eyes opened briefly to the sound of his true name. The nurses who attended Ron said he died the next day without regaining consciousness, at the Third Field Hospital in Saigon.

*   *   *

The Special Forces–led Mike Forces counterattacked at dawn on November 8. Those tough little warriors killed four NVA soldiers and captured a first sergeant. At 0800 hours a chopper landed. Chaplain Thompson alighted and said, "Get aboard the chopper. I'm here to relieve you."

It was hard to leave while LZ Jerri was under siege, but I did so because I suspected someone higher up had ordered it. The battalion photographer/reporter Chuck Harris waved goodbye to me from the helipad as I flew off.

At LZ Vivian, I transferred to a Chinook. The Chinook dropped me off at Quan Loi, on-loaded some supplies and passengers, and took off, only to be shot down during its final reapproach to LZ Vivian. The Chinook crashed about thirty feet outside the perimeter, where a whirling rear rotor blade beheaded a 1–5 Cav trooper as he and the other passengers and crew scurried out of the burning aircraft. Sergeant Elvin Jackson, who had just returned from the hospital, witnessed this horrible death of a great trooper and close friend. "He was a fine young man. We'd visit for hours every time we came on the LZ. He was married, and lived in Florida, I believe. I wish I could remember his name. Watching his head fly off was probably the worst thing I witnessed while in Vietnam," Jackson said. No doubt this experience would contribute significantly to Jackson's postwar suffering.

LTC Robin Mangum died violently on December 6, killed by the same pistol he'd lent to me a month earlier during the first NVA attack on LZ Jerri. The four snipers who found the Chinese klacker died on LZ Jerri early in the morning on November 11. Chuck Harris, the combination photographer and reporter, lost a shoulder and the sight out of both of his eyes in the same barrage. Captain Robert C. Beckman, the Green Beret leader, was killed in sight of LZ Jerri on November 10 or 11, along with another American and five MSF soldiers.

In the early morning hours of November 11 a heavy

barrage of rockets and mortars hit LZ Jerri. Harris and the snipers were in positions on the northwest side of the perimeter, and probably felt fairly secure there beneath several giant tree trunks, any one of which would deflect the biggest rocket in the NVA arsenal. Again the vagaries of war came into play.

According to one source, a 120mm rocket hit at just the right angle to pass between the logs and get to the four snipers, one of whom was reported to be Pfc. Charles Joseph Keitt of New York. Another grunt who was nearby at the moment said, "A 122mm rocket hit among the logs and made a partial opening. A second 122mm came in on the exact same trajectory as the first one—like lightning striking twice in the same place—blasted the rest of the way through the logs and killed five troopers, including the four snipers."

Another trooper, Larry Touchstone, recalls that the four snipers were not all killed by the same rocket. "One other thing I will never forget—two of the snipers you talked about were in the bunker next to mine. . . . Their bunker took a direct hit. . . . It was a sad experience putting them into a poncho. One was black and one white, which is the only way we could separate the pieces, to tell which body parts belonged in which poncho."

Harris the photographer was hit in the same barrage. Again, my original source said he was hit by a 90-recoilless while standing on the helipad where I last saw him and that he lost both his eyes.

The rest of the story came out a few months before the thirtieth anniversary of this action. We passed each other in a Holiday Inn hallway during a 5th Cavalry Regiment reunion in Peoria, Illinois. It was May 1999. "You look familiar. Where did we know each other?" I asked.

We established only that I had been his chaplain when he served with Alpha 1–5 in 1969. We parted, then I turned and called to him. "In early November 1969 at LZ Jerri, there was an enlisted battalion photographer. . . ."

"That was me!" he blurted.

Couldn't be. "The man I was remember was blinded in both eyes a couple of days after I last saw him."

"Yes. I was blind for a long time, until a world-renowned ophthalmologist took me on as a special case and restored the sight in one of my eyes. I am Chuck Harris," he said as he extended his hand again. A name for a face after all these years!

As other Alpha 1–5 veterans gathered about us, Harris explained what happened in the early morning darkness on 11 November 1969. "A heavy barrage of 122mm rockets hit us at 0240 hours. One came in right on top of the other. The first rocket blew an opening in the overhead cover and the second rocket went right through the opening and killed five men inside their perimeter bunker. I was in a bunker nearby. Another 122 rocket hit near me and ruined my shoulder and blinded me in both eyes." Chuck showed us the shrapnel-damaged lens of the camera he was using that night. He also showed us X rays of his upper body. An artificial shoulder was quite easy to see as were scores of white spots that indicated shrapnel, gravel, and other debris that was blown into his body.

The First Air Cavalry History Book, 1965–1969 contains a picture that was retrieved from Harris' damaged camera after he was evacuated. It is an excellent shot of a medevac operation that took place out in the jungle the previous day. Perhaps the casualty in the picture was Captain Beckman.

Sp4 Clark Robert Douglas received the Distinguished Service Cross for his actions during the attack on LZ Jerri that night, posthumously. He gave his life trying to reach the wounded whose buddies cried out "Medic!" at the height of the enemy barrage.

On the previous day, November 10, Green Beret Captain Beckman, standing almost head and belt buckle above his Mike Force troops, had assaulted uphill against the NVA on Hill 153. The attack lasted all afternoon and ended about 2400 hours, after the Special Forces–led Mike Force was reinforced by an element of the 11th Armored Cavalry Regiment. The attack was a tactical success, though Beckman gave his life in the effort, as did another American and five Mike Force strikers.

Later that same day at a hospital something of a miracle occurred, and my appreciation of God's love and blessings increased. I visited the pilot of a pink team LOH that was shot down the day before near LZ Vivian. Today he lay in the hospital in very bad shape, delirious and writhing in agony despite being heavily sedated with morphine. After praying for him, I yielded to spiritual guidance and placed my hands on his head to bless him. He stopped writhing and fell into a deep, peaceful sleep the instant my hands touched his head.

Soon after the action at LZ Jerri, three 1–5 Cav troopers were brought to Quan Loi to await transfer to LBJ for court-martial for refusing to do their combat duty. At Quan Loi they went about spouting black-power slogans and tossing black-power salutes, trying to increase racial tensions. Robin Mangum's task was to control and care for the three men until they could be incarcerated at LBJ.

Bad incidents rapidly increased in number and frequency as soon as the three *mutineers* arrived at Quan Loi, including threats and fragging attempts against Mangum, the battalion sergeant major and a first sergeant.

An eighteen-year-old replacement arrived in the battalion rear at Quan Loi one evening, where he remained overnight to await a flight to his new company the next morning. A generous first sergeant gave his bunk to the replacement for the night. During the night a fragmentation hand grenade exploded under the wooden floor, directly beneath the first sergeant's bunk. The blast completely blew off the young soldier's genitals and seriously wounded him in other ways.

At the 2nd Surgical Hospital that day, the young trooper declared to me that he was a virgin and born-again Christian. He appeared to be free of any ill feeling toward whoever had robbed him of ever having a normal marital relationship, of ever siring children of his own. That the young man lost so much to a fellow soldier or soldiers rather than to the enemy didn't seem to matter to him.

LTC Robin Mangum was found dead in his hooch on December 6, 1969, gut shot by his government-issue .45-caliber pistol. Officially, Mangum died of an accidental self-inflicted gunshot wound in consequence of a defective seer pin in the weapon, according to Lieutenant Colonel Rasmussen. That pistol had functioned quite well four weeks earlier, when Mangum lent it to me on LZ Jerri. I suspect that a "fragging" occurred.

For days Bravo Troop scouts had been reporting the smell of elephants in the area northeast of LZ Buttons. The Third Brigade commander, Colonel John P. Barker, under whom I'd served at Fort Bragg, opined that the scouts were showing off and bragging—that they couldn't possibly smell elephants while whipping over the jungle in choppers. Apparently Colonel Barker hadn't seen the LOH choppers hover and buzz around and under the trees the way they often did, nor did he know Captain Lou Niles. "I tracked elephants by smell . . . never smoked, which gave me an advantage. I could smell elephant urine. I'd go out at lunch and dinnertime and fly sideways, upwind until I picked up the scent of food. Then I would continue until I could smell it no more. That's where the enemy would be. I found hospitals the same way, by the odor of alcohol," said Niles.

Anyhow, during a daily briefing, Colonel Barker lashed into Major George O'Grady, Bravo Troop Commander: "I'm tired of hearing reports about scouts smelling elephants from the air, and I'd better not hear another such report unless you bring me some fresh elephant [manure]."

"I was in that briefing. The reports about elephants were getting to George O'Grady, my troop commander, too," said Niles.

Two days later, the scouts found and killed twenty-seven elephants. The beasts were being used by the NVA to haul war supplies down the new, yet to be discovered trail, a partially bamboo-paved route that skirted the 1st Cav AO on the east, toward Saigon. There were those in high places that designated the newly discovered trail as the Surges Jungle

Highway. The 1–9 Cav people preferred to call it the Jolly Jungle Highway. This was in honor of Major Jolly, who had replaced George O'Grady as Bravo Troop Commander, and whose scouts found the trail.

On November 18, I visited Steve Blake at Tay Ninh and also conducted a memorial service for the rangers. An LRRP team in support of Apache Troop had lost two men the previous day during a very bad fight.

The mission went as follows, as Sergeant Jim McIntyre described it to me a few days later, and as it was told by Sergeant Kregg P. J. Jorgenson in his intriguing book, *Acceptable Loss*.

McIntyre and four other team members were inserted in the jungle to recon for five days in the vicinity of Song Be and LZ Buttons. Each man carried nearly a hundred pounds of supplies, ammunition and arms. As per standard operating procedure, to confuse the enemy, the liftship made some fake stops in the area before hovering above a preselected insertion LZ. In an instant, the LRRPs were off the skids and on the ground, driven by their heavy loads to hands and knees by the five-foot drop.

On the ground, "Mack motioned for us to move into the tree line. Torres took off first, followed by Zaporozec, McIntyre, and me. Rogers covered the rear," wrote Jorgenson.

On the third day of the operation, McIntyre moved his team to higher ground to regain radio contact. After reestablishing commo, the team took a short break to gain its breath following a hard climb. Fifteen minutes later, McIntyre, who was at the point, shot his hand into the air, fist clenched. He'd found a well-used trail. Ten minutes later, after carefully crossing and re-crossing the trail, McIntyre selected a spot between a two-foot high anthill and a fallen tree. "Barely moments after we sat down, we heard Vietnamese moving up the trail," said Jorgenson.

Ten NVA soldiers came along the trail. They passed within fifteen feet of the team members. The rangers hadn't had time to set out claymore mines and adequately camouflage their position. After the NVA passed, Jorgenson barely had time to call in the sighting before more NVA came along. "I gave up counting at thirty and prayed they'd keep on going, only God wasn't listening," Jorgenson said.

McIntyre said the NVA had approached slowly and quietly, obviously searching, not moving like a unit that was intent on covering distance. He said the NVA column stopped for a break after some soldiers had passed the rangers' hiding place. Then an NVA soldier stepped to the side of the trail, perhaps to relieve himself, and squatted to investigate something. Jorgenson wrote that the NVA soldier had spotted the red pin on one of Torres' grenades. A squadron officer who was privy to debriefing information said the NVA had relieved himself and bent down to investigate the sound of liquid splattering off Torres' uniform and equipment. Whatever his reason, the NVA soldier looked into Torres' eyes, screamed, and swung his AK-47 on target. Jorgenson wrote, "Before he could pull the trigger, Torres opened up with his M-14, killing the NVA soldier instantly."

Jorgenson said Torres suddenly sat up holding his chest where blood gushed from a bullet wound, and yelled, "Oh, Jesus! Jesus!"

Up on one knee, Zaporozec fired away, as did the rest of the team, including the mortally wounded Torres. "I felt Zap's arm grabbing mine . . . a bullet had hit him above the upper lip. . . . Rogers was screaming, too, and rolling over and over on the ground, holding onto his left leg. . . . 'Keep firing! Keep firing!' yelled McIntyre, pulling me back to the tactical situation," said Jorgenson.

Though pink teams were en route and the Saber Blues were scrambling in response to frantic radio messages, the rangers were on their own for several minutes, and receiving fire from all sides. Returning withering fire for withering fire, the LRRPs fought off repeated NVA attempts to destroy them before help could arrive.

Quickly, pink teams arrived on-station to add their fire to that of McIntyre's team. The Blues stayed out of the fight because there was no place near enough for them to be inserted in time to affect the outcome.

It took several minutes for the combined fire of the LRRPs and pink teams to suppress the NVA enough for the LRRPs to try to disengage and get to a usable pickup zone. To make the move possible, someone recommended that McIntyre leave Zaporozec's body behind and attempt to escape and evade to a place where the liftships could land and extract the rest of the team. McIntyre refused to leave Zaporozec, so the decision was made to extract the LRRPs using a McGuire rig.

McGuire rigs were used as a last resort to extract LRRPs and other special operations troops from harm's way. These extractions were very exhilarating, especially at night. A 120-foot rope (or four ropes) with a D-ring attached was dropped to the ground, weighted by a sandbag or other weight when necessary to get it down through the jungle canopies. The pilot had to hold the chopper in a near-perfect hover while the rope was lowered and a passenger hooked on. Booth explained, "Our lift-helicopters did not have a pulley. They extracted by lifting straight up to raise the ranger above the treetops, and then moved forward to gain airspeed. The ranger was then flown some distance to a relatively safe area, then let down into an open area where the ranger could unhook from the D-ring and climb aboard the helicopter."

Once the decision was made to use the McGuire rig, a liftship quickly came to a hover above the jungle immediately over the LRRP team. The crew chief and door gunner dropped the rope. McIntyre sent up Zaporozec's body. Rogers, the severely wounded medic went next. The mortally wounded Torres followed Rogers up through the tree branches, and then Jorgenson. Like the fine leader he was, McIntyre was hoisted up last of all.

Following this tragic mission, Sergeant McIntyre was taken out of the LRRPs and assigned to Operations in the Apache Troop TOC at Tay Ninh. He told me he'd had enough, but that's not what Lieutenant Colonel Booth remembers: "About a month before McIntyre's last LRRP mission, I considered moving a great young pilot out of the scouts. Major Bob Hardin and Captain Paul Funk—commander and XO of Apache Troop—agreed, so I met with the pilot. After an hour of talking with him in Apache Operations, he pleaded with me to leave him in scouts. I relented. Two or three days later, this young pilot's LOH was hit and went straight into the jungle at very high speed, killing him and all aboard."

Booth said, "With this weighing on my mind, and considering how many really tough contacts he'd survived recently, I ordered McIntyre transferred out of LRRPs. Like the pilot before him, Mack objected to the transfer out of his sense of duty and obligation to his men and buddies. This time there was no talking me out of it. I told McIntyre, 'I want you to leave Vietnam standing up, to return to your family alive.' We sent him to Apache Troop to work in operations.

"I visited McIntyre in the TOC frequently when I went to Tay Ninh. During one of those visits he admitted, 'Colonel, you were right. It was time for me to get out of the LRRPs.'"

McIntyre's close calls hadn't all been recent, either. During one of his first missions—perhaps the first one—McIntyre saved his team members by throwing his rucksack and himself on top of a chicom grenade.

Jorgenson came down with malaria the day after he received an impact award of the Silver Star for this action. Like McIntyre, he transferred to the Apache Troop Blues upon his return from the hospital, where he was wounded twice more. Though I didn't know it until years later, both Jorgenson and Zaporozec had been part of the LRRP team that the Blues and I had *rescued* a couple of weeks earlier on 30 October, the day Carroll was killed.

On November 23, a soldier came to me and confessed to a recent act of immorality while he was on R&R. Though he seemed repentant, I counseled with him and advised him to discuss the matter with a chaplain or ecclesiastical leader of his own faith. Afterward I thought and wrote in my journal: "I'd rather be dead than unchaste. Must not read or willingly allow anything in mind that degrades sacred things. An unchaste mind is first step to an unchaste body." Translation: I'd rather die than face the pain that unfaithfulness on my part would cause Helga and the children. As for sinning against God and one of His daughters, regardless of her willingness or motives, I echo Joseph of old when he was tempted, "How then can I do this great wickedness and sin against God?" (Genesis 39:9)

It was about this time that Alpha Troop choppers frequently took small-arms fire from a single weapon as they arrived and departed the western perimeter at Tay Ninh. The shots came from a vast field of rice or grass growing out of water. Naturally, the chopper crews tried repeatedly to find and get rid of the NVA that was shooting at them, to no avail. So one day a patrol went out with a tracker-dog team at the point. The patrol had gone out about two or three hundred meters when a shot rang out and the last man in the patrol fell dead. The shot had come from someplace in the grass between the patrol and the perimeter. To get that shot, the NVA soldier had managed to avoid detection by the sharp eyes of the troopers *and* the extraordinary nose of the black Labrador tracker dog. A few days later an LOH swept down when the crew spotted something. A crewmember jumped out into the grass and water and captured the evasive, ghost-like shooter, a badly wounded NVA soldier who apparently was determined to keep fighting until his infected wounds killed him—which he almost succeeded in doing.

Notes

7 November 1969, 1–5 Battalion Journal, 0935: "15 sorties of C Co touched down LZ Jerri. Completed 0947."

1012: "LZ Jerri receiving 82mm and AK-47 at this time."

1027: "Fr GM6: Request 2 sniper teams . . . for FSB Jerri (Snipers reported at approx 1100 hrs)."

8 November 1969, "2nd Battalion, 3rd MSFC, Operation Shaker, 0220 Hrs...LZ Jerri...5 kilometers south of Bu Dop, received 20 rounds of 82mm mortar and 50 rounds of B-40 rocket fire. One MSF was killed and nine were wounded..."

8 November 1969, 1–5 Battalion Journal, 0310: "Fr GM (LZ JERRI): At 0235 hrs. reports receiving 50 B-40, some 82mm and a ground probe on the NW side of LZ Jerri...15 line 2s, 1 line 1 (little people), (06 line 2s U.S., 05 US line 2s, litter)."

0320: "Fm 3d Bde—G-2: "C/1–5, FSB Jerri 0240 H. Rec'd 30x 82mm mort, SA, B-40 rkt fire and ground probe frm N. W. (rec'd 50x B-40)...at 0420 7x US WIA were medevaced and 9x MSF were awaiting medevac. Contact broke 0319 H, 1 × MSF KIA."

11 November 1969, "2nd Battalion, 3rd MSFC, received sniper fire from an unknown number of enemy...five kilometers south of Bu Dop. One USASF and five MSF were killed, and one USASF and 11 MSF were wounded."

12 June 1970, 1st Cav G-3 Op Reports—Lessons Learned for Nov-Jan 1969–70, paragraph (3)(d): "FSB Jerri received 30x 82mm mortar rounds, 5 B-40 rockets and light ground probe commencing at 0240H on 8 November. Friendly casualties totaled 7 US WIA, 9 MSF WIA and 1 MSF KIA."

Paragraph (3)(f): "On 10 November, FSB Jerri received another heavy stand-off attack consisting of 15x 120mm and 15x 82mm mortar rounds and a ground probe from the southwest. Friendly losses included 5 US KIA and 7 US WIA [including the four snipers]."

forty-four

In Memoriam

About 0200 hours, November 25, someone blew up the Squadron Executive Officer's latrine, just behind my sleeping area. The XO wasn't using the latrine at the time.

For a week Warrant Officer Hodson had begged me to accompany him on a scout mission, saying he'd be shot down if I didn't. Hodson had transferred from the navigator seat of an Air Force B-52 bomber into the pilot's hot seat of an Army scout LOH, to get nearer the war. Having already flown scout missions for several months without taking a hit on his aircraft, Hodson said he believed his numbers must be about up. He asked me to fly a mission with him, else he would die. I agreed to fly a mission with Hodson. As observer, I'd be in the copilot seat on Hodson's left.

Mister (WO) Hodson, his torque (door gunner) and I departed from Phuoc Vinh before dawn on November 26, flying low with a Cobra trailing high and to the rear. By dawn we were north of LZ Buttons conducting first-light recon over thick bamboo. Hodson hadn't told me the observer was supposed to keep a smoke grenade in hand with the pin pulled, and to be ready to drop it at the first sign of enemy.

Thus, when we spotted a smokeless campfire beneath the bamboo I wasn't ready to "mark the target" for the Cobra. Though the campfire was out by the time we turned around, the Cobra put in a couple of rockets where we thought the fire had been.

At 0900 we were ordered west of LZ Buttons to scout for Charlie 2–12 Cav, which was in contact and had sustained three KIAs from NVA mortars. We arrived on-station and began circling at two hundred feet, intent on drawing fire to give the Cobras something to blast with their grenade launcher, mini-gun, and rockets. We quickly succeeded in drawing fire, and this time I had a smoke grenade ready to mark the target.

After a few minutes, the commander on the ground called for a resupply of smoke so he could continue to mark his position. Hodson headed us back to LZ Buttons where we refueled and took on extra smoke grenades while the Cobra rearmed. We were about five hundred meters from the Charlie 2–12 Cav position when a 60-caliber machine gun opened up and punctured the LOH in two places. "What's that?" asked Hodson when the machine-gun rounds began cracking around us.

"Thirty cal," I answered.

"I think," Hodson said, "this is the first time I've been shot at by anything that big."

While I knew gun sounds, Hodson and his torque knew the chopper. Because of changes in aircraft vibrations, changes well below my level of sensitivity to such things, they knew we'd taken a hit in the main rotor blade. Despite the hits, we continued the mission.

After kicking off the smoke at the feet of a squad of harried troopers, we stayed on-station another hour, doing what we could for the hard-pressed grunts. For an hour or more we flew in monotonous circles over the contact area. For the first and only time in my life, I almost became airsick.

We left the LOH at Buttons to be repaired in place or sling-loaded to Phuoc Vinh. Mr. Hodson was quite pleased, though he'd taken his first hit by enemy fire to his aircraft while I was aboard. "Your being with me kept me from being shot down and killed," he insisted.

The next day was Thanksgiving. As was expected, I blessed the Thanksgiving meal in the 1–9 Cav mess hall. General George Casey dined with us, sitting between Pete Booth and me. His comments and questions during the meal reflected a lot of interest in my religious support efforts and attitudes.

Following Thanksgiving activities with Apache Troop at

Tay Ninh and Bravo Troop at Quan Loi, I returned to Phuoc Vinh and learned that an assignment in Germany would be mine following this tour. A letter from Germany arrived a couple of months later to inform me I would be assigned to Graffenwöhr, Germany, where my high school-age children would have to board away from home during the school season. *This assignment is not acceptable. I'll resign first. No need to weigh the pros and cons. There are no pros, not after spending 24 of the last 42 months away from James and Jeannie.* I so informed the necessary military and church officials and wrote to Helga to explain my position and intentions in the matter.

On 29 November two Bravo Troop pilots were killed when their Cobra, part of a pink team, was shot down north of LZ Buttons. The NVA also shot down an LOH as its crew fought to keep them away from the crash site until another pink team and the Blues arrived. The Blues inserted successfully and reached the Cobra in time to sustain casualties when it exploded.

This little blurb appeared in a 1st Cav newspaper, in an article titled, "Traveling Cav Chaplains Bring Church to Boonies," *Cavalair*, November 19, 1969:

> One example of the chaplain's willingness to get out in the field with the grunt is Chaplain (CPT) Claude Newby.
> Chaplain Newby spent six months with a line company. Given a choice in rear area jobs, he selected the Airmobile 1st Squadron, 9th Cavalry. His 'rear area' assignment still keeps him in the field most of the week.

On December 1, I began my tenth month on this tour by conducting a memorial service at Quan Loi. From there I flew to Tay Ninh and spent the day and night with Apache Troop, which kept me away from Phuoc Vinh in the early hours of December 2, and out of a nasty and accurate mortar attack. Two 1–9 Cav troopers died and twenty-one were wounded during the barrage. One KIA, a member of Delta Troop, died when a mortar exploded directly over his cot. His room was about fifty feet from mine. I visited wounded troopers at Long Bien before returning to Phuoc Vinh.

One day in late November or early December, Apache Blues platoon leader Lieutenant Gary Qualley came to me following a worship service and said in essence, "Chaplain Newby. I used to believe in God, but I can't anymore."

"What brought you to this opinion?" I asked.

"This war, chaplain. If there were a God, he wouldn't allow horrors like this to happen."

The man's confusion seems understandable, provided one believes in a God whose mercy robs justice, a God with no more plans for His children than to use them in a gigantic harp orchestra. For more than an hour, I tried to help the lieutenant understand the principles of agency and consequences and how vital these are in the eternal scheme of things. But he departed sorrowing, his doubts apparently unresolved.

On December 7, Pearl Harbor Day, Lt. Qualley and his Apache Troop Blues were inserted to check out a bunker complex: "One of our Apache scout birds was guiding us toward a suspected NVA base camp. I had the troops on line, and we'd just entered the tree line. I dropped behind a small tree—about 5 inches diameter—when the squads on our right reported occupied bunkers. 'Frag them,' I ordered, and still had the radio handset to my ear when, from about five meters away, an NVA jumped from a hidden bunker and sprayed us with AK-47 fire. That first burst hit Sp4 Sanchez, got me in the thighs—shattered both femurs—gut-shot Sp4 Timothy McCreight of Aledo, Illinois, and hit another trooper. To get into a prone position to fight, I had to pull my legs around one a time—they were bent at strange angles, like I had a second pair of knees. We killed one or two NVA while fighting them off so we could be medevaced.

"The NVA, my platoon, the Apache Scouts, and the medevac crew kept up intense firing while they hoisted us out. To this day I cannot believe how medevac hovered up there just above the treetops—right over the enemy bunkers—and brought us up while firing those M-60s to protect us. Anyhow, after they hoisted up Sanchez and McCreight using a cable or rope, I turned my platoon over to Platoon Sergeant George Busch, and they started hoisting me out, but the cable was shot or broke and dropped me back to the ground. Finally, somehow, they got me up and flew me to the hospital at Tay Ninth Base Camp. There, they got me on a gurney and cut my clothes off while rushing me to the OR. Top Sgt. Williamson was there to meet our medevac. He visited several times. I was evacuated to Japan then to Fitzsimons Army Medical Center in Denver. Eighteen months—three months in traction, eight months in casts of various types. The people of Denver were terrific, once I was able to get about on crutches—free movies and dinners and just lots of friendly people. I made captain there, which I didn't expect because I was ROTC and should have been out in two years instead of three. I went on to graduate school in Arizona, married, have three terrific sons and a great wife. And I became very religous!"

The next day I visited Timothy McCreight at the hospital on the Tay Ninh base camp. He sat up while we visited and a nurse cauterized bleeding vessels in his abdomen. I thought Timothy looked good and had a fair prognosis; he died of his wounds on December 13.

The Army tested my ears on December 8 or 9, declared me deaf in several high frequency ranges, and placed me on a medical profile that forbade exposure to loud noises! For a few days I honestly tried to avoid loud noises (combat), but I repented on December 16. *As long as I am in the Army, I will do what needs doing, profile or not*, I decided.

On December 10, I accompanied a Delta Troop platoon on an overnight operation southwest of Phuoc Vinh. We rode in vehicles to a site near a village. The vehicles returned to base and we set an ambush along the west side of a road, *right* where we were let off. To make matters worse, in my view, civilian children hung around until dark. I thought surely we would move to another location after dark; but no, we stayed exactly where the natives last saw us at twilight. The objections I expressed to the lieutenant served only to wear out my welcome. A few nights later, Delta Troop was attacked and the same lieutenant received the Purple Heart and Silver Star.

In Apache Troop on December 21, almost two months after his twentieth birthday, SSG Christopher James Gray was shot down and died in a flaming crash; along with Thadius Yanika, the pilot of the scout LOH; and Barry Paul Kaletta of Ohio, door gunner.

I've said little about worship and memorial services in the past chapters. Suffice it to say I held worship services often, with more focus on Sunday than had been the case with infantry battalions. Memorial services, like the one for Yanika, Gray, and Kaletta, were held almost as often as regular worship services. My work in the 1–9 Cav left me feeling like a circuit-riding memorial service provider.

It was hard to objectively gauge the effects of memorial services on the troops. Most of the remarks by those who said anything at all suggested that the services helped a lot. Some appreciated that appropriate honors were provided to fallen comrades. Others insisted the services boosted flagging hope, even as close buddies kept getting killed. Others said the services reawakened—or gave birth to—faith to sustain them as they faced their own mortality and the high odds that they could be next.

I was concerned, however, that memorial services on an almost weekly schedule, with the same men standing in the same formation—each man intensely aware of who was missing—might lose their effect and even become counterproductive.

Kregg Jorgenson describes one of the memorial services I conducted. "The mounted bayonet held the M-16 rifle in place in the hard-packed, orange soil. The helmet rested on the upturned butt of the rifle's stock, while a pair of polished jungle boots stood beside the rifle, forming a quiet monument, an outdoor altar.

"The battalion chaplain was reciting a final prayer. . . . When he finished, he looked into the faces of the soldiers who stood in formation before the memorial; somber faces, some still with adolescent acne. But their eyes made them different, they had the cold, hard stares of people who'd seen too much in too short a time. . . . The memorial service was more for us than it was for the fallen soldiers.

" 'Take solace in that Thaddeus, Chris Gray, and Barry Kletta—'

" 'His name was Kaletta!' someone yelled from the rear of the formation as heads turned. An officer scowled at the soldier who'd interrupted the service.

" 'And Barry Kaletta,' the chaplain said, carefully pronouncing the name. 'To those of you who knew them, they were special people, performing a special mission. Though I didn't know them, I don't intend to let their memory die without pausing to think of the personal sacrifice they endured—'

" 'In a bull sh— cause!' someone else said.

"The ceremonies were never easy, and usually very emotional. Though the senior NCOs and officers would yell, 'At ease!' they knew they could do little to quell the feelings that arose.

" 'This war is more than politics, more than duty. It is a commitment to friendship between you and those who have died. Yours is a personal war with personal tragedies and extraordinary sacrifices for that friendship. I urge you to not let those friendships or memories die in this war. Remember Tad Yanika, Chris Gray, and Barry, and remember their names and their sacrifices for you, rather than to a cause or political purpose. Speak their names and share your stories about their friendship.

" 'I . . . I wish you safety and peace in your lives as well as in the war, and I pray to God to this end. I know that God understands and loves him who lays down his life for a friend. These men's sacrifices of life and of future on earth

will weigh heavily on the side of mercy when they stand before their Creator to give an account of their lives.'

"The chaplain walked off toward the command post. His
was an awkward, uncomfortable gait."

The service Jorgenson describes stands out in my memory precisely because the trooper corrected my pronuncia-
tion of Barry Kaletta's name. Though I don't recall the other
interruption, I understand it very well. The word was out.
American forces were pulling out of Vietnam, leaving the
job undone. It is no wonder that soldiers had a hard time
seeing any meaning in their own or their buddies' deaths
and sacrifices.

This description reinforces my concerns that memorial services held too frequently for the same small group might become counterproductive. Imagine a family that had to endure
almost weekly funerals for one of their own. How would they
handle it? How would it affect their relationship with the officiator? How would the officiator handle it? Not well, I expect.

Now-retired Lieutenant General Paul Funk, who replaced Bob Hardin as Apache Troop Commander, told Colonel Booth that he lost thirty-eight men during the four
months he commanded Apache Troop, compared to seven
out of a whole division in Desert Storm.

The services continued in the First of the Ninth in a
seemingly never-ending sequence. They had to, regardless
of the difficulties involved, for the troopers and leaders
wanted—needed—the chance to pay final tribute to their
friends. We owed our comrades and their families that—and
those soldiers were accustomed to hard things.

By the way, Jorgenson nailed me on one point. The
"awkward, uncomfortable gait" he described was the result
of a combat-assault injury back in January 1967. Sometimes
the awkward gait became quite pronounced when things
weighed heavy on my soul.

December 25, Christmas Day! I spent the morning providing worship services at Phuoc Vinh, Quan Loi and Tay
Ninh. In the afternoon I visited hospitals at Long Binh and

Saigon. In the evening I returned to Tay Ninh because of
spiritual distress I'd detected earlier in Sp4 Blake.

My impression proved correct. Blake really needed to talk.
He'd slumped into deep melancholy, a combination of
Christmastime homesickness and remorse over how some
around him observed Christ's birthday. From my journal:
"Encouraged him to realize that our duty is to continue because honest people seek the light. Increased darkness
will . . . make our light more noticeable. . . . Well, the muddy
river [world] is now more like a cesspool. All the more reason
to cast out to those who call for help." I needed my own advice. All around me were young men who daily laid their
lives on the line, who honored their heritage, and who needed
all the support they could get. I was so thankful at this
Christmas season to be privileged to serve them as a chaplain,
and to help them remember the good things they knew before
the war.

In my first post-Christmas mail from home, Helga related how on Christmas she had answered the door and
found Elder Marion D. Hanks and Keith Garner (former
head of the Southeast Asia LDS Mission) singing Christmas
carols on her doorstep. Hanks and Garner took the children
shopping for clothing and gifts, including Skittle. The Skittle
game, which we still have, is a favorite of three generations
of the Newby family, and a reunion tradition.

Happy thirty-third birthday to me! Happy birthday,
Helga! I celebrated my birthday on December 27th and
Helga's on the 30th. *I'm now old enough to mourn, rather
than celebrate birthdays.* But I still felt young and didn't
dread aging. *I'll be pleasantly surprised if I have the privi-
lege,* I sometimes thought.

While I relaxed briefly on my birthday and dreamed of
wife and home, Apache Troop lost four choppers and sustained two KIAs in the Tay Ninh area. Because of the intense fighting, it took a while to find the bodies of two
crewmembers. We thought they'd been captured. That was
the day a mysterious fixed-wing aircraft flying out of

Cambodia fired on an Air Force plane. American fighters forced it down. I heard nothing more about it.

I celebrated the end of 1969 at Phuoc Vinh, in company with troopers David Van Outen, Harold Lewis, Russell Rinehart, Wandler, McDill and three others. We gobbled hamburgers and sodas and pretended we were ten thousand miles away. All around the base camp, troopers fired weapons into the air to welcome in the new year, the year that every one of them was due to rotate home. A few soldiers on perimeter guard even fired on an ARA gunship as it patrolled the perimeter. The shooting stopped quickly, however, when the ARA pilot radioed, "Be advised. I am receiving fire and will roll hot on its source if it doesn't cease immediately." A staff officer became very excited at the pilot for threatening to return fire. My sympathies were with the pilot.

At 2230 hours, January 3, the NVA attacked the 1–9 Cav at Phuoc Vinh with rockets, recoilless rifles, and mortars. When the attack began, I rolled under my cot and watched through the open door as rockets and recoilless shells exploded among the revetments and choppers of Charlie and Headquarters Troops. Meanwhile, several 82mm mortar shells landed squarely on and among the troops' living areas. Four rounds burst directly behind my room. Delta Troop sustained direct hits on three sleeping areas. In a December attack a mortar had crashed through a roof, killing a trooper. This time, in the exact same spot, another man was killed in the same spot as he took cover beneath his mattress. We sustained one killed and eight wounded in the attack.

The NVA shot down three 1–9 Cav choppers on January 9 and also hit the 1–9 Cav area at Phuoc Vinh. We sustained no casualties this time, though eighteen choppers were damaged on the ground. The next day I flew with LTC Clark Burnett, the new 1–9 Cav Commander. After patrolling all morning north of LZ Buttons, we ate lunch there during a rocket attack. After lunch we joined up with some pink teams and made several rocket and mini-gun dives against NVA forces that were attacking an ARVN convoy. Then, being low on everything, we headed for LZ Buttons to refuel and rearm, only to be waved off because the base was under attack. So we refueled at Duc Phong and made it back to Phuoc Vinh in time for a religious meeting at 1900 hours.

For the remaining two months of my tour, the pace and intensity of combat continued unabated for members of the 1–9 Cav. But the chronicles stop here because my journal and memory are blank.

forty-five

A St. Valentine's Day Massacre

About February 20, Major Hefner, the division psychiatrist, sent an LDS trooper to me for counseling. A few weeks earlier Pfc. Jerry Clayton had transferred out of the rangers to Charlie 2–8—part of my battalion during the 1966–67 tour. The account of what brought Clayton to me is reconstructed from his recollections and from official and unofficial documents.

On Valentine's Day, February 14, Charlie 2–8, commanded by Captain Joseph Gasker, was working with a unit of the 11th Armored Cavalry Regiment. They were operating a few klicks north of the Black Virgin Mountain. That area in Tay Ninh Province consists of large open areas pockmarked with large, irregular-shaped clumps of jungle and bamboo.

On this day, the tanks and APCs stopped in a clear area so a platoon of infantry could dismount and move through a stretch of jungle, one of several that jutted finger-like into the clearing. While the infantry moved into the first stretch of bamboo, the tanks and APCs skirted wide around it and passed beyond yet another protruding stretch of jungle. Suddenly the tanks and APCs spun around and headed the other way. The infantry platoon they'd just dropped off was in heavy contact and taking casualties.

The tanks and APCs came under small-arms and rocket fire as they approached the near side of the first stretch of jungle, opposite from where they had dropped off the platoon earlier. Quickly the ACR commander and Captain Gasker decided to reach the beleaguered platoon by charging straight through the bamboo rather than circling around the end of it again. The infantry dismounted, and the tracked vehicles charged into the jungle in two columns, knocking down everything in their path.

Apparently, in anticipation of the armored reaction, the NVA hunkered down in well-hidden bunkers and spider holes and waited for the tracked vehicles to pass over them. The charge ground to a quick halt when, within moments, the NVA knocked out a tank and two APCs, while the infantrymen lumbered over downed vegetation and struggled to keep up.

The shooting on the near side of the bamboo thicket slacked off after the charge halted, allowing the platoon that Pfc. Jerry Clayton was in to catch up. Soon, the point man moved cautiously forward, passing to the right of the disabled tank. He probably noted that the right front of the tank was stopped atop a bunker. A few feet past the tank, the point man passed around a termite hill. About ten meters beyond the mound, he discovered a trail and commo wire running across his direction of advance. Platoon leader Lieutenant Gregory C. Schoper moved forward in response to a whispered message from the point. The NVA resumed firing and Schoper and two troopers fell dead even as they were examining the commo wire.

From farther back in the platoon, a trooper ahead of Clayton was hit by gunfire. Clayton reacted by running forward. "I saw the tank on my left and an APC on my right as I ran forward and went over the termite hill—not a very smart way to get past it under the circumstances. In front of the mound, I found a wounded machine gunner fighting off the NVA alone, surrounded by the bodies of the lieutenant and the two troopers," Clayton said.

After dragging the wounded machine gunner back around the mound and pushing him into waiting arms, Clayton went forward again and manned the machine gun. He was determined to hold the NVA off his buddies and the NVA seemed just as determined to take out the American and machine gun that blocked their advance. Though he now has no idea how long he stood off the NVA, Clayton

kept firing for what seemed like an eternity, pausing only to
ram in fresh belts of ammunition that his buddies scavenged
from the disabled vehicles to his rear. Clayton didn't realize
he was being attacked from the rear too. The grunts back behind the termite hill saw a chicom grenade hurtle in
Clayton's direction from the partially collapsed bunker beneath the tank. They ended that threat by tossing a grenade
of their own into the bunker, but not before Clayton sustained wounds to his right side and arm.

Sometime during the standoff, "[a] very brave medic
crawled up to me and was tending wounds on my arm when
a burst of enemy fire split open his head, killing him instantly, and spraying me with his blood. I became very
scared after the medic was killed, not of dying but of dying
alone. I prayed. Something, almost a voice, answered, 'You
are not alone.' All fear left me then, and I kept firing because I realized that the NVA fired at me only when I
paused to reload. Though the NVA and I were very close to
each other, I couldn't see them or even the trail. Apparently
they thought I was shooting from behind the protection of
the termite hill, for their fire was high, which probably
saved my life.

"That machine gun and I were one. It was as if there
were nothing else in the world—just me, the gun, and the
NVA," explained Clayton.

The machine gun became so hot that it burned him wherever he touched it, but, "I was oblivious to pain and everything else," Clayton recalls. He stopped shooting only when
the machine gun blew up in his face. Only then did Clayton
realize that he was the only grunt still alive anywhere near
the termite hill and destroyed vehicles. "I *lost it* and fled
wildly to the rear, with green tracers cracking all around me,
my buddies told me later," Clayton said.

His wild flight ended when he broke into a clearing and
came upon his surviving comrades as the last of them scrambled aboard armored vehicles to get out of the area ahead of
an air strike. Clayton's buddies may have presumed him
dead when the machine gun fell silent, or may have written

him off. The citation for the award he would receive read, "When a platoon came under intense fire, he moved forward to lay down a heavy base of fire, enabling the platoon to move back to safety." Before withdrawing with the 11th ACR, Clayton's buddies doused him with five gallons of water to combat heat exhaustion and ease the pain of his burns. Clayton says eight Americans gave their lives in the fight. The Army Casualty Information System names Lieutenant Schoper, eight enlisted infantrymen (MOS 11B), and two with infantry MOS 11D as KIAs on Valentine's Day.

Of this action the *Cavalair* wrote, "The firefight began on the afternoon of Feb. 14. Charlie Company, 2nd Battalion, 8th Cavalry, conducting a joint operation with 11th Armored Cavalry Regiment tanks and APCs came upon enemy bunkers 13 miles north of Tay Ninh City at 2:45. . . . Twenty minutes later, said Sp4 Ralph Branzalli, 'The tanks kept moving up. . . . when RPGs started flying at the tanks.' At the same time, the skytroopers were caught in a crossfire. . . . The two forces maneuvered for advantage. . . . The battle flared sporadically until 6:40, when contact finally broke. By then, 31 North Vietnamese had been killed."

For his part in the fight, Sp4 Jerry Clayton was recommended for the Medal of Honor (MOH). Following medical and psychological treatment, Clayton returned to the 2–8 Cav for about a week, then became the 3rd Brigade Commander's driver; this was to keep him out of the field pending the outcome of the MOH recommendation. After the MOH was downgraded to a Silver Star, Clayton extended his tour in Vietnam six months to became a door gunner on a brigade scout chopper. He finished his tour back in the 1–9 Cav as a door gunner on a scout LOH.

In June 1970 Clayton had been selected to star in an Army documentary, but his movie career was cut short when he sustained second- and third-degree burns over most of his body. Clayton recovered and served in the Army and National Guard for twenty-five years. He resides with his wife, the former Kimberley Belt, at their home in Sandy, Utah.

*   *   *

I recall three tragic incidents that never made it into my journal. The first incident occurred back in June and the other two toward the end of my tour. In the ranger billets at Phuoc Vinh a team of LRRP rangers prepared for a mission. At least one of the rangers placed a detonator in a claymore mine—each team member carried a claymore and they always armed them before hitting the ground at the beginning of a mission, the better to set up rapid defenses, if necessary. The rangers deemed the advantages of being prepared to outweigh the dangers inherent in this risky practice. But this time the negative vagaries of war won out. There in the barracks, one or more claymore mines exploded in a rucksack and, "Three rangers died," recalls Pete Booth.

Natural human tendencies during those moments toward the *end*—the end of patrols, the last hours of the night, the end of a war—aid and abet the negative side of the vagaries of war. A motorized Delta Troop element returned to base camp from patrolling around Phuoc Vinh. The lead vehicle mounted a 106mm recoilless rifle. The gun, a breech loader, should have been cleared before the patrol reached the gate. But with a flechette round still in the chamber, the vehicle stopped at the south gate with the gun pointed slightly off to the right, toward a quadrangle or parade field of sorts. The gunner, instead of opening the breech of the recoilless rifle from above and forward, stood directly behind it. The gun fired accidentally, spraying the division chapel and chaplain's offices with steel arrows. The back-blast blew the gunner in half and wounded the platoon leader and a sergeant who were in the jeep right behind the recoilless rifle.

From experience and such memories, I maintain that anything one can imagine happening in war will happen.

One afternoon an element of the 11th Armored Cavalry Regiment pulled a tank up to the south-gate of Quan Loi, near the south end of the airstrip. At that point the tank cannon accidentally fired a flechette round. *Down range*, to the west or left of the airstrip, about eight shirtless grunts were soaking up sunshine atop a bunker. Those men quietly fell over dead with their bodies covered on one side by small, almost blood-less wounds, entry points of hundreds of steel darts.

I conclude my chronicle of the actions, heroics, and va-garies of the war in Vietnam by recounting a tragedy that occurred in one of my former companies two years after I left the field for the last time.

By May 10, 1972, the 1st Cavalry had essentially stood down from the war. That same day, Captain Kenneth Rosenberg and his Delta 2–8 Cav troopers lifted out of the field for the last time. Rosenberg boarded a Chinook with his First Platoon (former call sign, White Skull), thirty sol-diers in all, to fly to the in-country R&R center at the beach-front city of Vung Tau. The Chinook crashed en route, killing all aboard. Thus on its last day on the field of battle, Delta 2–8 lost more men than it had during the past two years of combat. The remainder of Delta Company returned to the United States a month later along with the rest of the battalion.

Notes

26 November 1969, 1–9 Cav Journal, Summary: "A OH6A rec'd fire at 50 ft and 80 knots . . . took two hits and no-fly at LZ Carolyn . . . C Trp OH6A rec'd fire at 40 ft and 50 knots, 1 hit, no-fly at P.V. . . . C Trp OH6A rec fire at 50 ft and 40 knots, neg hits. Also B trp UH1C rec fire at 1500 ft and 80 knots, 11 hits, no fly at Bu Dop. A Trp had OH6a rec fire at 60 knots and 30 ft, no hits. . . ."

February 14, 1970, Army Casualty Information System, KIAs: 1LT Gregory C. Schoper; Sp4s William L. Cline, Rivera Ernesto Cuevas, Harold P. Fesperman, and Wayne D. McRay; Pfcs. Jerold B. Day, Joseph H. Duncan, Gary Smith, Ferdinand J. Sochurek III, Earl C. E. Tidwell Jr., and James H. Wilbanks.

May 10, 1972, from the Honor Roll, Angry Skipper web site, roster of Delta 2–8 Cav troopers who were killed in a Chinook crash on the last day of that company on the field of battle in Vietnam:

Sgt. Mike John Aguilar of Compton, California; Sp4 Oscar Aguilar of Fairfield, California; Sgt. William Arvel Boatright of Abbott, Arkansas; Pfc. Steven Edward Bowersock of Lima, Ohio; Sgt. Edward Denzel Burnett of Jay, Oklahoma; Pfc. Clint Edwin Carr of Alexandria, Louisiana; Sp4 Dennis Guyman Dunning of Raymond, Mississippi; Sp4 David Cruz Flores of Agana, Guam; Sgt. Deiter Kuno Freitag of Ft. Dix, New Jersey; Pvt. James Douglas Groves of Marysville, Kentucky; Pfc. Dale Lamont Hayes of Detroit, Michigan; Sp4 William Frederic Henaghan of Bethpage, New York; Sp4 Frank Theodore Henson of Massapequa, New York; Sp4 Donald Edward Howell of Los Angeles, California; Sp4 Freddie Jackson of Cocoa, Florida; Sp4 Thomas Allen Lahner of Eau Claire, Wisconsin; Captain Kenneth Rosenberg of New York, New York; Pfc. David Allen Lydic of Johnstown, Pennsylvania; Sp4 Gary Robert Monteleone of Saugus, California; Pfc. Dean Anthony Phillips of Tiro, Ohio; Sgt. James Christian Jensen of Elsinore, Utah; Pvt. Jackie Ray of Jackson, Mississippi; Sp4 Richard Ridgeway of Bloomington, Illinois; Pvt. Errain Rivera-Agosta of Sabana Grande, Puerto Rico; Pfc. John Tenerio Sablan of Agana, Guam; Sp4 Clarence L. Saulsberry Jr. of Chicago, Illinois; Sp4 Raymond Joseph Shiko of Kingston, Pennsylvania; Sp4 David Wesley Sulser of Galion, Ohio; and Pfc. Thomas Eugene Wood of Tacoma, Washington.

forty-six

Peace Without Honor

It was March 2, 1970 and my last day with the 1st Air Cavalry Division. General Casey's jeep stopped near where I was saying goodbye to Division Chaplain (LTC) Charles F. Powers, his staff and several others. On impulse, and perhaps contrary to protocol, I jogged over to General Casey, saluted, and informed him of my admiration for his demonstrated leadership and care for the troops.

General Casey graciously accepted my compliments, said he regretted I was leaving so soon, and promised he'd be watching my great future in the Army. He and all aboard his C&C helicopter gave their lives a few months later. He went down in the Central Highland mountains during a trip to Cam Ranh Bay to visit his troops in the hospital.

Sp4 Bill Ellis, a trooper in Alpha Company 1–5 Cav during 1968–69, composed ballads about the grunt's life. Jim Miller, Public Information Officer for the Third Brigade, "discovered" Ellis as the latter was singing and strumming a guitar during one of the company's rare breaks at a "VIP" Center like the one at Quan Loi. Before he knew it, Ellis was pulled away from his buddies to sing for all the troopers in the 1st Cav AO. Probably, Ellis' most popular ballad was about the civilian charter airplane that took veterans home. "Freedom Bird," he called the ballad. Ellis cut a record of his ballads for the 1st Cavalry Division, on condition that each sky trooper then serving in the division would get a free copy. My copy is a choice treasure to my wife, children, and me.

On March 2, 1970, I boarded a "freedom bird" and left

Vietnam for the last time—a day late, sad and tired but without personal regrets for the way I served. My first tour had started slowly and ended with a bang. This tour began with a series of gigantic bangs and petered out during the last couple of weeks. In 1967 I had returned to an America where patriotism was still somewhat in vogue. Now, in 1970, I returned to an America where both patriotism and America's heroic young soldiers were increasingly held in disdain. Where in 1966–67 and early 1969 infantrymen were infantrymen without regard to race or color, by 1970 even they showed evidence of succumbing to civilian and rear-area trends, of dividing into *us* and *them*.

Leaving the 1st Cav for the last time was difficult. Staying would have been harder. It was especially hard to leave while the grunts and aircrews continued to die, for nothing anymore but one another, betrayed by their civilian leaders. Gone was much of the unit cohesion and esprit of 1966–67, with the exception, perhaps, of the 1–9 Cav—and esprit was suffering there. Staying longer would have been torture because I couldn't bear to watch this slow *death*, at least not without a break.

In September 1967 my colonel had *thrown* me out of the field to go home. The men, the war, everything had pulled at me. Only as I drew nearer to home could I let go for a little while. Now, in 1970, I just went home, hurting for those I left behind, dead and alive, but having to go.

Psychologists speak of combat veterans and others suffering from survivor's guilt, feelings of having let their fallen buddies down. Well, for a long time I thought I had escaped survivor's guilt. I knew about "survivor's surprise" and "survivor's gratitude," but felt no guilt, or so I believed. I was wrong. In part, this work, *It Took Heroes*, is a product of that guilt, my way of apologizing in a sense to men who died while I lived.

This might seem strange coming from a former chaplain, but I cringe when I hear someone boastfully attribute his survival to God's recognition of his prayers and those of his family, as above the prayers of another family. I know that men fell in battle whose families, present or future, needed them as much as mine needed me. I know that men fell whose hopes were buttressed by the prayers of loved ones as faithful and righteous as mine. Yet I laid my life on the line as a sacrificial offer and lived to pick it up again, while others laid their mortal lives down for keeps. Why them and not me?

Of this I am certain: God in His loving and incomprehensible way can and sometimes does intervene to deflect bullets. He always answers prayers, and always from His higher perspective.

In His great love and wisdom, our God understands that though many heroes survived Vietnam, few of them can escape. So perhaps I survived precisely because of my ability to remember. Perhaps God allowed me to come home to pay tribute to the heroes, to help others understand the horrors of war, and to chronicle the unsung heroism of so many of America's best and brightest of the era who stepped forward when their country called. Perhaps I lived to provide a bit of healing balm to the veterans whose inescapable suffering would increase with the passing of decades, and to the loved ones of some that never returned.

Fortunately I was, and am, keenly aware of the advantages and privileges of coming home when so many others didn't. I'm very blessed to be physically whole when so many are maimed and mangled, to be mentally and emotionally functional, and to have my faith in God intact. So many became emotional and spiritual basket cases—others just as deserving and capable as me. I'm grateful I could return and father a seventh child, Daniel Bryan, who in turn has fathered two grandchildren for me thus far. So many young men gave their all, leaving not even posterity behind to remember them and carry on their name or their line. I'm left feeling eternally grateful to God, to my family, and to those heroes that paid so much more than I did.

That I came home was consolation in years to come after chaplains replaced line officers in the efficiency rating scheme and career advancement slowed. How could I complain? I came home from the *wars* at least.

Only after many years and the writing of this book did I fully awaken and realize that I returned from Vietnam an alienated man in many respects. I was alienated from the Army for policies, like six-month commands in combat, that all too often deprived soldiers of experienced officers. I was alienated from civilian leaders who sent us off to war with our hands tied and later welcomed home the draft dodgers before expressing thanks to the faithful who served. I was alienated from the American people who participated in or tolerated public abuse of its faithful sons and daughters, and from the whole system for pursuing "business as usual" while heroes suffered faithfully, and died. I was alienated from myself for feeling relieved to be going home while so many grunts, medics, scouts, pilots, dog handlers, rangers, green berets, artillery men and others remained behind. But *I'd* be okay, though the images, smells and feelings of wars in Vietnam would linger, perhaps forever.

For me, perhaps the most difficult adjustment to peacetime life had to do with the pace of events. Life in "the world" was agonizingly slow after two years of living on the fine edge between mortality and eternity. Time in "real life" seemed to stand still after two years of repeatedly living lifetimes in minutes. Civilian life was surely just as different for the former infantryman coming home, cut off from his buddies, both living and dead. He was disdained by peers and constrained by *rules of life* that hadn't applied in combat. He had to endure each day, perhaps in a boring job or no job, facing and dealing with people who didn't—couldn't—understand. Many of these people judged him and refused him work because of his *employment history* the past year. Undoubtedly returning from war was easier for me than for the infantryman. But I never escaped without scars.

There was a lot to adjust to besides the maddeningly slow pace of postwar life and tales of returning soldiers being spat upon and called baby killers. Some of the events most difficult for me to adjust to included the pardoning and welcoming home of draft dodgers in 1974; the fall of South Vietnam in 1975; and the deployment in 1990 of the First Cavalry Division to Desert Shield and Desert Storm—without me. I had a hard time, too, on most of those occasions when protocol forced me to mingle in social gatherings.

Eventually I volunteered for a third tour in Vietnam, in an attempt to assuage my mixed feelings. "Request denied."

Colonel Rasmussen would call in 1973 and ask me to join his staff at the US Army Sergeant Majors Academy. That did not work out because the people in the Office of the Chief of Chaplains had other plans for me. He called again in August 1974 from Fort Carson, Colorado. I was at Fort Ord, California. "One-Niner? This is Motors [short for General Motors] Six." He wanted me to be his brigade chaplain. Again, the chaplain branch didn't cooperate. The next to last call came from his brigade chaplain, a Catholic priest. He said in essence, "Please come to Fort Carson as soon as you can. Colonel Rasmussen has suffered a severe heart attack, and Mrs. Rasmussen would like you at his side."

I took leave and hurried to Colorado, only to find Ron conducting a brigade staff meeting from his bed in the cardiac intensive care unit. In counseling with Ron's wife, I discovered in her the source of much of Ron's greatness.

The last call came the day after I left Colorado. "The colonel suffered another heart attack and did not survive. Mrs. Rasmussen and the commanding general of Fort Carson request that you return and deliver the funeral sermon," said his brigade chaplain, as I recall. The funeral and that very difficult duty, willingly performed, occurred in the Fort Carson Post Chapel on October 4, 1974.

At the conclusion of the funeral service, a strikingly attractive woman introduced herself to me. The lady was one of those heroic souls who waited for the man that never came home—the widow of General George Casey.

Helga and I were at a conference in early April 1975 when the South Vietnam forces crumbled and the NVA and

Vietcong stormed into Saigon. The news was full of pictures of Vietnamese clamoring to board departing American helicopters, of choppers being pushed into the sea to make room on American ships for "withdrawing" forces and refugees. Sensing, sharing the turmoil I was experiencing, Marion D. Hanks greeted Helga and me. "I thought you'd be swimming to Saigon." He seemed to understand what I was going through.

Another tragic image was on our minds, that of a USAF C-5 transport aircraft that crashed soon after lifting off from Saigon with a load of Vietnamese children. "We might try to adopt some Vietnamese orphans," we said to Chaplain Robert Cordner and his wife Karen at dinner that evening.

Hearing this remark, Elder Boyd K. Packer, a high ecclesiastical official, said, "No, you don't want to do that. That part of your life is behind you, and it is time for other things." We heeded his counsel.

The events I describe in this book involved America's best and brightest as they served in great units. Mine were but five of scores of combat battalions. The heroics and actions I describe were occurring—and would continue to occur—to greater or lesser degrees at any given time across Vietnam and throughout the war. I was but one of hundreds of chaplains serving and witnessing these faithful, heroic Americans as they answered the call of their friends and neighbors, even when those neighbors seemed to turn on them.

I'm sustained by memories of great men, and strengthened by the belief that they appreciated my service to them. I'm glad I went to serve the draftee soldier who in most cases, knowing what he knows now, would go again. He would go because someone would have to take his place if he dodged his lawful duty—even to die in his stead. He could neither value his doubts—which were as real as those of the protestors and politicians—above the life of another, nor his own life above personal responsibility. I served the regular-Army soldier who went to Vietnam again and again because he'd vowed to obey lawful orders, and that was his duty, as he saw it. I believe many of us at ground and air level went to Vietnam in part for altruistic reasons. I don't accept that the results disproved the domino theory that was in vogue then in some circles. For example, communists nearly took over in Indonesia. Instead the non-communists prevailed—in great part because American forces were in the area. Perhaps historians will someday realize the Vietnam War marked the high-water mark for communism's expansionist plans to bury America and dominate the world—that things would have turned out very differently for the world, had American blood not been sacrificed with honor in the jungles, rice paddies, deltas and mountains of Vietnam.

At the conclusion of the "peace" talks in Paris, an American military officer said to his North Vietnamese counterpart, "American forces won every time on the battlefield."

"That is irrelevant. We won the war," said the NVA officer.

The American officer was correct and the NVA officer only partly so. Communist forces didn't win victory in the war. Rather, America grew tired of the infringement of the war and its protestors on their consciences via the nightly news. Her civilian leaders ceded an unearned victory to North Vietnam in the pursuit of a so-called peace with honor that was neither.

forty-seven

Invisible Heroes

Look around you, children of the World War II and Great Depression generation. Search carefully and you will find three kinds of true, almost invisible heroes walking in your midst.

You will not be able to see the first type of hero, except as he is reflected in the eyes and demeanor of the other two. He is the hero who never returned from the terrible wars of the twentieth century, or who came home in a metal box. He is very real, but invisible to all but a very select few—family members who grieve still and buddies who accompanied him through the carnage. The memories of him dim each time a loved one or former comrade-in-arms passes from this mortal stage. Those who keep track of such things say that some twelve hundred World War II veterans die each day, taking their stories and memories with them.

The second type of hero is visible to all, but seen by very few. He goes successfully about the daily pursuits of life as farmer, janitor, banker, and clergyman. He is the retired person fishing along a river bank. This hero survived the war but cannot escape it. He can't forget the carnage or erase the ethereal presence of buddies who fell around him. He suffers quietly as he re-experiences things that none should have to endure. Frequently he flashes back to those anguished last moments when death entered the face of a buddy by his side, or in his arms, or in his place.

Mostly this hero succeeded in taking up his life where he left off when he responded to his friends' and neighbors' call and marched away to war. Though we all see him moving in our midst, few recognize him for the true hero that he is.

Although the actual percentage is small, far too many combat veterans, especially those of the Vietnam War, find the memories unbearable. Some remain trapped in a 1960s stunted growth stage booby trapped with drugs and alcohol, and littered with shattered relationships. You'll find many of these sad heroes on the streets and in our prisons. Others of them, often the most heroic in combat, escape into seclusion or suicide.

This second hero, almost to a man if he saw combat in Vietnam, yearns to understand: "Why do I feel guilty for doing what you selected me to do on your behalf? Or if I'm not guilty, why did you take so long to begrudgingly welcome me home?" To assuage this hero's longing—need—to feel welcome at home, he often greets a fellow Vietnam veteran with "Welcome home!" and a firm handshake and probably a hug.

Freddie Owens of Knoxville, Tennessee, is a good representative of these invisible heroes. Freddie, a friendly, outgoing former sergeant, has been deeply involved in the leadership of the 5th Cavalry Regiment Association since its inception in the early 1990s. But his memories and grief overcame him after thirty-five functional and successful years. On August 6, 2000, he wrote me: "The battles in Nam . . . will not escape your mind, but I had to bring those memories back to start my life all over. Ia Drang and Bong Son were hellholes as those of us who were there can attest. I [just] spent six long weeks in therapy trying to put some of those memories in perspective, and have finally gotten some inner peace. I never had the opportunity to say 'goodbye' to some of my dearest friends who lost their lives alongside of me in battle, but I finally did. . . . Cannot make the reunion at Fayetteville because the doc says it's too early to converge with the crowds."

The third type of hero, certainly making up the largest and probably the bravest group, includes the families of those who served. Their lot was hardest because while their loved one served, they wondered and worried, seldom knowing just what he endured. Even when their soldier had a chance to relax, they couldn't because they had no way of knowing. Because it took time for the word to reach them, these heroes often continued to pray for the safety of a son, husband, or father for days after he fell dead or wounded. Many of these heroes on the home front endured the brunt of anti-war protests and disdain with nowhere to escape.

Barbara Conrad and her children and grandchildren represent these heroes. Barbara, the widow of Sp5 (Doc) Andrew Conrad, resettled her family in Flint, Michigan, following his death. None welcomed her there. "My neighbors resented me because my husband was killed in Vietnam. Our daughter, Cynthia (Cindy), the oldest of three children and ten at the time, still suffers from being taunted at school because, 'Your Daddy was stupid enough to get his head blown off in Vietnam.' Andrew did volunteer for Vietnam. We were stationed in Japan in 1967, where he tended the steady stream of wounded guys pouring into the Army's 249th Station Hospital. Often, Andy brought guys home with him, those who were recuperating and getting ready to return to combat. Andy volunteered for combat duty in Vietnam because of these experiences, over the objections of loved ones. Then he gave his life trying to reach wounded soldiers on a terrible *hell*-top called LZ Pat. Stupid? No! Noble and extremely heroic? Yes," avowed Barbara Conrad. Barbara wrote the following poem the day she received notification that her husband had been killed in action (used with her permission):

> *You've gone ahead before us,*
> *To well earned rest,*
> *Having given to this life*
> *Your very best.*

> *There's a private place, Darling,*
> *Where you'll never depart.*
> *And there you're very much alive—*
> *It's a special corner of my heart.*

> *You volunteered for combat,*
> *Leaving the children and me,*
> *You went to help the battle*
> *To keep other people free.*

I know, could we turn back the years,
You would do it all again,
In your quiet gentle manner
You died helping your fellow man.

You won't go down in history books
Or ever remain immortal.
But I know God said: "Well done,
My son," when you entered Heaven's portal.

So in my own way, Darling,
I've written this remembrance to you—
No one here can know how much
I miss you—
But I somehow feel you do.
I love you,

—Babbie

You will do well, America, to seek out the heroes among you. Find them, especially those among your own kin, and sincerely welcome them home. Help them to feel what they probably know but haven't heard very clearly—that the guilt of a nation and its politicians, if such there is, belongs not on their once-young and faithful shoulders. In his book, Tom Brokaw called your great-grandparents—those who endured the Great Depression and shouldered the burdens of World War II—the *Greatest Generation*. Most of the un-sung veterans of Korea and Vietnam are true sons of the greatest. They are America's sons, who honored the legacy left them.

forty-eight

A Benediction for Heroes

My first objective in writing *It Took Heroes* was to pay tribute to heroes in the field and on the home front. Second, I wanted to help others understand what they called you to do, what sacrifices were demanded of you, and how faithfully you performed your duty. I wanted your fathers and grandfathers, veterans of other wars, to know that you always fought to the end and never surrendered as a unit, no matter the overwhelming odds against you. Naturally I also desired to preserve our mutual history for my posterity and yours.

In appreciation for your efforts, I hoped to provide aids in this book to help you find answers to your questions. What happened after you or a buddy or both of you fell, or disappeared into the medical evacuation system. I wanted to help you, the gold-star mother, to identify others involved in the action that your son gave his life in, to help you find solace and answer questions that next-of-kin telegrams and official reports did not always address to your satisfaction. To these ends, these books contain the best descriptions that I could manage, along with chapter notes and an extensive index of names. Veteran, these tools may help you find a buddy when all you recall is his face, nickname, shared experiences, and how important you once were to each other.

As your former chaplain, I desire to bless you one last time. I want you to know that I know that, no matter your faith or lack thereof, there is a God in Heaven who loves you and knows what you endure. As a son or daughter of the "Greatest Generation," you inherited a mantle of respon-bility and a sense of duty to country, which values pro-

you to swim against the growing tide of public opinion and to fight rather than to flee.

I'm certain that a loving and just God smiles very favorably upon you for making an honorable, value-based choice to go and do service that required you to "lay down [your] life for a friend." That same loving God understands the great courage and sacrifice involved when a parent, spouse, or child surrenders a loved one to the sacrificial altar of service. If it were possible, I would wipe pain and irrational guilt away with a word. I can't do that, but I assure you, as one who knows, that you have paid the price long enough.

Fellow veterans and families, heroes, we've endured the darkest hours, the worst of the vagaries of war and the aftermath. We don't have to stay "down there" forever. Former Captain Lou Niles reminded me that, "To every thing there is a season, and a time for every purpose under the heaven . . . a time to kill, and a time to heal; a time to break down, and a time to build up . . . a time of war, and a time of peace" (Ecclesiastes 3:1–8). You fought when you had to. You returned home and helped build. Now it is time to heal and to let yourselves be healed. To this end, I offer these words of prayer and sacred hymn by Jeremiah E. Rankin (1828–1904):

"God be with you till we meet again; by his counsels guide, uphold you; With his sheep securely fold you. God be with you till we meet again . . . When life's perils thick confound you, Put [God's] arms unfailing round you, God be with you till we meet again . . . Keep love's banner floating o'er you, smite death's threatening wave before you. God be with you till we meet again."

To each of you, whichever type of hero you are, "The Lord bless thee, and keep thee. The Lord make his face shine upon thee, and be gracious unto thee. The Lord lift up his countenance upon thee, and give thee peace" (Numbers 6:24–26). Amen.

Glossary

A/C:	Air Craft, also Aircraft Commander
Air Cav:	Air Cavalry; 1st Cavalry Division, Airmobile
Alpha:	Letter A in Army phonetic alphabet, as in Alpha (A) Company
Alpha 2–8:	Thus used, *Alpha* refers to company, the numbers to the battalion and regiment the company belongs to
AO:	Area of Operations
APC:	Armored personnel carrier, light skinned, tracked vehicle used as mount for various weapons and to transport troops
ARA:	Aerial Rocket Artillery
Area Support:	Army principle whereby certain assets are provided across unit lines, for example legal services and religious-denominational assets
Arclight:	B-52 strategic bomber strike (raid); carpet bombing of an area one-quarter-mile wide by one-mile long; often ineffective because enemy had advance warning—USAF registered B-52 flights with international agencies favorable to Hanoi
Arty:	Abbreviation for artillery
ARVN:	Army of the Republic of Vietnam
AWOL	Absent without official leave
B-40:	Rocket propelled grenade. A nasty weapon used by the NVA and VC against armor and personnel
Barrier:	Primary base defenses; used at the An Khe Base Camp, 1965–68
Battery:	Basic unit of artillery, persons, guns and

	equipment; comparable to a Company in non-artillery organizations
Beehive:	An artillery round containing steel flechettes, or tiny steel arrows; see Flechette
Berm:	Earth barrier around defensive perimeters and bunkers
BF Goodrich:	Footwear cut from car tires and worn frequently by NVA and VC soldiers; also called Ho Chi Minh sandals
Bird:	A helicopter; see *Chopper*, LOH, Cobra and gunship
Blue:	Infantry color
Blues:	Infantry rifle platoon, one-each in each Air Cav Troop in the 1st Squadron, 9th Cavalry; member of Blues
Bravo:	Letter B in Army phonetic alphabet
Bubble:	OH-13, a light observation helicopter; a deathtrap that was replaced by the LOH
C-Ration:	Individual Combat rations
C-47:	Fixed wing cargo aircraft, see Chinook
C-130:	Air Force Hercules Transport Aircraft, see also C-133 and Caribou
CA:	Combat Assault; also *Charlie Alpha*
Cav:	(1) The 1st Cavalry Division (The Cav); (2) Troopers of the division; (3) Infantry battalions in the division; (4) First Squadron, 9th Cavalry (the "real" Cav, as its members referred to the unit)
C&C:	Command and Control; also, *Charlie-Charlie*, the Commander's command and control helicopter
Call Sign:	Radio call sign name for units in the field; also identified commanders, leaders and staff at each echelon when followed by a number, as in Fence Post (Charlie Company 1–5 Cav) and Fence Post-6 (Company Commander)
Canister:	Rounds containing steel ball bearings for tank and artillery cannon, and the M-79 grenade launcher
CG:	Commanding General

Caribou:	CV-2, a light cargo aircraft, capacity about 32 persons
Charlie:	Letter C in Army phonetic alphabet; short for Viet Cong
Charlie Model:	Huey chopper used primarily as gunship, replaced by Cobra
CONUS:	Continental United States
Chieu Hoi:	Vietnamese for "Open arms," a program to entice enemy soldiers to change sides in the war
Chinook:	CH-47 tandem-rotor transport helicopter; also, *Hook*
CIDG:	Civilian Irregular Defense Group; home guard; Natives recruited to serve with U.S. Special Forces
Chopper:	Helicopter; see Huey, LOH, Cobra, gunship and *Bird*
Claymore:	Anti-personnel mine. American, spews out hundred of steel balls in a fan-shaped arc, lethal at fifty meters
Close Air Support:	Airforce operations in support of ground forces (see also Danger-Close)
Clover Leaf:	Pattern utilized to keep friendly patrols from accidentally engaging each other in combat
CO:	Commanding Officer, also Conscientious Objector
Cobra:	Nickname for the AG-1G helicopter gunship
Combat Trains:	Battalion forward support site, usually on a firebase during the Vietnam War; see Field Trains
Company:	Basic unit of Infantry and other non-artillery, persons, weapons and equipment; usually with between one and two hundred men—Infantry companies, about one hundred and forty
Conex	Metal shipping container with double doors, also utilized as storage, office, makeshift stockade, etc.
CP:	Command Post
CS:	Tear gas

Daisy Cutter: Ten thousand-pound bomb used by USAF to cut instant landing zones in thick jungle

Danger-Close: Fire support against enemy positions that creates a serious risk of danger for nearby friendly forces. Danger-close support is any fire delivered by friendly land- and sea-based aircraft, and by land- and sea-based artillery. By its nature, Danger-close requires special procedures and care

Delta: Letter D

Det-cord: Explosive fuse-like cord used to explode multiple charges simultaneously

DivArty: Division Artillery, may mean headquarters or all artillery organic to the Division

Division: The major maneuver element of the Army, ranging in strength (during Vietnam era) from eighteen to twenty-four thousand personnel

Door Gunner: Machine gun operator on a helicopter

Echo: Letter E

EM: Enlisted man (men); later, EP for enlisted persons

EPW: Official designation for captured enemy prisoners, more commonly called POWs

FAC: Forward Air Controller; an officer who direct air strikes while flying in his own aircraft

Field Trains: Rear-support area, usually located at a major base camp; see Combat Trains

FIX: To entrap or confine an enemy so he can be destroyed

Flagpole: Jargon for a position under the direct influence and/or sight of a commander, at echelons above companies

Flak Vest   Body armor

Flare: Illumination device (noun); or the landing attitude of an aircraft (verb)

Flechette: Small steel arrows or darts in canister or beehive shells

FO: Forward Observer. Usually artillery officers attached to infantry companies to call and adjust artillery fire; also an individual member of mortar platoons in support of rifle platoons

FOB:	Forward operating base for an infantry company, often used interchangeably with NDP (night defensive position) earlier in the war
Fougasse:	Homemade napalm used for defense around American firebases
Frag:	Fragmentation grenade (noun); part of an operational order or *frago* (verb); criminal act of attacking one's own leaders in a war zone, usually by hand grenade, but the term expanded to include other attacks against one's own leaders during the Vietnam War
Friendly Casualties:	American and allied persons that become killed, wounded, or captured, by enemy or friendly action
Friendly Fire:	Munitions of all types fired by American and allied forces, having nothing to do with relational qualities
FSB:	Fire Support Base; usually a battalion-size operational base which included the battalion combat trains, TOC and a battery of howitzers; also, officially called an LZ prior to mid-1969, and unofficially after that
Full Metal Jacket:	Standard, copper small-arms bullet, intended to wound and kill without messing up the body the way soft-nose munitions do
GI:	Term for American soldier, carried over from World War II
Gook:	Derogatory word some American soldiers used to refer to the enemy. It is used in this book only in direct quotations, and then only when necessary to the action being described
Grease Gun	Simple and reliable .45-caliber automatic weapon that resembles a device for lubricating vehicles
Greenline:	The generic term for the outer defensive ring of bunkers, wire, towers, etc., at most base camps
Grunt:	American Infantryman; popularly believed to have arisen from the infantryman's grunting as he hoisted his heavy rucksack
GSW:	Gun shot wound

Gunship	Helicopter armed with mini-gun, machine guns, rockets and some with 40mm grenade launchers
H-13:	Light observation helicopter, a two-seat bubble with fuel tank right over the crew's head, a firetrap; replaced by the LOH
HE:	High Explosive ammunition
Hoi Chanh:	VC or NVA soldier that joins South Vietnamese; see Chieu Hoi
Hooch	Mackeshift accommodation
Hotel:	The Letter H
HQ:	Headquarters
Huey:	UH-1 utility helicopter. Also, *HUEY*
Hump (verb):	Maneuver by foot, tactical march or patrol by dismounted soldiers. May have derived from the large, heavy rucksacks that infantry and LRRPs carried, reminiscent of a camel's hump
In-country:	Military phrase (jargon) meaning physically present in Vietnam
In-process (verb):	Military phrase meaning to process into a new unit or onto a military installation
IO:	Information Officer; also PIO (Public Information Officer)
KIA:	Killed in Action
Kit Carson Scout:	Former VC or NVA who served as scout for American units in the field
Klick:	Kilometer, slang
Leg:	A non-airborne infantryman; also called a *straight leg*
LNO:	Liaison Officer
LOH:	Light Observation Helicopter, used primarily as a scout bird
LP:	Listening Post, usually two men placed in front of friendly forces to listen for approaching enemy under cover of darkness. See OP
LRRP:	Long-range Reconnaissance Patrol member or team; member of ranger company such as H Co. 75th Rangers that was attached to 1–9 Cav, 1st Cav Division; also called LRRP

LZ:	Landing Zone; any place used for aircraft to land, once or more times. See also PZ and FSB
M-1:	Clip fed, semi-automatic rifle, WW II and Korean vintage
M-14:	U.S. Caliber 7.62-mm, predecessor to M-16, and in use in Vietnam
M-16:	U.S. Caliber 5.56-mm, the basic US forces assault rifle
M-60:	U.S. Caliber 7.62-mm machine gun; platoon and company weapon, also used on Hueys and Armored Personnel Carriers (APCs)
M-72:	LAW (Light Anti-tank) weapon. HE round fired from a throwaway tube; used in Vietnam to attack bunkers
M-79:	40-mm grenade launcher, breech-loaded, shoulder-fired
Machine gun:	Crew-served automatic weapon
MACV:	Military Assistance Command, Vietnam; commanded advisors, special operations, etc.
MARS:	Military Affiliate Radio System. Pre-internet/e-mail system by which soldiers call loved ones
MG:	(1) Machine gun; (2) Major General, two stars
Medevac:	Aerial medical evacuation, 1st Cavalry term
Medic:	Medical Aid man; also, affectionately called *Doc* by many troopers
Mike force:	Mercenary strike forces, frequently Cambodians, led by American Special Forces; also called MSF and *strikers*
Mini-gun:	Multi-barreled machine gun with firing rates of 2,000 and 4,000 rounds per minute, every fourth round a tracer
NDP:	Night Defensive Position, used interchange-able with FOB or forward operations base, especially in 1969
Net:	Short for radio network. All tactical radios operated within a defined network on a des-ignated frequency
OER:	Officer Efficiency Report

OP:	Observation Post; usually one or two men posted in front of friendly forces to watch for approaching enemy during the daylight; see LP
OPCON:	Operational Control
Pace man:	Individual designated to keep track of a unit's location in the trackless, featureless jungle
Palace Guard:	Relatively safe duty protecting base camp from attacks
Picket Line:	The defensive area several kilometers beyond a base camp barrier line or perimeter; also, Rocket Belt
Pink Team:	Two-helicopter team, Cobra gunship and LOH scout helicopter
Point:	Person or element in the lead during movement, also called point man
Police *(verb):*	To clean up or search an area
Pony Team	Five-man patrol, precursor to the LRRPs
Popular Forces:	Local Vietnamese Force (PF)
POW:	Prisoner of War
PRC-25:	FM radio, back-packed; basic communications for nearly every level of command within the division
Prep:	Short for preparation of an LZ by artillery, ARA and, occasionally, by air strikes
Prone Shelter:	One-man position; shallow, body-length trench used frequently early in the war in place of foxhole
PSP:	Perforated sheets of steel that joined together to provide a runway for fixed-wing aircraft; also used to reinforce overhead cover on bunkers
Punji Stake:	A small sliver of bamboo, stuck in the ground and in punji pits to impale "enemy" forces; sometimes tipped with feces and other matter to cause the wound to fester; Used by VC forces
PX:	Post Exchange, on-base store for military people
PZ:	Pickup zone, temporary site where choppers pick up soldiers, as opposed to a place to drop them off (LZ)

QRF:	Quick Reaction Force, usually a platoon or company, sometimes a larger unit which might be designated a reserve force
Quad:	Four guns, M-60 machine guns, 40-mm launchers, etc., configured to fire together
R&R:	Rest and Relaxation leave
Recoilless:	Called a rifle, but more like shoulder- or vehicle-mounted and fired artillery, recoilless because a dangerous back blast when fired equalized forward blast to prevent *kicking*
Recon:	Reconnaissance
Reconstitution:	Operations to rebuild a fighting unit, to reconstitute its numbers, material, readiness, stamina, morale and spiritual, etc.
Rocket Belt:	Area from which rockets can reach a target.
Roger:	Formerly, the letter R, and radio language for "yes" or "affirmative." Grunts often shortened it to "Rog" or "That's a Rog"
Rome Plow:	A standard D7E tractor, equipped with a heavy-duty protective cab and tree-cutting blade. Rome-plowing was carried out to deny the enemy sanctuary by removing jungle and to enhance base defense by clearing around bases
RPD:	Soviet 7.62-mm machine gun (NVA)
RPG:	Soviet 82-mm rocket-propelled anti-tank grenade; used by NVA as an anti-personnel weapon; see B-40
RTO:	Radio Telephone Operator
RVN:	Republic of Vietnam
S/A:	Small arms or small-arms fire
Sandwich:	One who wore patch of 1st Cavalry Division on both shoulders, signifying being in combat with unit previously to current tour
Sapper:	Soldier (originally an engineer) who attacks fortifications. VC and NVA used sappers extensively and effectively
Satchel:	Explosive package fitted with a handle for ease of handling charge and throwing; favorite weapon of the NVA sapper
Sitrep:	Situation report

SIX:	Designation for a commander at company and above
SKS:	Soviet carbine
Spider Hole:	Small, easily concealed NVA and VC foxholes
TOC:	Tactical Operations Center
Torque:	Crew chief/door gunner on a scout LOH, credited with being one of the most combat-effective positions on the Vietnam battlefield
Tracer:	Bullets that burn, leaving a *trace* of fire in their wake. Ours burned red, NVA burned green
Tube Arty:	Tube artillery. Also, field artillery and Naval guns
USAF:	U.S. Air Force
USARV:	U.S. Army Vietnam
Vagaries:	Unpredictable manifestation, action, or outcome
VC:	Viet Cong, also Vietcong, Victor Charlie or Charlie
War Zone C:	North, Northwest of Saigon along the Cambodian border
WIA:	Wounded in Action
XO:	Executive Officer, "first officer" at echelons below division
37-mm:	Soviet anti-aircraft weapon, electronically aimed and fired
40-mm:	Projectiles or rounds for the M-79, for a four-barrel launcher, and launchers on gunships
51-cal. MG:	Heavy machine gun favored by NVA forces
82-mm:	Medium size mortar favored by Communist forces in Vietnam
90-mm:	Recoilless rifle, shoulder-fired artillery
105-mm:	Field artillery piece and/or shell
107-mm:	Recoilless rifle, often jeep mounted; also, rocket used by the NVA for stand-off attacks
122-mm:	Heavy "artillery" of the NVA forces

Don't miss this dramatic story of the
Army's eyes, ears, and deadliest hands
by Michael Lee Lanning

INSIDE THE LRRPs
Rangers in Vietnam

*They did what others only dream about and
walked where others didn't dare.*

Vietnam was a different kind of war, calling for a
different kind of soldier from that of other wars. The
LRRPs were a perfect example of the new breed of
fighting man. Operating in six-man teams deep
within enemy territory, they were the eyes and ears
of the units they served. Their enemy body count
often exceeded that of much larger combat units.
The LRRPs—characterized by perseverance under
extreme hardship, extraordinary attention to detail,
absolute professionalism, and uncommon bravery—
may well have been the most effective use of manpower in the entire war. This is their story—how
they were staffed, how they trained, how they carried out the war's most hazardous missions.

Published by Ballantine Books.
Available wherever books are sold.

Look for this mesmerizing account of
suffering and courage in Vietnam
by Gary A. Linderer

EYES BEHIND THE LINES
L Company Rangers in Vietnam, 1969

*In Vietnam, nightmares came true.
The only question was whether
they killed you or not.*

In mid-December 1968, after recovering from
wounds sustained in a mission that saw four members of a twelve-man "heavy" team killed and five
more sent home, Gary Linderer returned to Phu Bai
to complete his tour of duty as a LRP. The job of the
all-volunteer Rangers was to find the enemy, observe
him, or kill him—all the while behind enemy lines,
where discovery could mean a quick but violent
death. Whether inserting into hot LZs, ambushing
NVA soldiers, or rescuing downed air crews, the
Rangers demanded—and got—extraordinary performance from their dedicated and highly professional
troops.

Published by Ballantine Books.
Available wherever books are sold.